An
Essex Tribute

Dr. F. G. Emmison, M.B.E., F.S.A.

An
Essex Tribute

Essays presented to
Frederick G. Emmison
as a tribute to his
life and work for
Essex history and archives

Edited by
Kenneth Neale

LEOPARD'S HEAD PRESS
1987

First published in 1987 by
Leopard's Head Press Limited
69, Aldwych, London WC2B 4DY

© 1987 Kenneth Neale

ISBN 0 904920 13 5

Typeset by Oxford Print Associates Ltd.,
The Studio, Kennington, Oxford

Printed in Great Britain at the
University Press, Cambridge

CONTENTS

		page
List of illustrations, maps and tabulations		vi
Editorial Note		vii
Biographical Notes		ix
Foreword	A. G. Dickens	xiii
Frederick G. Emmison: Archivist and Scholar	Kenneth Neale	1
The County Record Office: The unfolding of an idea	V. W. Gray	11
Essex Boroughs and their Records	G. H. Martin	27
The making of the Essex Landscape	William Addison	47
The Ealdordom of Essex	Cyril Hart	57
Two Charters of King Suebred of Essex	K. N. Bascombe	85
'Richer in land than in inhabitants'. South Essex in the Middle Ages, c.1066–c.1340	Jennifer C. Ward	97
The Bounds of the Forest of Essex	William Liddell	109
Blackchapel, Great Waltham	A. A. Dibben	115
The Letter of the Law Hatfield Peverel in the Lay Subsidy of 1524–5	Julian Cornwall	143
Those Greedy Hunters after Concealed Lands	H. H. Lockwood	153
New College, Oxford and its Hornchurch Estate, 1391–1675	Marjorie K. McIntosh	171
'Dear Betsey': Reflections on two letters from the First Carlist War	Ian G. Robertson	185
Four Colchester Elections: Voting Behaviour in a Victorian Market Town	Andrew Phillips	199
Essex and the 1871 Fairs Act.	John H. Boyes	229
Aspects of Local Cartography in Kent and Essex, 1585–1700	Felix Hull	241
Essex: An Appreciation	Kenneth Neale	253
INDEX		261

ILLUSTRATIONS, MAPS AND TABULATIONS

Frederick G. Emmison   *frontispiece*
The Families of Ealdormen Aelfgar and Byrhtnoth of Essex   58
Essex and the Danes 880–920.   61
Estates of the Essex Ealdormen c.950–1000.   64
Estates of Ealdorman Byrhtnoth.   67
King Athelstan's Ealdormen.   82
King Edmund's Ealdormen.   83
King Eadred's Ealdormen.   84
Topographical interpretation of Suebred's charters.   91
'The finger of suspicion?'   153
Official Election Returns for Colchester (1859–1870).   222
Appendix B, Colchester Elections.   222
Essex Fairs Act 1871: Applications for Abolition.   238

EDITORIAL NOTE

Volumes of commemorative essays are, so it has been averred, apt to be the bane of their editors and the curse of librarians struggling to classify diffuse and anomalous material. That these disabilities have, in this case I trust, been largely avoided is due to the excellent cooperation I have had from those concerned with its production.

Thanks are therefore due to the essayists who responded with their scholarship and good grace to the editorial disciplines of design and timetable. Their work would not, however, have come to early fruition were it not for the initiative taken by the Essex Archaeological and Historical Congress in launching the project and the enthusiastic responses of other important contributors. I must also acknowledge the generous and major financial support of the Friends of Historic Essex and two other private guarantors which has under-pinned the enterprise. Financial contributions have also been gratefully received from the Essex County Council Library, Museums and Records Committee, the Essex Society for Archaeology and History, the Essex Society for Family History, the Friends of Historic Essex and the Essex Archaeological and Historical Congress. The administrative burdens have been eased with the help of Dorothy Lockwood, Secretary of the Essex Congress and Michael Tiernan, Treasurer, to whom I am very grateful.

Finally, the expert advice and positive cooperation from Roy Stephens and the Leopard's Head Press have been indispensable. All this has made the editorial task both agreeable and professionally rewarding.

Great Sampford, 1987   Kenneth Neale.

BIOGRAPHICAL NOTES

William Addison Kt., J. P., D. L., F. S. A.

At eighty-two, having lived more lives than the proverbial cat, William Addison recalls with most satisfaction the fifty or more years spent, in association with Derick Emmison, promoting the study of local history in Essex. The list of county causes in which they have worked together in one capacity or another is too long to list here and selection would be invidious. All continue to flourish. William Addison's other chief interests have been with crime, which, he insists, have been much less rewarding!

(Ed. Details of Sir William Addison's career will be found in Who's Who)

Kenneth Bascombe M. A., D. Phil.

Born in 1932 at Poole, Dorset. Educated at Poole Grammar School and Balliol College, Oxford. He came to work in Waltham Abbey in 1961 as a scientist in the government service. Secretary, Waltham Abbey Historical Society 1966–78; Curator of its Collections since 1978. Chairman, Essex Archaeological and Historical Congress 1969–70; Secretary, 1978–84; President, 1984–7. Vice-President of the Friends of Historic Essex and of the Royal Archaeological Institute. Most of his publications are concerned with the archaeology and local history of the Waltham Forest area.

John H. Boyes A. R. Hist. S.

Retired Civil Servant. Rolt Memorial Fellow, Bath University; Past President, Essex Archaeological and Historical Congress; Bulletin Editor, the Newcomen Society for the Study of the History of Engineering and Technology; Joint author, *The Canals of Eastern England* (1977); Member, VCH Essex Editorial Committee; Member, Wind and Watermill Section Committee of S. P. A. B.; President, Lee and Stort Rivers Committee; Lecturer for, inter alia, the National Trust and the Inland Waterways Association.

Julian Cornwall M. A., F. R. Hist. S.

Born 1926; educated Brighton and Hove Grammar School and University College, London; archivist, 1951–6; teaching, 1956–82, finally as Senior Lecturer in History, Colchester Institute. Came late to Essex, with strong interests in other counties already developed, and as usual ineluctably drawn to the fiscal records for the age of Henry VIII. Now engaged on research and writing, editing the Subsidy Rolls, 1524–5 for *Essex Historical Documents* series. Other than articles (mostly on 16th and 17th century economic and social history), publications include Subsidy Rolls, 1524–5, for Sussex Record Society, *How to Read Old Title Deeds* (1964), and *Revolt of the Peasantry, 1539* (1977).

Alan A. Dibben M. A.

Read history at Caius College, Cambridge. Worked as Assistant Archivist in the Essex, West Sussex, and Ipswich & East Suffolk Record Offices. City Archivist of Coventry, 1965–1974 and County Records Officer of East Sussex, 1974–81. Chairman, Society of Archivists, 1972–5; member of the Council of the Historical Association, 1959–63, 1968–85 and Vice-President, 1976–85. Has edited the *Suffolk Review* and been Secretary of the Sussex Record Society. Secretary of the Record Users' Group. He wrote three parish histories for *VCH Essex* vol. iv; other publications include the Historical Association pamphlet *Title Deeds* (rev. ed. 1971) and *Coventry City Charters* (1969).

Arthur Geoffrey Dickens C. M. G., D. Litt., F. B. A., F. S. A.

Educated at Hymers College, Hull and Magdalen College, Oxford. First Class, History 1932. Fellow, Keble College, Oxford, 1933–49. Served, Royal Artillery, 1940–45. Professor of History, Hull, 1949–62 and King's College, London 1962–7. Director, Institute of Historical Research, University of London, 1967–77. Foreign Secretary of the British Academy, 1969–79. Author, 16 books and numerous articles, mainly on the Reformation, British and Continental.

Victor Gray M. A.

Victor Gray became County Archivist of Essex in 1978 after nine years working in county record offices in Devon and Suffolk. He is a past Chairman of the Association of County Archivists and is currently Vice-Chairman of the Society of Archivists. His interest in the early history of county record services has grown from an active involvement in current thinking on future developments in archive provision in England and Wales.

Cyril Hart M. A., D. Litt., F. R. Hist. S.

Cyril Hart is a Cambridgeshire general practitioner and an amateur historian of pre-Conquest England. He is a native of Essex and has published extensively on its early history. As a young man he was taught palaeography by Derick Emmison at the County Record Office.

Later he was a pupil of Professor H. P. R. Finberg at Leicester. His publications include *The Early Charters of Essex* (1957) and *The Early Charters of Eastern England* (1966).

Felix Hull B. A., Ph. D. (London), Hon. D. Litt. (Kent), F. R. Hist. S.
Worked in Essex and Berkshire Record Offices. County Archivist, Kent, 1952–80. Chairman of Council, Society of Archivists, 1960–3; President, 1976–82; Vice-President from 1982. Member, Council of Kent Archaeological Society, from 1953; subsequently, Vice-President and Patron from 1984. Chairman, Kent Archives Fellowship, 1981–6. Publications: *Guide to Berks. R. O.* (1952); *Guide to Kent County Archives Office* (1958) and *Ist. Supplement* (1971); *Catalogue of maps in Kent Archives Office* and *Kentish Maps and Map-makers* (1973); *Handlist of Kent County Council Records* (1972); Ed. *Calendar of White and Black Books of the Cinque Ports* (1966); UNESCO, RAMP Study – *The Use of sampling techniques in the retention of Records* (1981); Various articles, especially in *Archaeologia Cantiana* and in *Journal of the Society of Archivists*.

William Liddell M. A., F. R. Hist. S.
Senior Lecturer in History, Department of Extra-Mural Studies, University of London. Past President of Essex Society for Archaeology and History (formerly the Essex Archaeological Society); Chairman, Essex History Fair Committee (1986); Chairman, Association of Local History Tutors.

Herbert Hope Lockwood B. A. (Hons.), A. K. C.
Educated at University of London, King's College; formerly Lecturer in History and Social Studies at Tottenham College of Technology. Founder member of Ilford and District Historical Society and Chairman since 1978; contributor to *Topography and Manors in Barking and Ilford*, *VCH Essex* vol. 5 (1966) and author of other studies in the local history of the area.

Geoffrey Martin C. B. E., M. A., D. Phil., F. S. A., F. R. Hist. S.
Keeper of Public Records since 1982, was born in Colchester and educated at Colchester Royal Grammar School, Merton College, Oxford and the University of Manchester. From 1952 he lectured in history at the University of Leicester where he was Professor of History, 1972–82 and Pro-Vice Chancellor, 1979–82. He is the author of several studies in urban history, including a history of Colchester published in 1959, and a Vice-President of the Essex Society for Archaeology and History (formerly the Essex Archaeological Society).

Marjorie K. McIntosh Ph. D.

Professor of History at the University of Colorado, Boulder, U.S.A. Having completed several works on the royal manor and Liberty of Havering in the medieval and Tudor/Stuart periods, she is now engaged in a study of how English local communities responded to the poor between 1388 and 1598.

Kenneth Neale O. B. E., F. S. A.

Author, lecturer, consultant; served in the Royal Navy, Civil Service, Colonial Service and Diplomatic Service. Chairman, Essex Archaeological and Historical Congress, 1984–7; Vice-Chairman, Friends of Historic Essex, 1983–6, Chairman since 1986. Member of Council of the Essex Society for Archaeology and History (formerly the Essex Archaeological Society) since 1984. Published books include, *Discovering Essex in London* (1969), *Victorian Horsham* (1975), *Essex in History* (1977) and *Her Majesty's Commissioners 1878–1978* (1978). He has also published studies and articles on local history, natural history and penology.

Andrew Phillips B. A., Dip. Ed.

Head of School of Humanities at the Colchester Institute. President of the Essex Society for Archaeology and History (formerly the Essex Archaeological Society) 1984–6. He has published many articles on Colchester and Essex and is author of *Ten Men and Colchester: Public Good and Private Profit in a Victorian Town* (1985).

Ian G. Robertson M. A., F. M. A.

Read Modern History at The Queen's College, Oxford; Museums Diploma with Archaeology option; Assistant Curator, Chelmsford and Essex Museum, 1965–7; Curator, Passmore Edwards Museum, 1967 to date; President of the Society for Post-Medieval Archaeology, 1982–5; Member of the Statutory Ancient Monuments Advisory Committee of the Historic Buildings and Monuments Commission for England, 1984 to date; President, Museums Association, 1986–7.

Jennifer C. Ward M. A., Ph. D.

Senior Lecturer in History at University of London's Goldsmiths' College. She has published various articles on the Clare baronial family and on Essex history, and has edited *The Medieval Essex Community – The Lay Subsidy of 1327*, for the Essex Record Office series, *Essex Historical Documents*.

FOREWORD

Contemplating an exhibition of paintings by Sir Joshua Reynolds, one of his contemporaries exclaimed 'Lord, how *various* the man is'! Extremely few archivists can have aroused this emotion. In one sense or another they have to be specialised and even localised. They tend to be highly essential but unglamorous members of learned society, people who make possible the achievements of minds more original – or should we rather say more pretentious? To this mild stereotype Dr F. G. Emmison bears little resemblance: he is incisive, creative, indeed sometimes quite assertive, yet nevertheless armed with a saving generosity of spirit which has consecrated his highly energetic life to a cause, and consequently to the service of others.

Dr Emmison's career began with the Bedfordshire archives where he was trained by Dr G. H. Fowler. Yet after three years of apprenticeship he began to work wonders on his own account. He surveyed the outlying parish records, drew in many valuable family and estate collections and attracted to Bedford a rising number of attendances by members of the public. As early as 1929 he foreshadowed his own lifelong mission by publishing a short article with the title *The County Record Office – its Educational Function*. Since then this broadening view – admittedly promoted also by a few others – has done much to change attitudes both within and outside the profession. At heart Emmison has always been a teacher, intent to share with scholars of all ages and degrees of proficiency his own vision of archival and historical studies, to broaden horizons, even to create a fresh dimension of citizenship and identity. If the common man has achieved his due place in history, if the value of our roots and their growth out of local history are now far more widely appreciated than in the last century, this is largely due to the smallish body of archivists and university lecturers in the Adult Education movement. Unfortunately, while converting many thousands of people, often rather unprivileged people, these teachers failed to convert that group of politicians and civil servants who in later years – and for the most trivial reasons – were to slice up, rename and even abolish our ancient counties and other territorial divisions: those profound symbols of familial identity and historical consciousness. Emmison himself has laudably coined the word 'Comitatism' to be set alongside 'patriotism', even though his own county did not suffer the irrational mauling we have undergone in Yorkshire and other northern regions.

These malign events lay far in the future when in 1938 Emmison left Bedfordshire to become County Archivist of Essex, which office he held until 1969. During these three decades he was responsible for more than fifty Essex Record Office publications: books and pamphlets on an astonishing variety of subjects, together with maps covering many periods and places. With his flair for publicity he accomplished this feat with a financial profit to the County Council. Quite rightly, he was less interested in producing formal catalogues than in arousing the public mind to the many intellectual functions of archives. First of all he needed to imbue teachers – some of whom had long been prepared for such a lead – with a practical determination to use such aids in the class-room and in the open countryside. Here a milestone was reached when in 1946 the Essex County Council actually appointed an education officer to the staff of the Record Office. Seven years later the Council leased from Lord Petre a wing of Ingatestone Hall, where impressive local history exhibitions could be presented in a distinguished setting without disturbing the researchers at work in the Students' Room at County Hall.

The activities of a county archivist, even those of such a tribal leader, can scarcely assume the grand manner of our admired, mutual friend Maurice Bond, creator of the House of Lords Records Office so impressively stacked up the Victorian Tower in the Palace of Westminster. A county archivist is not called to such high places: he must remain close to the craftsmen in the county town and the tillers of the soil. He does not assemble the great documents of state but pursues such activities as Emmison's indefatigable publication of wills, inventories, maps and the like. People such as he – and for that matter the present writer – had to put forth hard and unspectacular effort to discover new methodologies in social history, often by empirical, hit-and-miss approaches. Fifty years, even thirty years ago, the uses and potentialities of regional sources were far less apparent than they have since become: a fact not invariably appreciated by the younger generation of 'revisionists'. Emmison did not rest content with merely doing the hard work: he also sought to publicise the results and induce others to make extra efforts. He was fully entitled to a national reputation. Inevitably there have been less ambitious and effective people who have muttered the words 'a bit of a showman', words which castigated their own inertness rather than his dynamism. It was emphatically not the business of our generation to blush unseen!

Fortunately, Emmison did not spend his whole career on the ground floor of history. That he could also accomplish a grand literary design became evident when in 1961 he published *Tudor Secretary: Sir William Petre at Court and Home*. It achieved a second edition and should achieve others, being a biography which any Tudor historian would be proud to have researched and written. Despite his high office in perilous times and under three monarchs, Sir William Petre is numbered among those laborious maintainers of low profiles to whom the great achievement of the Tudor state was so largely due. Emmison perceived that Sir William lacked those spectacular and superficial qualities which make for huge sales and television rights. But the book compensates for this lack by a remarkably solid realism, which renders faithfully the hard realities of daily life in Essex and at court. Being himself a good host and by no means unappreciative of the good things in life, Emmison uses even the extensive household accounts to describe what one ate at Ingatestone and elsewhere. To read this biography has made some of us – and by no means the *bon viveurs* alone – willing to spare a few of the record-volumes for some further biographies from the same author. But 'various' as the man is, we cannot reasonably demand much more than we have already been given in the course of his long and devoted lifetime.

A. G. Dickens

Frederick G. Emmison: Archivist and Scholar

KENNETH NEALE

When we, Derick Emmison's friends and colleagues, gathered in the 'fayr and . . . stately gallery or walke mete for any man of honour to come into' at Ingatestone Hall in mid-Essex, on 17th June, 1969, it was fitting in both period and academic context. The welcoming roseate mansion, traditional home of the Petre family from the mid-sixteenth century, seemed to symbolise his love for Tudor Essex and the most conspicuous facets of his scholastic achievements. Some might have been forgiven for thinking that the occasion of his retirement party, as it was somewhat inaptly described, marked the culmination of his massive contribution to Essex archives and history. So much of high excellence had already been given: there was still much to come from his spacious mind and fecund pen.

County archivists, like country parsons, are a natural focus of respect and affection. They are contemplated by the devotees of local and family history with the 'umility, h'admiration and h'awe of a Dickensian character. These are the gratuitous accoutrements of the office. A few, like Derick Emmison, extend the range and degree of those generally muted sentiments to an appropriate coterie of national and international students of their scene. Almost uniquely, if I may be allowed that trifling ambiguity, he enlarged his audience to include thousands of people who, on the periphery of local history, none the less derived pleasure and instruction from his work in this field. As we shall see in this brief biographical tribute, his versatile intellectual flair combined with a compelling personality and a truly Elizabethan style to intrude a strand of genius into his thought and work.

The duty of an editor and writer of a biographical note demands that he should first record the prosaic details of his subject's birth and career. Frederick (Derick to his friends) Emmison was fortunate enough to have been born at no great distance from Essex, at Bedford on 28th May 1907, and to have inherited from his father a love of history. He entered Bedford Modern School in 1918. In 1922 he distinguished himself by gaining the only First Class Honours in the Cambridge and Oxford Senior Locals Examination awarded that year at any of the four public schools in Bedford. He intended to go up to Cambridge. However, his father's sudden belief that he had lost a great deal of capital in a bad investment, falsified by events, caused him to abandon the plan and the Bedfordshire County Council was the recipient of this able and ambitious young historian. When it later became clear that the investment had in fact prospered, it was too late to reconsider going to Cambridge. The prestigious degree that would doubtless have awaited him was thus forfeited. In retrospect, the constraining educational rigours of formal degree courses seem almost irrelevant in the glare of a career of such manifest brilliance. Nevertheless, he has often regretted the mischance that deprived him of the benefits of academic discipline and wider opportunities for reading and learning that the University would have offered. Emmison thus came to be appointed in 1925 Bedfordshire's first Clerk of Records (an honourable term drawn from the House of Lords Record Office) and received the unique tuition of Dr G. H. Fowler, Chairman of the Council's Records Committee and the 'Father of Local Archives': an eminent medieval historian and editor, who virtually forbad Emmison to seek a London University external degree!

He transferred to Essex in 1938 and was County Archivist until 1969. In 1935 he had married Margaret, daughter of Dr Hamilton Langwill. An Edinburgh history honours graduate who then qualified as an archivist at London University, she helped him with various editorial tasks until her eyesight began to deteriorate. The pair were blessed with two talented children, Lesley and Martin. Derick's illustrious career as an archivist led him to Fellowships of the Society of Antiquaries, the Royal Historical Society and the Society of Genealogists. In 1932 he became a founder member of the British Records Association and in 1947 of the Society of Local Archivists. A number of admiring societies honoured him with the offices of President or Vice-President and thereby added the lustre of his name to their own. These have included the Historical Association, the British Record Society, the British Records Association, the Society of Archivists, the Society of Genealogists, the Committee of the Victoria County History of Essex, the Essex Society for Archaeology and History, the Essex Archaeological and Historical Congress, and the Essex Society for Family History. Several local history societies in Essex have similarly honoured his exceptional status in county history. I know that he was pleasantly surprised to be elected the first President of the Bedfordshire Family History Society, of which he is now Patron, in succession to the Lord Lieutenant. Nor has he shirked the working roles. He has also served as Honorary Secretary and Treasurer of the Friends of Historic Essex and is now their Editor. As a Liveryman of the Worshipful Company of Scriveners of the City of London, he finds himself among people of his own ilk. As to the symbolic trophies with which distinguished careers are embellished, he was, in 1974, awarded the Julian Bickersteth Medal by the Institute of Heraldic and Genealogical Studies. In 1970 an honorary Doctorate was conferred on him by the University of Essex in recognition of his work in Essex history and he is one of the few elected members of its Court. Emmison's most recent mark of academic distinction was the award by the Historical Association of the Medlicott Medal for 1987 in recognition of his 'outstanding service to history, both in the record office field and as a local historian.' Membership of the Order of the British Empire was conferred on him in 1966, a well-merited award by the sovereign that afforded those who knew and admired his work a great deal of pleasure.

Under Emmison the Essex Record Office prospered with a dynamic stream of initiatives and unambiguous purposes. These, by common consent, put the office in the lead in pioneering fresh approaches and in developing new standards of methodology in the growing sphere of archival administration. The groundwork had been laid in pursuit of his own youthful enthusiasms and later, more definitively, in the formative experience he gained at Bedford working under the redoubtable Dr Fowler. During that period his tireless application had urged him to survey the ecclesiastical and civil parish records of Bedfordshire, all of the work being done in his own time. These efforts, inter alia, put that county in the forefront of the still embryonic business of archives. It was from the early 1930s also that his devotion to manuscript maps and Tudor records, in both of which the Bedfordshire office was rich, was ignited to burn brightly for ever after.[1] This almost obsessive specialisation on cartographical and social (but seldom political) history has tended to obscure his other work. It was his happy acquaintance with north-west Essex, conveniently near to Bedfordshire, that drew him eventually to Chelmsford, where there was, at that time (unimaginable now), no county record office. Emmison, making excellent use of the weekends, listed the parish records of that part of Essex and discovered its delights as a pleasant corollary to the self-imposed task – with the blessing and awakening interest of the Clerk of the Council. The opportunity, for Essex as much as for himself, to work at Chelmsford and to exploit his experience and aspirations in developing an Essex Record Office came in 1938. Almost at once his plans were constrained by the outbreak of war. Those years were not, however, wasted, for although himself seconded full-time to national duties, he continued to lay stronger foundations. For much of the war he and his wife were the only staff at the E.R.O.. It was a period during which large quantities of archival material were being deposited. Following the advice of the sixteenth-century writer Hilles, who inscribed in his Commonplace book the injunction 'when you proffer the pigge open the poke', the Essex archives were soon after the war made fully accessible.

Despite the problems and the formidable scale of the work (a truly Herculean task), the first E.R.O. *guides* were published in 1946 and 1948. In between them came Emmison's pioneer publication, the detailed and luxuriously illustrated *Catalogue of Maps*, in which incidentally he first gave publicity to his important discoveries of the handsome and remarkably accurate estate maps of John Walker father and son. Few, apart perhaps from Emmison's closest colleagues, would have then foreseen that the E.R.O. was on the threshold of major advances and the achievement of a prestige that, notwithstanding the undoubted excellence in other counties, is still acknowledged by professionals. Dr Gladys Ward, in the younger days of the *Essex Journal*, has recollected the pride and affection that the old, crowded but thriving office attracted.[2] How agreeable it is that her daughter, Jennifer, now a distinguished scholar herself and one who is indebted to the old E.R.O. and its doughty leader, should be a contributor to this volume. We all, indeed, recall the flavour of those earlier days with gratitude. Now we witness, under the inspiring leadership of Victor Gray, the recent developments at the E.R.O. to new levels of sophistication and the continuing manifestations of the successive changes that have endowed Essex with such eminent archivists and splendid facilities. It is no indulgence at this point of my narrative to recollect the scholarship of the much-loved medievalist Ken Newton, who succeeded Derick Emmison as county archivist and made his own valuable contribution to this path of progress. It is not possible here, to go beyond these brief references in tracing the development of the E.R.O. and Derick Emmison's unique contribution to it. He was always in the forefront of the struggle for full recognition of its professional status. It is significant that nine county archivists had been members of his staff at Bedford and Chelmsford.

On that note I shall turn to a major dimension of Emmison's career: the scholarship and versatility displayed in his publications, a field in which his formidable armoury of knowledge has been readily acknowledged by the wider public audience. The considerable and growing corpus of published work has put his professional career into an impressive relief. For well nigh sixty prolific years his pen has enriched the historical scene with a vast range of original and re-organised material recovered from the complex obscurity of the archives. Essex has been particularly favoured by this and of course by the munificence and scholarship of Dr Marc Fitch, whose support for much of this work and his own immense body of edited indexes and texts have earned the gratitude of numerous students who have benefited from these invaluable reference books.

As Professor Dickens has remarked in his foreword Emmison when only 22 wrote a four-page article prophetically entitled, 'The County Record Office: Its Educational Function',[3] and four years later his book *The Relief of the Poor at Eaton Socon, 1706–1834*[4] appeared. These were but the beginnings: it would hardly be feasible to list all the Emmison publications here. The Society of Archivists published a bibliography of his work in 1977[5] covering the period 1927–1976; it embraced five pages and the run has since been extended by numerous articles and several major works. It is, however, a pleasing necessity to highlight some of the more important offerings and to seek to conjure some of the flavour and erudition that pervades them. All of this work is generally characterised by that sparkling presentational flair which reflects his personality. It also exhibits the intellectual disciplines demanded by the standards of his profession. This rare combination of values in works of academic purpose testifies to the masterful touch and agile mind that created the Emmison bibliography.

The current guides to the E.R.O.[6] have been among the essential tools for every practising Essex historian for several decades. Apart from the clearly tabulated data, they are enriched with excellent, readable and instructive explanatory texts that have stood the tests of time and reference. From the readers' point of view they are good examples of how to furnish information that could so easily belong – albeit at the upper end – to that prosaic genre that normally accommodates railway timetables and telephone directories! It was, nevertheless, *Tudor Secretary: Sir William Petre at Court and Home*[7] that reminded us of what we ought to have assumed, namely, that Derick Emmison was not only a master craftsman and scholar but an artist of style and sensibility. This book is a biographical study of the dextrous and tenacious Secretary to four sovereigns of the capricious House of Tudor. Its impeccable scholarship has ensured a significant account of an important and interesting secondary figure of the period. The continuity of Petre's involvement in the affairs of state at the highest levels, alone establishes his historical interest and validity. The insights the author has extracted from his subject's working relationships with Thomas Cromwell and William Cecil embroider the rich tapestries of administration and daily life in Tudor court circles. Invited by Professors Sir John Neale and S. T. Bindoff to join their Tudor seminars while researching on Petre he was later to see his *Tudor Secretary* included in the short list of recommended Tudor biographies in Bindoff's *Tudor England* (Pelican), a high compliment indeed. Emmison's international reputation as an archivist and Tudor social historian was reflected in invitations to make a number of lecture tours in the U.S.A., where he spoke at numerous universities including a public lecture at Harvard, and to historical and genealogical societies.

As a diversion from reciting Emmison's publications, I interpolate here a pleasant note of what I know he regards as one of the most colourful episodes in his life. His acquaintance with Miss Christina Foyle, who lives at Beeleigh Abbey in Essex, is long standing. Invited to one of her famous literary lunches he was seated not far from Mr Paul Getty, the guest speaker. Two weeks later, Derick and Margaret were hastening from a royal garden party to their car in the Mall, when Derick noticed Mr Getty a few yards behind, searching in vain for a taxi. Grateful for a lift to his hotel in a severe thunderstorm, he enquired his fortuitous chauffeur's name. 'I've read your *Tudor Secretary*' was the surprising remark. In appreciation, Derick was invited to Sutton Place, the Surrey mansion, where Mr Getty gave him a two-hour talk about his collection of pictures and furniture as well as a memorable lunch.

Before returning to the bibliography there is a second anecdotal episode worthy of record here and which provides an agreeable link with another of Derick's major books. The life of a local government official with all its restraints may not be regarded as attractive by everyone. But *Home, Work and Land*, volume III of the *Elizabethan Life* series, brought the author two totally unexpected literary bonuses. It was included in 'Books of the Year' in a national newspaper on the recommendation of Elizabeth David, the author of the well-known cookery books. The colour frontispiece of *Queen Elizabeth the Queen Mother*, the luxurious biography by Godfrey Talbot (1978), shows Her Majesty holding a copy of *Home, Work & Land*, the title and author's name conspicuously visible. It was a charming coincidence that it had been the Queen Mother who visited Ingatestone Hall and who presided at the investiture when Derick received his M.B.E.

If *Tudor Secretary* is the most rewarding and enjoyable of Derick Emmison's books, *Elizabethan Life* is the most memorable and remarkable in scale and sustained scholarship.[8] These five impressive volumes are valuable increments to our knowledge and understanding of social life in the long reign of Queen Elizabeth I. Mainly from the rich Essex sources, some of which are unique, the series reveals, on a wide canvas, the remote recesses of life with authentic records of the mundane but vital aspects of the daily round, family and domestic circumstances, religious observances, public disorder and social misconduct. Facts, vividly portrayed and documented, cascade from almost every page in accessible volumes of essential reference that in other hands could so easily have been diminished into turgid clutter.

The last two volumes of *Elizabethan Life* were replete with abstracts of the wills of the Essex gentry, yeomen and the more affluent merchants. In another series[9] of several volumes, still in current production as I write, Emmison has enlarged the scope of his work on Essex wills to the delight of historians and genealogists alike. In the new *Essex Wills* series, from 1558, the range has been extended to include the lesser gentry, husbandmen, labourers, craftsmen and trades people. The detailed abstracts of the wills of these Elizabethan social classes have, with masterly concision, been made readily available for the study and analysis of the relevant details of thousands of testaments in the vast repository in the E.R.O. Published with American support, especially that generously given by John B. Threlfall of Wisconsin and guaranteed by the Friends of Historic Essex, county history has been endowed with a massive array of full abstracts for 1558–1603 far in excess of any similar corpus of information open to students in any other English county. When one has seen, as I have, the physical and mental problems of coping with such a great volume of material, much of it drawn from barely legible records, one marvels at the intellectual stamina and moral courage involved in compiling the books to such high standards of accuracy and presentation.

Not as prestigious as *Elizabethan Life* or the Petre biography, but more widely known and used have been the publications on the use and understanding of archives. The one that predictably has run to several editions was *Archives and Local History* (1966). Written with clarity and an attractive text, it was also presented with quotations and illustrations from many counties and cities.[10] This book and its more modest but also excellent, literary siblings, *Introduction to Archives* (1964)[11] and *How to Read Local Archives, 1550–1700* (1967)[12] have harvested and retained numerous now devoted adherents for local history who learned the elements of their craft from them. I find myself, as others no doubt do, still turning to them for pleasure as well as instruction in those odd half hours with which only the busiest of local historians can contrive to indulge themselves.

It is not only his prodigious output of publications that distinguishes this author and advocate of the printed text. He has also encouraged, as appreciative prefaces testify, many students and other writers to follow in his well-trodden paths. At the E.R.O. he promoted many excellent in-depth studies by his able staff and other scholars and the popular 'half-a-crown' booklets that covered many interesting specific aspects of Essex history. They must be among the best buys of all time in the field of local history. Even the most assiduous bookshop browsers are unlikely to find any of Derick Emmison's work on the remainders shelves. I hope, however, that others will share my luck in finding, as I did in Tony Doncaster's shop on North Hill in Colchester not long ago, some of his earlier publications that are no longer in print. All discerning local historians must surely enrich their own bookshelves with these works and ensure that they are within easy reach of eager hands and enquiring minds.

Emmison's passion for history in a variety of its numerous aspects and entire devotion to his profession have never excluded his love and talent for music. Those who know of his comprehensive grasp of the technical side of music speculate that he could have enjoyed a career as distinguished in that art as in his chosen work. He is an accomplished pianist and a licentiate of the Royal Academy of Music (1925). It has been an important component in his cultural life. His playing of the mid-sixteenth century virginal at Ingatestone Hall will long be remembered with admiration and was, fortunately, recorded for sale in 1964. As that notable performance was given under the auspices of the Friends of Historic Essex, who had purchased the instrument in 1958 because of William Byrd's close links with Ingatestone Hall, I may appropriately allude here to Derick Emmison's thirty-year service to that important county body. No one has done more to inspire and support the Friends by dint of personal exertions in office and financial generosity. It is one of the success stories of Essex history and archives and, as such, a matter of considerable satisfaction to him for it is a product of his time and policy at the E.R.O. That it flourishes and now has an impressive record of major aid for the office is an adequate monument to the closer associations that he himself encouraged between practising local historians in the county and the Record Office staff.

At the beginning of this essay I wrote of the admiration and awe that, in the introspective attitudes that all areas of intellectual endeavour have, are attached to the person of the county archivist. Emmison worked indefatigably to ensure that the social and academic importance of that profession was established. With all his diverse pre-occupations with the essential bureaucratic processes that burden public administration, research and authorship, he consistently found time and energy to support the subject at local level. Also high in his priorities was always the encouragement of interest in local history among young people. This led Margaret and Derick Emmison to endow an annual essay prize, now almost forty years ago, for work based on research by Essex schoolchildren. With the advantage of Hilda Grieve's expertise and enthusiasm, this was soon an established success and in its wake there are many now successful and devoted historians and historical geographers including Dr William Petchey, Dr Sarah Tyacke and Dr Jennifer Ward. Emmison's passion for research was also reflected in a booklet[13] listing much available material for theses to be found in the various local archive repositories. On another level, he could even find time, his own, as I know for I was one of his appreciative students many years ago, to teach the rudiments of palaeography. Whether he was involved with policy, practice or people, his approach embraced an impressive grasp of scale and detail that could transmute ideas and purpose into reality and achievement.

I turn now to the inevitable but daunting task of summing up this complex, comprehensive man. We may ask first, with some astonishment, how has he done so much? The explanation must begin with, as Anthony Trollope put it in allusion to his own prodigious output, 'the frugal use of time'. That, complemented by professional pride, that precarious attribute itself tinctured with an admissible vanity that impels him towards achievement, application and robust health answer the question I have posed. Such traits, indulged in full measure and with precious little restraint, account for some of the irrepressible foibles of the man, who, up to this point of the essay, has emerged as a paragon of the professional virtues. So he is; but the equally credible portrait is one whose own virtues of enthusiasm, commitment and the pursuit of excellence impose burdens, not always tolerable, on others; he never sought easy popularity with his staff. An assertive unconventionality and an occasional petulance or extravagance are not easily absorbed by more sensitive people. Those who know and therefore like him best, realise that they are matched by the friendly warmth of the guiding hand and an absence of malice. Such extrusions of personality are only to be expected. He has plied his trade and pressed his beliefs with directness, but, there is delicacy too, and a punctilious regard for etiquette and protocol. A transparent and unsubtle humour has also tempered these rigidities to advantage. Few people of Derick Emmison's status or distinction altogether avoid those occasional alienations that roughen the edges of human relationships. One can only say that in his case they are forgivable and almost always forgiven. I have known many perfectionists in my own various spheres of work and most of them have struggled with the incompatibility of high performance and undiluted commitment on the one hand and an easy, undemanding relationship on the other. Not all have exhibited the kindly and generous traits that vie with Derick Emmison's other, sometimes more conspicuous personal attributes. That generosity and the sincerity of his love for his profession and dedication to its objectives were manifest in his gift to mark his retirement in 1969 as an archivist of £1,000 to be shared between the Historical Association and the British Records Association. He stipulated that this sum should be devoted to improving the facilities for the study of local archives and to encourage better publications, exhibitions and other amenities. It was a characteristic act of gratitude.

Heroes and heroines are necessary in all societies, groups and for individuals. For many local historians and genealogists Derick has been that. On a more historical plane, one of mine, in English literature, has been John Milton, whose buoyant spirit, glorious prose and poetry have been uplifting. I recollect studying the *Areopagitica* in my youth, in particular the reference to books an enduring obsession for which I can but plead guilty. Milton opined in that towering essay 'For Books are not absolutely dead things, but do contain a potency of life in them to be as active as that soul was whose progeny they are.' How well that reflects Emmison's written work. Its scale of purpose, the embodiment of industry and academic rigour, the sparkling reference, the Elizabethan emphasis, the devotion to Essex history, and the use and study of archives epitomise the massive contribution he has made and the style and personality of the man.

That said, it would be ungracious not to remark upon the importance of the support and influence of his gifted wife Margaret. It has often occurred to me that there is a neat and coincidentally felicitous touch in Derick Emmison's intellectual love affair with the age of England's great Tudor Queen and his good fortune in having a Scottish wife whose own name, Margaret, is cognate with that of two Queens of Scotland of happier historical connotation than that of some of that generally sad coterie. One, at least, Margaret – the 'perfect Princesse' – the wife of Malcolm Canmore, rightly earned the appellation 'blessed'.

Thus, his friends and colleagues over half a century and more have combined to pay their tribute to Derick Emmison in this volume of essays. To me has been given the privilege of contributing this biographical note and editing the tribute. I have done so in the spirit of Miles Coverdale, the Tudor prelate who, in completing the translation of the bible into English, expressed himself with sincerity and an appropriate modesty thus: 'Though I could not do as well as I would, I thought it yet my duty to do my best, and that with a good will.'

References

1. 'Poor Relief Accounts . . . in Bedfordshire, 1563–1598' in *Economic Hist.* Rev., vol. iii, pp.102-116 (1931); *Types of Open-Field Parishes in the Midlands, with three Maps*, Hist. Assoc., (1937), revd. edn., Phillimore (1965).

2. *Essex Journal*, Vol. 4 (1969), p.120.

3. *County Councils Assoc. Gazette* (Dec. 1929).

4. *Beds. Hist. Rec. Soc. Pubns.*, Vol. XV (1933).

5. *Journal of Soc. of Archivists*, Vol. 5, No. 8 (1977), p.527.

6. *Catalogue of Essex Parish Records, 1240–1894*, 2nd edn. (revd. 1966); *Guide to the Essex Record Office*, 2nd edn. (revd. 1969).

7. *Tudor Secretary: Sir William Petre at Court and Home*, Longmans (1961).

8. *Elizabethan Life*, 5 vols., Essex Record Office (1970–80).

9. *Essex Wills*, Vol. 1 (1558–65), Nat. Geneal. Soc., Washington, U.S.A., (1982); Vol. 2 (1565–1571), New England Hist. Geneal. Soc., Boston, U.S.A. (1983); Vol. 3 (1571–77) (1986), New England Hist. Geneal. Soc., Boston, U.S.A. Also a separate book, *Elizabethan Wills of South-West Essex*, (in Guildhall Library, London), Kylin Press (1983).

10. *Archives and Local History*, Methuen (1966).

11. *Introduction to Archives*, B.B.C. (1964).

12. *How to Read Local Archives, 1550–1700*, Hist. Assoc. (1967).

13. *Material for Theses in Some Local Record Offices*, (jointly with W. J. Smith), Phillimore (1973); revd. edn., Hist. Assoc. (1980).

The County Record Office: The Unfolding of an Idea

VICTOR GRAY

In August 1938, Derick Emmison took up his appointment as the first County Archivist of Essex and the Essex Record Office opened its doors to the first of the hundreds of thousands of researchers who have since drawn upon its resources. For Essex it was a new venture, the acceptance by the County Council of a new responsibility to be carried out on behalf of the people of the county and the recognition of a broader obligation to what would nowadays be succinctly described as 'the heritage'.

County Councils are, however, seldom reckless in the shouldering of new community roles and if, now, the opening of the searchroom door by the very first researcher takes on a birth-like significance, we should be wary of concluding that the concept of a record service leapt spontaneously and fully formed from the conciliar head. The idea had been a long time maturing.

To begin with there were precedents. Immediately to the west, in Hertfordshire, a records service, effectively maintained by the County's Record Agent, Captain William le Hardy, had been operating for many years. Across the Thames, Kent had appointed an archivist in 1933, while just over the River Lea, the Middlesex County Council had, for half a century been taking steps to ensure the well-being of its records. Throughout the country, more than a dozen County Councils were already making some sort of provision for the care of a range of local records and others were on the point of taking up the challenge. Only the imminent war was to slow up the acceleration of the movement towards the point where, by 1955, 70% of the English and Welsh counties were actively involved with archive care.[1] But this was the flowering of an idea. For the planting of the seed we must look further – considerably further – back in time.

It is one of those accidental neatnesses of history that exactly one hundred years before the Essex Record Office opened its doors, Captain Richard Sprye of Bath took up his pen and, in a letter to Lord John Russell, the Home Secretary, set out what may well be the earliest exposition of the idea of locally based repositories for historical records.[2] The son of a Devon vicar and a keen and active historian, Sprye had been shocked by the condition of parish registers in churches close to his father's living and catalogued for the Home Secretary, in tones which re-echo through successive campaigns on behalf of local records, the many types of neglect which he and others throughout the country had encountered: decay, mutilation, misappropriation and wanton destruction. Such observations were even then by no means uncommon but his solution was novel: 'to rescue these Records then from such certain injury and decay, to take them from the exclusive custody of persons so negligent of them and so little disposed to render their contents readily available to the public for their

11

proper purposes to the utmost extent, to make them indeed national records instead of as now merely parochial, and of great public utility instead of almost none . . .'. The machinery by which this was to be achieved was neatly built on the back of the national registration service, set up only in the previous year. A Commissioner should be appointed under whom would work county or diocesan 'Assistant Commissioners or Clerks of Old Registries'. Each of these, working with a team of transcribing clerks, should gather in, in alphabetical order, the registers of each of the parishes within its area. The clerks, some with 'accurate knowledge of old writings' and others with 'a good English round hand', all of them sworn in to make accurate transcriptions, should make two copies of each register, the first to be forwarded for central storage in the office of the Registrar General, the second to be supplied to the parish of origin. The registers themselves, after appropriate repair and rebinding, were to be 'transmitted to the Bishop, or other authority, to be lodged in a Diocesan or County Registry Office' where they would be open to public use on payment of a fee.

The approach by Sprye was skilfully timed. Barely a year before, the new civil registration system had come into operation and Sprye's proposals had all the feel of a complementary tidying up of the records of pre-1837 registration. Non-parochial registers were already the subject of a Royal Commission report and only months before, the Record Commissioners had issued their final General Report which included the detailed results of an enquiry into the nature and extent of surviving records of municipal and county authorities throughout England and Wales. Local records and registration were clearly in the air. And was not this, 1838, to be the year in which, with the passing of the Public Records Act, the foundation was to be laid for a national archive repository?

With everything going for it, Sprye's suggestion slipped quietly into the Home Secretary's files where it slumbered, to be re-awakened only momentarily 80 years on, for a brief appearance as an appendix to a new enquiry. It may have been that Russell was now fully occupied on the record front with plans for the central records of state. It may have been that, alerted by the strong church opposition to civil registration, led by the Archbishop of Canterbury himself during the passage of the 1836 Bill, he was anxious to avoid further impositions upon the freedom of the Established Church. Either way, the time had not yet come for the birth of a system of local repositories to complement that shortly to rise in Chancery Lane.

It was to be upon parish registers, which, for four centuries or more, seem to have spoken to the world at large, eloquently and with the greatest immediacy, of the importance, fragility and irreplaceability of the local written record, that attention was to return time and again later in the century. In 1878, a Bill was placed before the House of Commons with a view to putting pre-1837 parish registers and Bishop's transcripts under the control of the Master of the Rolls, by now of course recognised as titular head of the Public Record Office.[3] Such a step would merely have extended to the records of the Established Church the measure of centralisation which had been imposed upon nonconformist registers under the Non-Parochial Registers Acts of 1840 and the 1858 Registration Act. It would also have set England on a comparable footing to Scotland where all pre-1854 registers had been gathered in to the General Register House in Edinburgh, and to Ireland where most registers had been passed to the Public Record Office in Dublin. Once again, the move was destined to fail.

By this time, however, there had begun one of those subtle shifts of climate, difficult to date and impossible to quantify, which warm the soil just enough to generate new growth and activity.

Exactly why a society from time to time focuses its attention more and more upon its past is a matter for discussion. One could posit any number of reasons for the late Victorian preoccupation with former days and ways. That there was such a tide of interest, broadly based in its appeal and widespread in its effects, is beyond dispute. Since so much of that interest was focused on the minutiae of social history, attention was often turned to the local evidence for specific practices. Already the regular reports of the Royal Commission on Historical Manuscripts, established in 1869 to seek out and report on the contents of the numerous collections of archives which were known to be scattered throughout the country and which fell outside the scope of the Public Records Acts, were quarrying into what appeared to be an unfailingly rich and endless seam of hitherto unsuspected historical detail, uncovered on expeditions into country houses, town halls and diocesan registries. Newly awakened to the fact that the local and particular – and moreover their own local and particular – could have a wider and more general relevance, local record societies and individually inspired and financed publishing ventures sprang up everywhere. At the national level new genealogical and antiquarian periodicals appeared, to meet a growing market.[4] At the same time the rising tide of concern in the last two decades of the century with the past, present and future shape of local government gave rise to a whole new body of serious study, again concerned with the assembling of local evidence.

Caught up in this tide (or perhaps riding it in those cases where local enthusiasm already existed among the elect or appointed) a new awareness began to dawn among local authorities both of the historical significance of the contents of their own muniment rooms and of their responsibilities towards their well-being. Undoubtedly this bloomed most vigorously among the boroughs where it was enriched with civic pride,[5] but in the shires too, where, until 1888, the burden of responsibility could fall only on the less promising shoulders of the magistracy, there were some signs of life. When, in the early 1880s, enquiries were made by the Middlesex Sessions of 41 other counties, 19 of them reported expenditure on the care of their records within the last twenty years. In some cases this amounted only to reboxing costs, but in others sums had been spent on commissioning indexes and calendars and in 11 counties new, additional or improved storage, frequently boasted of as 'fireproof', had been or was on the point of being provided for the records.[6]

The Middlesex response to the problem was more enlightened and better organised than most, but in the extent of the responsibilities which it acknowledged and in the manner in which it set out to shoulder them, it provides a useful case study.

In November 1882 the Sessions appointed a special committee to assess whether any improvement could be made to the accommodation of the records and what might be the best way of sorting and listing them. At their first meeting they inspected the basement of the Clerkenwell Sessions House where the records were piled from floor to ceiling. Seeking professional advice they wrote to the Royal Commission on Historical Manuscripts who sent down the redoubtable John Cordy Jeafferson recently back from a sortie among the Sessions records in Chelmsford.

Unable to make a detailed examination because of the chaos in which he found the records, Jeafferson drew attention to the mould and damp attacking them ('Left as they are, their destruction is merely a matter of time') and tantalised the Committee by hypothesising, on the strength of similar records elsewhere, as to the rich and colourful picture of the county's past that the archives, properly sorted and listed, would reveal. It was too much for the Committee to bear. Hastily they appropriated a committee room for three months, tore down the curtains and rolled up the carpet, covered the tables and brought in trestles. Under Jeafferson's direction, A. T. Watson, Superintendent of Workmen at the Public Record Office, moved in with two assistants and for 45 days worked on sorting the collection, ferrying them from the Record Room by way of a ladder and a hole specially cut through the wall. At the end of the work, Jeafferson's report gently lured the Committee into deeper water. 'The Custos Rotulorum and Magistrates of Middlesex still possess a body of muniments which would enable a zealous and competent antiquary to produce an adequate history of the county from Elizabeth to Victoria.' They needed cleaning, repairing and further sorting, and housing in a larger and better ventilated room. Other records at Westminster needed examination. The Committee followed enthusiastically; all was agreed. The County Surveyor set in motion improvements to the Record Room, totalling £566 8s, and leaving it, by April 1884, 'warmed, ventilated and lighted' and fitted with new glass shelves. By July, Watson was able to report the arranging of 10,118 volumes and 4,916 rolls or bundles. The work had cost around £360, over 60% more than the original estimate, but the Committee were more than content with the full schedule of the records which Jeafferson appended to his report.

It was only when Jeafferson moved into the next phase of proposals that the Committee began to look closely at how far their involvement might take them. The logical next step should be a calendar of the 16th-century records, he argued, 'a work of labour and expense', but 'to glance at the roll of the present Justices of the Peace for Middlesex – a roll brightened by the names of statesmen honourably distinguished by their concern for the interests of Historical Research . . . is to be confident that the Custos Rotulorum and Magistrates of the County will not from mere pecuniary considerations decline to render literature the important service that is asked of them by men of letters and all other men of enlightenment.'

This time Jeafferson had misjudged. The 'hard sell' had been a little too vigorous. The Committee approved the expenditure to date and made not a comment on the latest proposal. Within five months it had met for the last time.[7]

With variations, the short life of this first Middlesex Records Committee typifies the extent of involvement that county authorities saw as appropriate in the years leading up to the First World War. The arrival of democratically elected county government in 1888 made little difference to the nature of this involvement. The improvement of accommodation to a level which was acceptable by contemporary standards was the first step. The calling in of outside expertise to advise on this and on the arrangement of records was the normal response. The major variation lay in the degree to which the authority was prepared to go down the line of sorting-calendaring-publication which was the pattern almost invariably suggested to them.

In Bedfordshire, a Sub-Committee of the General Purposes Committee began to look at what should be done with and for the county records in 1897.[8] By the following year, they had called in a report from Hardy and Page, the London record agents, and set up a County Records Committee. Hardy and Page had immediately offered a price for sorting and calendaring the Sessions records but quickly fell in line with the new Committee's obvious need to go more slowly. Their report on storage suggested the need for no more than regular ventilation and cleaning. A start could be made on improving things by sending the Sessions Books to the P.R.O. for repair and cleaning. By 1899, the Committee were ready for the next stage; a clerk was taken on for three months to arrange the documents physically along lines suggested by Hardy and Page.

For the next few years activity was desultory but positive: minor improvements to storage conditions, continuing repair and notes on the more interesting items compiled by Hardy and Page. The practice of regular expenditure on the records – usually £100 more or less – was becoming well established. By 1907, Hardy had completed his notes up to the reign of William IV and it was decided to print these, together with an Introduction by the Committee chairman, the Rev. Paul Williams Wyatt, for limited circulation, primarily to members of the Council.

At this point, Hardy was himself invited to meet the Committee. The opportunity seemed ideal and, on the surface, fruitful for, by April 1909, the Committee had approved the full calendaring of the Sessions minute books. By now, however, enthusiasm was quietly waning. When the Committee met on 25 April 1910, the Chairman was the only member present. Unconcerned, it would seem, about inquoracy, he proceeded to authorise further expenditure on sorting and shelving, but took the step of mothballing work on the calendar. For the moment, Bedfordshire had set the bounds of its commitment to its archives.

In Hertfordshire, a Records Committee had been set up in 1895, two years before neighbouring Bedfordshire and a mere six years after the County Council had come into being.[9] At its very first meeting, chaired by Sir John Evans and held at the Inns of Court, the seemingly ubiquitous W. J. Hardy (himself a resident of St. Albans) was invited to make a preliminary inspection and report. Three months later it was on the Clerk's desk. With an assistant to help dust and sort, Hardy had visited and prepared a preliminary list of records in the Records Room and in the roof of the Shire Hall, in the Clerk's own solicitor's office in Hertford and in the Court House and Town Hall at St. Albans. Hardy, predictably, suggested bringing the older records together in a single fireproof room. The more recent papers could easily be sorted by an untrained hand leaving only the pre-1750 Sessions Rolls to be dealt with by a professional. These the firm of Hardy and Page would be ready to work on. At the same time, repair and binding should be undertaken. In the longer term, Hardy pointed out, other counties – Middlesex and Worcestershire, for instance – were compiling lists for publication. Should the County wish to follow these examples, Hardy, as editor of *Middlesex and Herts. Notes and Queries*, would be only too ready to provide a publishing outlet to reduce costs.

Work on cleaning and binding began straightaway, using the St. Albans firm of S. Austin and Sons. Hardy arranged for the sorting of the documents prior to binding. By December 1899, the rolls had been sorted and bound up to 1770 at a total cost of £268 3s 10d. (The original intention of working up to 1750 seems to have been quietly forgotten). Five years later, in October 1904 the Committee finally called a halt at the year 1880. Not that this was to be the end of the story. Far from it. Hardy and Page were already now hard at work compiling a more detailed calendar of the early rolls at a newly negotiated rate of pay. Furthermore it had, one suspects, taken little persuasion to bring the Committee to the view that the increasingly lengthy series of extracts presented to each Committee meeting would be easily assembled to form prestigious volumes of County Records. The first two, covering the period 1581 to 1698 and 1699 to 1850 appeared in 1905.[10] Five hundred copies were printed and put on sale at 15 shillings a piece. In vain did the County Accountant point out that the Committee had already spent £1,125 on the records and was about to venture a further £513 on publication. The presses rolled, the volumes appeared, work went on on a third volume (published in 1909) and began on a fourth, to cover the Sessions of the Liberty of St. Albans. With £2,175 spent in total and the St. Albans calendar ready to 1833, the Committee met in March 1914, for the last time before the War. By the time they reassembled in December 1919, Hardy was dead.

In the meantime, there had been, if not major new developments on the national front, at least a flurry of activity. In 1891, a body of private persons interested in local archives and their preservation, drafted proposals for an Act which would impose new statutory controls. The attempt was repeated in 1898 but support was not sufficient and the matter was dropped.[11] Not, however, from the minds of everyone. Among those who had become increasingly concerned was the Bishop of London, the Rt. Rev. Mandell Creighton.[12] In March 1899, Creighton wrote to Arthur Balfour, then First Lord of the Treasury, on the subject and received an indication both that the matter would be put before the Cabinet and that Balfour considered it would be a good idea to have a question raised in the House. He was as good as his word. In August a Treasury Committee was set up 'To enquire and report as to any arrangements now in operation for the collection, custody, indexing and calendaring of local records, and as to any further measures which it may be advisable to take for this purpose'. The members were to be the historian and politician James Bryce, M.P.; Sir Francis Mowatt, Permanent Secretary of the Treasury; Sir Courtenay Ilbert, Parliamentary Counsel to the Treasury; S. E. Spring-Rice, Principal Clerk in the Treasury and – to provide the weight of expertise – Sir Henry Maxwell Lyte, Deputy Keeper of the Public Records. In the Chair was the Bishop himself.

In the meantime, Creighton had begun attacking on another front. He had now got himself made chairman of an Episcopal Committee looking into the nature and adequacy of the storage provision made for diocesan archives throughout the country. In December 1899 he sent out a circular to bishops on the subject and early in 1900 presented to the Ecclesiastical Commissioners a report on the replies. As a result, a Bill was drafted placing upon the Commissioners the responsibility for providing adequate storage for diocesan records, giving them the power to make rules as to the terms of care and custody and guaranteeing arrangements for public access on payment of a fee which should be paid into the common fund of the Commission. In return, all expenses connected with the provision should be met from the same fund. The Bill was introduced by Lord Belper but did not meet with widespread approval. In July the Congress of Archaeological Societies came out in favour of deferring the Bill until the Local Committee on Records had reported. A few days later Stanley Leighton, M.P. for Oswestry and founder of the Shropshire Parish Register Society, published a letter in the *Manchester Guardian* criticising the vagueness of the wording of the Bill, doubting the abilities of the Ecclesiastical Commissioners as record keepers and urging, instead, a pause for further thought. Might there not be a case, for instance, for considering an alternative arrangement involving the appointment of Diocesan Record Committees charged with the provision of a diocesan record office, the classification and possibly the printing of the records? The costs might be met by voluntary subscription and local incumbents might be invited to deposit their records there.

The climate was obviously running against the Bill. It went no further. All eyes were now fixed on Creighton's other Committee with its broader remit.

It is clear that, even before Bishop Creighton set his Committee to work on their deliberations, he had already formulated the idea which was to form their central recommendation: that of a network of record offices to cover the country and to provide a readily available repository for local archives of every nature. In a letter to Count Ugo Balzani in Italy, written on 10 July 1900, Creighton speaks of having written some time previously 'about a plan which I had started for constituting local archives in England. I prevailed on the government to give me a committee'. Indeed the final report of the Committee conceded that, from the beginning they had seen such a network as a possible remedy for the problems and that the questionnaire which formed the nub of their enquiries, and which had been sent out in November 1899 to more than 850 potentially interested parties had been couched in such a way as to gather responses to the idea.

The Report itself was, according to Creighton's widow, drafted late in 1900 but its eventual publication, in 1902, was delayed by the untimely death of Creighton in January 1901. It was left to his successor as Chairman, James Bryce, to pull together the loose ends. The proposals clearly did justice to Creighton's ambitions.[13] Local record offices should be set up in the wake of enabling legislation. That the basic idea was sound, the Committee had had no doubt. A majority of responses to their questionnaire had been in favour of such a step. The problem had been to decide on the appropriate level of catchment area and the type of authority which should administer them. A range of suggestions had been made. Urban and rural districts, boroughs, poor law unions, district probate registries and county courts had all had their advocates. The Historic Society of Lancashire and Cheshire had proposed a system based on universities which should link a chair of palaeography to the keepership of a central muniment room for the area, an idea rejected by the Committee on grounds both of the size of the area so created and of the difficulty of maintaining central control. Some individuals and organisations had seen some merit in wider, regional repositories, comprising groups of consenting counties.

In the event, the scheme favoured by the Committee was one which placed the responsibility for archive care on county councils but allowed to boroughs the option of retaining their own records. In this the Committee were recognising not only the fact that, outside the larger towns, there seemed to be little archive-consciousness but, perhaps more to the point, the strength of local feeling for retention within the towns, best summed up by the succinct response of the town clerk of Arundel to the notion of establishing local archive-collecting repositories: 'The Corporation of Arundel would not part with their documents'.

In the Committee's eyes the County Councils formed the natural authorities upon which to build a network. Their powers of inspection of Parish Council records, under section 17(9) of the 1894 Local Government Act provided a natural starting point, and the present activities of some counties in indexing, listing and in some cases publishing the Sessions records provided evidence at least of a potential. The new county record offices might be administered by a committee of the council (precedents already existed). As to the custodians, they and their assistants 'should have sufficient knowledge of palaeography to decipher the records in their charge and to make certified copies in return for fees; and this requirement of itself postulates the existence of some school where the necessary training could be supplied'.

The Committee had to tread gently on the delicate ground of ecclesiastical records. No ready answer presented itself to the question of how far the clear independent right of the Church of England to legislate for the care of its own records might be reconciled to the position proposed. In the event the Report contented itself with the hope that diocesan and archidiaconal authorities might wish to unite with the counties in the provision of joint repositories for both civil and ecclesiastical records and that, in the case of the much-prized parish registers, the deposit of pre-1837 volumes should be 'permitted and encouraged', with power reserved to the bishop to order deposit where desirable.

As to the owners of private and semi-private records, the voluntary use of local record offices should be encouraged by emphasising the continuity of ownership; loan deposit upon terms established in a table of regulations should be the norm and with their rights secured owners would no doubt be all too ready to take advantage of the safe custody offered.

Thus far, the Committee, armed with a crystal ball, would have been able to recognise in the situation which eventually (but oh so eventually) emerged in this country the scheme to which they had aspired. In one important respect however their hopes were not to be realised. It was, thought the Committee, 'eminently desirable' that, in the interests of uniformity of approach to the task before them, local record offices should be subject to inspection by officers from the Public Record Office. The suggestion had itself been put forward in their returns to the questionnaire by several local authorities and by a number of scholars, in particular the highly influential Congress of Archaeological Societies which had submitted a return to the Committee following a special meeting to consider the matter in March 1900. Inspection would serve to provide expert assistance in archive administration, would provide the channel through which reports on conditions and performance could be received centrally and considered locally by administering committees and, above all, would serve to encourage uniformity of approach in such matters as fees and indexing, which the Committee had listed under their essential requirements for an archive systems; 'to secure this it would be necessary to place the various local offices under the supervision of one central department'.

The 1902 Report distilled and focused a good deal of the thinking on the subject of local records which had been going on at the turn of the century. The ideas it embraced were to re-emerge, sometimes as theories, sometimes as practices, over successive decades. The reasons for its becoming the subject of almost immediate governmental apathy or calculated silence remain to be traced. In one respect, however, its conclusions refused stubbornly to be ignored and when, in 1910, a Royal Commission was set up to look into the workings of the Public Records Act, its terms of reference included an inquiry into 'the custody of local records of a public nature'.

It is clear that the 1899 Committee provided the Royal Commission with a valuable starting point in many areas of its considerations. In almost every respect they came to agree with the findings of their predecessors.[14] If they had any quarrel with them it was in the matter of their diffidence when it came to suggesting legislative change. These new Commissioners were less inclined, both by their status as individuals and by the weight of their Commission, to hold back out of modesty. Under the chairmanship of an Admiralty Court Judge (Sir Frederick Pollock) their membership embraced, inter alia, the Directorship of the British Museum, the Presidency of the British Academy, the Provostship of Eton and formerly of Kings, the sometime Vice-Chancellorate of Cambridge University, the editorship of the

Dictionary of National Biography, the past presidency and the current vice-presidency and treasurership of the Royal Historical Society, membership of the Historical Manuscripts Commission, three University Chairs, two governorships and the treasurership of the National Library of Wales, two high sheriffdoms, a recordership and the Chair of a Quarter Sessions.[15] Whatever it chose to say, the voice would be authoritative and articulate. In method of consideration, too, this was altogether a weightier body, proceeding not only by circular but also by interviewing 62 witnesses in 31 separate sittings and inspecting more than 100 collections of records in 30 towns, the extent and number of such visits limited only by wartime exigencies.

Armed with no established definition of what comprised local records of a public nature, the Commissioners took a broad view, commenting specifically on quarter and petty sessional records, the papers of local courts of record (which they described as being scattered in some 2,000 separate repositories), county, borough, town and civil parish records, the archives of a whole range of statutory authorities, including Turnpike Trusts, Boards of Guardians, River Conservators and Income Tax Commissioners, as well as those of semi-public bodies like charitable trusts, friendly societies, canal and railway companies and water boards. Nor, having ventured into these more tentatively public fields, did they hesitate to comment on the situation regarding diocesan, ecclesiastical court and parish records.

Perhaps inevitably, given their remit for considering the whole spectrum of activity of the Public Record Office and their consequent detailed knowledge of both the intent and workings of the Public Records Acts, the Commissioners had a different stance from the members of the 1899 Committee. Their concern for local records was based less exclusively on their historical worth and took into account their legal and evidential status. The need to administer current records properly in order to provide for the future survival of a balanced and adequate public archive featured more prominently in their deliberations. To this end, they placed much weight on toughening up existing provisions for ensuring that authorities exercised their responsibilities thoroughly in this respect: the county councils should be compelled to take more seriously their role in supervising the care of civil parish records for instance and the Guardians of the Poor should be taken to task where they made inadequate provision for the care of records in district registries.

Despite these differences of approach, their overall conclusions were remarkably similar to, if more clearly defined, than those contained in the 1902 Report. Local record offices, usually based on and administered by counties and county boroughs should be established in proper fire- and damp-proof buildings where facilities for access by students would be guaranteed at reasonable fees and where the records would be properly arranged and listed. Such a system would build upon local patriotism and help stimulate 'provincial schools of history'. 'It should be regarded as a point of honour for a well-managed and progressive county or municipality to possess a record office, just as much as a public library and a museum'.

But local patriotism needed to be assisted by central government. State funds might be used to assist in setting up local record offices which might, after all, serve the additional purpose of providing sub-repositories of the Public Record Office for the storage of locally generated public records, a suggestion which the Commissioners had already put forward in their second Report. And if, on the one hand central government should come bearing gifts, it should also, on the other, wear the mailed glove. For the situation which the Commissioners had both heard about from their expert witnesses and seen for themselves on their visits was very far from satisfactory. Standards of archive care throughout the country were uneven and often lamentable. There were no established criteria in matters of building construction, methodology of listing or conservation. There was no measure of competence for custodians. 'We are clearly of opinion that no remedy short of a central controlling power will be effectual'. The power of the Master of the Rolls should be extended by Order in Council to local records of a public nature. The importance of calling upon local patriotism to provide the motive force for the provision of an adequate repository was one thing, but in case it did not prove enough there would, once the records concerned had been declared public, be the ultimate sanction of the Master of the Rolls' power to remove them from unsatisfactory conditions. This should be sufficient to incense local opinion into improving inadequate standards. To keep an eye on local provision, a new section of the Public Record Office for dealing with local records would need to be set up to monitor standards, and provide advice and supervision where necessary.

Local archivists of today will recognise the birth here of the concept of 'improvement by persuasion' which is still current today. If they find it hard, however, to relate the somewhat modest reality to the much more grandiose conception, that must be laid at the door of the Commissioners' total failure to secure the extension of the definition of public records, upon which the whole 'stick and carrot' system was to depend. No doubt, as Dr. Emmison suggested as long ago as 1929, the timing of the report was inopportune.[16] Though the Commissioners finished their deliberations in 1916, it was not until 1919 that the Report was published and, in the immediate post-war period, priorities lay elsewhere. (When, one begins to wonder, would the timing of a report on archives be 'impeccable' or 'exactly opportune'?). No doubt also, the mere publication of such a consideration gave succour and encouragement to those who were striving towards the same goal. The ideas it contained would, from time to time, break cover and take on a new life. For the moment however it was left, as before, to individual and local effort to forward what was increasingly being seen as a legitimate objective. And in one corner at least, those objectives were moving towards practical reality.

It is to Bedford that we now return and to the arrival on the scene of a new archival flag-bearer, this time in the unlikely guise of a retired marine zoologist. George Herbert Fowler had retired from his work at University College, London in 1909 at the age of 48. His father's death having left him with adequate independent means, he set to work to restore his 16th-century house in Aspley Guise and, discovering a new passion in local history, began not only to write the village history but to found the

Bedfordshire Historical Record Society. At the same time, he stood in a 1912 County Council bye-election and within a year had been made Chairman of the by now somewhat exhausted Records Committee.[17]

Nothing that Fowler ever took on was done half-heartedly and clearly his chairmanship was to be no mere sedentary pastime. Within three months of his appointment he produced, in January 1914, a report on the state of the county archives which cut, like a knife through butter, into the torpor which had overcome the Committee. There was, said Fowler, a need for a comprehensive arrangement of the archive. Non-county material should be cleared out of the muniment room, the floor strengthened, rolling presses introduced to increase capacity. He himself was ready to give of his own time, but he would need an assistant. Together they would arrange the room by classes. The Committee were swept up by this new tide of energy; by the end of the meeting the County Surveyor had been instructed to set to. Before war had time to break out in August, the room had been re-equipped and newly ventilated, an assistant had been taken on at 30 shillings a week, irrelevant material had been removed, a scheme of classification prepared and destruction schedules for managing current records drawn up. Moreover, with an eye to the future, Fowler had drawn up both a draft form of agreement for the receipt of deposited collections and regulations for researchers seeking access to the records.

That Fowler brought to his new interest a much-needed scientific approach, an instinctive organisational talent and a useful natural hyper-activity cannot be doubted. But, given his training, it would be unlikely that he undertook his onslaught without first assessing the state of the art. Even from his first brief report it is clear that he visualised the county taking on the wider role of custodian of local deposited records proposed in the report of the 1899 Committee.[18] It is also clear that he was already in touch with the Royal Commission. Though, according to their Report, the Commissioners did not begin to consider the subject of local records until June 1914, Fowler was in January of that year leaking to his Committee the news that 'it will probably recommend that the Counties should accept, on deposit, private collections of papers and deeds which have local interest'. He urged the committee to make provision for such a step whether or not it formed a final proposal of the Commission. It was, after all, a good idea. As so often, both before and after in the history of archive services, a seemingly innocuous suggestion, quietly slipped before the eyes of a committee, was ready to open the door to a whole new level of activity.

It was in fact while Fowler was away from Bedfordshire, preoccupied with war work at the Admiralty, that the county's first deposit of private archives appeared. In 1917 Miss Elinor Lucas presented to the Committee a number of local deeds and in so doing set in train a new phase in the history of archive care at the county level, not only in Bedfordshire but, ultimately, throughout the country. Outside the town and university libraries, such an arrangement was almost without precedent.

Fowler was released by the Admiralty in March 1919. 'I at once resumed work in the muniment rooms', he told the Committee. There, for four and a half years, while the fate of Europe was being settled, Mr. W. D. Baker,

Fowler's assistant had been at work rough sorting the collections (Fowler was later to talk of this early work as 'peculiarly filthy and disheartening'). He was soon back in his stride and by October 1920 had completed the cataloguing of the County Council's records. Over the next few years, quietly but with a firmness of touch, he took a series of steps which were to be emulated, often much later, in one after another emerging record office. The development of the scope and nature of a new public service was being worked out in prototype.

In 1922, for instance, the Committee spent £3 9s 6d to acquire its first purchased items; Fowler began to talk of numbers of students in a way which has since been repeated *ad nauseam* in countless annual reports; he began to concern the Committee with recent records by instituting a class of war records; he purchased materials and equipment to enable him to carry out first-aid repairs; and he introduced the committee to the idea of training up a professional staff. Already in the previous year, he had persuaded the Committee of the desirability of accepting custody of the records of the Archdeaconry of Bedford by warning them that the alternative would be for them to go to St. Albans where they would be 'lost to Bedfordshire'.

In 1923, Fowler produced the first treatise on local archive care, *The Care of County Muniments*, published by the Association of County Councils. It took the principles of Jenkinson's *Manual of Archive Administration*, published the previous year and moulded them to local needs, wrapping them around with exactly the no-nonsense practical detail that would be needed by any beginner establishing a county service and adding a brief historical account of local administrations. The descendents of Fowler's classification scheme, his searchroom regulations and deposit receipts, first set forth here, are still embedded in a surprising number of record offices sixty years on.

This too was the year in which Fowler appointed his first trainee Clerk of the Records, at an initial salary of £52, rising by increments to £300 per annum. Of the seven candidates for the post, he chose one F. G. Emmison, a pupil of the nearby Bedford Modern School, a step the significance of which for the future development of the local record office ideal even Fowler could scarcely have foreseen.

It was by now all coming together. Fowler's steady advances towards the broad-based county record office envisaged in the 1919 Commissioners' Report received a welcome stimulus with the new procedures for recognising repositories for manorial documents, 'rendered historical' by the Law of Property Acts of 1922 and 1925. In Hertfordshire and Middlesex, Hardy's son, Colonel W. H. C. le Hardy, carrying on his father's business, urged the County Councils to assume the wider role. Other counties also took up the call.

This later period of more increased activity has, however, already been well documented.[19] The activities of the British Records Society and Association, and of the Institute of Historical Research, the spread of repositories and the appointment of archivists, the acceptance of manorial and diocesan roles now shifted development into an altogether higher gear. At the end of this phase was to lie, for Essex, the appointment of its first

County Archivist and, for the country, the achievement of an almost comprehensive network of county repositories.

We have slipped from concept into practical development, from blueprint to prototype. The idea had been a long time developing below ground and if, now, it was able to break the surface and to spread and flourish with increasing speed and vigour, it was because of the slow and careful nurturing it had received from Fowler and the Commissioners, Bishop Creighton and the Hardys, the investigators of the Historical Manuscripts Commission and ultimately, in its earliest glimmerings, from Captain Sprye, whose 'County Registry Office', had, finally, nearly a century on, become a reality.

Notes and References

1. The point at which a county archive service can be said to be properly established is hard to define. The figures here are compiled from *British Archives: a guide to archive resources in the United Kingdom*, J. Foster and J. Sheppard, (1982).

2. Transcribed as Appendix II.15 to the Third Report of the Ryl.Cmsn. on Public Records (Vol. III, Pt. II) Cmd. 368, (1919).

3. The 1902 Local Records Committee report (see n. 13 below) draws attention (p.22, n.1) to an article by T. P. Taswell-Langmead in the *Law Magazine and Review*, (May 1878), in support of the Bill. Further evidence of its content and passage has not yet been collected.

4. The 1880s were the great period of initiative for local record publication. New local societies venturing into record publication in the second half of the 19th century included: The Manx Society (1859), Wilts. Arch. and Nat. Hist. Soc. (1862), Cumbs. and Westm. Antiq. and Arch. Soc. (1877), Lancs. and Cheshire Rec. Soc. (1879), Staffordshire Rec. Soc. (1880), N. Riding Rec. Soc. (1884), Middx. Rec. Soc. (1884), Yorks. Arch. Soc. (1885), Oxfordshire Hist. Soc. (1885), Somerset Rec. Soc. (1887), Hants. Rec. Soc. (1889), Thoresby Soc. (1891), Hon. Soc. of Cymmrodorion (1892), Worcs. Hist. Soc. (1893), Wilts. Rec. Soc. (1887). For fuller details see E. L. C. Mullins: *Texts and Calendars*, R. H. S. (1958).

On the genealogical front *Miscellanea genealogica et heraldica* first appeared in 1868 and the *Genealogist* in 1877.

5. The pioneering work of some boroughs and cities in developing the care and publication of local archives is outside the limited scope of this essay but should in no way be underestimated or overlooked. It was from precedents set here that both theorists and practitioners of county archive services must have drawn many ideas. Earliest and most advanced in the collection of local archives was the Guildhall Library which took in manuscripts from 1824 and the archives of local bodies from 1863 (see the Introduction by Raymond Smith to Part II of *A Guide to the Records in the Corporation of London Records Office and the Guildhall Library Muniment Room*, P. E. Jones & R. Smith, (1951)). Others early in the field were Liverpool, Leicester and Cardiff. A useful summary of early work by the boroughs is contained in *Appendix II to the Report of the Committee on Local Records*, Cd. 1333, (1902), which details replies by Town Clerks and others to enquiries made by the Committee as to the extent of surviving records and steps taken to care for and arrange them.

6. An undated summary of replies appears in the Miscellaneous Committee Book of the Middlesex Sessions, Gtr. London R. O.: MA/C/MISC/1) from which the account in the following paragraphs is compiled.

7. Jeafferson's work was next taken up by the short-lived Middlesex County Record Society, founded in 1884 for the purpose and wound up in 1888. Calendaring and publication resumed when the Standing Joint Sub-Committee set up a Records Sub-Committee in 1900 and brought in W. J. Hardy, the Record Agent, to carry forward the work along lines paralleling those adopted in Hertfordshire and Bedfordshire.

8. This account of activity in Bedfordshire is based on Beds. R. O.: CRM1, County Records Cmtee. minutes and CRP1, Records Cmtee. papers.

9. Details taken from Herts. R. O.: HCC18 1 and 2, minutes of the County Records Committee.

10. *Hertford County Records: notes and extracts from the Sessions Rolls, 1581 to 1698* and *1699 to 1850*, W. J. Hardy, Hertford (1905).

11. The 1891 and 1898 proposals are mentioned by Sir Hilary Jenkinson in 'Archive developments in England 1925–1950' published originally in *Miscellanea Archivistica, Angelo Mercati*, 37–361, (1952) and reprinted in *Selected writings of Sir Hilary Jenkinson*, 271–292, (1980).

12. Some account of Creighton's efforts can be found in *Life and letters of Mandell Creighton sometime Bishop of London*, written by his wife and published in 1906. See particularly Vol. II, 436–7. See also Lambeth Palace Library: Creighton FP65 for some of the documents cited here.

13. Published as *Report of the Committee appointed to enquire as to the existing arrangements for the collection and custody of local records, and as to further measures which it may be advisable to take for the purpose* Cd. 1335, (1902).

14. The Commission's findings on local records were published as the *Third Report of the Royal Commission on Public Records appointed to inquire into and report on the state of the public records and local records of a public nature of England and Wales*, Cmd. 367, (1919).

15. The members were: Sir Fredk. Pollock (Chairman), Sir E. Vincent Evans, Prof. C. H. Firth, M. R. James, Sir F. G. Kenyon, Sir Sidney Lee, Henry Owen, H. R. Tedder and W. Llewellyn Williams.

16. 'The County Record Office: its educational function' in *County Councils Assn. Official Gazette*, (Dec. 1929), 344–348.

17. A useful biographical note on Fowler is contained in the Report of the Bedfordshire Records Committee for 1967.

18. The following details are taken from the minutes and papers of the Beds. County Records Cmtee (Beds R. O.: CRM1 and CRP1).

19. For this later stage see Sir Hilary Jenkinson's account (*vide* n. 11) and 'The development of local archive service in England' by Elizabeth Ralph and Felix Hull in *Essays in memory of Sir Hilary Jenkinson*, ed. A. E. J. Hollaender, (1962).

Essex Boroughs and their Records

GEOFFREY MARTIN

The year 1988 will mark some notable anniversaries, two of which will be much in the minds of those who contemplate such occasions from the vantage-point of Essex. The first is the centenary of the Local Government Act of 1888 (51 & 52 Vict. c.41), which against some more recent events stands out as a strikingly successful contribution to the ordering and management of local affairs. The second is the fiftieth anniversary of the decision taken in 1938 by the County Council's Record Committee to establish a record office in Essex, and consequently to recruit F. G. Emmison from his native Bedfordshire to devise and manage it.[1]

The two events are closely related, and they open large vistas forward and backward in time. The Record Office has so far maintained its territory rather more successfully than the county. Its policy of acquisitions under successive directors has ranged freely over the historic ground of Essex, whilst the county itself has endured much administrative surgery. Travellers from London now leave Stratford bridge, and even Romford market, far behind them before they cross the border into Essex. The holdings at Chelmsford, however, reflect both such recent and more remote changes, and they present even the most disruptive of them in an apprehensible form. Although the face of Essex today would, at least momentarily, surprise Chapman and André, or Philip Morant, they like many others would readily find themselves at home in the company both of the records and of those who frequent them.[2]

Amongst the many constituents of Essex, from its barely-imaginable beginnings as the kingdom of the pagan East Saxons, its boroughs have been a numerous and varied company. As a group they have been relatively long-enduring, though subject individually to widely contrasting fortunes. They have also been objects of interest throughout their existence, and latterly beyond it, to archivists and a variety of students. Even within the life-time of the County Record Office, a period which though packed with incident is brief in comparison with the historical perspectives of St Peter's, Bradwell, or Greensted church, borough records have flowed in and out of the premises in Chelmsford. Their disposition today is complex and historically interesting: a microcosm of Essex as a collection of communities.

The word borough has always been an elastic one, and its literature is extensive. It is taken here to mean a community with urban qualities, or at least urban aspirations, which imply certain administrative arrangements, and which lead on to an ascertainable status in law when law itself can be discerned. Essex is taken to be the historic county in all its manifestations. Although untidy in their origins, early history, and some of their more specialised forms, boroughs could down to their general extinction in 1973 claim to have had a longer tradition of record-keeping than any other local community in the country. Indeed, as counties joined the archival race at a rather later date, and metropolitan boroughs have lingered on beyond the life-time of metropolitan counties, it may even be that the boroughs will retain that distinction. Whether they do or not, they have produced a wide range of texts since their inhabitants first took to writing and, in however modest a way, filing.[3]

The East Saxons encroached early upon the Middle Saxons, and their power probably extended into Surrey. It is certain that London was for a time the chief settlement of their kingdom. When Essex subsequently became a unit of the larger kingdom of Mercia, however, it found itself confined to the east of the Lea, and it has always been more or less content to lie south of the Stour. Within those bounds there have been at least 35 boroughs, of all sorts and conditions, over the centuries. Five of them survive today as the London Boroughs of Barking, Havering, Newham, Redbridge, and Waltham Forest, which have swallowed ten municipal boroughs between them, and the present district of Colchester has retained the formal title of Borough. Even to summarise them in that fashion, however, uses terms and involves ideas that require closer definition.[4]

The word borough, the Old English *burh*, originally meant a fortified place, and in its origins probably no more than a fortified farmstead. In that sense there would have been many *burhs* in the lands of the East Saxons, and there are traces of some in place names, such as the stronghold of the Daenningas, now Danbury. Originally there were probably as many as there were units of settlement, though there may have been fewer as the early tribal units like those commemorated by the names of Vange, the *ge* or region of the fen-dwellers, or the interesting group of *ingas* and *ge* place-names round Ingatestone, coalesced into a kingdom.[5] The East Saxon kingdom in turn became a client of Mercia, and lost its outlying territories beyond London, and even the great *Lundenburg* itself. The primitive *burhs* had by that time long served their turn, but with the emergence of a kingdom of the English after the Danish wars the *burh* became generally something more than a strongpoint, and the borough emerged.

As the West Saxons reconquered the areas occupied by the Danes they consolidated their gains with the first recognizable system of local administration in England. The major unit was the shire or county, such as the former kingdom of Essex became. The shire was managed for the king by a shire-reeve, or sheriff, and sub-divided into units called hundreds, of which Essex eventually contained twenty. Boroughs, which served both as administrative and trading centres, were fitted into the pattern as they developed. Edward and Elder campaigned in Essex in 914–917, building *burhs* at Maldon and Witham, and expelling the Danes who had occupied Colchester and were holding it as a strong point. He may have built another *burh* at Horndon-on-the-Hill during one of those campaigns. Horndon had some such status, and it is difficult to think of a later date at which it might have had some strategic significance.

The shapes of the hundreds that emerged in the liberated and resettled county cut across such indications as we have of the earlier tribal settlements. The pattern was still incomplete at the end of the eleventh century, but in the meantime the nascent system had assimilated a new institution. The borough was now a trading place with a market licensed and protected by the king, the site of a mint and of a court distinguished from the courts of the surrounding hundreds, and known as a borough because it was usually, probably invariably, enclosed by fortifications. Of Edward's foundation in Essex the *burh* at Witham may only have been a fort, but the name of Chipping or Market Witham seems to have attached to the area by the church before the market at Newland was laid out in the early thirteenth century, and Witham does give its name to a hundred. Horndon appears to have had a mint, however, whilst Colchester and Maldon figure in Domesday Book with features that set them clearly apart from the general pattern of rural settlements.

Colchester had its own territory in 1086, rated as a hundred, which included the village of Lexden and was apparently carved out of Lexden Hundred, as was the borough of Maldon's half-hundred from Dengie. It also had strong fortifications, its Roman walls, repaired by Edward the Elder, and not improbably, although Domesday Book does not mention it, some part of its enormous castle. Both boroughs had a mint, both paid special dues to the king. Domesday does not mention any markets in Essex, but there is no reason to believe that either Colchester or Maldon functioned without one. Above all both are marked by concentrations of population, and their inhabitants are described as burgesses.[6]

Domesday Book is a uniquely valuable source of information, but its approach to the boroughs is tentative and often puzzling. In recording them it uses a variety of terms, and it frequently omits information about them which we should not only have wished, but might from other indications reasonably have expected, to have. At the same time we know from pre-Conquest sources, chiefly the Old English laws, that the king had sought to control trade and secure revenue by granting privileges, or imposing special duties, on townsmen. The uncertain indications of such functions in Domesday Book, such as its sparing and uneven references to markets, reflect the fact that in the eleventh century wealth was observed and thought of as a matter of agrarian resources. There was evidently little curiosity amongst the aristocracy or the clergy about the ways in which the value of those resources was realised, although the proceeds were always welcome. The fact that they impinged as far as they did upon the Domesday survey, which was not directly concerned with administrative arrangements, is evidence that the boroughs proved a more powerful and prominent feature of English society than the Conqueror's advisers had supposed or expected.

What gave towns importance was their access to money and supplies, which arose from their crude but decisive monopoly of trade. The surpluses of the countryside were wasted unless they could be converted into cash or credit, and the markets and mints of the boroughs provided the principal means. Their specialism meant that the inhabitants, the burgesses, had to be left to their own devices in a manner then unthinkable for rustics. In trade there were no prescribed courses like those of the farmer's year. There is evidence in Domesday Book, at Cambridge and elsewhere, that the king's agents, like those of other lords, exacted manorial services from townsmen when they could, but for much of the time it was simply more profitable to take the money, and increasingly less than worth-while to enquire closely into the manner of its making. In a society which defined men by the nature of the services which they performed, burgesses were therefore characterised by rents and the communal render of tolls, whilst their numbers and propinquity led them into associations and forms of common action more ambitious than those found outside the borough walls. They evidently had some sense of community at the time of the Domesday Survey, and by the end of the twelfth century they can be found negotiating directly with the king, with some confidence and success.

The earliest borough records from Essex, as opposed to notices in other documents, are royal charters. Maldon received one from Henry II in 1171, Colchester a more elaborate charter from Richard I in 1089, exempting and burgesses from the jurisdiction of courts outside the borough, and granting them freedom from toll throughout the kingdom, and the right to elect their own bailiffs, or chief officers. Richard and his brother John, who were each constantly short of money, though for different reasons, granted privileges to the principal boroughs much more liberally than had their father Henry II, and it is not to be supposed that they pressed them unsought upon the burgesses. Behind every charter there lay negotiations between the leading townsmen and the king's officers in which the townsmen's desire for privileges was closely measured against their willingness and ability to pay for them. Colchester's charter followed upon several years' accountancy by the burgesses at the royal Exchequer, where the Pipe Rolls recorded an annual statement of the king's income and expenditure in the shires, and it is likely that both the negotiations and an earlier grant or grants from the king stretched back to the time of Henry I.[7]

Certainly by the end of the twelfth century burgesses in the royal boroughs had experience both in dealings with the king and in managing the internal affairs of their communities in ways that made their applications and promises convincing. They had conducted their own courts for more than two hundred years, and had found in them a setting for public discussion and simple administrative business. They also had in the gild a highly adaptable institution, which they used as we now use committees, for the advancement of any cause that required concerted action. There is at present no evidence in Essex of the gild merchant which has been regarded by some scholars as an essential ingredient in the making of boroughs, and which at Leicester (1196) and Shrewsbury (1209) produced the earliest surviving administrative records from the English municipalities. However, unacknowledged gilds would have sustained the perilous business of bargaining with the sheriff or the king, just as social and religious gilds, like the Trinity Gild at Saffron Walden, subsequently provided the means of holding the ruling townsmen in informal but powerful association with each other. Whatever the means, the royal boroughs began a significant enlargement of their public responsibilities in the century following the Domesday survey.

In the meantime other places were acquiring some of the chacteristics of the royal boroughs. The process had started elsewhere by the time of

Domesday, and it might well be that just as the return for Essex takes no account of markets so the presence of burgesses on seignorial manors was not felt to be a matter of consequence. In the course of the twelfth century, however, the number of markets grew everywhere with the population, and lords enfranchised their tenants on selected manors, perhaps not always on carefully selected manors, to take advantage of new commercial opportunities. The process is unevenly documented, as royal grants of market rights, which undoubtedly were often confirmations of existing markets, were not systematically enrolled until the reign of John. There were nevertheless more than 70 markets licensed in Essex by the middle of the fourteenth century, and in many instances they were in manors which had probably engaged in trade in the twelfth century, or even earlier.[8]

In some of those places we find references not only to markets and fairs, but to privileged tenants called burgesses. They included Pleshey, where the ramparts of the Norman castle, reconstructed and strengthened in the later twelfth century, embrace the site of the borough. There were also burgesses at Berden, at Great Bardfield, on the bishop of London's estate at Chelmsford, at Harlow, where the abbot's tenants were granted the same terms as his burgesses at Bury St Edmunds, and at Harwich, Manningtree, Newport, Thaxted, Waltham Holy Cross, and Writtle. Hatfield Regis may have had some burgages, as it was represented by its own jury before the king's justices itinerant in 1198, but there seems to be no other signs of that status in its later history. It would at any time be possible to extend the list, if references to burgesses were found in any of or all the other sixty places in the country which had markets or markets and fairs during the Middle Ages. For the moment, however, the company is a closed one, determined by the accidental survival of documents and the use by their clerks of one word rather than another. Its constituents represent one particular stage in the development of the economy and social structure of England.[9]

The time during which a lord could create a borough by enfranchising his tenants and securing a market charter was effectively over before the latest Essex names appear in the list. The creation of parishes by the assignment of tithes had a similar efflorescence, for much the same reasons. Between the eleventh and the thirteenth centuries a growing population created unprecedented demands for food, commodities of all kinds, and services. The towns existing at the time of the Domesday Survey offered a model, the willingness of the king to grant or confirm markets enabled many lords to establish small boroughs, and a few, like the bishop of Norwich at Lynn, to nurture what came to be major settlements. Then the very success of the movement began to change its terms. Royal government grew in sophistication and power as it marshalled the reserves of society; the established use of written records strengthened routine and the force of precedent. The emergence of Parliament during the fourteenth century gave the king new resources, and imposed a new pattern upon the localities.

Parliaments evolved from the practice of enlarging the king's council by consultations with distinct groups of his subjects. The lords, as tenants in chief, were summoned individually but assembled as a body, and representatives of the commons of the realm, that is to say of the gentry and other free-holders, were summoned in the name of their county. On occasions merchants were summoned as a group, but the usual form was for the sheriff to call for representatives of the boroughs in the shire at the time when he prepared the return of the two knights who were to speak for the community at large. The sheriff evidently exercised a good deal of discretion, and in general he named what was later called the county town, as the seat of the shire court, and then any other borough that commanded attention.[10]

Essex was unusual in having as its principal borough, in Colchester, a town that did not house the shire court, although its huge castle served as a gaol and no doubt on occasions as secure quarters for the sheriff. However, although Chelmsford had attracted the court, as it did the later assizes, by its central position, and although it had been enfranchised with burgage tenure and had come to overshadow its neighbour Writtle, it was never recognised by the sheriffs as a borough to be represented in Parliament. The only places in the medieval county to be ranked with Colchester were Maldon, regularly, and on one occasion Harwich. The others, varied in their individual fortunes, remained in the second rank.

It is not difficult to see why the sheriffs decided as they did: they were generally disposed to define boroughs as royal, ancient, and named in Domesday Book. Harwich, developed as a hamlet of Dovercourt and no larger than any of the other successful market towns, probably attracted attention as a port. The other small boroughs might well not have wished for the distinction, even if they had won an autonomous status, for the costs of representation in Parliament were a charge upon the community itself, and parliamentary boroughs regularly sought townsmen who would be willing to pay their own costs, and sometimes petitioned for exemption from the obligation to return anyone at all. It might even be that Chelmsford evaded rather than missed representation, as merchants from Chelmsford attended a council in 1337, but that was a time when Edward III was furiously intent on raising finance for his opening campaign against France, and the wool-producing and wool-trading parts of the country were scoured for those able to pay or to propose schemes for making others pay for soldiers and supplies.[11]

The Chelmsford merchants, themselves not numerous, probably had few congeners elsewhere in the county at that time, outside Colchester and Maldon. The smaller Essex boroughs were manors with markets, their tenants in burgage rather craftsmen and chandlers than wholesale dealers, and members of a community that was predominantly agrarian. Colchester and Maldon themselves had open fields with common pasture and meadows within their bounds, though in both the principal manorial rights came to be vested in the community of the burgesses. Townsmen in general were as interested in farming, and especially in grazing and commoning rights, as anyone else. With all their other preoccupations, the burgesses of Colchester pertinaciously urged their claims to Kingswood Heath, which now largely serves their successors as an industrial estate, just as those of Maldon defended their rights in Tiptree Heath, another part of the royal forest. They did so, however, because at least outside London the life of every town had an agrarian setting, and even London had its Moorfields outside the wall, and many orchards and garden grounds within. In a world of manorial lordships, therefore, the question was with whom local authority lay, and where it lay with the burgesses themselves even a sheriff could discern a borough.

The distinction was duly reflected in the records. Public business throughout the Middle Ages remained judicial in character, and the court roll or court book was for long the principal register of the borough's administration. The burgesses of Colchester were given cognizance of ordinary pleas by Richard's charter, but none of their rolls has survived before 1310, when the long series now begins. It is clear from Morant's *History*, however, that there were written muniments in the town in the thirteenth century, and by the late fourteenth century the town clerks were drawing up volumes of memoranda of which two survive as the Red Paper Book and the Red Parchment or Oath Book. Both contain collections of constitutional texts, ordinances and memoranda, including a town chronicle in the Red Paper Book, and a calendar of the court rolls from 1327, eventually extended to 1564, in the Oath Book. Colchester maintained a single continuous record of all kinds of business in its courts, rolling the membranes together and filing them at the end of each year. A medieval register or custumal known as the Black Paper Book has since been lost, and there may well have been other guides to the contents of what was evidently a substantial collection of muniments. The earliest records from Maldon are rather later in date, and there court books precede the earliest surviving court rolls. Again however the burgesses conducted the whole business of the town, answerable to the king only for an annual rent in discharge of all dues.[12]

In the lesser boroughs the burgesses lived and worked as the tenants of lords who were not necessarily resident, but whose officers oversaw the community and in particular kept its courts and its records. In many such instances the borough was a short-lived institution. Not all markets prospered, and those that did could often function without close support beyond the immediate presence of a craftsman or two. Berden and Great Bardfield, even Pleshey by the end of the Middle Ages, exemplified that process.[13] At Hatfield Regis and Waltham the borough may never have been more than an aspiration, a matter of a status granted to or even assumed by manorial tenants, and then repented or resisted by their lords, or simply ignored by the rest of the world and at last by themselves. There were other places, however, where the mysterious ingredients of growth were present, as in Great Dunmow, Saffron Walden, and Thaxted.

Thaxted had burgesses, burgage tenure on its principal manor, in the fourteenth century when, apparently, Dunmow and Walden did not. All three places had chartered markets and fairs, but at Thaxted the grants, made between 1296 and 1327, seem to have been more closely associated with a perceptible urban growth. By the middle of the fourteenth century, Thaxted housed a cutlery-making trade which was on a substantially larger scale than the metal-working crafts that were to be found in many other and larger towns. Its origins are undocumented, and its resources unexplained.

There was no steel-working nearer than the north Midlands, and no grit-stone any closer to hand. Wood for knife-handles could have been cut as readily anywhere else in Essex, and horn anywhere else in the kingdom. The manor was in the house of Clare down to the death of Gilbert de Clare at the battle of Bannockburn, was then held by Bartholomew de Badlesmere, and was later long disputed between his heirs and the Clare co-parceners. Its affiliations offer no ready suggestion about any immigration of craftsmen, whilst a native growth seems even more unlikely. Nevertheless, there was a cutlery industry in Thaxted, and the indications of the splendid parish church are that the community was a prosperous one throughout the fourteenth century and as far into the fifteenth as the reign of Edward IV, whose Mortimer ancestry had brought the manor to the crown. The movement of both the raw materials and the finished products challenge the notion that inland traffic in the Middle Ages was spasmodic and localised.[14]

What we know of the medieval borough of Thaxted comes from manorial documents and from the records of the national poll-tax of 1381. By 1393 the burgesses were well enough established to rent the market stalls and tolls from the lord of the manor, to have an elected officer to represent them, and to dispute matters of right with the lord's steward. It is unlikely that they maintained no records of their own, but none has survived. In the early sixteenth century, when the town's trade was probably in decline, the bailiff was known, at least to his fellow burgesses, as mayor of Thaxted, and presided over the lord's court in company with the steward. Even those intimations come, however, from a manorial extent made for the earl of March in 1393, and from evidence in a dispute between the burgesses and the lord of the manor in the 1560s, which followed the formal incorporation of the borough by a royal charter in 1556.[15]

The burgesses' object in securing that charter was probably to offset their economic difficulties. If so, their new dignity did them little good, and it brought new responsibilities with it. The doctrine of municipal incorporation developed over several hundred years and found full expression in the fifteenth century. It gave townsmen a corporate personality which enabled them to hold common property with perpetual succession, to sue and be sued without hazard to individuals, to regulate their own affairs by making by-laws, and to express their unity by the use of a common seal. The earliest charter of incorporation in Essex was granted to Colchester in 1462, and largely expressed in due legal form the rights and privileges which the burgesses already enjoyed. Its principal innovation was the grant of a separate Commission of the Peace to the magistrates of the borough, a device that reflected the gradual growth of a new system of local jurisdiction, and also established a new test of a borough's autonomy.

Maldon did not acquire the same status until 1553, by which time another community had been enfranchised, though without a Commission of the Peace. The newcomer was one of the older manorial boroughs, Saffron Walden, a name which says something, though not everything, of its history. Walden was a market settlement at the centre of an important manor. In the fifteenth century it had been enriched by the cloth trade, which flourished widely in north Essex during the later Middle Ages, as it did in Suffolk and Norfolk. By the early sixteenth century the cultivation of the autumn crocus in the town fields was so intensive that Market Walden became better known as Saffron Walden. The stamens of the plant were used both as a dye-stuff and in medicine and cookery, and the specialism survived locally as long as the cloth trade itself, disappearing only in the course of the eighteenth century.

Walden's rise to incorporation was as remarkable as, and rather better founded than, that of Thaxted. The burgesses had their tenurial privileges confirmed by Henry IV in 1402 and by Henry VIII in 1512, and a charter two years later in 1514 gave the leading townsmen, as members of the gild of Holy Trinity, control of the market and mills. The use of a social and religious gild as a supplement or alternative to municipal authority, somewhat in the style of later statutory commissioners in later centuries, was one found in many other places, but on the eve of the Reformation it entailed particular risks. The burgesses of Saffron Walden, however, contrived to extricate themselves with some adriotness. In 1549, two years after the suppression of gilds and chantries, they secured a charter of incorporation from Edward VI, and with it the management of a town school and almshouses of earlier foundation, with endowments of a kind that they might have lost in the general confiscation.

The Burgesses of Colchester, from a stronger base, had contrived ten years earlier to continue their medieval grammar school by a timely reassignment of chantry lands, and Walden may have learned something from their example. It certainly looks as though others learned from Walden. Despite a change of regime and religious doctrine, the borough prevailed upon Queen Mary to confirm her brother's charter of incorporation in 1553. Two years later Great Dunmow, a market town with a similar though less imposing stake in the woollen trade, was also incorporated. Against that background the action of the burgesses of Thaxted has something of emulation about it, despite their claim, duly echoed in the charter, that they had had a mayor at their head since time immemorial.[16]

The doctrinal convulsions of the 1550s, when Mary tried to restore the country to Rome and Elizabeth thrust it into her own style of Protestantism, were accompanied by a serious economic crisis and a sharp contraction of the cloth trade. There was widespread unemployment which was most evident, and least readily offset, in the towns. Colchester was one of the East Anglian boroughs which experimented in 1555 and 1556 with a compulsory rate for poor relief, and so set a pattern for the national system developed by statute between 1572 and 1601. The standard unit of administration was the parish, an institution upon which the Tudors had imposed a variety of duties since the late fifteenth century, and in which the Christian virtue of *caritas* eventually found some strange expressions. Whilst the Poor Law is not in all its aspects the most engaging manifestation of the human spirit, however, it transformed English local government, and it would be difficult to suggest a more plausibly effective use of the resources with which the Elizabethan parliaments sought to meet the needs of their day.[17]

For the moment, therefore, the magistrates in Colchester wrestled with the problem of recruiting the means of sixteen parishes to relieve the distress which was unevenly spread through them, and in so doing began a process that has left its marks on modern local government. In the smaller boroughs, as in the villages, the community was contained within a single parish, and parish government, especially in the all-important business of poor relief, existed alongside and often outlasted the ritual management of courts for small claims and closed annual elections into which unextended municipal government usually lapsed. Where there was wider business to be done, however, both the means of accomplishing and of recording it responded to its demands. The ready availability of paper, cheaper and more adundant than parchment, encouraged the use of casual memoranda, and of books, bound volumes, rather than rolls. A conservative feeling in Colchester preserved the form of the roll for some purposes down to the nineteenth century, but the Court Books appeared alongside the court rolls in the late fifteenth century, and the minutes of town assemblies were removed from them into a separate series of Assembly Books from 1576 onwards.

Colchester, with substantially the largest population and territory, had the most complex system of records to inform its administration, but Maldon could match many of its activities, including an Admiralty Court, on a smaller scale. Maldon's clerks used books for current business from the late fourteenth century onwards, and the sixteenth century saw a similar multiplication of paper documents for draft accounts and memoranda of all kinds. The other incorporated boroughs have less to show beyond their charters, which were usually kept with particular care. Thaxted has some late sixteenth century accounts, but a confirmation of its by-laws at the Assizes in 1607 is a reminder of its minor role status.[18]

By that time another Essex borough had been incorporated. Harwich had secured several confirmations of its liberties as a free borough down to 1547, but in 1604 it obtained a full charter of incorporation with a Recorder for its courts, control of a second market and two fairs, and the right to return two Members of Parliament. The last provision was one sparingly granted by that time, and may be a reflection of the strategic importance of the town as a crossing point to the Low Countries. From the seventeenth century onwards Harwich has a continuous history as a packet station and, down to the end of World War II a naval base, an association that gave the Crown a long interest in the borough as a constituency. The medieval borough of Harwich is documented in a long series of manorial rolls from the fourteenth to the sixteenth centuries, and the new corporation conserved its own court and assembly books with some care from its inception. As at Saffron Walden the church provided a focus of public work and record keeping which was quite substantial, although St Nicholas's in Harwich was for many centuries only a chapel-of-ease to the parish church of Dovercourt.[19]

The political stresses of the seventeenth century would have left comparatively little mark on the Essex boroughs if it had not been for the quirk which brought a Royalist army to Colchester in 1648 to stand siege there from the Parliamentary forces under Fairfax. The county was a notable centre of Puritanism from Elizabeth's reign onward. The Puritans were probably not greatly more numerous than those who supported or sympathised with the king and the Anglican church, but they were notably better organised, and Essex passed quite smoothly under the control of its parliamentary Committee and stayed there until it welcomed Charles II in 1660. Opinion in the towns was often finely divided, and by the end of the destructive siege in August 1648 the burgesses of Colchester had no great enthusiasm for either side. The war dislocated the clothing trade and recovery was slow, although Colchester merchants began and continued to make money again over the next century, and the town's looms drew on a spinning industry that spread over the whole northern part of the county. In the meantime the aftermath of political and sectarian strife was expressed in the growth of Nonconformity and the imposition of religious tests for municipal and other public offices. Sacramental certificates lingered on to the abolition of tests for Protestant dissenters in 1828, and appear in many places in addition to Bundles 125 and 133 in the Harwich borough archives.[20]

The economic recovery of the late seventeenth century was the beginning of a complex process that has continued, despite the varying fortunes of individuals and localities into the present time. The changes in the historic community, though masked by the conservation of institutions and the natural strengths of tradition, were deep and portentous. Improvements in transport began not with the Bridgwater canal in 1761 but with the first experimental turnpike works, on the Great North Road and the Harwich road, in the 1660s. The flurry of commercial activity in the city of London was accompanied by a steady growth of wharves along the banks of the Thames and a new value for land in the south western parishes of Essex as merchants began to seek relief from 'the thick air and hurry of London'. Sir Josiah Child's mansion at Wanstead set a standard to which few could aspire, but it was a portent.[21]

So were some other episodes of the time. When James II attacked the corporations in his efforts to contrive an obedient House of Commons, Thaxted surrendered its charter and then failed to regain it either from James or from his successors. The other boroughs were more resilient, although they had trying times to comes. Colchester in particular, faced with the vulnerability of an industrial population, procured a private Act in 1698 to establish a union of its parishes for the purposes of poor relief. The experiment lasted only half a century, and by the time it was abandoned the municipality itself was in difficulties. For the moment, however, Colchester was again, as in the 1550s, leading a movement which slowly and painfully became a national policy. Like other municipalities, it then fought a long rearguard action to maintain its traditional forms and functions, a tradition which looked back to a closed and would-be autonomous community which had won privileges and wished only to preserve them. The parochial base of the poor law was another, though powerfully enduring expression of the same principle. In Colchester disputes over the nature of the freemen's privileges and elections to the council reduced the corporation to legal incapacity in 1742, and it had to be reconstituted by charter in 1763 to avoid dissolution.[22]

That low point in its fortunes coincided with the first serious work on the history of the town. Philip Morant's *History and antiquities of Colchester* was published in 1748, as he moved to achieve his larger design of a history of the whole county, *The History of Essex* was published in parts from 1763 and completed, with a second edition of *Colchester*, in 1768. Morant's work on the county was based on earlier antiquarian collections which originated in the sixteenth century, but since his arrival in Colchester as rector of St Mary's-at-the-Walls he had worked extensively on the historic archives of the borough. In doing so he removed material from the strong room which his executors subsequently failed to return, but his interest and careful work probably preserved more records than were lost. His *History*, which expresses a view of the past which is closer to our own than to that evidenced in earlier centuries, is an interesting picture of a community in the early stages of a major change.

There is a marked advance in technique to be seen if one sets Morant's work beside Samuel Dale's edition of Silas Taylor's *History and antiquities of Harwich and Dovercourt* which appeared in 1730 and was republished in 1732. Dale was celebrated as a botanist, rather than as an antiquary. Taylor, who appears under his pseudonym of Domville in the *Dictionary of National Biography*, was an early collector of historical manuscripts who served as keeper of the naval stores at Harwich from 1665 to 1678. He read extensively amongst the borough's muniments, and made extracts of material for a history of the town, which after his death came into Dale's hands. Many of Taylor's notes are still amongst the archives. A calendar of council acts made by the clerk about 1690, which includes material from act books which have since been lost, suggests that Taylor's interest either coincided with, or perhaps stimulated, some offficial concern with the records.[23]

The eighteenth century saw one of the two historic industries in Essex, farming, in a state of increasing prosperity, and the other, the woollen trade, in gradual decline. The processes were not readily detectable from year to year: agriculture is never free from risk, and there were substantial fortunes still to be made, at least for Colchester merchants. Over the whole period, however, the rebuilding of farmhouses and rectories, and the spread of neat Georgian facades in villages and market towns speak of the vigour of farming and marketing. The absence of substantial innovation in the cloth industry, and perhaps also the presence of some handsome houses such as the Minories in Colchester, as representing a clothier's capital investment, tell the rest of the tale.

The other boroughs showed something of the same process. Harwich was sustained by the naval yard and by traffic to the Continent. The Guildhall was handsomely rebuilt in 1749, and by the end of the century the town had public baths to cater for the new fad of sea-watering bathing. Dunmow, which was a collecting point for yarn to be used by the Colchester bay-makers, was able to compensate the decline of that trade by general marketing, though not as successfully as Saffron Walden. The rise of farming against cloth-making is shown in Saffron Walden by the development of the corporation properties around the new Guildhall, the accounts for which survive from 1761 onwards (Borough Archives, 86) alongside the records of corn sales and prices in the years of the French wars (Borough Archives, 75–85). The beginning and last phase of an interesting stage in the town's history are marked by a survey of property taken in 1670, and a census of occupancy preserved from the second year of the Decennial Census in 1811.

If those had been the county's only manifestations of the great changes that took place at that time, Essex would have presented a very different face to our own age. A steady growth of population, at least from the 1730s, offered a growing market for farming produce, and conditions favoured the countryside and the smaller markets rather than the established towns. The bay-and-say trade looked traditionally to exports in markets that were not themselves expanding, while cotton from Lancashire had begun to capture business at home and abroad. Commercial and industrial activity everywhere, however, was reflected in and sustained by London, and London pressed unrelentingly on Essex. As the docks spread down the river, both the riverside and inland parishes filled with people. There was work for all comers, but the rewards were uneven, and the organisation of the local communities was of the simplest kind. The vestries were active and enterprising in Barking and West Ham in the seventeenth century, and late in the eighteenth, in 1786, Barking and Romford secured Acts of Parliament to establish corporations to manage poor relief, the directors of which in Barking were given powers to manage the town wharf. Those were significant gestures towards a municipal status that took many more years to realise.[24]

The French wars of the late eighteenth and early nineteenth century brought a further stimulus to farming and the final eclipse of the cloth-trade. Cromwell's *History of Colchester* in 1824 speaks of the bay-and-say industry as entirely decayed, and not even a subject of regret amongst the townsmen, whom he judged more likely to miss the business that the Napoleonic barracks had brought them. However, the 'recent climax of wealth and refinements' had brought 'a demand for the productions of the general shop-trade', and although there was some depression in the markets in the early years of the peace, Cromwell foresaw a return to a 'healthy state of moderate prosperity'. The phrases are bland, but the general perception quite acute. Farming remained in an uncertain and distressed state for more than another decade, but the town had some new functions, and as a centre of retail trade, itself a comparative innovation, was beginning to enjoy some of the dividends of an industrial society. Its corporation was less far removed from the realities of life than some others. The continuing records of the borough court and council are largely formal, and may give a less lively impression of the community than do the medieval rolls, but its assets, which included the oyster fishery, were quite substantial in relation to the general economy of the town.[25]

One measure of harmony lacking in some other boroughs appears in the working of the Improvement Act of 1811 (51 Geo. 3, c. 43) which provided for paving, lighting, cleansing, and some other services, including the care of the harbour and its channel. The commissioners, who were obliged to publish their accounts annually, numbered the borough magistrates together with those county magistrates resident in the borough. They were not an inactive body, and the state of the town centre, including a system of gas-lighting from 1818, seems to have been creditable to them. Their presence, however, was also a reminder of the unresolved problem of a general modernisation of municipal government comprehended, with other questions, under the catchword of Reform. The industrialising society needed a competent system of local administration, but the close association of the parliamentary franchise with municipal incorporation meant that the management of the towns would have to wait upon parliamentary reform. Although only Colchester, Harwich, and Maldon returned Members of Parliament, they and the other communities of the shire, whether incorporated or not, had to remain as they were.

Parliamentary reform came, after bitter delays, in 1832 (2 & 3 Will. 4, c. 45). Essex was given a northern and a southern division each with two Members, whilst the boroughs also kept their two each. By the time of the Reform Act of 1867 (30 & 31 Vict., c. 102), when the county constituency was divided into six, and Harwich and Maldon lost a member each, the boroughs had been reformed by the Municipal Corporation Act (5 & 6 Will. 4, c. 76) of 1835. Uniform corporate bodies appointed by staggered annual elections, meeting virtuously in public and publishing annual accounts, were established in four of the five surviving boroughs. Great Dunmow was excluded from the benison of the national scheme, though its twelve chief burgesses were still elected annually and controlled the market which their predecessors had acquired from the lords of the manor.

The municipal boroughs with their committee minute books, valuation lists, and proliferating printed forms were still in some sort islands of a distinctive administration. Around them, and to some extent within them, however, the Poor Law Amendment Act of 1834 (4 & 5 Will. 4, c. 76) had created what became, by default, the basis of English local government. Unions of parishes, on the model of such earlier municipal unions as those of Bristol and Colchester, administered a system of poor relief which corrected the defects of the old system with an often ugly display of officious small-mindedness. The architect of the new system, Sir Edwin Chadwick, was a caricature of the man whose intellectual perspicuity blinds him to practicalities. He was also abundantly punished by his countrymen's subsequent indifference to the issues of public health to which he turned, with genuine and deep concern, when the misapplication of his ideas had made the lives of all paupers, as opposed to some in the past, adequately miserable. In positive terms, the Unions enlarged the franchise by allowing women to vote for the Boards of Guardians, and provided, though often enough in a repugnant form, a setting for the first substantial essays in the amelioration of public health.

The new administrative units were groups of parishes broadly but not consistently modelled upon the old Hundreds and their analogues, the rural deaneries. In the event Colchester remained a Union of itself, whilst Maldon and Saffron Walden were joined with their neighbouring parishes in Unions of their own names, and Harwich, though still a distinct community, was absorbed by Tendring Union. In default of a new form of government for urban communities the vestries continued, at first beside the Unions, but from the middle of the century beside other public bodies, from which a new system eventually emerged.

A powerful new factor in the development of the county appeared in 1840 when the Northern and Eastern Railway, later called the Eastern Counties and Norfolk, was opened. That first line was of less immediate consequence to Essex than the Eastern Counties line to Colchester, opened in 1843 and extended to Ipswich by the Eastern Union Railway in 1846, and the London, Tilbury and Southend Railway, opened in 1856. The Eastern Counties line had its first terminus at Bishopsgate and its principal works at Canning Town, Stratford, which in 1863 became the depot of the Great Eastern Railway. The railways had a strong effect everywhere, and are particularly associated with the growth of seaside resorts, which in Essex began late in the eighteenth century on the Thames, notably at Southend, and continued on the Tendring Hundred coast, encouraged first by steamships from London and then by the railway, at Walton, Dovercourt, and Clacton-on-Sea. Dovercourt, which had been first the mother parish and then a mere rural appendage of Harwich, grew strongly from the opening of the line from Manningtree to Harwich in 1854, which also stimulated the packet traffic and led to the opening of Parkestone Quay in 1883.[26]

In simple terms of numbers, however, the chief effect of the railways was in the area outside London. By 1861 West Ham had 37,639 inhabitants, a figure which Colchester matched only in 1901, although it had trebled its size during the century. The old ecclesiastical parish of West Ham was divided into three in 1844, when Stratford and Plaistow were established as full parishes, and district churches were built in all parts. The whole was then unified administratively by a Board of Health and Burial Board established in 1856. The Burial Acts of 1852 and 1863 (15 & 16 Vict., c. 85; 16 & 17 Vict., c. 134) were important agents of local reform, which allowed the closure of churchyards and the establishment of cemeteries under elected authorities. As the century progressed, Local Boards were charged with wider responsibilities under legislation culminating in the Public Health Act of 1875 (38 & 39 Vict., c. 55), and as Urban Sanitary Authorities began to exercise the powers which ought generally to have been applied fifty years earlier. West Ham developed so rapidly that it was incorporated as a borough in 1886, a transformation which owed something to its enfranchisement as a Parliamentary Borough the previous year in the wake of the Reform Act of 1884. By that time the inhibiting factor in the promotion of municipalities was no longer the parliamentary franchise but control of the police. West Ham had evidently passed the test.[27]

In 1888, the Local Government Act created County Councils in place of the old county magistrates, with aldermen and councillors elected on the municipal model of 1835. In the same year, Chelmsford, now the seat of a busy council and its administrative offices, was chartered as a borough. So in 1892 was Southend-on-Sea, which had not only grown as a sea-side resort but was now a substantial dormitory town.[28] In 1894 another Local Government Act established a network of Urban and Rural District Councils in place of the sanitary authorities, and the south-western parishes in particular could be assimilated in a uniform system. Formal incorporation followed more slowly. East Ham became a borough in 1904, but Ilford and Leyton had to wait until 1926, although each had been given a Member of Parliament, together with Southend and Walthamstow, under the Representation of the People Act of 1918 (7 & 8 Geo. 5, c. 64). The pace of development was in fact quite uneven, as the siting of West Ham's Isolation Hospital on the outskirts of Dagenham in 1892 shows.[29] The new boroughs, which were joined by Walthamstow in 1929 and Barking in 1931, took over the functions and the records of their predecessor authorities, and were able to celebrate the centenary of the Municipal Corporation Act in 1935 with varying degrees of emphasis. In the years before the outbreak of World War II Romford (1937), Wanstead and Woodford (1937), Chingford (1938) and Dagenham (1938) all received charters.[30]

In those same years the Essex Record Office was established, and its energetic incumbent began to gather in the records of the county and its constituent communities. When the heavy duties of the wartime years were laid upon the local authorities there was an added urgency in the task, and the appearance of the first *Guide* to the Office in 1946 showed how much had been done in an unpromising time. Since then the reorganisation of the government of London in 1964, and of local government at large in 1973 has changed the shape of the county, but not of its archivists' beneficient interest in its records. That interest was well expressed by the establishment of branch record offices for Southend-on-Sea (1974) and Colchester (1985) to house the records of those municipalities. And, whilst much else has come into the county archivist's purview, the districts of Harwich and Saffron Walden still keep at their own charges the muniments which have come down to them.

In that present disposition the archives of the boroughs of Essex well express the variety of their history. Between Colchester and Dagenham, or between Thaxted and Southend, they offer for our instruction an exceptional range of communal experience, and an endless tale of the devices by which the troublesome but so far indispensable entities called towns have had to be managed. That a substantial number of their records should be in Chelmsford, that former manorial market-town, now a cathedral city, with as unconventional a history as any shire town can show, is a fitting outcome to the labours which F. G. Emmison began.

Notes and References

1. F. G. Emmison, 'Early years in county record offices', *Journal of the Society of Archivists*, 7 (No. 8), (October 1985), pp. 534–536.

2. For the Record Office, see F. G. Emmison, ed., *Guide to the Essex Record Office*, 2nd ed., Chelmsford, (1969), and the other publications of the Office at large.

3. For a conspectus of published work, see G. H. Martin and S. C. McIntyre, *eds.*, *A bibliography of British and Irish municipal history: 1, General works*, Leicester University Press, (1972). For material deposited in the Essex Record Office, see the *Guide to the Essex Record Office*, and F. G. Emmison, *Essex parish records, 1240–1894*, 2nd ed., Chelmsford, (1966).

4. They are, or were, in their earliest manifestations, Barking, a Municipal Borough from 1931; Berden, a manorial borough; Castle Hedingham, a manorial borough; Chelmsford, a Municipal Borough from 1888; Chingford, a Municipal Borough from 1938; Colchester, a borough by prescription; Dagenham, a Municipal Borough from 1938; East Ham, a Municipal Borough from 1904; Great Bardfield, a manorial borough; Great Dunmow, a manorial borough incorporated in 1555; Harlow, a manorial borough; Harwich, a borough incorporated in 1604; Hatfield Regis, a putative manorial borough; Horndon-on-the-Hill, the site of a pre-conquest mint, and a putative *burh*; Ilford, a Municipal Borough from 1926; Leyton, a Municipal borough from 1926; Maldon, a borough by prescription; Manningtree, a manorial borough; Newport, a manorial borough; Pleshey, a manorial borough; Romford, a Municipal Borough from 1937; Saffron Walden, a borough incorporated in 1549; Southend-on-Sea, a Municipal Borough from 1892; Thaxted, a manorial borough incorporated in 1556; Waltham Holy Cross, a manorial borough; Walthamstow, a Municipal Borough from 1929; Wanstead and Woodford, a Municipal Borough from 1937; West Ham, a Municipal Borough from 1886; Witham, a *burh* in 912; and Writtle, a manorial borough. Romford was the *caput* of the liberty of Havering-atte-Bower, which was regarded by the Municipal Commissioners in 1835 as a manorial corporation, and by Ll. Jewett and W. St John Hope, in *Corporation plate and insignia . . . of England and Wales*, London, (1894), as a borough. It might be better to say that all boroughs were liberties, rather than that some liberties resembled some boroughs.
Of the present London Boroughs, Barking has absorbed Barking and Dagenham; Havering has absorbed Romford; Newham has absorbed East Ham, West Ham, and part of Barking; Redbridge has absorbed Ilford, and Wanstead and Woodford; and Waltham Forest has absorbed Chingford, Leyton, and Walthamstow.
The manorial boroughs, except for Castle Hedingham (Record Office *Guide*, p. 122), are listed in M. W. Beresford and H. P. R. Finberg, *English medieval boroughs: a hand-list*, Newton Abbot, (1973), and M. W. Beresford, *New Towns of the Middle Ages*, London, (1967). For a general bibliography of places in Essex, amplified by the individual studies subsequently published in the *Victoria History*, see W. R. Powell, *ed.*, *A History of the County of Essex: Bibliography*, London, (1959), which also contains a useful survey of public libraries in the county and its boroughs as they were then constituted.

5. P. H. Reaney, *ed.*, *The place-names of Essex*, English Place-Name Society, 12, Cambridge, (1935), pp.xx-xxiii.

6. H. C. Darby, *Domesday England*, Cambridge, (1977), p.365. See Also G. H. Martin, *The Story of Colchester*, Colchester, (1959).

7. For charters at large, see the works cited in Martin and McIntyre (n.3, above, especially p. 143). Colchester's charters are translated in W. G. Benham and I. H. Jeayes, *The charters granted to the borough of Colchester*, Colchester, (1903).

8. For a comprehensive survey, see Wendy Walker, *Essex markets and fairs*, Essex Record Office Publication 83, (1981). See also R. H. Britnell, 'The proliferation of markets in England, 1200–1349, *Economic History Review*, 2nd ser., 34, (1981), pp. 209–221, and further references there.

9. See the references cited in Beresford and Finberg, n.4 above, and the manorial documents listed in the *Guide to the Essex Record Office*.

10. See M. McKisack, *The parliamentary representation of the English boroughs*

during the Middle Ages, London, (1932). For the individual constituencies, see the accumulating volumes of *The history of Parliament: The House of Commons*, London, HMSO, (1964).

11. P. Morant, History of Essex, (1768), i, p.2.

12. On the physical forms of borough records, see G. H. Martin, 'The origins of borough records', *Journal of the Society of Archivists*, 2, (1960–64), pp. 147–53. For the records of Colchester, see H. Harrod, *Repertory of the records of the borough of Colchester*, Colchester, (1864), and R. H. Britnell, *Growth and decline in Colchester, 1300–1525*, Cambridge, (1986), which includes a schedule of the medieval rolls, and cites further studies by the author.

13. Morant. *History of Essex*, 2, pp. 451–2.

14. For the records of medieval Thaxted and its cutlers, see K. C. Newton, *Thaxted in the fourteenth century*, Essex Record Office Publications, 33, Chelmsford, (1960).

15. *Calendar of the Patent Rolls, 1555–1557*, London, HMSO, (1938), pp. 154–6.

16. Maldon's charter of incorporation, with *inspeximus* confirmations from Henry II's charter onwards, is in *Calendar of the Patent Rolls, 1553–1554*, London, HMSO, (1937), pp. 136–7. For Saffron Walden, see *Calendar of Patent Rolls, 1548–1549*, London, HMSO, (1924), pp. 211–12, and for Dunmow *Calendar of Patent Rolls, 1555–1557*, London, HMSO, (1938), pp. 166–9. On Colchester school and the appropriation of chantry lands, see G. H. Martin, *History of Colchester Royal Grammar School*, Colchester, (1947).

17. See Sidney and Beatrice Webb, *English poor law history*, English Local Government, 7–9, 3 vols., London, (1927–1929), and W. Holdsworth, *History of English Law*, 4, (1936).

18. Harrod, *Repertory of the records of Colchester*, pp. 7–31; *Guide to the Essex Record Office*, p. 64. See also R. H. Britnell's paper, 'Colchester Courts and Court Records', 1310–1525, *Essex Archaeology and History*, 17, (1986).

19. (L. Weaver), *Calendar of Muniments . . . of the Borough of Harwich*, Harwich, (1932).

20. *Ibid.*, pp. 117, 24.

21. Morant, *History of Essex*, 1, p. 1.

22. G. H. Martin, *The story of Colchester*, Colchester, (1959), pp. 74–8.

23. Weaver, *Calendar of muniments*, p. 101. For Taylor's collections, pp. 19–20, 101.

24. W. Ashworth, 'Metropolitan Essex', *Victoria History of the County of Essex* (= *V. C. H.*), 5, London, 1966, pp. 1–92. The present distribution of the records of the former boroughs in the metropolitan area is noted in. J. Foster and J. Sheppard, *British archives: a guide to archival resources in the United Kingdom*, London, 2nd ed., (1983). It is particularly appropriate that the administrative records of Walthamstow should be lodged in the Vestry House Museum there.

25. Cromwell, *op. cit*, p. 165.

26. B. Carlyon Hughes, *The History of Harwich harbour, particularly the work of the Harwich Harbour Conservancy Board, 1863–1939*, Dovercourt, (1939).

27. On the assimilation of the police forces of Harwich and Maldon, see the Record Office *Guide*, p. 15. For the administrative history of West Ham, down to the creation of Newham, see *V. C. H.*, 6, (1973), pp. 96–112.

28. Chelmsford became the seat of the new diocese of Essex in 1908: J. C. Cox, *The cathedral church and See of Essex*, London, (1908). Southend was advanced to the status of a County Borough in 1914.

29. For East Ham, see *V. C. H.*, 6, pp. 18–24; for Ilford, *V. C. H.*, 5, pp. 255–7; for Leyton, *V. C. H.*, 6, pp. 205–14. For a curous sidelight on the Isolation Hospital, see the account of the demise of the Romford Canal in M. Denney, *London's Waterways*, London, (1977), pp. 158–9.

30. For Walthamstow, see *V. C. H.*, 6, pp. 275–85, for Barking, *V. C. H.*, 5, pp. 219–43; for Romford, *V. C. H.*, 7, (1978), pp. 75–79; for Wanstead and Woodford, which were each Urban Districts from 1894 to 1934, when they were amalgamated, see *V. C. H.*, 6, pp. 330–32, and 351–2; for Chingford, *V. C. H.*, 5, pp. 108–9; and for Dagenham, *ibid*, pp. 292–4.

The Making of the Essex Landscape

WILLIAM ADDISON

The Essex landscape is uniquely the creation of glacial drifts that reached the north-west of the county at the end of the Ice Age, and in gliding southwards either split to form inland lakes, or pressed forward to gouge out channels for slow meandering rivers. The most dramatic effect of what happened is seen in the west where, when an ice-sheet split on the high bank of the Roothings, one lobe scooped out a channel for the Roding, the other for the Stort and Lea, squeezing the land between them into the rugged contours of Epping Forest, so different in character from the Thames plain to the south and the gently undulating boulder-clay country to the north and east.

In mid-Essex the water accumulated on clay to wash against banks of gravel and loam, depositing flints that had travelled immense distances, until by sheer weight of mounting pressure the obstructed water broke through, eventually to be discharged into the sea by way of either the Thames or the Blackwater. Only the action of water over a long period could have produced the smooth surfaces of the low hills that are so typical a feature of the mid-Essex landscape. And only the volume of that water could have produced the wide fringe of marsh and reedy waterway, which has saved so much of the Essex coast from the disfigurement of a continuous promenade and consequent building sprawl.

When this slowly evolving landscape began to attract settlement it would be covered inland by a dense forest of oak, small-leaf lime and ash, sustained from a sub-soil of boulder- and London-clay. Settlement would therefore start where the geological process had started, in the north-west.

When metal was found, the proximity of woodland would be of prime importance because the ore had to be smelted. Evidence of this has been discovered in the Bronze Age cemeteries in Brambleshot Field to the east of the Roman station at Great Chesterford, and near the railway viaduct at Wendens Ambo.

Of the two impediments to progress, marsh and forest, marsh was far more obstructive than forest can ever have been. Primitive man could neither ford it as he could a river, nor climb it as he could a hill in order to survey the way ahead. He lacked the means to measure its extent; to drain it was beyond his skill. Marsh, therefore, barred his way inland from the sea along the greater part of the coast more effectively than the inland forest barred land approaches. So seen as a whole, the clues to the development of the man-made landscape of Essex were in the clearing of the forest, where the red deer, the wolf, the badger, and the wild cat had their home, and more slowly in the draining of the marshes.

Many of the coastal heaths – those round Colchester particularly – were clearings made by Neolithic farmers. Horns and bones of deer, as well as tusks of boar, have been found where sites of early occupation have been excavated. When the Romans invaded these ancient settlements would be expanded by tribesmen who had been cultivating pockets of land in mid-Essex, and had fled when news of the invading legions reached them, to join Belgic farmers in the north.

Under Cunobelin, Shakespeare's Cymbeline, who gave the tribesmen their first strong government, there must have been an impressive increase in crops raised by farmers of Celtic-Germanic origin, who had found in south-east England a countryside similar to that of the north German plains from which they had come. They were knowledgeable about the use of iron and introduced a heavy ox-drawn plough, fitted with coulter, share and mouldboard capable of turning the stubborn clay. That the raising of crops had already created wealth for chieftains in the cultivated parts of Essex before the Romans came is proved by such burial mounds as those of the Bartlow Hills in the north-west, and it is worth noting that coulters of this first ox-drawn plough have been found in that neighbourhood. But the most convincing evidence of Essex having a highly developed agriculture in prehistoric times is the fact that Caesar, on landing, rapidly made his way to Belgic settlements in Hertfordshire and Essex, as they became, where he was able to feed four legions, their auxiliaries, and seventeen hundred cavalry off the land, and shortly afterwards had a surplus for export from Colchester to the Continent.

The most important contribution of the Romans themselves to the making of the Essex landscape was in the planning of towns and the surfacing of roads. In surveying the region they would see that it fell into natural divisions defined by ancient riverside tracks and hilltop ridgeways. As water had been so determining a factor in the formation of the landscape and the early selection of places for settlement, fords became key points for urban expansion. The names of Romford and Chelmsford are evidence of ford-towns frequently predating bridge-towns. To this day all the most historic Essex towns are along Roman highways, especially along those linking Colchester with London, and Stane Street, which links Colchester with St. Albans, crossing the county boundary near Bishop's Stortford. Neither is along a ridgeway. There is, however, a fascinating east-west ridgeway from Maldon, supported by the range of hills running westward through Danbury, Fryerning, and South Weald to cross the river Lea and continue into Hertfordshire.

Another important ridgeway, the one through Epping Forest, is still the forest's spinal chord; but ridgeways are rare in the heart of Essex. Only in the downland of the north-west can inland tracks of any considerable length be found on high ground. The main routes in the west before the Romans came were along the gravel terraces of the rivers. Stone Age implements have been found near all the principal streams. After the Thames, the most important of these river routes were the one along the Lea and Stort, linking the Thames Valley with the great Fenland Basin in Cambridgeshire, the one along the Stour forming the northern boundary of the county from the coast to Haverhill, and a third, which branches from the Blackwater estuary in two streams, one following a circuitous route beyond Chelmsford into the denser parts of the ancient forest before reaching the watershed of the other, the Colne, which meanders through a valley in which every village is Saxon to the core. All these streams gave access to ancient trackways across East Anglia and the Fens, of which the most important was the Icknield Way.

An examination of the one hundred and fifty Essex parishes that have Roman remains credited to them indicates a preference for the gravel terraces of the valleys, or for hill tops overlooking them. We seldom find evidence of Roman settlement in the old forest belts, although there must have been considerable felling of trees to extend the Roman towns, and pig breeding was developed in England under the Romans as it had been in Gaul, which meant that great herds of swine roamed through the woods to feed on beech mast and acorns, restricting regeneration by cutting off seed supply.

The Saxons, who succeeded the Romans in control and gave Essex its enduring character, had no interest in Roman culture. Urban social life meant nothing to them, and even in their rural life they had little of the sense of community that inspired the Celts. Soil was in their blood, and with them the clearing of the forest began in earnest. In every glade they were to be seen: men of immense strength, swinging their axes to bring down the great oaks, then stooping to grub out the stumps. And in every clearing they made, a family settled down to a free unhampered way of life.

The distribution of Norman churches with Roman material in their walls shows how little respect the Saxons must have had for the life that had been established in the towns during the Occupation. Colchester fell into decay when the Romans withdrew; the smaller towns were deserted and vandalised. Their buildings were used as quarries. One explanation of this is that the Saxons settled the land from the rivers rather than the roads. They were a valley loving race, using the low-lying land where their ploughs cut deepest and the richest crops could be grown. Their pride in the land they made is shown in the frequent substitution of the Saxon personal name of the new holder for an earlier name now lost. An even stronger explanation of this complete transformation of the landscape in Saxon times is the inbred character of these rural settlers, who came from Schleswig-Holstein, a countryside near the mouth of the Rhine where towns were regarded as 'the defences of slavery and the graves of freedom'.

Partly for safety, and partly to leave the rich loam along the river bank free for crops, Saxon villages were built a short distance inland, but close to a spring or feeder stream. They were approximately circular in form – the best shape for defence, and had an enclosing palisade for the protection of the cattle folded in them at nightfall. The country inland was steadily cleared and improved as pasture for the oxen, which are notoriously greedy feeders. As the grazing was poor, it is calculated that ten times as much heathland pasture would be needed to provide the nourishment one small field of rich grassland would provide today. Behind this grazing land was the woodland from which the villagers took their fuel for heating and timber for building. At the same time the oxen would steadily tear at the undergrowth and eat the seedlings. So the woodland was gradually cleared, eventually producing the narrow strips which survived into the 20th century as the elongated parishes typical of the Thames Estuary. Dagenham, for example, was five times as long as it was wide, extending across Hainault Forest to Chigwell Row.

In course of time cattle were being fed too far away from the homestead for convenience and new settlements had to be started. It was these that gave Essex its innumerable small hamlets called 'ends' and 'tyes', until by Domesday they covered the entire county, with the only exceptions in the uncleared forest of the south-west and the heathland of the north-east. These 'ends' and 'tyes', strung out across an intricate web of winding lanes and green tracks, clearly indicate in their names family enterprise. Only when land has been hewn from forest piecemeal do we get this diffuse kind of settlement. In Cambridgeshire, by contrast, most of the villages are of the compact, or nucleated, type, surrounded by fields. In Essex we usually find a nucleus round a church or manor house, with open fields nearby, linked by a tangle of lanes connecting isolated farmsteads and scattered hamlets. The parish with the largest number of these was Great Waltham, in the heart of the forest north of Chelmsford. At one time it had ten 'ends' or 'greens', and four Roman 'streets', now forgotten: Howe Street, Buck Street, New Street, and Oldfield Street. Where villages were compact, the name in conjunction with the site usually indicates a defensive origin. Stock and Danbury are examples, and two miles from the abandoned Roman town of Billericay the Saxons built a new defensive town at Great Burstead.

The evolution of this man-made Saxon landscape is traced in place-names, working on the principle that the oldest are the -hams, -ings, and -tons with Saxon personal prefixes. Descriptive names ending in -field, -stead, -ley, etc., are later, and most of them are in the heavily wooded heart of the county. If we examine local Ordnance Survey maps we see how few names there are in Essex which are not Saxon. Celtic, or British, place-names are extremely rare. In no other part of England is the proportion smaller, and despite the Viking ravages only in the Walton-on-the-Naze district do we find in the Sokens a pocket of names that are indisputably Scandinavian. Although the Saxons, who founded their kingdom in 527, were harried by the Danes for two centuries and finally conquered, there can be no disputing the Saxon character of this, their eastern kingdom!

But an examination of place-names also reveals how long it took for this rural occupation to be completed. Greensted, with its Saxon nave dated c.845, marks the outpost of early settlement from the Thames in west Essex. There can have been little in the Roothings, with their Norman names, which means that the towns along the Roman road through Dunmow were cut off by forest throughout most of the Saxon period from those along the London to Colchester highway, except by lonely trackways, like the one we call the Suffolk way, and the Roman road from Chelmsford to Braintree. It is also to be noted that the Colchester through Dunmow road (Stane Street) marks the southern limit of the drift country favoured by the Romans for their villas in Essex. Most of the sites that have been excavated are north of it.

The marshes along the coastal fringe, which were to bring wealth to the abbeys in the Middle Ages as sheep pastures, were already assessed as such at Domesday; but then the sheep were kept chiefly for milk. Reminders of this are preserved in the place-name element 'wick', a dairy farm, especially in the Tendring Hundred. There were four in St. Osyth parish, eight in Canvey and Benfleet, many of these in Essex, as in Kent, belonging to inland parishes.

On the fringe of the marshes were the saltpans: forty-five of them between Manningtree and Maldon. Salcott (Salt-cote) is a reminder of these, and it is significant that the village stands on the creek separating the two hundreds of Thurstable and Winstree.

The third transformation of the scene came with the Norman Conquest. The new overlords would find a rural life adequately organised, which could be adapted to their own manorial system, although the people who sustained it would soon discover that a Norman lord was a much more autocratic ruler than the Saxon thane had been. At the Conquest about ninety Essex landowners were deprived of their estates and Norman favourites installed in their stead. The great mound at Pleshey and the smaller one at Great Canfield are reminders of two of the most powerful families who imposed the symbols of their rule upon the loosely evolving landscape of 'ends' and 'tyes', 'wicks' and 'steads'. The de Mandevilles moved from Pleshey to Walden, the de Veres to Castle Hedingham, where their massive keep stands as a memorial to the family Macaulay described as 'the longest and most illustrious line of nobles this country has ever known'. The last de Mandeville to rule from Pleshey was the Duke of Gloucester who figures in Shakespeare's *King Richard II.*, where the duchess, after the murder of her husband, who had been kidnapped in Epping Forest, says:

Commend me to my brother, Edmund York.
Bid him – ah, what?
With all good speed at Pleshey visit me,
Alack! and what shall good old York there see,
But empty lodgings and unfurnished walls,
Unpeopled offices, untrodden stones.

There is little of Norman pride to be read into what survives today at Pleshey, one of the most charming Essex villages, except the Norman castle plan, which survives in the shape of the village, as, to an even more remarkable degree it does at Ongar, where the old town is still within the bailey of the castle Richard de Lucy built on the Saxon mound he found there. But the castle keep at Hedingham has no superior in provincial England, and Colchester has a keep considerably larger than the White Tower of London and, incidentally, one which incorporates much Roman material. These, however, are isolated memorials of Norman power. More pervading as symbols of Norman rule are the ancient parish churches sited near the manor house, even when at a distance from the village they serve. Two-thirds of the pre-Reformation churches in Essex retain substantial Norman features.

The other inescapable reminder of Norman rule is in the two groups of place-names, the Rodings (or Roothings) and the Colnes, in both of which we find titular names like Abbess Roding and Earls Colne. These groups also signify land holdings larger than those characteristic of the Saxons. The

Age of 'take-overs' had begun, and life was gradually being industrialised as well as organised. The Norman lords began the process of substituting for the primitive log-cabin type buildings of the Saxon, thatched timber-framed houses, and churches of flint rubble. By the end of the 13th century Essex was already acquiring buildings of types still retained, which were eventually to give the county its distinctively domesticated as well as intensively cultivated landscape.

The Royal Commission on Historical Monuments which reported in the early 1920s found the amount of medieval carpentry in old farmhouses in Essex so outstanding that it formed 'a remarkable commentary on the social and economic history of the county'. The characteristic Essex farmhouse still to be seen in every parish is the timber-framed hall-house of single room depth, with service rooms under a catslide roof at the rear descending to within a few feet of the ground. The retention of so many such houses is due to the county having been so much poorer in the early Middle Ages than either Suffolk to the north or Kent to the south. This original hall in which the entire family fed by day and slept by night was extended in the 13th or 14th century by adding a room at one end to serve as a bedroom or private chamber for the head of the household and his wife. Many of these can still be identified by having two windows on one side of the door, only one on the other, and a curved roof-ridge. Either one or two cross-wings were added later, usually in either the 16th or 17th century. A common reason for the retention of the original site and the core of the first building, which in most counties would be either demolished or converted into out-buildings, was the scarcity of well-drained sites near springs or dependable streams. Moats, which in some parts of England were only dug out for defensive reasons during the Wars of the Roses, in Essex were primarily for practical domestic and farm use. But the chief reason for the retention of the core of these early medieval buildings was that although Essex had no building stone it had an abundance of stout oak to give the primitive narrow hall firmness which continued to support additions built on to it over periods of up to four hundred years. The showpiece is the 13th-century manor house at Little Chesterford; but there are examples in most of the parishes with -field, -stead, -ley etc. as terminals of their place-name. Felsted is one of the richest.

In the final stages of the development of the Essex timber-framed farmhouse the spaces between the studs were infilled with wattle and daub. In the oldest the wattles were of oak, which were sprung into grooves scored into the framework. Clay would then be pressed into them. Later, the wattles were woven of unpeeled hazel sticks, called 'rizzes', and the clay was pressed into them by two men working together, one on the inside, the other on the outside, pressing the clay against each other through the wattles laterally between the timbers. William Harrison of Radwinter, in his *Description of England* (1577) tells us that the Spaniards who came to England during the reign of Mary 1. marvelled to see these houses built, as they said, of 'sticks and dirt'. But they marvelled still more to see how well the people who lived in them fed!

In Essex it was usual to cover the entire outside of the house with a protective layer of smeared clay, which was later superseded by plaster and decorated with the early form of pargetting. In the 16th century this was in simple patterns, of which the most popular were derived from the imprint of a bird's foot or a shell, which could easily be pricked out over the panels with a hard stick. The elaborate patterns seen on the former Sun Inn at Saffron Walden and houses at Wivenhoe and Earls Colne came after the Restoration of Charles II in the 17th century.

Even more typical of Essex 'cladding' to keep out the wind was the weather- or clap-boarding, which like the tile-roofing, was imported from Germany and Holland. This was carried by the Pilgrim Fathers to America and became the local style there in small towns, many of which were given such Essex names as Wethersfield, Toppesfield, Dedham, and so on. Essex weather-boarding is still seen at its best in surviving windmills and riverside watermills.

These long, low, timber-framed houses, thatched in traditional style, contribute their own serenity to the prevailing mood of the Essex landscape. They are seldom showpieces in the way the timber-framed Wealden houses of Kent are; but as the Spaniards noted, they were the homes of a friendly, hospitable people who were more interested in the stocking of the buttery and pantry than in the furnishings of the parlour.

With the dissolution of the monasteries came another parcelling out of the land on a similar scale to that suffered at the Conquest, and William Harrison of Radwinter describes it vividly. The sporting interest of the Norman lords continued but in more sophisticated style. The newly enriched gentry provided themselves with 'greate plentie of parkes . . . . . wherein greate plentie of fallow deere is cherished and kept. As for warrens for conies, I judged them almost innumerable', he wrote.

The labourer's lot improved little. Old cottages in village streets are often described as formerly inhabited by them. There are, in fact, no genuine labourers' cottages in Essex earlier than the 18th century. Earlier ones described as such were the homes of independent farmers, many of whom would be small-holders. One Essex parson, Joseph Hall of Waltham Abbey (1574–1656), later Bishop of Norwich, describes the labourer's cottage early in the 17th century as

Of one bay's breadth, God wot, a silly cote
Whose wretched spars are furred with sluttish soote
A whole inch thick, shining like blackmoor's brows,
Through smoke that downe the headless barrel blows.
At his bed's feete feeden his stalled teame,
The swine beneath, his pullen o'er the beame.

It is this wealth of half-timbered and weather-boarded houses that explains why early brick farmhouses are not common in Essex, although we now know that brickmaking was revived in eastern England in the second half of the 13th century. The building of large brick houses started with Faulkbourne Hall in 1490, followed by Layer Marney Tower in 1520. The Royal Commission found brick barns so imposing a feature that they recorded no fewer than two hundred of the 16th and 17th centuries, all of which were seen as testifying to the prosperity of Essex farming. We now know that several of those were earlier than the Royal Commission thought. But again the pioneering work in the refurbishing of the landscape was done by the Church. Red brick church towers remain the county's most impressive architectural feature, and they were all constructed in two comparatively short periods: the first between 1500 and 1530, during which the most magnificent were built across an area extending from Layer Marney in the east to Theydon Garnon and Nazeing in the west, the second during the reign of James I, with the finest at Castle Hedingham. Most of them are in dark red brick with diaper work in blue. The outstanding exception is Ingatestone, where the diapers are black.

Agricultural prosperity continued throughout the 18th century, guided by the farming gentry who throughout took an intelligent interest in land drainage and stock breeding. The landscape became more diversified. In the north-west the gracious old town of Saffron Walden was the market centre for the villages of the chalk downland: Clavering, Arkesden, Elmdon, Wendens Ambo, all similar in character to their neighbours in Hertfordshire. The predominant crop on the light soil was barley. From Saffron Walden to Thaxted the road crosses breezy upland with fine old farmhouses on the old Audley End estate, and road signs bearing the names of Suffolk towns and villages in the 'Constable country', reminding the traveller that Constable was himself the best interpreter of the Stour Valley landscape.

At Thaxted, with its 15th century Guildhall, windmill, and noble church, we sense something of the character of the county in the 14th and 15th centuries when this was a centre of the cutlery industry. The appeal of this proud church is all the greater for being built in true Essex style of flint rubble. The explanation of Essex retaining so rural a landscape is that it lacked the underground wealth, coal, which fed the furnaces of the Industrial Revolution and blackened the landscape of the North. The 19th century found Essex still farming country. When Arthur Young toured it in 1807 he reported that for the past twenty or thirty years scarcely an estate had been sold which, if divided into moderate size lots, had not been bought by farmers, living in good style houses.

This general aspect of affluence and well-being continued until depression came in the 1870s, when much of the land became derelict. Once fertile fields were choked with thistles. Charlock and henbane displaced oats and barley. The hedgerows, formerly so trim, became ragged and broken, and the farmworkers in their smock frocks and leather buskins had to get what they could out of their cottage gardens, while depending for milk on the goat that tore up the hedgerows, and on the pig in the sty at the bottom of the garden for winter bacon. Much of this depression was due to the magnet of an expanding London drawing off the enterprising young people.

With the 20th century the tide turned. London now spills over into the densely populated boroughs that Dickens saw being transformed when he called the region London-over-the-Border. But within ten miles of the East End of London is Chigwell, which Dickens described as 'such an out-of-the-way rural place', and from Chigwell a curious motorist might still spend a whole day driving through parishes in which Tudor farmhouses are as much part of the contemporary scene as wayside inns and cornfields. But Chigwell is on the edge of the Green Belt, which itself is coming under threat. The whole of the north bank of the Thames is now what is euphemistically called 'developed', with the ruins of Hadleigh Castle standing sentinel over the south-west approaches to the historic Rochford Hundred, symbolically guarded in the north by the massive tower of Canewdon's stately church, traditionally held to have been built to celebrate the victory at Agincourt. North of this the Essex landscape remains substantially as Matthew Arnold described it after a visit to Copford in 1861: 'I hardly know any county', he wrote, 'with the rural and secluded character of north Essex. It seems immensely old, and is full of old halls and woods and hollows and low ranges of hills, and then eight or nine miles off, across the deeply quiet part of the county is the sea'. Long may it remain so!

The Ealdordom of Essex

CYRIL HART

I *From Kingdom to Ealdordom*

The course of Essex history in the ninth century is notoriously obscure. It is generally assumed that the bounds of the ancient kingdom had been reduced to those of the modern county well before its governance by its own royal dynasty came to an end in 825, when King Sigered of the East Saxons was expelled by King Ecgberht of Wessex. For some generations the local kings had ruled under the suzerainty of the Mercians, but King Ecgberht's campaign cleared these overlords from the whole of South Eastern England.[1] The Mercians, who remained in control of London and of the territory to the west of the River Lea, may well have continued for a while to support surviving members of the East Saxon royal family as pretenders; indeed, as late as 827 x 839 a Sigeric *rex Orientalium Saxonum* witnesses a Mercian lease of land at Braughing;[2] but it appears very probable that the West Saxons were in effective control of Essex at this time.

The main course of events in Essex may be inferred from the account in the A text of the Anglo-Saxon Chronicle, supported in all its essentials by the version preserved in the B text, which made some use of a lost A text precursor for these years.[3] It seems that Essex was included, together with Sussex, Surrey and Kent, in a subkingdom which King Ecgberht created for his son Æthelwulf. When Æthelwulf succeeded his father as king of Wessex in 839, he handed over this subkingdom to his own son, Athelstan.[4] In 858 this appears to have become an independent kingdom for another son, Æthelberht, but it was reunited with Wessex in 860, when Æthelberht succeeded to the whole.[5] In 867 we find King Æthelred I of Wessex disposing of land in Essex,[6] and it has been claimed, not unreasonably, that Essex formed part of the kingdom inherited by King Alfred the Great in 871.[7]

Clearly, the West Saxons having displaced the indigenous royal line were in need of some representative to uphold their power in Essex. Ealdordoms had been created already within their territories, and from various entries in the A text of the Anglo-Saxon Chronicle it appears that initially their areas of jurisdiction were coterminous with those of the shires. Thus as early as 755 we find reference to an *aldormon* named Cumbra who seemed to have held office in Hampshire, and (less ambiguously) we encounter *alderman* Weohstan leading the men of Wiltshire in 800, *ealdorman* Æthelhelm those of Dorset in 840, and *alderman* Eanulf those of Somerset in 845; Huda of Surrey appears in 853 and Æthelwulf of Berkshire in 860. There is some dispute as to the handwriting of this section of the A text, but it can hardly date from much later than the early tenth century; so even if the scribe were translating into Old English annals written in Latin, his use of the term

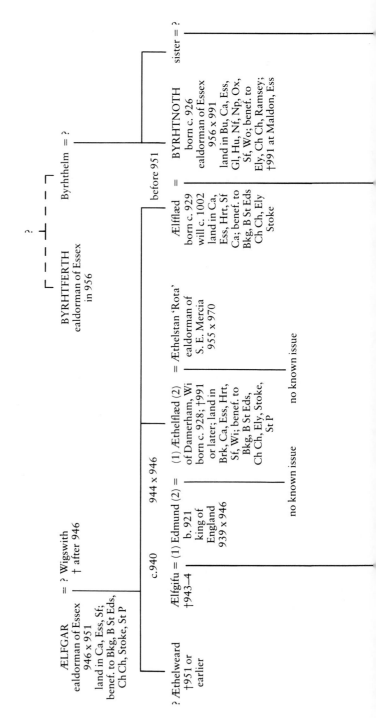

THE FAMILIES OF EALDORMEN ÆLFGAR AND BYRHTNOTH OF ESSEX

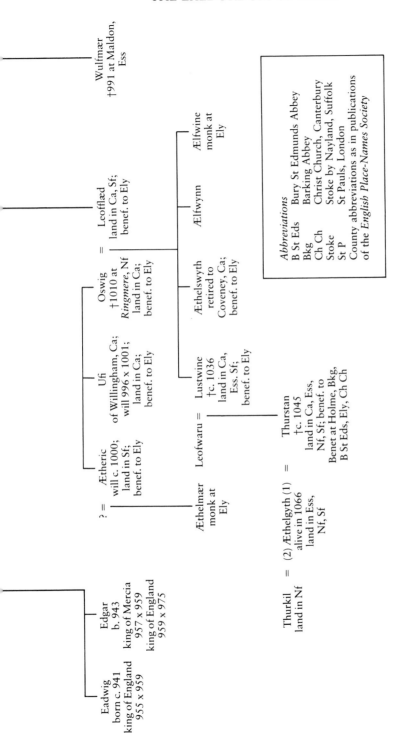

Abbreviations
B St Eds   Bury St Edmunds Abbey
Bkg   Barking Abbey
Ch Ch   Christ Church, Canterbury
Stoke   Stoke by Nayland, Suffolk
St P   St Pauls, London
County abbreviations as in publications
of the *English Place-Names Society*

ealdorman is unlikely to have been anachronistic for annals of the second half of the ninth century. In the Latin charters of the period we find these self-same men referred to variously as *dux* and (less commonly) as *princeps*.[8]

Returning now to our East Saxon charter of 867 we find that King Æthelred I made his grant of land at Navestock at the request of his bishop Deorwulf and of his *dux* Ealdred. In later records we find the shire bishop and the ealdorman acting jointly.[9] Deorwulf was bishop of London, the diocese of the East Saxons, and one may reasonably postulate that Ealdred's ealdordom included Essex. We encounter him witnessing as *dux* West Saxon charters of 860–2,[10] and as there appears to be no record at this or any other period of an ealdorman changing his sphere of office, we may, I think, reasonably suppose that Ealdred was ealdorman of Essex from 860 to 867, if not for longer. Furthermore, he may perhaps be equated with the thegn named Ealdred who witnessed West Saxon charters in 854,[11] and who received land at West Woolston in Berkshire from King Æthelwulf in 856, soon after the West Saxons had won back Berkshire from the Mercians.[12]

We are indebted to the A text of the Anglo-Saxon Chronicle for our next identification of an ealdorman of Essex, and this time our evidence is unequivocal. Writing under 896 and reviewing events of the preceeding three years, the chronicler tells us that among the distinguished Englishmen who died at this time was Beorhtwulf, ealdorman of Essex. Attempts to identify this individual with persons of the same name who appear among the signatories to West Saxon charters of the period are confounded by the fact that a second Ealdorman Beorhtwulf appears as witness in 903 and 909.[13] It seems profitless to debate which (if either) of these two was the *dux* Beorhtwulf who witnessed a will and several West Saxon charters whose texts survive (sometimes in modified form) for the years 860 to 882.[14]

Even if we confine ourselves to accepting the evidence for the existence of an ealdorman of the East Saxons at some time during the period 892 x 895 however, we are still fishing in troubled waters. It has always been assumed by historians that Essex was under Danish control at this period, following the settlement in 880 of a large Danish army in East Anglia, which shared out the land. Nowhere else do we hear of English ealdormen holding office in territories under Danish rule.

The tradition that the East Anglian Danes also occupied Essex goes back a long way, for the early twelfth-century Worcester chronicler records that when King Edward the Elder recovered Colchester in 918 (*recte* 917) 'many of the English in East Anglia and Essex, who had been enslaved to the brutal Danes for more than thirty years, joyfully submitted to him'.[15] The Worcester chronicler here may have depended on an account drawn up at Ramsey Abbey in Cambridgeshire as early as the end of the tenth century.[16] Nevertheless, apart from a royal genealogy there is no evidence that its author had at his disposal any ninth-century Essex sources of evidential value; his statement seems rather to have been drawing on local legend at this point in his narrative.

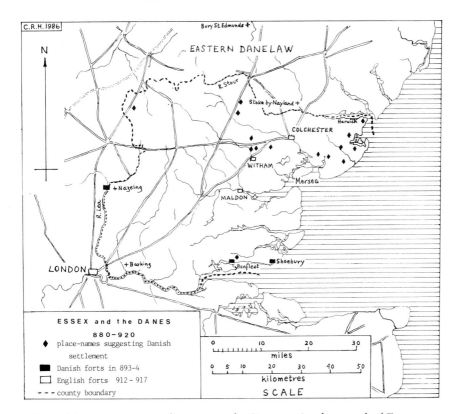

In seeking to assess to what extent the Danes gained control of Essex, we have also to take into account the late Barking tradition that the nunnery founded there in the seventh century was destroyed by the Danes in the late ninth century; and to this we must now add archaeological evidence that a small nunnery at Nazeing ceased to function at about the same time.[17] Against this however we must remember that some early Barking muniments survived this supposed destruction of the abbey.[18] Property and institutions could be destroyed during raids, without the attacking forces necessarily settling in the area.

Both the A and B texts of the Anglo-Saxon chronicle have annals for the opening years of the tenth century which lend some support to the view that part at least of Essex remained under West Saxon control after the Danish settlement of East Anglia. They record that when King Alfred died his nephew Æthelwold competed unsuccessfully for the succession in 899, then fled to Northumbria, where he was accepted as king by the Danish settlers. Two years later he sailed southwards with a fleet which landed on the Essex coast, where the local inhabitants submitted to him. In a recent paper Dr David Dumville has argued persuasively that Æthelwold's expedition was aimed at securing the defection of Essex from its West Saxon rulers.[19]

Æthelwold's insurrection was short-lived, and West Saxon authority was soon restored. However, there is no reason to assume that either before or after the insurrection the West Saxon *dominium* extended over the whole of Essex. It seems rather to have covered chiefly the north bank of the Thames and its hinterland. Further to the north and east, the Danes appear to have held effective control over a substantial portion of the county.

The next two decades witnessed a great resurgence of English power, in a long series of campaigns mounted by King Edward the Elder against the Danish settlers in Eastern and Northern England. The fighting at that time was characterised by occupation and fortification of strategic strongholds, often on major roads or river crossings. Those in Essex comprised Witham on the London-Colchester road, occupied and fortified in 912, Maldon on the Blackwater fortified in 916, and finally Colchester itself, whose occupation in 917 set seal to the recovery of the whole of Essex by the West Saxon forces. Recording the Witham campaign, the A text chronicler claimed that 'a good number of people who had been under the rule of the Danes submitted to King Edward'. According to the Worcester chronicler, men from Essex joined the West Saxons in their 917 campaign in Bedfordshire, and later than autumn, according to the A text chronicler, men from Essex formed part of King Edward's forces in the battle for Colchester.

The complete absence of land charters for this period, together with the vagueness of the chroniclers on points of detail, prevents us from reconstructing with certainty the tenure of the Essex ealdordom throughout King Edward the Elder's reign. His son Athelstan succeeded in 924. The run of charters then resumes, and it is apparent that the old tradition of each ealdorman holding jurisdiction over a single shire had disappeared. Instead, we find that for most of the period 930 x 955 there were three ealdordoms south of the Thames, three or four in Mercia, and one or two in Eastern England. The southern ealdordoms comprised those of the Western Provinces (Cornwall, Devon, Somerset, Dorset), Wessex (Hampshire, Wiltshire, Berkshire), and the South Eastern shires (Surrey, Sussex, Kent). The limits of the Mercian ealdordoms are less easy to determine, but it appears that one covered Central Mercia, another South East Mercia (including Hertfordshire, Middlesex, and probably Buckinghamshire and Bedfordshire), and there were one or two ealdordoms in Northern and Western Mercia. A powerful ealdordom was created for East Anglia,[20] and we now have to consider whether or not Essex was ruled (uniquely for the period) by a separate ealdorman during Athelstan's reign and that of his successor Edmund.

The issue hinges on the identity of the various *duces* named Uhtred who appear in charters of the period. In an appendix to this paper I have listed the subscriptions of all the English ealdormen to the known charters of King Athelstan and of his successors Edmund and Eadred. It will be seen that a *dux* Uhtred (here given the designation *Uhtred I*) witnesses from 3 April 930 right through to at least the beginning of 946. He fails to witness in the early years of King Eadred's reign, but the *eorl* Uhtred who witnesses two charters in 949 and one in 950 is probably the same man. Elsewhere I have suggested that he be identified with the person of that name who received Hope and Ashford in Derbyshire in 926 while still a thegn, and with the *dux*

Uhtred who received Bakewell in Derbyshire in 949.[21] It is interesting that in this Uhtred's last appearance, as witness to the newly discovered Barking charter of 950, he was placed next to Osulf, the high reeve of Bamburgh. This gives some credence to the late W. H. Stevenson's supposition that he was the Uhtred, son of Eadwulf or Athulf, the reeve of Bamburgh and friend of King Alfred.[22] Athulf died in 913. Ten years later his son Uhtred survived a massacre at Corbridge, where he was fighting on the English side.[23]

It seems likely that the person named Uhtred *cild* who received Chesterfield in Derbyshire from King Eadred in 955 was the son of the *dux* Uhtred I.[24] P. H. Sawyer has suggested, rightly I think, that he was the *dux* of this name who witnessed four Midland and Northern charters in 956–8.[25]

As long ago as 1905, H. Munro Chadwick postulated that the *dux* Uhtred who witnessed during King Edmund's reign was ealdorman of Essex.[26] However, if the identifications suggested above be accepted, Chadwick's attribution can no longer be sustained. It remains to consider the possibility that the *dux* Uhtred designated in the appendix to this paper as *Uhtred II* was ealdorman of Essex. I first suggested this in 1975,[27] but on further examination of the lists the attribution appears unsound. Uhtred II witnesses as last of the ealdormen from 23 March 930 to 28 May 934. During the same period, ealdormen named Alfred and Æthelstan witness in succession, both apparently from East Anglia,[28] together with an Ealdorman Ælfstan whose jurisdiction appears to have been in South East Mercia. If Uhtred II ruled Essex, he was therefore ealdorman of a single county. No other ealdorman of the period ruled a single shire, and there seems no particular reason why Essex should have been treated as an exceptional case. With the aid of our collection of witness lists, it now seems more likely that Uhtred II's area of jurisdiction lay in those parts of North Western Mercia not ruled by his namesake Uhtred I. An Ealdorman Æthelmund ruled there from 940 to 965,[29] and by process of exclusion we arrive at the name of Uhtred II for his probable predecessor. Certainty is impossible, but it appears that we have now eliminated all the Uhtreds as ealdormen of Essex for the period from 930 to 945.

This leaves us free to explore other possibilities. For example, Essex might have formed part of the East Anglian ealdordom, held from 932 right through to 956 by Athelstan 'Half King'. Certainly he possessed a very wide-ranging area of jurisdiction.[30] There remains, however, an alternative solution which appears to me to be a good deal more likely. From 940 to 946 the Half King's younger brother Æthelwold I (the number serves to distinguish him from a second Ealdorman Æthelwold who was the son of the Half King) held an ealdordom embracing Surrey, Sussex, and Kent. It could well be that it was Æthelwold I's ealdordom, rather than that of his brother Athelstan, which included Essex within its bounds. As the surviving charters of 946 show, Ealdorman Ælfgar of Essex (discussed below) commences to witness immediately after Ealdorman Æthelwold's attestations cease. Admittedly the surviving copy of Æthelwold I's will does not dispose of any named estates in Essex or Kent, but this copy appears to be concerned only with those lands which had been left to him by the king; he

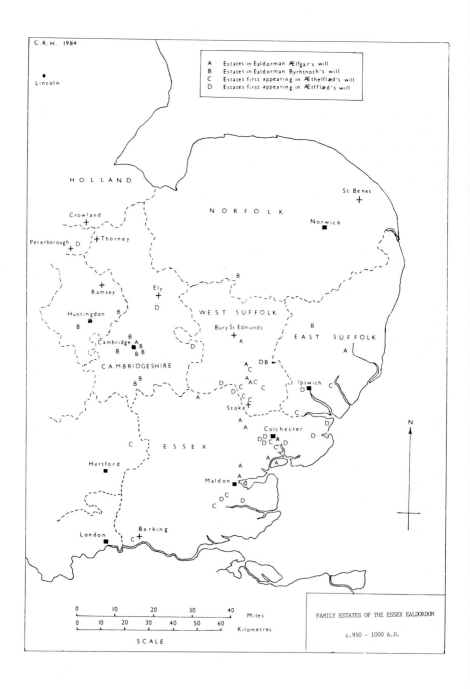

C.R.H. 1984

A   Estates in Ealdorman Ælfgar's will
B   Estates in Ealdorman Byrhtnoth's will
C   Estates first appearing in Æthelflæd's will
D   Estates first appearing in Ælfflæd's will

Lincoln

HOLLAND

St Benet

NORFOLK

Crowland

Norwich

Peterborough D   Thorney

Ramsey   Ely   B

Huntingdon   D

WEST SUFFOLK

Bury St Edmunds   EAST SUFFOLK

Cambridge   B   A   C

CAMBRIDGESHIRE   B   Ipswich   C

Stoke   C

Colchester   D

ESSEX   D   C   A   D

Hertford   A   A

Maldon   C

London   Barking   C

N

SCALE

0   10   20   30   40   Miles

0   10   20   30   40   50   60   Kilometres

FAMILY ESTATES OF THE ESSEX EALDORDOM

c.950 - 1000 A.D.

could well have held other property as his patrimony, or by other forms of title.[31] The fact remains that of all the ealdormen of this period, Æthelwold I appears by far the most likely one to have held jurisdiction in Essex. It is not until the witness lists are collected and tabulated as in the appendix to this paper that conclusions of this sort can be reached with any reasonable degree of probability.

The argument does not rest here, for the witness lists show further that Æthelwold I was preceded in Sussex, Surrey and Kent by an ealdorman named Osferth to whom we must now turn our attention, for if Æthelwold I might have held Essex, so too might Osferth before him. We know a good deal about Osferth, who first appears in the will of King Alfred the Great, which was drawn up in 888 or earlier.[32] King Alfred left him 100 mancuses, the same sum as he left to each of his ealdormen. Osferth witnessed as a thegn from 898 to 904, usually heading the thegns in the lists.[33] He stood in some specially close familial relationship to King Edward the Elder, for although the title *frater regis* given him in a charter of 904 is certainly a mistake, he witnessed this charter after the king's son and before the archbishop; he also witnessed another of the same date before all the ealdormen.[34] Again, he witnessed a charter of 909 as *propinquus regis* before the ealdormen; still more remarkably, he witnessed in 929 as *Osferth comes cum ducibus et ceteris optimatibus*,[35] a phrase paralleled in later charters witnessed by Athelstan 'Half King' *cum ceteris suffraganeis*.[36] From his first appearance as an ealdorman in 909 onwards, he nearly always headed the ealdormen witnessing. He last witnessed a charter dated 7 June 934, and it seems probable that he died during King Athelstan's Scottish campaign that summer. He may have been over 60 when he died, a great age for a tenth-century ealdorman.[37]

We must return now to the beginning of this paper, to remind ourselves that from the explusion of its indigenous royal line in 825 right down to 860, Essex formed with Sussex, Surrey and Kent a subkingdom of Wessex. Moreover, both Ealdred (who was probably Ealdorman of Essex from 860 to 867 or later) and Beorhtwulf (who was probably Ealdorman of Essex from 892 to 895, if not for longer) witnessed West Saxon charters. A pattern is beginning to emerge, for we have now postulated that Ealdorman Osferth (909-934) and Ealdorman Æthelwold I (940–946), both of whom held Sussex, Surrey and Kent, might both have held Essex also.

We are now in a position to put forward the fully developed hypothesis that from 825 to 946, Essex formed together with Surrey, Sussex and Kent a single administrative unit subordinate to the kings of Wessex, first as a subkingdom and then from 860 onwards as an ealdordom. The strategic importance of such an administrative unit for the defence of the West Saxon kingdom, controlling as it would the Eastern and South-Eastern seaboard and the estuary of the Thames, will be apparent. The Danish army of East Anglia succeeded in settling the North East corner of Essex in 880, but were driven out by the West Saxons between 912 and 917 when Colchester was recaptured. It seems however that the great bulk of Essex remained under West Saxon administration throughout the period of Danish autonomy in East Anglia. No doubt the Danes penetrated deeply into this West Saxon territory during their raids, but they never settled there.

It must be stressed that what has been presented here is no more than a hypothesis; the evidence is insufficient for dogmatic assertions to be made. Nevertheless, it seems to me to fit the known facts better than other reconstructions of the administrative history of Essex at this period hitherto put forward.

II *The Ealdordom at its Zenith*

Before examining the Essex ealdordom in its heyday, it is convenient to pause here to consider briefly in general terms the status and responsibilities of the English ealdorman. Unlike those of his continental counterparts, the ealdorman's office was not hereditary, although on occasion it might be passed down within a family. The appointment lay in the gift of the king, acting usually on the advice of his council. The ealdorman was often related to the king, either by marriage or by membership of a cadet branch of the royal house. He was a regular attendant at court, where he held an established precedence relative to his peers, as is shown in the attestations to royal diplomas. He sat on the king's council and tendered advice on matters of state, helping to formulate and implement laws and policy. When (as was often the case) the king was sick or a minor, the ealdormen between them held effective power. Throughout much of the tenth century there was a tendency for one particular ealdorman to play a dominant role in council, often supported by members of his family and other followers. For half a century from 943 onwards this power was contested by two great families; Ealdorman Athelstan 'Half King' of East Anglia was dominant until 957, then Ealdorman Ælfhere of Mercia gained control, supported by his brother Ealdorman Ælfheah of Wessex; finally in 983 power passed back to the Half King's son, Ealdorman Æthelwine 'Dei amicus' of East Anglia, assisted by Ealdorman Byrhtnoth of Essex. Byrhtnoth died in 991, and Æthelwine in the following year.

As the king's representative the ealdorman was responsible for raising the local levies and leading them into battle. These consisted firstly of his own *comitatus*, thegns owing him direct allegiance by reason of tenure of his land or of office within his household; secondly other thegns holding estates within his ealdordom; and thirdly such local peasantry as could be mustered and armed.

The ealdorman's duties included overseeing the administration of justice and the execution of the king's writs within his territory. He would sit (often with the bishop) to hear pleas in the courts of the boroughs, shires, and hundreds (or groups of hundreds) within the ealdordom. He was entitled to a share of the profits of justice within these courts. Probably too he had an overall responsibility for enforcing the collection of the geld or royal tax, although normally the administrative task was supervised by the reeves of the royal estates within the ealdordom. The ealdorman was usually a substantial local landowner, and might also hold properties outside his ealdordom. Often the farm of a number of estates within his area of jurisdiction would be set aside for the support of his office. His own

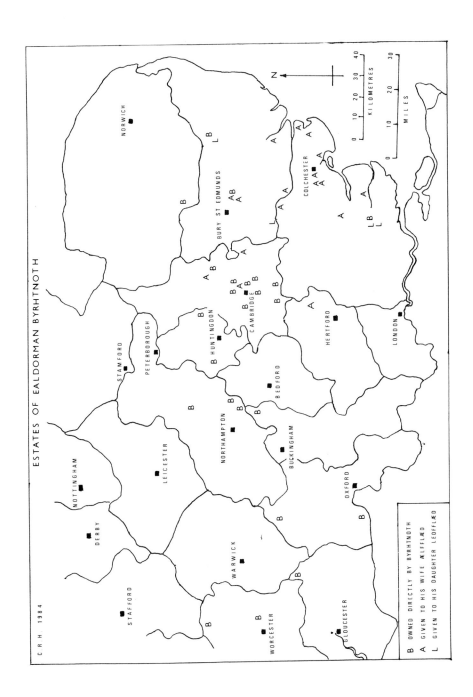

ESTATES OF EALDORMAN BYRHTNOTH

B OWNED DIRECTLY BY BYRHTNOTH
A GIVEN TO HIS WIFE ÆLFFLÆD
L GIVEN TO HIS DAUGHTER LEOFFLÆD

C.R.H. 1984

household was substantial, with officials such as butlers and stewards, craftsmen such as goldsmiths and weavers, and a host of clerics, reeves, huntsmen, and other hangers-on. All depended on his patronage, and his power over them was all but absolute.

After a long period of obscurity, in the mid-tenth century the history of the East Saxon ealdordom suddenly springs to life, thanks largely to a series of wills preserved in the archives of the church of Bury St Edmunds in Suffolk. In the early years of the century a small collegiate minister was founded at Bury to house the relics of St Edmund, the last English king of East Anglia, who had been martyred by the Danes in 870. Its endowment increased gradually throughout the next hundred years until 1020, when King Cnut granted it substantial estates and liberties and put monks there, so turning it into a major monastic foundation.

Among the earliest muniments kept at Bury was the will of Ealdorman Ælfgar, drawn up some time between 946 and 951.[38] In his will Ælfgar gives himself no title, but the D text of the Anglo-Saxon chronicle calls him ealdorman in an annal dated 946, when referring to the marriage of his daughter Æthelflæd with King Edmund of Wessex and England. No surviving contemporary or near-contemporary source locates his ealdordom in Essex, but his will shows him to have been a man of the eastern counties, and since the East Anglian ealdordom is known to have been held at that time by Athelstan 'Half King', and since Ælfgar's son-in-law Byrhtnoth became ealdorman of Essex, it has been assumed, with good reason, that he took his title from that shire.

Ælfgar's origins are obscure. We known from his will that by 951 at the latest, his wife and son were dead, and that his younger daughter Ælfflæd had already married Byrhtnoth, who was to succeed him in the East Saxon ealdordom. It appears also that at the time the will was drawn up, his elder daughter Æthelflæd was still the widow of King Edmund, and had not yet married Athelstan 'Rota', who became her second husband at some unknown date, and was ealdorman of South East Mercia from 955 to 970. One cannot identify Ælfgar with certainty with the thegn of that name who witnessed two Kentish charters in 943 and 946.[39] Nor can we be sure that he owed his appointment as ealdorman to his daughter's marriage to King Edmund, for the earliest surviving charters which he witnessed as ealdorman date from after Edmund's death. King Edmund did however give Ælfgar a sword heavily embellished with gold on its hilt and silver on its sheath, which Ælfgar presented subsequently to Edmund's brother, King Eadred. Ælfgar held the ealdordom from 946 to 951.

Throughout his tenure of office, Ælfgar witnessed consistently as last of the seven ealdormen attesting King Eadred's charters, and it appears very likely that he was to some extent subordinate to Athelstan 'Half King', the powerful ealdorman of East Anglia. How far his jurisdiction extended outside Essex cannot be determined from the surviving sources. His will, and those of his two daughters,[40] show him possessed of considerable estates in Essex and Suffolk. Those in Essex were concentrated in the north east of the county, with a subsidiary group in the Maldon area. His Suffolk properties lay mostly near the Essex border. All this territory must have been in Danish hands until its reconquest by King Edward the Elder some forty years before the date of Ælfgar's will. Some of it may have been given him directly by King Edmund or King Eadred, or it could have been given first to his parents, and passed on to him by inheritance, though his will makes no reference to any patrimony. A third means by which he may have acquired some of his estates is from his predecessor in the Essex ealdordom, whoever that may have been. To accept this third theory would involve one in a presupposition that King Edward the Elder or one of his sons set aside some properties recovered from the Danes for the endowment of the ealdordom. We shall consider this again when we come to look at the estates of Ælfgar's son-in-law Byrhtnoth.

The most remarkable feature of Ælfgar's will is the strongly religious nature of his bequests. Practically everything he possessed was left to one of five ecclesiastical foundations, a tradition to be continued by the next four generations of his descendants. Most of his properties were left in reversion, with the usufruct remaining with his daughters and their children for their lifetimes – a policy that had stored within it the seeds of trouble for his successors. He had a strong sense of family, and his chief provisions related to the endowment of a collegiate foundation at Stoke by Nayland, just to the north of the Suffolk border, in the midst of his estates. It was here that his ancestors (presumably his parents) were buried, together with his wife and only son; eventually he was to join them. Altogether seven properties in Essex and six in Suffolk were left in reversion to Stoke, an endowment that would have eclipsed that of St Edmund's college at Bury, had Ælfgar's intentions not been thwarted. The wills of his two daughters show that they did their best to carry out their father's intentions. In this they could call on powerful supporters, but it was all to no avail, and the endowment of Stoke was totally dispersed in the reign of King Cnut.[41]

Whether Ælfgar died in office, or relinquished his appointment because of ill health or retirement, we do not know. It seems likely that Athelstan 'Half King' then took over the direct administration of Essex, for there is no room in the witness lists for any other successor until 955, when in the closing months of Eadred's reign three of his charters were attested by a certain Byrhtferth.[42] Very little is known about Byrhtferth. He is generally thought to have held the ealdordom of Essex, and to have been related to Ealdorman Byrhtnoth.[43] Not without some misgivings, I have followed this tradition here, assigning to him a provisional place in the pedigree as Byrhtnoth's uncle; there is however no firm evidence in support of this. Byrhtferth continued to witness the charters of Eadred's successor King Eadwig until 13 February 956, after which his attestations cease.[44] Ealdorman Byrhtnoth began to witness Eadwig's charters on 29 November that same year. His ealdordom is given as Essex in the Worcester chronicle.[45]

Byrhtnoth was undoubtedly the most illustrious incumbent of the East Saxon ealdordom, which he held for thirty five years until his death in 991, in battle against the Danes near Maldon. His origins seem to have been Mercian, and it is possible that he was descended from the Mercian royal line, represented by Kings Beornwulf (823–825), Beorhtwulf (840–852), and Burghred (852–874), the last-named having been driven into exile by the Danes. From the poem on *The Battle of Maldon* (11. 214–9) we know that Byrhtnoth was related to a descendant of Ealhhelm, ealdorman of Central Mercia in 940–951, and father of Ealdormen Ælfhere of Mercia and Ælfheah of Wessex, Byrhtnoth's contemporaries and political opponents. Of Byrhtnoth's own father Byrhthelm we know nothing; no thegns or ealdormen of the name appear in surviving charters of the period.

Our records of Byrhtnoth's earliest landed interests show them to have been exclusively Mercian. While still a thegn, he had some interest in Phepson in Himbledon, Worcestershire, which he persuaded King Eadwig to donate to St Mary's, Worcester, in 956.[46] Byrhtnoth's estates included Tadmarton in Oxfordshire, granted to him in 956 and used for the endowment of Abingdon Abbey,[47] Cookley in Wolverley, Worcestershire, granted in 964,[48] and Brafield on the Green in Northamptonshire, granted in 967.[49] He owned also Whiston and Denton which bordered on Brafield, and were probably included in the 967 grant. These he gave to Ramsey Abbey, together with Isham, also in Northamptonshire.[50] Byrhtnoth held in addition Shifford in Oxfordshire and Mickleton in Gloucestershire, which were given to him by King Edgar and which he passed on to Leofwine, a relative of Ealdorman Æthelmær the lay patron of Eynsham Abbey, to which these estates descended.[51] Records of these holdings have come down to us only by chance, and one cannot doubt that he held many more Mercian properties of which no muniments have survived.

All the information on Byrhtnoth's possessions so far considered derives from charters. For knowledge of the remainder of his properties, mostly in Cambridgeshire, Suffolk and Essex, we are dependent on the will of his wife Ælfflæd, preserved at Bury, and on post-Conquest records of benefactors preserved at Ely, Ramsey, and Christ Church, Canterbury.[52]

Examination of the accompanying maps will show a pattern in the distribution of those estates which lie in Eastern England. First, there is a concentration of properties round Cambridge. These formed part of Byrhtnoth's patrimony,[53] but how they came into the possession of Byrhtnoth's father Byrhthelm we cannot tell. We shall return to speculate on this shortly. Secondly, there is another concentration round Colchester. These six estates – Dovercourt, Stanway, Byrton in Stanway, Beaumont, Alresford, and Lexden – together with Elmset and Buxhall north of the Stour, were given *en bloc* to King Æthelred the Unready in the will of Byrhtnoth's widow Ælfflæd, dated around 1002. One supposes that they descended to her from her husband because none of them occur in the wills of her father Ealdorman Ælfgar or her sister Æthelflæd. These estates lay in that part of Essex which had been occupied by the Danes, and in my view they formed the remnant of the endowment of the Essex ealdordom, handed down, perhaps, to successive incumbents from the time of King Edward the Elder or King Athelstan. It is significant, I think, that Hadleigh in Suffolk, another of Byrhtnoth's estates, had been the burial-place of Guthrum, the Danish king of East Anglia, in 890.[54] Moreover, Byrhtnoth's sister-in-law Æthelflæd endowed the church of Hadleigh for the souls of her ancestors, and this suggests that her father Ealdorman Ælfgar of Essex may once have held the estate.[55] When we come to examine the estates of Ælfgar in detail, we find another collection of properties close to Colchester, including the Mersea holding, strategically placed to control the seaward approaches both to Colchester (via the River Colne), and to Maldon (via the River Blackwater). This had within its bounds the meeting-place of the local hundred of Winstree, so it carried rights of jurisdiction; it also possessed a town house in Colchester, as we find in Little Domesday.[56] These properties too may once have formed part of the endowment of the ealdordom.[57]

It is well known that in the areas of Danish settlement – particularly in the territory of the Five Boroughs of Stamford, Leicester, Nottingham, Derby and Lincoln, and in the Danish shires of Bedford, Cambridge, Huntingdon and Northampton, administration and mustering of the Danish settlers at the beginning of the tenth century was controlled by the local earl, seated in the county town. I would suggest, tentatively, that the estates surrounding Colchester that came into the possession of Ealdormen Ælfgar and Byrhtnoth represent properties sequestered from Guthrum's Danish successors by King Edward the Elder in 917, and used for the endowment of the Essex ealdordom.

Whether the Cambridgeshire properties of Byrhtnoth and his father derived ultimately from a similar sequestration of estates belonging to a Danish earl, is more problematical. It is a curious fact that whereas Ealdorman Byrhtnoth's estates surrounded Cambridge and those of his contemporary, Ealdorman Æthelwine of East Anglia, surrounded Huntingdon, the *Liber Eliensis* shows Byrhtnoth exercising jurisdiction in Huntingdon, and Æthelwine in Cambridge. Perhaps it was easier that way, since the ealdormen would thus be spared the difficult problem involved in adjudicating the rights of tenure of their own estates.

Not all of Byrhtnoth's Essex properties descended to him with the ealdordom, for we know that Rettendon was given by him to his wife Ælfflæd as her *morgengifu*, or marriage gift, and that he was married to her by 951, five years before he was made ealdorman.[58] It has to be stressed that although we have evidence of his possession of over forty estates scattered over ten shires, only fragments of the details of his will have survived, and our knowledge of his holdings is probably far from complete.

Byrhtnoth's long tenure of office was marked by the occurrence of two series of events of great national importance, in which he played a full part. The first of these was the long-delayed revival of Benedictine monasticism, which finally reached England from the continent in 964, and which led among other things to a radical change in the pattern of landholding throughout Wessex, Mercia and East Anglia as many monasteries were founded (or refounded) and endowed. During the first decade of the reform, the five great fenland monasteries of Ramsey, Ely, Peterborough, Thorney and Crowland were established. Of these, Ely in particular, the greatest of them all in terms of landed wealth, enjoyed the patronage of Byrhtnoth and his family. When King Edgar died in 975 there was a considerable reaction against these endowments on the part of the dispossessed landowners. Byrhtnoth was in the van of those supporting the reform movement and protecting the abbeys against the usurpation of their newly acquired lands. His activities in this direction are well documented in the Ely archives and have been widely discussed, so we need not dwell on them here.

The second great series of events, from 980 onwards, was the renewal of viking raids on England from Scandinavia, after a lull of many decades. The early raids were on the south coast, and it is doubtful if Byrhtnoth was personally involved in repelling them. Although they did much damage, the forces deployed were not large; seven shiploads are mentioned in 980, and three shiploads in 982.[59] The great force of 93 ships under the command of Olaf Tryggvason, later king of Norway, which arrived off Folkestone in the early summer of 991 was a menace of a totally different order.[60] They moved up to Ipswich, where they landed and overran the countryside, and then sailed southwards along the Essex coast to the mouth of the River Blackwater. It seems that they travelled upstream as far as Northey Island, a flat and fertile piece of marsh land where the citizens of Maldon grazed their sheep. Here, some if not all of the raiders disembarked. In previous expeditions of this kind the vikings had developed a technique of seizing an island off the coast and establishing a base there, from which they would set out on raids penetrating deeply into the hinterland.

We do not know for sure what was their intention on this occasion. Handled with skill and resolution, their force of perhaps 3,500 men (40 from each of their ships) might have been sufficient for them to seize complete control of the country. Probably however their intention was no more than to probe the defences, to loot, and to raise tribute before sailing away. Perhaps their prior visit to Ipswich had proved disappointing, for there is no evidence that their numbers were swollen by the addition of Danish settlers from East Anglia.

Even without local reinforcements, it seems to me that the Danes at Maldon substantially outnumbered the English forces. Facing them, Byrhtnoth led an army drawn from Essex (Battle of Maldon 1. 69: *Eastseaxena ord*). He had with him a hostage from Northumbria and a relative whose ancestors were Mercian, but there is no evidence to suggest that his force consisted of contingents from counties other than Essex. The one warrior whose home is located securely came from Sturmer in Essex, on the Cambridgeshire border, which was on Byrhtnoth's approach route to the battle site.

Supposing Byrhtnoth's forces at Maldon to have been mainly East Saxon, let us make a guess at their numbers. A document known as the Tribal Hidage, dating perhaps from the second half of the eighth century, allocates an assessment of 7,000 hides to the East Saxons, but in addition to Essex their territory then included Middlesex and a sizeable chunk of Hertfordshire. By the time of Domesday Book, the hidage of Essex had been reduced to c. 2,650. If (aided by the newly-discovered Barking charters) we compare the early hidages of individual Essex estates with their Domesday assessments, we are left with the general impression that at the end of the tenth century, the county may have answered to the geld for 3,000 to 3,500 hides – certainly no more. Assuming that levies were mobilised from the whole county, and allowing the conventional assessment of one man from every five hides, we arrive at a total of 700 fighting men. Even if we allow Byrhtnoth a personal retinue of 300 followers from his own household and estates (several of which were in the vicinity of Maldon), the Danes at Maldon still probably outnumbered the English warriors by at least three to one. Yet according to the poem on the battle (discussed below), Byrhtnoth allowed the Danes to cross the River Blackwater from their encampment to the southern bank, so that the two opposing forces could do battle. No wonder the Maldon poet considered him over-confident to the point of foolhardiness (1. 89: *ofermode*). But it must be remembered that this was the first arrival on the shores of England for a whole century of a viking force of this size. Byrhtnoth may have been totally unaware of their true numbers – we just cannot tell.

It seems likely that Byrhtnoth was in Huntingdonshire, within his ealdordom, when news reached him of the location of the viking force. His route to Maldon passed by the abbeys of Ramsey and Ely, and monks from Ely, led by their abbot, followed him on his journey; subsequently they were to carry his headless corpse back to their abbey.[61] There is no need to question the Ely tradition on this point; twenty five years later, monks from Ramsey accompanied Edmund Ironside to his battle with King Cnut at *Assandun* and brought back the bodies of their abbot and his predecessor. The presence of monks from Ely at Maldon has to be taken into account when considering the genesis of the poem, which would appear to have been written by an eyewitness of the battle.

III *The Poem on the Battle of Maldon*

On 10 August 1991 we shall be celebrating the millenary of the battle of Maldon.[62] This was one of the decisive battles of English history, but it is remembered today chiefly because of the great Old English heroic poem about it that has survived. Since its *editio princeps* by Hearne in 1726 the poem has generated an enormous literature.[63] Besides the editions and translations there have been numerous commentaries by paleographers, philologists, and historians, not to mention the literary critics. The roll of historians offering interpretations of the poem commences with Freeman and continues with such illustrious names as Steenstrup, Stevenson, and Liebermann through to the present century, when most writers on the period have had something to say about it. I think I have read them all, or nearly all. What strikes me most is the wide variety of opinions that have been expressed. No two commentators, however renowned, end up with precisely the same interpretation. If anything, controversy as to the date and place of composition, the purpose of the poem, and its evidential value, is greater today than ever before. It is with trepidation that I enter the fray, spurred on by the immortal lines ascribed in the poem to one of the fallen warriors:

Hige sceal þe heardra   heorte þe cenre
mod sceal þe mare   þe ure mægen lytlað

The poem praises Byrhtnoth and those who fought and died with him; it was composed, one feels, for those who had been closely associated with him by ties of kinship, obligation, or common purpose. The national interest is indeed touched on at one point (ll.52–54), but the bias is overwhelmingly local. One can only speculate as to the circumstances attending its composition, but it appears to me that the surviving text of the poem stems primarily from a literary rather than an oral tradition. The impressive prayer ascribed to Byrhtnoth in his death throes is surely the work of a cleric, deriving inspiration from the offices of the church rather than the impromptu boastings of the mead hall. In short, I think the poem was composed at leisure in an ecclesiastical centre where there was a library and a scriptorium. The surviving text could well be the end result of a theme developed and revised (like *Beowulf*) extensively during composition; a carefully balanced eulogy written for a patron by someone well versed in the conventions of poetic writing, able to innovate, yet competent also to draw upon a considerable stock of existing Old English verse for some of his half lines.

It has to be remembered that in the surviving text we have only a fragment of 325 lines, incomplete at the beginning and at the end. Most commentators assume that the loss has been minimal, particularly at the end of the poem, but there is really no warrant for this. It is well known that the original fragment of the poem was destroyed in the Cotton library fire of 1731; our present knowledge of it depends on a transcript made, most fortunately, by David Casley a few years previously.[64] The late N. R. Ker, whose opinion commands respect, thought it likely that the original leaves on which the fragment was written owed their survival until the eighteenth century to their having been used as binding leaves.[65] It could well be, therefore, that the intact poem was twice or three times as long as the surviving fragment, and (like the tapestry presented by his widow to Ely) described the deeds of Byrhtnoth over a number of years before his death. Possibly too the poem was completed by a description of the recovery of Byrhtnoth's body from the battle site, and its carriage by the abbot and monks of Ely to its final resting place at their abbey.

The Latin account of Byrhtnoth which appears in the *Liber Eliensis* book II, chapter 62, written about 1154, could well have utilised the complete poem as its major source; if so, its compiler misinterpreted his text in places, due perhaps to insufficient command of Old English. Conceivably therefore, this late Latin narrative preserves within it a garbled outline of the whole content of the poem in its original state. That the compiler of the Latin account made use of the poem is suggested by his inclusion of a number of details of the battle which appear in the poem, but for which no other source is now known. These comprise references to fighting on the *bricg* (here rendered as *pontem*), not yielding a foot of ground (as in ll. 147, 175), and other items, discussed on page 11 of Scragg's edition. The poem appears also to have been known at Ramsey Abbey at an early date, for there are echoes of it in Byrhtferth's *Vita Oswaldi*, a product of that house.

Turning now to the content of the poem itself, there is a classical source, not previously identified as far as I know, which seems to me to have been utilised by the poet as the framework for part of his composition. This is

Sallust's *Conspiracy of Catiline*. The events portrayed in this work occurred in 63 B.C. and were recorded by Sallust some twenty years later.[66] Chapter 59 describes the final battle at the foot of the Alps, in which Catiline was defeated and killed. Sallust describes how, before the battle began, Catiline dismounted his cavalry and drove away the horses, so that the foot soldiers should know that their danger was shared by all alike. Similarly, the opening lines of the Maldon poem (in its surviving fragment) tell of Byrhtnoth ordering his mounted soldiers to get off their horses and drive them away from the scene of the action. A few lines later, Byrhtnoth is made to ride among his troops, arranging them in correct order and encouraging them to stand firm. Speeches are put into the mouths of the participants. Byrhtnoth announced his readiness to guard the realm, the people, and the land. Having arrayed and harangued his host, Byrhtnoth alighted from his horse and took up his position in the midst of his loyal bodyguard. There he fought to the death, as did most of his companions and retainers. All this is to be found in Sallust's description of Catiline's last battle.

Lest this claim of a classical model for the poem should appear far-fetched, I would mention that the tradition of using Sallust's writings as a framework for descriptions of contemporary battles appears to have originated on the Continent with the historian Widukind, writing at Corvey some twenty years before the battle of Maldon. It was taken up by Richer, the chronicler of Rheims, a decade or two later. The Maldon poem marks, I think, the first appearance of this literary device in England, but it was copied soon afterwards by a monk of Ramsey, the neighbouring abbey of Ely, who utilised the same chapter from Sallust's *Catiline* in his description of the final battles of Cnut and Edmund Ironside in 1016.[67] Subsequently the conceit was developed by the encomiast of Cnut's widow (herself a visitor and benefactor to Ely), writing perhaps at St Bertin's early in 1042.[68] At Ely itself the tradition lay dormant for a further century, only to flower once again in the writings of the monk who recorded a revolt by Bishop Nigel's steward in 1154.[69]

When one considers that Byrhtnoth's family lands were centered on Cambridgeshire; that he and his family, for successive generations right up to the Norman Conquest, supported Ely's interests and endowed it with lands and treasures whose value was exceeded only by Bishop Æthelwold's foundation endowment; that Byrhtnoth, his wife Ælfflæd, and his daughter Leofflæd were all buried at the abbey, to which Ælfflæd had presented a tapestry describing her husband's deeds; that his granddaughter Æthelswyth supervised a group of women servants who devoted their lives to making embroideries and vestments for the abbey; and finally that his grandson became a monk there; when one takes all this into account, it appears to me that an Ely provenance for the compiler of a poem eulogising Byrhtnoth is very likely indeed. According to a mid-twelfth-century tradition at Ely, Old English poems concerning its benefactors were composed and chanted by the monks in choir as early as the reign of Cnut.[70] One supposes that like the tapestry, the poem described Byrhtnoth's activities and eulogised his virtues over a considerable period of his life. Indeed, one cannot wholly discount the possibility that the poem and the tapestry were interdependent, each being created to illustrate the other to an audience – a sort of *son et lumière!* All we have left is a noble fragment, a great battle poem to be used only with circumspection as an historical record.

IV *From Ealdordom to Earldom*

With the deaths of Ealdormen Byrhtnoth of Essex (10 or 11 August 991) and Æthelwine of East Anglia (24 April 992), the balance of power in the court of King Æthelred the Unready underwent a profound change. At the time of their deaths, these two ranked second and first respectively among the ealdormen; the only other ealdormen witnessing Æthelred's charters at this time were Æthelweard of the Western Provinces and Ælfric of Wessex. Clearly, fresh appointments had to be made for England north of the Thames. We find Ealdormen Ælfhelm of Deira (southern Northumbria) witnessing from 993 onwards, and Ealdormen Leofsige and Leofwine from 994 onwards.[71] Leofwine's ealdordom covered Western and Central Mercia.[72] That of Leofsige, named as Essex in a charter of the period,[73] appears to have covered in addition East Anglia proper (that is, Norfolk and Suffolk)[74] and some at least of the East Midland shires, including probably Northamptonshire, Huntingdonshire, Cambridgeshire,[75] Bedfordshire, Hertfordshire,[76] Buckinghamshire, and Oxfordshire.[77] His sister Æthelflæd held estates in Huntingdonshire,[78] and probably Hertfordshire and Essex.[79]

Of Leofsige's activities as ealdorman we know very little; the late Sir Frank Stenton discussed some charters bearing on this.[80] In 1002 he was sent by King Æthelred to negotiate a treaty with the Danes investing the south coast ports.[81] In return for their departure he organised provisioning of their ships and payment of 24,000 pounds in Danegeld – a remarkable change of approach from that of his predecessor Byrhtnoth, who died rather than render the Danes tribute of this kind.

Very soon after his Danish negotiations, Leofsige killed the king's chief reeve Æfic in the course of a quarrel, and was banished by the witan 'because of his pride and rashness'.[82] We do not know where he went, but he is likely to have maintained contact with the Danes. Ten years later, at a time when the country was in turmoil due to the widespread depredations of the Danish army, his sister Æthelflæd was stripped of her estates for aiding Leofsige in his banishment.

From closer inspection of some of the sources for the period one can perhaps uncover a little more of the circumstances attending Leofsige's downfall. The reeve Æfic whom he killed is probably to be identified with the man of that name who had been the steward to the king's sons, or æthelings, and was involved in a lawsuit to be dated 990–2.[83] King Æthelred is known to have promoted Leofsige in two steps, first to *satraps* (probably an official in the royal household), and then at some indeterminate time later to ealdorman.[84] He may therefore be identified with the Leofsige to whom were left Standon, Offley and Tewin in Hertfordshire, and Weedon in Northamptonshire, by the will of the noble lady called Æthelgifu, which is probably to be dated 985–990.[85] This Leofsige may have been related to Æthelgifu. In her will, she appealed to the queen mother to help him to secure a position as steward to 'the ætheling', by whom Æthelgifu appears to have meant Athelstan, the king's eldest son, who died in 1014. Leofsige may therefore have been Æfic's predecessor in the ætheling's household. Athelstan's will shows him to have possessed Tewin, perhaps due to Leofsige's forfeiture. He also owned another estate, named Norton, which may have been the Hertfordshire property of that name which Leofsige is known to have acquired, and which may similarly have been forfeited to Athelstan.

In themselves these matters are of no great interest, but if the various identifications have been made correctly, they show that Leofsige gained his position as ealdorman through service as steward in charge of the estates set aside for the king's children. It is noteworthy that many of these estates were within the area of jurisdiction of his ealdordom, and that the Æfic whom he killed in a quarrel may have been his successor as the ætheling's steward.

A remarkable feature of the East Saxon ealdordom that has been highlighted by this enquiry is that every ealdorman of Essex for whom sufficient evidence survives, appears to have held jurisdiction over a much larger territory than that of the shire from which he took his title. Byrhtnoth and Leofsige, both named in contemporary sources as ealdormen of Essex, certainly governed a much wider area. Beorhtwulf, the first named ealdorman of Essex, also appears to have ruled a territory embracing several shires. This application of the title of a single shire to an ealdorman having a wider area of jurisdiction is not confined to Essex; for example, Æthelmær and Edwin, whose deaths are reported in the C text of the Anglo-Saxon Chronicle under the year 982, are described as 'on Hantun scire' and 'on Suth Seaxum' respectively, but the former certainly governed Wiltshire and Berkshire as well as Hampshire, and the latter's ealdordom must have covered Kent, and possibly Surrey, as well as Sussex. Perhaps the Essex title derived from its former status as a kingdom; Cambridgeshire and Huntingdonshire had been ruled only by princes in the time of the Heptarchy.

Leofsige was the last ealdorman of Essex. After Cnut gained the English crown in 1016, subsequent rulers of the county were called earls. As with the ealdormen who preceeded them, each earl had control of more than one shire, but they no longer took their titles from Essex. As with the ealdordoms, the territory held by each earl appears to have been decided independently at the time of his appointment, and the permutations and combinations of shires were constantly changing. Thus in 1017 when England was divided into four, Essex was included in the portion alloted to Thorkell the Tall, Earl of East Anglia.[86] By 1045 the jurisdiction of Earl Harold was a good deal smaller; with Essex went East Anglia, Cambridgeshire, Huntingdonshire, and probably Middlesex. Leofwine who took over in 1057 held a very different earldom; Essex and Middlesex were detached from East Anglia and lumped together with Hertfordshire, Buckinghamshire, Surrey and Kent.[87]

It was not until the reign of King Stephen in the early twelfth century that earls took their titles from single counties over which they held jurisdiction.

A century ago, J. Horace Round's great study of Geoffrey de Mandeville appeared.[88] All subsequent writers on the earldom of Essex have started where he left off.

ACKNOWLEDGEMENTS

My interest in the East Saxon ealdordom was initiated by Dr F. G. Emmison, during my visits to the Essex Record Office in 1950–51. My grateful thanks are due also to Professor Helmut Gneuss, Dr Simon Keynes, and Dr Donald Scragg, all of whom have read this paper and contributed helpful criticism. Professor Gneuss drew my attention to an important paper of his on the battle of Maldon, little known to English scholars, which appeared in *Studies in Philology*, 73 (1976), pp. 133–137.

Notes and References

The following abbreviations are used in these footnotes:
ASC   Anglo-Saxon Chronicle. The various texts are listed as A, B, C, D, E.
         They may be consulted conveniently in translation in D. Whitelock (ed.), *The Anglo-Saxon Chronicle*, London, (1961).
S   (followed by a number) refers to charters listed in P. H. Sawyer, *Anglo Saxon Charters*, R. Hist. Soc., London, (1968).
s.a.   (followed by date) = *sub anno*.

1. ASC A s.a. 825; B. Yorke, 'The Kingdom of the East Saxons', *Anglo-Saxon England* 14 (1985), 1–36, esp. 24 n. 142.
2. S 1791; M. Gibbs, *Early Charters of the Cathedral Church of St Paul, London*, R. Hist. Soc., Camden Third series, 58 (1939), 7.
3. C. R. Hart, 'The B text of the Anglo-Saxon Chronicle', *Journal of Medieval History* 8 (1982), 241–299, esp. 249–252.
4. ASC A s.a. 836, supported by 'Florence of Worcester', see C. R. Hart, 'The early section of the Worcester chronicle', *Journal of Medieval History* 9 (1983), 251–315, esp. 279–285; D. Dumville, 'Alfred and Guthrum' n. 12, to appear in his *Wessex and England from Alfred to Edgar*, Woodbridge, (1986).
5. ASC A s.a. 855, 860; D. Dumville, 'The ætheling', *Anglo-Saxon England* 9 (1979), 1–33, esp. 21–24.
6. S 337; C. R. Hart, *The Early Charters of Essex*, Leicester, 2nd edn., (1971), 10–11. The text has suffered at the hands of a late interpolator, but the original text can easily be reconstructed, and there is no reason to question the authenticity of this restored version.
7. Dumville, 'Alfred and Guthrum', n. 15.
8. For example, Eanulf is *princeps* in S 292, *dux* in S 304, 1196.
9. A. J. Robertson, *The Laws of the Kings of England from Edmund to Henry I*, Cambridge, (1925). III Edgar, 5, 2; II Cnut 18, 1; Cnut 1020, 8.
10. S 327, 335.
11. S 304–5, 307, 381–3.
12. S 317; M. Gelling, *The Early Charters of the Thames Valley*, Leicester, (1979), 28.
13. S 367, 375–8, 381–3.
14. S 327, 337, 1203, 1508.

15. B. Thorpe (ed.) *Florentii Wigorniensis monachi Chronicon ex chronicis*, 2 vols., London, (1848–9), 1, 126.
16. Hart, 'Worcester Chronicle', 280.
17. See K. N. Bascombe, *Two Charters of King Suebred of Essex*, elsewhere in this volume.
18. C. R. Hart, *The Early Charters of Eastern England*, Leicester, (1966), 145.
19. Dumville, 'Alfred and Guthrum', *passim*.
20. C. R. Hart, 'Athelstan Half King and his Family', *Anglo-Saxon England* 2 (1973), 115–144.
21. C. R. Hart, *The Early Charters of Northern England and the North Midlands*, Leicester, (1975), 362.
22. A. S. Napier and W. H. Stevenson, *The Crawford Collection of Early Charters and Documents now in the Bodleian Library*, Oxford, (1895), 74–5; A. Campbell, *The Chronicle of Æthelweard*, London, (1962), 53.
23. Symeon of Durham, *Historia de Sancto Cuthberto*, in *Symeonis Monachi Opera Omnia*, ed. T. Arnold, London, Rolls Series no. 75, 1 (1882), 209.
24. S 569; Hart, *Charters of Northern England*, 362.
25. S 659, 674, 677, 679; P. H. Sawyer (ed.), *Charters of Burton Abbey*, Oxford, (1979), 22.
26. H. M. Chadwick, *Studies in Anglo-Saxon Institutions*, Cambridge, (1905), 188.
27. Hart, *Charters of Northern England*, 287–8.
28. Hart, 'Athelstan Half King', 121.
29. Hart, *Charters of Northern England*, 287–8.
30. Hart, 'Athelstan Half King', 122–3.
31. S 1504; F. E. Harmer, *Select English Historical Documents of the Ninth and Tenth Centuries*, Cambridge, (1914), 33 (no. 20).
32. S 1507.
33. S 350, 364, 1284, 359, 367; Hart, *Charters of Northern England*, 355.
34. S 1286, 367.
35. S 378, 399–401.
36. S 605, 597.
37. S. Keynes and M. Lapidge (eds.), *Alfred the Great*, Penguin, (1983), 173–4, argue that the section of King Alfred's will in which Osferth's name appears represents a revision made between 888 and Alfred's death on 26 October 899. This would certainly make the chronology of Osferth's career more plausible.
38. S 1483; D. Whitelock, *Anglo-Saxon Wills*, Cambridge, (1930), 6–9 (no. 2).
39. S 497, 510.
40. S 1486, 1494; Whitelock, *Anglo-Saxon Wills*, 34–41 (nos. 14, 15).
41. C. R. Hart, 'The Mersea Charter of Edward the Confessor', *Essex Archaeology and History*, 12 (1980), 94–102, esp. 95–7; C. R. Hart and A. Syme, 'The Earliest Suffolk Charter', to appear in *Proceedings of the Suffolk Institute of Archaeology and History*, (1987).
42. S 563, 565, 553.
43. Chadwick, *Anglo-Saxon Institutions*, 179–180. In S 1447, an Old English record of a lawsuit, Byrhtferth is shown to be adjudicating in a case involving theft of a woman living in Yaxley in Huntingdonshire, for which he demanded the sequestration of an estate in Sunbury, Middlesex, from the person whom he held responsible. Dr A. Robertson considered this transaction to show that Byrhtferth held jurisdiction in Middlesex. Charters indicate that the ealdordom of South-East Mercia was vacant at the time, and it is not impossible that Middlesex was being administered by the ealdorman of Essex; an alternative view, which I prefer, is that Byrhtferth was acting here as an ealdorman having jurisdiction in Huntingdonshire,

where the crime was committed. See further, A. J. Robertson, *Anglo-Saxon Charters*, Cambridge, (1956), 90–93, 336–7; Hart, *Charters of Eastern England*, 162.

44. S. Keynes, *The Diplomas of King Æthelred 'the Unready'*, Cambridge, (1980), 53–5.

45. Thorpe, *Florentii Wigorniensis*, 1, 149: *strenuus dux Orientalium Saxonum Byrhtnothus*.

46. S 633.

47. S 584, 611, 617.

48. S 726.

49. S 750, wrongly located by Sawyer at Cold Brayfield, Buckinghamshire; see C. R. Hart, 'A Charter of King Edgar for Brafield-on-the-Green, Northamptonshire,' to appear in *Northamptonshire Past and Present*, (1987).

50. S 798; Hart, *Charters of Northern England*, 58–9.

51. S 911.

52. S 1486, 1637; E. O. Blake (ed.), *Liber Eliensis*, R. Hist. Soc., Camden Third Series, 92, London, (1962), 422–3; W. Dunn Macray (ed.), *Chronicon Abbatiæ Rameseiensis*, Rolls Series, 83, London, (1886), 116–7; Hart, *Charters of Essex*, 15; *Charters of Eastern England*, 60.

53. Blake, *Liber Eliensis*, 134: *totum patrimonium suum conferebat*.

54. D. Dumville and M. Lapidge (eds.), *The Annals of St Neots with Vita Prima Sancti Neoti*, Cambridge, (1985), 95; C. R. Hart, 'The East Anglian Chronicle,' *Journal of Medieval History*, 7 (1981), 255.

55. S 1494. Could Guthrum have been one of Ælfgar's ancestors?

56. DB 22a. At the time of the Domesday Survey, the holders of the West Mersea estate had two thirds of the profits of justice of Winstree Hundred, and the king had one third, except for forfeitures, for which he was entitled to two thirds.

57. Hart, 'The Mersea Charter,' 95.

58. Hart, *Charters of Essex*, 19–20.

59. ASC D, E s.a. 980; ASD C s.a. 982.

60. ASC A s.a. 993, with a caret mark for 991. This entry was made at Winchester in 1002, but the chronicler appears to have used a source now lost. There is no reason to disbelieve the entry, which shows how important the battle of Maldon was considered by the English, ten years after it had been fought. See further, Hart, 'The B text of the Anglo-Saxon Chronicle', 258–60.

61. Blake, *Liber Eliensis*, 136.

62. Perhaps we should accept the Winchester date, 11 August, rather than that of Ely, 10 August; the Winchester source is much the earlier of the two, and is supported by the Ramsey tradition; see W. Dugdale, *Monasticon Anglicanum*, (1846 edn.), 2, 566: *tertio idus Augusti, obiit Brightnothus comes*.

63. The best edition is that by D. G. Scragg, *The Battle of Maldon*, Manchester, (1981), which has also a good bibliography.

64. H. L. Rogers, 'The Battle of Maldon: David Casley's Transcript,' *Notes and Queries*, 32, (1985), 147–155.

65. Scragg, *Battle of Maldon*, 42–3.

66. A. W. Ahlberg (ed.), revised by A. Kurfess, *C. Sallusti Crispi*, Teubner, Leipzig, (1968). Translation by S. A. Handford, *Sallust: Jugurthine War. Conspiracy of Catiline*, Penguin, (1963).

67. Hart, 'Worcester Chronicle,' 303–4.

68. A. Campbell (ed.), *Encomium Emmae Reginae*, R. Hist. Soc., Camden Third Series, 72, London, (1949), xxix-xxx. The Continental tradition was continued by William of Poitiers; when writing (in 1071 or soon after) of William the Conqueror's invasion of England, he referred to the concluding passage of Sallust's *Jugurtha*.

69. Blake, *Liber Eliensis*, xxxix, 287, 296–7.
70. Blake, *Liber Eliensis*, 153.
71. S 876, 880–2, 1379.
72. Hart, *Charters of Northern England*, 344–5.
73. S 891.
74. Hart, *Charters of Northern England*, 344.
75. Blake, *Liber Eliensis*, 138.
76. S 916.
77. S 883.
78. S 926.
79. Whitelock, *Anglo-Saxon Wills*, 176.
80. F. M. Stenton, *Latin Charters of the Anglo-Saxon Period*, Oxford, (1955), 76–80.
81. ASC C, D, E s.a. 1002.
82. S 926.
83. S 1454; Robertson, *Anglo-Saxon Charters*, 136–9, 379–82 (no. 66).
84. S 926.
85. S 1479; D. Whitelock (ed.), *The Will of Æthelgifu*, Roxburghe Club, London, 1968.
86. ASC C, D, E s.a. 1017.
87. E. A. Freeman, *The History of the Norman Conquest of England*, 3rd edn., revised, Oxford, (1877), 2, 383–4 and maps.
88. J. H. Round, *Geoffrey de Mandeville: a Study of the Anarchy*, London, (1892).

APPENDIX. EALDORMEN'S ATTESTATIONS TO CHARTERS, 925–955

Charters are quoted by the number assigned to them in P. H. Sawyer, *Anglo-Saxon Charters*, R. Hist. Soc., London, 1968.
Barking charters are quoted in Roman numerals by the number assigned to them in the forthcoming edition in the British Academy series.
The numbers assigned to each ealdorman represent his positions in the witness lists of the relevant charters. The period during which each ealdorman witnesses is indicated by round brackets.
Ealdormen having the same name are differentiated by Roman numerals in parenthesis.

KING ATHELSTAN'S EALDORMEN

DATE (year)	925	926	928	929	930	930	931	931	931	931	932	932	932	933	933	934	934	934	934	937	937	938	938	939	939	939	Suggested Jurisdiction
DATE	4 Sept		16 April		3 April	29 April	23 March	20 June	15 July	12 Nov	30 Aug	9 Nov	24 Dec	11 Jan	26 Jan	28 May	7 June	16 Dec	21 Dec								
CHARTER	394	396-7	399-400	401-2	403	405	412	413	1604	416	417	B VI	418-9	379	422-3	425	407	427	434-5, 1575	432	438	440-1	444	455	446	447-9	
Ordgar I	1	1)																									Western Provinces
Osferth	(2	3	1	2	1	1	1	1	1	2	2	2	1	1	1	2	2)			1	1	1)					Surrey, Sussex, Kent
Ælfwold II		2	2	1	2	2	2	2	2	1	1	1	2	2	2	1	1	1	1								Wessex
Wulfgar I		(4)																									Central Mercia
Ealdred					(3		5	6	3	3	4	4	3	4)		4	5										Central Mercia
Uhtred I					4	5	4	5	4	4	5	5		5	4	5	5)			2	2				4	5	North West Mercia
Æscbriht					(3	3	2	3	5	5	6	6	6	6	6	6	6)		5				2				Western Provinces
Ælfstan					6	4	3	4	6	6	7	7	7			7											South East Mercia
Uhtred II					(5		(6	7		7											4)						?: North West Mercia
Alfred II							7			8)	(3	3	3	4)													East Anglia
Athelstan I											(3	3		3	3	3	3	2	2					3	3	3	East Anglia
Ælfhere I																						1)		(1	1	1	Wessex
Wulfgar II																						2		(2	2	1	Western Provinces
Wulfstan																										(4)	Surrey, Sussex, Kent

KING EDMUND'S EALDORMEN

CHARTER	940	941	942	943	944	945	946	Suggested Jurisdiction
(charters)	469 465 467 470 / 461,463 / 452	471 478 475 476 / 511	514 496 485 480 483 482 / 479,484	491 486 1497 487 489 1811 488,492 / 512	500 494 503 493 495 / 497	507	508 / 510	
Ælfhere I	1 1 1 1	1 1 1 2	1 1 1 1 1	1 3 1 1 1 1 1	1 1 1 1 1 1	2	3	Wessex
Wulfgar II	2 2 2 2	1 1 1 1	1 1 1 1 1	3 2 1 2 1 2 2 5	2 1 2 2 3 7	1	2	Western Provinces
Athelstan I	3 3 4	3 3 3 7 5	8 6 9 3 6	7 8 8 3 5 3			8 1	North West Mercia
Uhtred I	4 7 5 6	6 2 2 2 4	8 3 5 6 4	2 3 3 5 7 4	5 4 5 6 7	3		Surrey, Sussex, Kent
Æthelwold I	(3 3 2	5 4 6 4 5	3 5 6 3 4	4 5 5 4 6 3	4 4 5 5 3 4	4	6	Central Mercia
Ealhhelm I	(5 4 4	(2	4 5 4	6 4 6 4 6	5 5 6 3 7 5	5	7	North West Mercia
Æthelmund	(6 4 5 5		5 6 3 7 4 (7 10)	3 5 7 3	3 3 3 3 5 (6)		5	North West Mercia
Athelstan II	(3			5				South East Mercia
Eadric I				3 6 7	6 4 7 5		4	Wessex
Ælfwold III								Unknown

CHARTER	518	519	B VIII	520	B VII	525	B IX	529	522	523	526	527	528	542	536	535	531	534	533	532	546	543	552, 578	550	544	547	B X	556	554	558	516	559	560	561	553	565	563	566	564	Suggested Jurisdiction
DATE	946	946	946	946	946	947	947	947	947	947	947	947	947	948	948	948	948	948	948	948	949	949	949	949	949	949	950	951	951	951	951	952	953	953	955	955	955	955	955	
Æthelwold I	1)					1	1	1	1	1	1	1	1	1	1	1	1	1	1	1	1	1		1	1	1	1			2	1	1	1	1	1				1	Surrey, Sussex, Kent
Athelstan I	2	3				R	2	2	2	2	2	2	2	2	2	2	2	2	2	2	2	2		2	2	2	1		2	2		1	1	1	1				1	East Anglia
Eadric I	4	2	2	3		2	3	3	3	3	3	3	3				4	3	3	3					5)	5)									1					Wessex
Athelstan II																							1		1															South East Mercia
Wulfgar II						3	4	4	4	4	4	4	4														4)													Western Provinces
Uhtred I																																								North West Mercia
Ealhhelm	3	2	3	4		4	5	5	5	5	5	5	5	4	4	4	3	3	5	5		2	3	4	4	4	2	3	3	3		2	2	2		2	2	2		Central Mercia
Æthelmund	4	1	5			5	6	6	6	6	6	6	6	5	5	5	5	4	6	6		4	3	3	1	1	3	4	4	1										North West Mercia
Ælfgar			4		6	6	7	7	7	7	7	7	7	6	6	6	6	6	6	7		5)	1	7	7	7	5	1	2	1	1	3	2	2			1		2	Essex
Edmund																									(5	(5	6				(5				3	3				Western Provinces
Æthelsige																																			4	4		4	4	Wessex
Byrhtferth																							1		(1 2 1										(3	5			4	Essex

KING EADRED'S EALDORMEN

Two Charters of King Suebred of Essex

KENNETH BASCOMBE

1 *Introduction*

In 1969 Mr H. H. Lockwood of Goodmayes, in the course of a study of Ilford Hospital, examined a 16th century MS on vellum (the 'Ilford Hospital Book') in the library of Hatfield House, Herts. Subsequent study (also by Mr. Lockwood) indicated that ff 1–27 of this volume, all apparently in the same hand, is almost certainly the MS referred to and exhibited in connection with a tithe dispute of 1593 relating to that Hospital. This book was described at that time by a witness, James Armorer, as having been transcribed by him out of a 'more ancient writing' (which was somewhat defaced) at the command of one J. Vaughan, Master of the Hospital from 1558 probably till his death in 1577. The contents of ff 1–27 suggest that Armorer had been instructed by Vaughan to select, from the 'more ancient writing', material which appeared to be relevant to the Hospital and its rights and properties.

The Hospital of St. Mary and St. Thomas at Ilford was founded for the poor and infirm by Alice, abbess of Barking from 1126 x 1133 to 25 January 1166 (Knowles *et al* (1972), 208). The Hospital remained under the control of the Abbey till the latter was dissolved in 1539 (VCH II, 120) and it seems very probable that the 'more ancient writing' selectively copied by Armorer was in fact a cartulary of the Abbey. The 18th century Ilford historian, Smart Lethieullier, certainly thought so, while Armorer's employer, Vaughan, was a Master in Chancery, and would certainly have been in a good position to obtain access to such a document, which having survived the trauma of the dissolution would have been held by the Augmentation Office (part of the Exchequer). The removal of the vellum MS from Ilford to Hatfield is accounted for by the fact that control of the hospital passed to the Marquess of Salisbury in the 19th century (VCH V, 228). The existence of extracts from a cartulary of Barking Abbey is of great interest since no complete text of one is known to survive, but we are here concerned primarily with f 15r which contains, under the heading *Carta Suebredi Regis*, two distinct charters of that monarch, followed in ff 15r – 18r by seven further charters, one of Athelstan, four of Eadred, and two of Ethelred the Unready, all lacking the boundary clauses, presumably because either Armorer, or the Barking cartulary copyist before him, could not cope with Old English, in which they would have been written. None of these charters has apparently been mentioned in print before, let alone published. The two charters of Suebred form the subject of this paper. They are written in a secretary hand, the glossed names being added later in italic.

2. *The Text*

Carta Suebredi Regis

Ego Suebredius Rex intellexi (et) consideravi cum q(u)anta festinac(i)o(n)e cuncta / p(re)sentia p(ro)perant / ad fine (m) Et ncil stabile in reb(us) humanis firmit p(er)manet / sed ea sola sine labestant p(er)hennit que p(ro) deo disperient(ur). Quap(ro)pt(er) p(ro) remedio / a(n)i(m)e mee trado tibi

Nasingum
Enodmerese

ffymme terram Juris mei hoc est xxx manentes in / Nasyngum cuius terr(e) aliqua p(ar)s appellat(ur) Enod-merese cum om(n)ib(us) ad / se p(er)tinentib(us) campis silvis p(r)atis pascuis et piscariis ut h(ab)eat(i)s (et) possideas/tam tu q(u)am posteri tui in sempit(er)nu(m) tulit et eo solo modo ut ibi aut tu ip(s)e / si p(i)(et)as ale(ret) ... domu(m) dei erigas aut ad hanc utilitate(m) alio cuicu(m)q(u)e desideras / anno(rum) tuo(rum) tradas ut dei sit et eius voluntati so(li)det(ur) iugiter cuius terre / terminus est Stanhemstede in australi p(ar)te/

Ettumende obre Ego Suebredus Rex Estsexano(rum) p(ro) remedio anime mee addo tibi ffymme / ad p(ri)ore(m) donat(i)o(n)em decem manentes terre iuris mei que appellat(ur) Ettunende / obre ad eundum usum et ad eandem utilitatem qui prior(em) dedi sub eisdem testib(us) / qui priori subscrip-ser(u)nt dationi et sub eadem confirmat(i)o(n)e et idem confirma qui / ad priorem terr(am) iuncta est. Et hoc consuetudo multo(rum) regn(um) et Episcopo(rum) / et principu(m) ut in fine cartule multos maledictiones (et) anathematizat(i)o(n)es / impon(e)nt. Nos hec amplius non dicimus qui hec servet (et) augeat / servetur illi requies r(ec)to(rum) et augeant(ur) dei misericordia hic (et) in futuro qui / hec minuerit miniat(ur) ab illo requies r(ec)to(rum) et fraudet(ur) pars eius de / terra vinecinum est hoc num(er)us terr(am) huius xl manent(ium) ... / + Ego Suebredus rex orientaliu(m) Saxonu(m) hanc donat-(i)o(n)em mea(m) sigillo s(anc)te crucis confirmabo. Signu-(m) manus Waldheri epi(scopi) + Signu(m) manus Sige-heardi + Signu(m) manus Eadburge + Signu(m) manus Offa + Signu(m) manus iusti abbat(is) + Signu(m) manus Edilredi Abbat(is) + Signu(m) manus Franca abb(at)is + Signu(m) man(us) Coelhere + Signu(m) man(us) Saba + Signu(m) man(us) Oedilredi + Signu(m) manus Tochta + Signu(m) man(us) Biba + Signu(m) manus misita + Signu(m) manus Cille + Signu(m) manus Patara + Signu(m) man(us) Iggnaldi p(resbyte)ris + Signu(m) manus Addan abbat(is)

The following translation is offered:

Charter of King Suebred

I King Suebred have perceived and considered how rapidly things perfect hasten to their end, and how nothing in human affairs is stable or remains unweakened save that which has been dedicated to God. Therefore for the salvation of my soul I grant to you *ffymme* my rights in 30 *manentes* of land in *Nasingum*, part of which is called
Nasingum *Enodmerese*, with all things appertaining to it, fields,
Enodmerese woods, meadows, pastures and fisheries, for you and your posterity to have and enjoy for ever, but only for the purpose that you may either share in erecting there a house of God, if the divine mercy sustains (you?), or that you may devote your years to this service in whatever other way you may see fit so that it may be devoted to God and his will for ever. The boundary of this land on the south end is *Stanhemstede*. (The remainder of the first charter is omitted).

Ettunende obre I Suebred, King of the East Saxons, for the salvation of my soul add to my earlier gift to you *ffymme* my rights in ten *manentes* of land which is called *Ettunende obre*, to the same / use and service as before, and the same persons witness this deed who confirmed the first donation, and I confirm that the same is joined to the land mentioned above. This company of many kings and bishops and princes is (gathered) so that at the end of this little charter they may set down many maledictions and anathemas. We say no more than these (words); may the peace of the righteous be preserved and augmented here and in the future, through the mercy of God, in him who preserves these gifts; (but) may the peace of the righteous be diminished in him who diminishes them, and may part of his own land be taken from him. This is the measure of this neighbouring 40 manentes of land (the actual bounds are omitted) + I Suebred, king of the eastern Saxons, will confirm this my gift with the impression of the holy cross. + The sign of the hand of bishop Walderus. (Etc.)

It will be seen that we have here two charters, confirmed by the same persons on the same occasion. The pious invocation to be expected at the beginning of each charter is omitted in each case. The bounds of the whole estate (40 *manentes*) were apparently included in the second charter, but these also are lost. The name *ffymme* is unfamiliar, and almost certainly corrupt: Hart (pers. comm.) thinks it is possibly female, but draws my attention to a thane *Imma* mentioned by Bede (1968, 238–40).

3. *Date of the Charters*

King Suebred, who issued these charters, was one of the later members of the East Saxon dynasty, recently discussed in detail by Yorke (1985), who questions the long held view that Suebred (which name is also glossed Swaefred) is to be identified with Swaefheard. Both are claimed as sons of Saebbi, the former by Bede (1968, 220) and the latter in a charter of 690, granted by him as King of Kent (Sawyer 1968, no. 10). Suebred and another brother, Sigeheard, add their confirmation to that of their father – all three witnessing as kings – of Œthelred's charter to Barking (ibid, no. 1171). This was given in c.686–8, but Yorke (p. 5) points out the possibility that they may have witnessed in confirmation after their father's death in 693–4 (p. 12). Other surviving charters of king Suebred include a grant (dated 704) in conjunction with a count Peogthath, of land at Twickenham, to Waldhere, bishop of London, (*ibid*, no. 65) and a grant of land at Dengie, Essex, to the next bishop, Ingwald, dated c.706–709 (*ibid*, no. 1787). Sigeheard, who acceded to the kingdom jointly with his brother on Saebbi's death (Bede, (1968), 220) consented to a grant (datable 704–709) of land at Fulham by bishop Tyrhtil (of Hereford) (Sawyer, (1968), 1785) to bishop Waldhere.

When Sigiheard and Suebred ceased to rule is unknown; the exact status of the next king, Offa, is unclear (Yorke, (1985), p. 22) but he abdicated and went to Rome in 709 (Bede (1968), 300). Since Offa also granted a charter to bishop Waldhere (of land at Hemel Hempstead) (Sawyer (1968), no. 1784), Suebred's reign must have overlapped with his. It is also possible that the two brothers' reigns overlapped with that of the next king, Selered (709–746) of whom very little is known.

The dating bracket for our charters can be defined by the presence as a witness of bishop Waldhere, who succeeded Eorcenwald as bishop of London in 693, and died not later than 709. The Iggnaldus, *presbyter*, who also signs, may be his successor Ingwald. Witnesses Sigeheardus and Offa are interesting; if these are the individuals who shared kingship with Suebred, it may be that the latter reigned originally alone and only later with co-rulers. Unfortunately, as will be seen, this does not positively narrow the date range on presently available evidence. One Pagara witnessed Sawyer no. 65 of 704 and might possibly be equated with Patara, but the two witness-lists have no other names in common. Oedilredus must be the grantor of Sawyer no. 1171, to Barking in 686–8 (d = th also in f.16 of the MS where the king's name Ethelred is written Edilred). Abbot Addan may well be Haddan, abbot of Medehamstede (later Peterborough) who witnessed a Mercian confirmation of Sawyer no. 233 – Swaefheard's Kent charter of 691. His witness of the Nazeing charter probably reflects Mercian influence in Essex at the date of the charter, as postulated by Hart (1966, 139) for the period 693–704. Cilli *principi* was also a witness to the Mercian confirmation of Sawyer no. 233.

Certainty for the date of our charters appears to be restricted to the date range 693 x 709, though there is some slight indication that the actual date is less likely to lie at the end of that range.

4. *Archaeological Significance*

In 1975–6 a Middle Saxon cemetary, with posthole evidence of two timber churches, was excavated at Nazeing (Huggins, P. J. 1978); the site showed evidence also of Romano-British occupation. The cemetery, which had been discovered in 1934, had contained at least 230 graves; the 118 interments which could be definitely sexed showed 86 females and 32 males, while analysis by age showed 17 children (aged 18 months to 15 years), 10 adolescents, 71 fully mature adults (29 aged 45+), plus 54 of mature age but not sufficiently complete to permit full ageing. These, an apparent absence of malnutrition and more detailed observations led the pathologist, Glenys Putnam, to postulate a hospice run by nuns. (Bede's record of Barking (1968), 221–2) indicates that that nunnery also housed aged and inform persons of both sexes). The earlier of the churches showed two primary interments in front of the altar, a situation normally expected for founders; both were female, aged 50 or over. One of these was dated to 670±80 by Carbon – 14 measurement, while an archaeologically later grave was similarly dated to 830±80. Further consideration reduced these date ranges to c.660–720 and c.760–870 respectively. The convent was considered to have been founded after Cedd's mission of 654, and possibly after Eorcenwald's arrival c.675, and to have probably been destroyed by the Danes after 870.

It would be difficult to avoid the conclusion that the charters under consideration represent the foundation of the Nazeing nunnery. The dates are in agreement, as in the presence of two female graves in the founder's position: *ffymme* (who was possibly female) was to share in the construction of a house of God on the first 30 manentes of land. The possibilty that more than one religious house in Nazeing could so adequately reflect the conditions of Suebred's grant must be very small indeed. The house is probably most appropriately described as a nunnery, since nunneries of the period acted *inter alia* as hospices, and separate hospices run solely as such were unknown in England at this time. At this period all nuns came from royal or noble families, and many became nuns after being widowed. (Hart, *pers. comm.*) Clearly, malnutrition is much less likely in such a community than in the population as a whole.

5. *Authenticity*

The archaeological significance discussed in section 4 is very strong evidence for the authenticity of the general content of the charters, and for the identification of *Nasyngum* in the first charter with the modern Nazeing, rather than Navestock, which in its oldest form (Reaney (1935), 69) is recorded as *Nasingestok*. This is reinforced by the presence in *Nasyngum* of fisheries (*piscariis*). Nazeing had 'half a fishery' in Doomsday, while Navestock had none; in fact, many fisheries are recorded on the Lea, but none on the much smaller Roding (on which Navestock abuts) except at Ilford, and possibly at Barking, near its mouth. (VCH I, 380). Dr. Hart has suggested (*pers. comm.*) that *Nasyngum* represents Nazeingbury (VCH V, 142 and f.p. 117), the 'bury' being the enclosure round the nunnery (cf. Peterborough).

That the originals of the charters are at any rate pre-Conquest in date is indicated by the fact that the letter *u* following *q* is shown in the great majority of cases (11 out of 14) whereas in later original medieval MSS it is consistently omitted. The 16th century copyist, Armorer, appears to have been much happier with the Latin than with the OE placenames (or personal names); it may have been this which induced him to omit the estate bounds – if an earlier copyist had not already done so. On the diplomatic, Dr. Hart has kindly supplied a preliminary comment: 'the diplomatic appears authentic; very many phrases reappear in other texts of the period' i.e. c.700.

6 *Topography* (see map)

The estate consists of 30 *manentes* in *Nasyngum* i.e. Nazeing (or Nazeingbury), and 10 *manentes* adjacent called *Ettunende obre*. Of the 30 manentes, part is called *Enodmerese*, and the southern extremity lies at *Stanhemstede*.

The total area is therefore 40 *manentes*; evidently a considerable estate, although at this early period it is not practicable to assign to it an equivalence in land area. Nazeingwood Common was enclosed from forest land only in 1229 (VCH V, 144) so that it is not likely to have been included in the grant. The estate therefore may reasonably be taken to lie between the rivers Lea and Stort and the boundary of Nazeingwood Common, but need not follow the present boundaries of Nazeing parish which will not have been defined at this early period. In spite of the absence of bounds from both charters an attempt will be made, using the scanty information available, to reconstruct the area occupied by the whole estate (see map).

Stanhemstede is 'a homestead, or site of a dwelling (Smith, I 217, 232) associated with stone' (Smith, II (1956), 153). A stone-built dwelling seems highly unlikely in this area at this early period. *Stan* would seem to indicate either (1) a Roman road, (2) some kind of stone monolith or (3) a boundary stone. For (1) we have the possibility of a road running eastward from the crossing of the Lea at Fishers Green, probably on the line of the existing road which continues the line of the Viatores' road no. 213 west of the river; road no. 212 also leads to the same river crossing on the west (Viatores, (1964), 114, 464). Option (2) might refer to one or more of the puddingstones, formerly extant in the Fishers Green area, and claimed by Rudge and Rudge (1952, 29) to mark a prehistoric trackway, also apparently leading to Fishers Green. Option (3) appears at first sight to be cyclic, but the fact that *Stanhemstede* already existed would indicate that the boundary stone antedated the first charter. Although this place-name, like many others containing *ham*- (or *hem*-) *stede* is lost, it will be seen that there is a very good chance that it refers to the Fishers Green area. It is

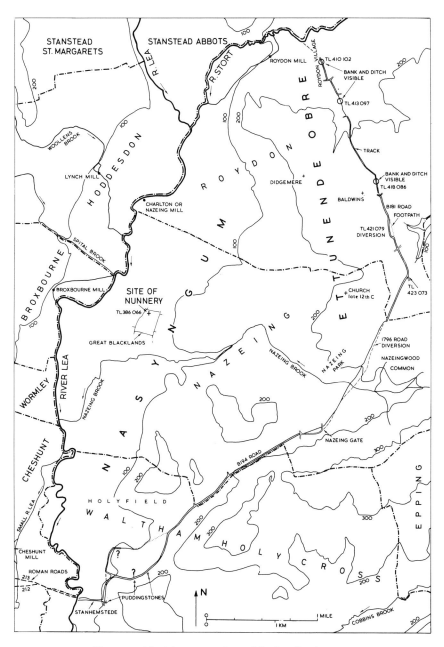

Topographical interpretation of Suebred's charters

interesting that Rutherford Davis (1982, 82) found that four place-names containing this element in the St. Albans area were in close proximity to known Roman sites.

This place name is recorded in two places by Sandred (1963). *Stanhaemstede* appears in a charter of 990 as a boundary landmark at Wootton St. Lawrence in Hampshire (p. 278); *Stanhamstede* in charters of 805 x 810 and 844 relating to Aldington, Kent (p. 226). The latter place-name is reduced to *Stanstede* in 993 and variants of this occur down to 1431 (*ibid*). Both place-names, like ours, are now lost, but it is clear that any *Standste(a)d* place-names may have been reduced in the same way, especially if no early forms are known. The nearest such name to Nazeingbury appears to be *Stansted* (*Great Stansted, Little Stansted, Great Stansted Spring, Little Stansted Spring*) in Epping (Essex Record Office D/DW P5). This group lies at TL/4405 (*ibid*. 151) about 5km almost due east of Nazeingbury, and cannot be identified with our *Stanhemstede*. The group is about 1km north of the Rudges' prehistoric trackway mentioned above. For none of the *Stanste(a)d* or related place-names does Sandred attempt any elucidation of the first syllable (or its link with the other(s)) beyond equating it with 'stone'. However, OE *stede* need not of itself imply habitation (*ibid*., 133ff.) so that the Epping *Stansted* group may refer to land containing one (or more) large stones (in an area generally lacking in them) or to stony soil (with a similar reservation).

The above identification of *Stanhemstede* places the Holyfield area of what is now Waltham Holy Cross in *Nasyngum*. By the later medieval period Holyfield was a separate manor, whose earlier history is obscure, but which apparently never belonged to Waltham Abbey (VCH V, 159–60) and it is at least possible that the first part of its name, which has never been adequately explained, may derive its association with the Nazeing nunnery. In addition it is at Fisher's Green that higher ground comes nearest to the River Lea in this area, while the shape of the Waltham Holy Cross/Nazeing parish boundary makes it at least plausible that Holyfield may once have been in Nazeing parish (see map).

Dr. Hart (pers. comm.) quotes *Ettunende obre* as representing *at tun ende ofer* i.e. 'at the *ofer* at the end of the *tun*'. *Ofer* is usually translated 'a bank, a river-bank, the seashore' but the river-bank here appears to form the western boundary of the whole of *Nasingum*, and it seems unlikely that one section of it (10 *menentes* out of 40) could be distinguished from the rest by association with the river-bank. In fact the association with water does not seem to be essential (Smith, II (1956) 53) and it seems plausible to connect the word with a previously unrecorded linear earthwork (a single bank with a ditch on its eastern side) running SSE from the modern Roydon village for at least 2km. along the higher ground; it has been seen by the writer at TL/410102, TL/413097, and TL/418086. Essex Record Office D/DCW P45 (c. 1825) shows part of its line as road, and it probably extended for a further kilometre in a straight line more or less along the modern B181 road. Essex Record Office D/DCW P31 (1798) provides evidence for a road diversion at TL/421079, where what is evidently the original road line still exists as a footpath.

This earthwork is not on or near the Roydon – Nazeing parish boundary (in fact it divides the parish of Roydon roughly into halves). Nor is it connected with the boundary between Waltham and Harlow hundreds, as shown in VCH V,93. It must predate both these boundaries, and may well have originated as a Roman or even earlier boundary; surely a candidate for 'the *ofer* at the end of the *tun*' (see map).

At TL/423073 the suggested boundary of Suebred's estate turns SSW and then SW to Holyfield (*Stanhemstede*). Part of the first section to Nazeing Gate was diverted in 1796 to improve the amenities of Nazeing Park (VCH V, 140). Another diversion from the road line is at Nazeing Gate, where field boundaries on the first edition of the Ordnance Survey 6 inch map (1880), hint at the possibility of a former straighter route passing to the north of the present road. The western boundary of the estate is shown running along the present Essex/Hertfordshire boundary, which follows the course of the old Rivers Lea and Stort. The river may have changed its course considerably in the past 1300 years; the Hertfordshire bank also would have been in Suebred's kingdom (Hunter Blair (1956), 22). However, any changes will not have seriously affected the block of land suggested for the estate, lying between the River Lea/Stort on the west and the higher ground to the east of the valley, with the north and south ends both defined by archaeological features. The nunnery, at TL/386066 is seen to be centrally placed, and the area may have been that of a Belgic and/or Roman farm since a Belgic field system and a Roman settlement had previously occupied the excavated area (Huggins, P. J. 1978).

The line dividing the estate into the two portions of 30 and 10 *mahentes* respectively has not been established but it may be pointed out that the brook running westwards from the eastern edge of Nazeing Common has been suggested as a boundary between two estates in the mid-11th century (Bascombe in Huggins, P. J., 1978, 33). Also the name *Enodmerese* appears to contain the element *maere*, 'a boundary', while Miss Elsie Woolard of Nazeing and Mr. Lockwood have independently drawn the writer's attention to Didgemere 'Old Cottage' (TL/407086), equated by Reaney (1935, 50) with *Dysmerefeld* mentioned in 1286. Although this name is unlikely to be derived from *Enodmerese*, these names also appear to contain the *maere* element, which in its position can scarcely be *maere*, 'a lake (mere) or marsh'. It seems possible that *Enodmerese* may occupy the northern end of the estate, and much of its area would then be in modern Roydon parish. A comparatively late date for the present Nazeing/Roydon boundary is suggested by the presence in Roydon (on e.g. the 1880 6-inch O.S. map) of two watermills, but none in Nazeing (see map); in Domesday, Nazeing and Roydon each had one mill. (VCH I, 539, 538).

7. *Discussion*

No other documentary mention of the Nazeing religious house is known. Much of the cemetery was lost to gravel-working before excavation and the archaeological evidence is therefore incomplete, but it was concluded that use of the cemetery came to an end before the late 9th century Danish invasions, (Huggins, P. J. 1978, 75) and no refoundation apparently took place. There is no means of knowing whether Suebred's 40 *manentes* constituted the whole endowment, but it falls far short of the 300 hides considered as suitable provision for a major monastery at this period (Hart, 1966, 118). Very probably Nazeing soon became – if indeed it was not from the start – a cell or dependency of Barking; this would account for the presence of Suebred's foundation charters in a later Barking cartulary. In this connection it is noteworthy that the nuns of Barking are recorded in Doomsday as holding half-a-hide in Parndon (VCH I, 448); this is now thought (VCH VIII, 215) to be represented by Baldwins in Roydon (TL/416084). This lies within the area postulated for the 40 *manentes*, and would appear to be the last remnant of that land not alienated from the heir (as it were) of the original grantee. Another pointer is the fact that Nazeing lay in the Deanery of Barking in medieval times, though separated from the rest of it by the peculiar jurisdiction of Waltham Abbey (VCH II, f.p. 84). Rhona Huggins (1975, 201) has suggested that Waltham (Holy Cross) was like Nazeing a royal estate in early times.

Rutherford Davis (1982, 76), referring to the Chiltern region (which is taken to include Hertfordshire) suggests the *-ingas* type place-names 'broadly occupy territory . . sometimes in the vicinity of a *-ham*. Many of these names signify expansion generally later than the *-hams*, infilling between them'. 'Most of the *-ingas* names probably belong to the years either side of 650, . . . such independent pioneer settlements are unlikely to have been made after 680' (*ibid*, 78). The first of these comments applies equally well to Waltham Holy Cross and Nazeing; the former, with a gravel terrace site near the Lea, and a causeway possibly already in existence across the valley to Ermine Street near the west bank, is likely to be an earlier re-occupation site than Nazeing. 'The coinage of the local-*ham* names . . . probably began about 600; the *-ingas* names (were) employed in the mid-7th century to describe small groups . . . under leaders who struck out widely and were the first Englishmen to venture into east and central Hertfordshire' (*ibid*, 108). If these groups came up (or down) the Lea or Stort it seems reasonable to extend these remarks to the east bank of the river; especially as the East Saxon kingdom is thought to have included, in the late 7th century, east Hertfordshire (Hunter Blair, (1956), 226), London and Middlesex as well as modern Essex, (Rutherford Davis, (1982), 10). It may well be that the higher land to the east of the Lea would be a more appropriate boundary for Rutherford Davis' Chiltern region than the navigable river itself.

8. *Conclusion*

These two previously unknown charters add about three and a half centuries to the recorded history of Nazeing, which previously began with its mention in the foundation charter (Sawyer (1968) no. 1036) of Harold's college at Waltham. This document is generally considered spurious, but includes at the end bounds in OE of some of the estates granted, including *Nassingum*. The 'new' charters add another two to the four Essex royal charters (two more of Suebred, two of Offa) previously known to survive (Sawyer (1968) nos. 64, 65, 1784, 1787) and should provide a stimulus for studies of middle Saxon Essex and of the contemporary diplomatic. They appear to document the foundation and initial endowment of the early religious foundation discovered by excavation of the early religious foundation discovered by excavation at Nazeingbury some years ago. The possibility of assigning bounds to the estate, however uncertain they may in fact be, is also of interest. It is confidently expected that the last word has not been said on any of these topics!

9. Acknowledgements

In the first place I must thank the Marquess of Salisbury and his librarian, Mr. Harcourt Williams, for enabling me to examine the Ilford Hospital Book and providing a photocopy of f.15r. I am very grateful to Mr. H. H. ('Bert') Lockwood for drawing my attention to the documents, and for making available all his research on the Hospital Book itself: Section 1 of this paper is almost entirely based on his unpublished work. Peter Huggins kindly drew the map, and with Rhona helped in various ways; Elsie Woolard discussed Nazeing topography with me, and made several helpful suggestions. Tony Burton provided a last-minute contribution. Finally I am particularly grateful to Dr. Cyril Hart, the well-known authority on Saxon charters, who very kindly read the paper in draft, pointing out slips and making useful contributions – including a proof-stage copy of a paper by Barbara Yorke, to whom also I express my thanks. For any errors that remain, and for the topographical interpretation put forward I am of course alone responsible.

10. Bibliography

Bede *A History of the English Church and People* translated by L. Sherley-Price, Harmondsworth (1968).
Hart, C. J. R. *The Early Charters of Barking Abbey*, Colchester (1953).
Hart, C. J. R. *The Early Charters of Eastern England*, Leicester (1966).
Hart, C. J. R. *The Early Charters of Essex*, Leicester (1971).
Huggins, Peter J. '*Excavations of Belgic and Romano-British Farm with Middle Saxon Cemetery and Churches at Nazeingbury, Essex, 1975–6*', *Essex Archaeol. Hist.*, 10, 29–117 (1978).
Huggins, Rhona M. '*The Significance of the Place-Name wealdham*', *Med. Arch.* XIX, 198–201 (1975).
Hunter Blair, P. *An introduction to Anglo-Saxon England*, Cambridge (1956).
Knowles, D., Brooke, C. N. L., London, V. C. M. *Heads of Religious Houses in England and Wales, 940–1216*, Cambridge (1972).

Reaney, P. H. *The Place-Names of Essex*, Cambridge (1935).

Rudge, E. A. & E. L. 'The Conglomerate Track', *Essex Nat.* 29, 17–31 (1952).

Rutherford Davis, K. *Britons and Saxons: The Chiltern Region, 400–700*, Chichester (1982).

Sandred, K. I. *English Place-Names in -stead*, Uppsala (1963).

Sawyer, P. H. *Anglo-Saxon Charters*, London (1968).

Smith, A. H. *English Place-Name Elements*, Cambridge (1956).

Viatores, The *Roman Roads in the South-East Midlands*, London (1964).

Yorke, B. 'The Kingdom of the East Saxons', *Anglo-Saxon England*, 14, 1–36 (1985).

Victoria County History of England: Essex: I (1903); II (1907); V (1966); VIII (1983), London.

'Richer in land than in inhabitants.' South Essex in the Middle Ages, c.1066–c.1340.

JENNIFER WARD

When Daniel Defoe started on his Tour through the Eastern Counties in 1722, he came through South Essex on which he commented, 'This side of the county is rather richer in land than in inhabitants, occasioned chiefly by the unhealthiness of the air, for these low marsh grounds . . . have been saved out of the River Thames . . . The flat country [beyond Tilbury] lies six, seven or eight miles broad, and is justly said to be both unhealthy and unpleasant. However the lands are rich . . . and it is very good farming in the marshes.' He went on to describe the 'large fat sheep' destined for the London food market.[1] Defoe's account is in many ways similar to Norden's description of the county in 1594 when he mentioned the growing of oats in Barstable and Rochford Hundreds and the 'most deep feedings' in the Hundreds of Rochford and Dengie; 'in these hundreds are the great and huge cheeses of such admiration for weight and magnitude made.'[2]

Many of these details were as true for the Middle Ages as for the early modern period. The parishes in the south of the Hundreds of Rochford, Barstable, Chafford and Becontree made use of the marshland along the River Thames particularly for the rearing of sheep, and the gravel terraces in that part of the county provided fertile and easily worked land for arable husbandry.[3] Yet there is more to this area in the Middle Ages than just sheep-farming and corn-growing, important though these pursuits were. Considerable changes took place between the eleventh and fourteenth centuries, with substantial growth in population, expansion of farming, the development of local trade, markets and fairs, and the establishment of small towns. As London grew, so contacts between South Essex and the City became more important.

The pattern of lordship established by William the Conqueror continued in some parts of the region until past 1340, and in the case of some of the Church manors tenures went back well before 1066. The principal royal holding according to Domesday Book was Havering which stretched north from the River Thames for nine miles and included the modern Romford, Hornchurch and Havering-atte-Bower. Monastic manors included South Benfleet, Wennington and East Ham held by Westminster Abbey, Southchurch and Milton in Prittlewell by Canterbury cathedral priory, and Barking and Mucking by the abbey of Barking; the bishop of London was lord of Corringham and Little Thurrock. In South-East Essex, the outstanding lay tenant-in-chief in 1086 was Sweyn of Essex who was sheriff of the county, and whose father, Robert fitz Wimarc, had been sheriff under Edward the Confessor. The *caput* of Sweyn's honour was situated at Rayleigh where he had built a castle and had a vineyard which produced twenty measures of wine in a good year.[4]

Over the next hundred years, the pattern of tenures changed substantially through forfeiture or the failure of heirs of many of the Domesday families. For instance, Sweyn's grandson, Henry of Essex, forfeited the honour of Rayleigh to the Crown in 1163. More property came into the hands of the Church through the endowment of new monastic foundations which proliferated in the twelfth century; the Cluniac priory of Prittlewell, for instance, founded by Sweyn's son Robert early in the century was granted the church of Prittlewell, the chapels of Sutton and Eastwood, and the tithes of Milton.[5]

By the late twelfth century at least a brisk land market had developed in South Essex which continued throughout the thirteenth and early fourteenth centuries. The amounts of land changing hands ranged from whole manors to a few acres; a fine of 1240 was concerned with one acre of marsh in Mucking.[6] In some cases, established lay and ecclesiastical lords were extending their possessions, and in an age when lords were farming their own lands and producing for the market there was every incentive for them to do this. Throughout the period, the abbot of Westminster was extending his holdings, both of land and marsh, in North and South Benfleet.[7] The de Rocheford knightly family, established at Rochford and elsewhere in the county since the twelfth century, followed a similar policy of expansion; thus in 1271 Guy de Rocheford acquired marshland in Foulness from John de Burgh, and more acquisitions were made by his great-nephew Robert in 1316–17.[8] Outsiders were also obtaining land in the area, and these included both Londoners and members of knightly families; land was regarded both as an investment and as the way to gain social status. Walter Turk of London, moneyer, acquired land and rent in Canewdon and Rayleigh in 1331, and he already had property in Canewdon four years earlier.[9] In 1314 John de Coggeshale acquired the manor of North Benfleet, and his son played a prominent part in county affairs in the first half of Edward III's reign.[10]

The period between the eleventh and early fourteenth centuries was a time of substantial population growth in Europe, and the population of England rose from about two to six million between 1086 and 1348. There are signs that the population of some places in South Essex was growing in the twenty years after the Norman Conquest. The recorded Domesday population in this part of the county mainly comprised villeins, bordars and serfs, and the increase is most noticeable in the bordar group. Partly this was because of a drop in the number of villeins and serfs and their probable absorption by the bordars, but the considerable rise in the number of bordars in several places must presuppose new inhabitants. At Little Thurrock, there were one bordar and six serfs in 1066, and six bordars and one serf in 1086,[11] but at Corringham the number of villeins had dropped from three to two, serfs from five to three, while the bordars had increased from seven to twenty-five.[12] The most marked increases were in South-West Essex at Barking and East and West Ham where the Domesday Survey gives 160, 59 and 51 peasants respectively in 1066, and 236, 72 and 130 in 1086;[13] the most significant rise was at West Ham where the bordars had increased from 16 to 79.

Only a highly approximate idea can be gained of the actual population of these places. If it is assumed that the peasants were heads of households, the figures can be multiplied by 3.5 to gain some idea of the number of inhabitants in a particular place, but it must be stressed that the figures can only be approximate;[14] such a calculation would give a population of 826 for Barking and 25 for Little Thurrock. Few places would have had more than 150 inhabitants; apart from Barking and East and West Ham probably only Hockley, Fobbing, Benfleet, Horndon-on-the-Hill, Rainham, and the Count of Eu's holding at West Thurrock come into this category.[15] It is significant that several of these places were on the River Thames or its creeks, and it was these places which were to develop most markedly over the next two hundred years.

It is unfortunate that it is not until the poll tax returns were made in 1377 that a further estimate of population is possible, although again the figures can only be approximate. By then, because of the Black Death and subsequent epidemics, the population of England had fallen from about six million to possibly as low as three million. The 1377 tax was levied at the rate of 4d. a head on all those over the age of fourteen, and approximate population figures can be arrived at by assuming that the age group under fourteen made up one-third of the population.[16] The tax returns for 1377 survive for Barstable hundred;[17] they are far more reliable than the 1380 returns for which only the West Ham list survives for this part of the county; this lists 240 names, but the 67 wives as compared with 173 men seems an impossibly low figure.[18]

The figures for the southern parishes in Barstable Hundred in 1377 show that in spite of the plague the population was in most places greater than in 1086, especially in vills along the River Thames or its creeks; it can be reckoned that the 1340 population would have been 30–45% higher. Thus, whereas there seems to have been little change at Horndon-on-the-Hill with a possible population of about 190 in 1086 and 1377, the population at Corringham had risen from 105 to 194, at Fobbing from 189 to 338, and at Mucking from 95 to 233. The biggest increase was at Tilbury where East and West Tilbury had only about 56 inhabitants in 1086, but about 242 and 120 respectively in 1377.[19] These vills were also among those with the highest density of recorded population. If we take the ten vills with the highest densities in Barstable Hundred in 1086, two of them were situated along the River Thames, Fobbing and Mucking.[20] In 1377, six out of the ten were Thameside vills, Stanford-le-Hope, Fobbing, East Tilbury, Mucking, South Benfleet, and Corringham.[21] If population growth and density were so marked in these parishes in Barstable Hundred, it is likely that the same was true of other Thameside vills as well.

The livelihood of the men of South Essex depended primarily on farming. According to Domesday Book, the economy was almost entirely agricultural, although reference was made at Barking and West Thurrock to houses in London. The only other occupation mentioned apart from farming was fishing, and this remained important throughout the Middle Ages. Fisheries were mentioned at a number of places, including Benfleet, Fobbing, Mucking, Little Thurrock, West Tilbury, Barking and Southchurch.[22]

Forest was a particularly important potential resource in South-West Essex, but it was markedly under-exploited in the late eleventh century. Thus there was woodland for 1000 swine at Barking but the abbey only had a herd of 150 pigs, and wood for 718 at East Ham but only a herd of 34 in 1086; in both places the woodland would have been in the north of the manors. In South-East Essex, woodland was only of major importance on a few manors, but again it was nowhere near fully used; at Fobbing Count Eustace of Boulogne had wood for 750 swine and a herd of 31.[23] It has to be remembered that the figures for livestock only apply to those on the lord's demesne, but, even if the size of peasant herds were known, the forest would still have remained under-used. With the growth of population in the twelfth and thirteenth centuries, however, forest was cleared to provide more land for arable farming, and was thus to become a source of greater profit to the lord.

The marshland was much more fully exploited in the eleventh century, and many lords had increased the size of their flocks of sheep to approximately the number their pasture was said to be able to support. It has been estimated that the Essex marshes in Domesday would sustain over 18,000 sheep, and many inland parishes had a stake in the Essex marshland, particularly on Canvey Island, Wallasea Island and Foulness. It is likely that, as in the twelfth century and later, the sheep were valued for their milk as well as their wool, and that Norden's 'great and huge cheeses' were being made in 1066.[24] A few examples suffice to show the extent of sheep farming on the marshes, and the contrast to the use of the forest; at Corringham there was pasture for 400 and the flock had been increased from 400 to 500, and at Fobbing there was pasture for 700 and a flock of 717; there had also been added to the manor the land of 22 freemen who had pasture for a further 400.[25]

Although the importance of the marshland must be emphasised, arable farming formed the basis of the economy, and its importance can to some extent be gauged by the number of ploughs recorded in the Domesday Survey. Thus at Barking there were three ploughs on the demesne in 1086 and 68 belonging to the peasantry, a drop of three altogether compared with 1066, and in contrast to the growth of population which had taken place.[26] On other manors, however, the number of ploughs had increased, and it is likely that this marked the beginning of the agricultural expansion of the twelfth and thirteenth centuries. The number had increased at both East and West Ham where, as already seen, the population had gone up substantially; moreover, the eight mills at West Ham in 1086 point to the importance of grain production in the area.[27] Similar expansion was taking place on smaller estates; at Rochford, held by Alfred of Sweyn of Essex, the demesne ploughs had increased from two to three and the men's from three to four, and again the number of peasants had gone up; in 1086 there were five villeins, twelve bordars and three serfs.[28]

Expansion of farming meant an increase in value of the estate for its Domesday lord; Domesday values often represented the amount received by the lord. At Rochford, the value had increased from £5 to £7, reflecting not only the probable expansion of cultivation, but Alfred's increase of his flock from 11 to 183, and of his herd of pigs from 8 to 21. However, increases of value could be a reflection of heavier burdens imposed on the peasantry and not an expansion of farming. This may easily have been the case at Barking, where the English on the Hundred jury thought that the value had not changed from the pre-Conquest figure of £80, while the French set the value at £100.[29]

The agricultural expansion of which there are signs in 1086 continued into the early fourteenth century, although its progress in the twelfth century is difficult to trace because evidence is sparse. An account for the manor of Rochford in 1185, however, shows that further expansion was taking place, and the emphasis remained on arable farming and sheep. At that time, the lord of the manor, John son of Guy de Rocheford, was a minor in the king's wardship, and the manor was said to be worth £12 a year when reasonably stocked; two demesne ploughs and 250 sheep were recommended with small numbers of other livestock. In fact, when restocking took place, 30 plough oxen were bought, and 585 sheep; 200 loads of oats were purchased for seed as against sixteen of wheat, an indication of the importance of oats as a crop in South Essex.[30]

During the thirteenth and early fourteenth centuries, lords were farming their own lands instead of leasing them out, and deriving their income largely from the sale of grain and stock. This demesne farming in South Essex is closely linked with the growth of markets which will be looked at later, and can be traced in the manorial accounts which become available from the late thirteenth century. For purposes of comparison, the accounts of three manors will be examined. One account survives for the manor of Westbury and Dagenham for the year Michaelmas 1321 – Michaelmas 1322; this was part of the larger Domesday manor of Barking and was held by the abbey.[31] A series of accounts for Edward I's reign and later survives for Eastwood which came into the hands of the Crown on the death of John de Burgh.[32] Thirdly, accounts survive for Sir John de Coggeshale's manor of North Benfleet for Michaelmas 1335 – Michaelmas 1337, and for Michaelmas 1338 – Michaelmas 1339; the account for 1338 only covers the months between January and September.[33] Ecclesiastical and major and less important lay lords are thus represented, and it is significant that there were strong similarities in the farming practised by all three in South Essex, with the emphasis being placed on arable husbandry and on sheep.

This is brought out by the receipts on these manors of which a sample is given in Table A, with details of rents received, sale of grain, stock and wool, and profits of the dairy.

Rents were of less importance than the other receipts; they comprised 12.9% of the total receipts at North Benfleet, but only 4.6% at Eastwood. Moreover, the profits of the manorial court were negligible, comprising 3.8% of the total at North Benfleet, and 2% at Eastwood.[35] Two sources of revenue were found at Eastwood but not at the other two manors; the sale of labour services brought in £4 16s 1½d, 4.2% of the total receipts in 1281–2, and the sale of pannage and herbage in Rayleigh park £5 11s 10½d, 4.8%. In other years, the profits of the park could be considerably higher, and in 1277–8 brought in £15 18s 7½d.[36]

Table A   Receipts at North Benfleet, Eastwood, and Westbury and Dagenham

Place & Date	Rents	Sale of grain	Sale of stock	Sale of wool & skins	Dairy	Total[34] receipts
North Benfleet 1338–9	£8 15s 0½d	£12 14s 9d	£4 3s 9½d	£5 19s 0d	£21 11s 7½d	£67 19s 3½d
Eastwood 1281–2	£5 6s 8½d	£81 9s 5¼d	£7 15s 8d	£0 6s 6d	£3 7s 6d	£115 7s 2¾d
Westbury & Dagenham 1321–2	–	£50 3s 3½d	£7 0s 8d	£6 14s 8d	£0 13s 4d	£91 1s 5½d

On all three manors grain production was important, the main crops being wheat, rye and oats, as shown in Table B.

Little barley was grown in South-East Essex, and the acreage for legumes was small. Apart from peas and beans, three acres of vetch was grown at North Benfleet in 1335–6. Yields were low. At Southchurch in 1362–3, 95 acres of oats yielded 12.6 bushels per acre, having been sown at the rate of three bushels per acre, and 8½ acres of barley produced 17.4 bushels per acre, but had been sown at 4½ bushels per acre.[37] Quite possibly, by 1300, soils were becoming exhausted. At both Westbury and Eastwood grain was purchased for seed, but this rarely happened at North Benfleet. The sale of grain made up 55.1% of the total receipts at Westbury, and 70.6% at Eastwood; at Westbury the profits from the mill, amounting to £19 16s 11½d, made up a substantial proportion of the total sum of £50 3s 3½d. At North Benfleet, the sale of grain only accounted for 18.7% of the receipts, and this was because a considerable proportion of the wheat was used for food allowances for the labourers, and because of low prices. Grain sales were bound to vary from year to year, because of the needs of the lord and the state of the harvest; at Eastwood in 1278–9 they only amounted to £49 19s 3½d.[38] Prices could vary dramatically; oats was sold at eight shillings a quarter at Thundersley in the famine year of 1316–17,[39] but at North Benfleet in 1338–9 it was sold at 14d.–16d. a quarter, and wheat at four shillings a quarter; the 1330s were years of falling agricultural prices.

Table B   Acreages under crops at North Benfleet, Eastwood and Westbury and Dagenham

Crop	North Benfleet 1338–9	Eastwood 1281–2	Eastwood 1289–90	Westbury & Dagenham 1321–2
Wheat	165	55	24	92
Rye		11	155	112
Mixed corn (probably wheat & rye)		116		
Barley	8	2	4	81
Peas	7			
Beans				37
Oats	171	174	173	178
Total	351	358	356	500

Although there is evidence at Westbury, Aveley, Sutton and elsewhere of marshland being used for arable husbandry,[40] the principal use of the marsh was for pasture. All three manors had marshland pasture, Westbury in the southern part of the manor by the River Thames, North Benfleet on Canvey Island, and Eastwood on Foulness and Wallasea;[41] John de Burgh had however granted marsh in Foulness to Guy de Rocheford. Profits from animal husbandry varied widely on the three manors under discussion. At Eastwood in 1281–2, the sale of stock and wool and profits of the dairy only made up 10% of the total receipts, and this figure is typical of the 1270s and 1280s. The numbers of demesne stock were small; there were 16 cows and 25 ewes at Michaelmas, 1278.[42] Amounts received for butter and cheese exceeded receipts for wool; in 1281–2, the figures were £3 7s 6d and £0 6s 6d respectively. In that year 288 cheeses weighing seven weys (1,568 lbs) were produced during the summer;[43] these would be from sheep's milk, as cows were milked for a longer season. In 1277–8 reference was also made to 31 rowan cheeses made after Michaelmas.

At Westbury, the sale of stock and wool and profits from the dairy in 1321–2 made up 15.8% of the total receipts, and it is likely that the figure would often have been much higher; only £0 13s 4d was received from the ewes' milk because of murrain, and 100 ewes were bought after lambing and shearing. Sheep were brought to Westbury from other Barking abbey manors to be fattened and sold. The amount of agricultural development since 1086 is emphasised when the figure of 114 sheep on the demesne at Barking in the Domesday Survey is compared with the 536 ewes and 121 wethers passing through Westbury (which was only part of the Domesday manor) in 1321–2. As well as sheep, pigs remained an important part of the stock here, and were brought from other Barking abbey manors to be fattened and sold; 376 passed through the reeve's hands during the year.

At North Benfleet in 1338–9, profits from the dairy, which was leased out, made up 31.8% of the total receipts, sale of stock 6.2% and sale of wool 8.6%. The figures in the other accounts of the 1330s are similar. Purchase of stock could prove a major expense, as when thirteen cows were bought for £6 10s 0d in 1336–7, and a lord would face serious problems if there was a bad outbreak of disease as happened at Westbury. Both cows and sheep were important at North Benfleet; at Michaelmas, 1337, there were 47 cows and 180 ewes on the demesne. Just as the Westbury economy was linked with other Barking abbey manors, there were close connections between North Benfleet and John de Coggeshale's other estates, as when lambs were driven to Little Coggeshall and Bocking in 1336–7, and three piglets received from Paglesham in 1338–9.

Animal husbandry could therefore be lucrative, but also entail considerable risks, and not only because of disease. Marshland farming could bring serious problems over flooding, as in 1339 when dower was being assigned to Marjorie, widow of John de Brianzoun, and part of Aveley could not be measured because of the inundation of water.[44] The most graphic description is found twelve years earlier when Canterbury cathedral priory made an eloquent plea to the bishop of Rochester to be allowed to appropriate Westerham church in Kent because of the losses they had suffered through flooding on Romney Marsh and at Milton in Prittlewell.[45] They asserted that they had lost at Milton 240 acres of salt marsh, 40 acres of land and a water mill, all of which was covered by the tide twice a day to a depth that merchant ships could sail over. The responsibility for sea defence rested with those who held the marshland, and at Westbury in 1321–2 £1 1s 8d was spent on forty perches of wall as a defence against flooding. There was however a need for this work to be coordinated and supervised, and from the thirteenth century the Crown was intervening to ensure that those who held marshland met their responsibilities.[46] In the fourteenth century local gentry were regularly appointed to royal commissions to oversee sea defence.[47]

The development of demesne farming leading to production for the market on a considerable scale was not the only way in which the wealth of South Essex was being increased in the thirteenth and early fourteenth centuries. Alongside this has to be considered the growth in the number of markets. Before 1200, there were probably only four markets in the area, at Barking, Horndon-on-the-Hill, Rayleigh and Stratford Langthorne. By 1349, markets had been licensed by the king at Aveley, Corringham, Fobbing, Grays Thurrock, Hadleigh, Prittlewell, Rainham, Rochford, Shopland, West Ham, West Thurrock, and West Tilbury.[48] The lords of these places must have been convinced that there was plenty of potential business before going to the trouble of obtaining a royal charter, and a successful market could provide a further addition to the lord's income. Not all markets would do equally well, and the profits would vary from year to year. Rayleigh market was leased out for £3 5s 0d in the 1270s, but only yielded £2 5s 0d in stallage and toll in 1302–3, while Prittlewell market then yielded five shillings; in 1320–1, Hadleigh fair produced 17d. and the market 4d.[49]

Good communications were essential for a successful market, and it is likely that the places which flourished most were those on the River Thames and its creeks. Several ferries operated across the Thames, such as the Tilbury ferry referred to early in Henry III's reign; the Aveley ferry where the lord had the right of carting goods from the market-place to the river; the ferry between West Thurrock and Greenhithe; and the ferry from Grays Thurrock.[50] There was a strong local trade between Essex and Kent. Canterbury cathedral priory shipped grain from its Essex manors across the river in 1226.[51] In 1313, 115 quarters of wheat and 115 quarters of oats were taken from the Templars' manor of Sutton to Leigh where a boat was hired to take the grain to Faversham; from there it was taken to Canterbury for the consecration of Archbishop Walter Reynolds.[52] Fullers and other merchants crossed the Thames from Dartford to come to Aveley market in the early fourteenth century.[53]

The Thames also provided a direct route to the Continent. In 1203, two ships taking bacon to Normandy took on part of their cargo at Barking, and in 1367 John Burgeys of Fobbing received a royal licence to ship sixty weys of cheese and sixty barrels of ale from Fobbing to Flanders.[54] All these examples point to the very close link between local farming and trading, and this is also brought out by a case of 1351 when various Essex wool and cheese merchants, including men of Fobbing and Benfleet, were accused of conspiring among themselves to fix the maximum price they would pay for a sack of wool and wey of cheese. They were also accused of using false weights so as to cheat any seller of wool and cheese of 1 lb. in 10.[55]

The Thames was certainly used to take supplies from South Essex to London, as is illustrated by a case of 1228. The Prior of the Hospital of St. John of Jerusalem impleaded Richard de Gray, lord of Grays Thurrock, for preventing him from bringing his ships into Thurrock and loading his corn there; the victuals were presumably on their way to the Hospitallers' centre at Clerkenwell.[56] What is not clear is how far London's food supplies were being drawn from South Essex before 1340, although, in view of the activities and interests of Londoners in the area, it is probable that much trading was going on. The places nearest to London were certainly supplying the City; in the fourteenth century poultry and wool were being bought for London in Barking market.[57] By then West Ham had established its meat trade with London, and the West Ham mills were producing flour for London bread; the Stratford bakers were often mentioned from the fourteenth century although it is not clear how many of these came from Stratford Langthorne in Essex.[58]

There are few references to industry in these South Essex towns. The most important activity apart from trading was fishing; these two occupations could easily be combined, and could be carried on from all Thameside towns and villages. By the fourteenth century Barking men were engaged in salt-water fishing in the Thames; in 1320, and again in 1349, Barking men were prosecuted by the London authorities for using kiddle nets with too fine a mesh.[59] Fisheries could be rented out by their lords, as at Rochford, and shellfish were obtained at a number of places; in 1362–3, £3 was received from the sale of mussels at Southchurch.[60]

Some idea of the wealth of the whole area can be gained from taxation assessments. There are difficulties over using these, but they provide a comparative picture for the region. According to the tax assessment for the 1/20 on movables in 1327, the two hundreds in Essex contributing the most tax per square mile were Chafford and Rochford, and Rochford had the second highest density of taxpayers.[61] Within the hundreds, there was great variety between vills, but it was very often the places with access to the Thames and with marshland pasture which were assessed at the highest tax per square mile. Thus in Becontree Hundred the vills can be divided between on the one hand the parishes in the forest, and, on the other, Barking and East and West Ham, and to a lesser extent Dagenham, which had far higher tax assessments to the square mile. In Chafford Hundred there is again a contrast between most of the Thameside and most of the inland parishes; thus the tax assessment at Grays Thurrock works out at 31.5 shillings to the square mile, in comparison with 10.7 shillings at South Weald and Brentwood. In Barstable Hundred, the ten places with the highest tax assessment to the square mile were East Tilbury, Fobbing, Mucking, Bulphan, West Horndon, Stanford-le-Hope, Horndon-on-the-Hill, Doddinghurst, South Benfleet, and Chadwell and Little Thurrock (assessed together); the concentration of wealth in the south of the hundred is clear, as is the fact that several of these places had the highest population density in 1377.

In view of all the developments which have been examined, it can be assumed that the wealth of South Essex was greater in 1327 than it had been a hundred years before. In fact this can to a large extent be proved by using the taxation assessment for the 1/30 on movables, levied in 1237.[62] This document does not give the names of individual taxpayers, but lists the assessments for most of the vills in the county. In view of the general tendency for taxation yields to fall as taxes on movables were levied more frequently, it might be expected that the amount of taxable property would be higher in 1237 than ninety years later. However, in a number of places in South Essex, the reverse was the case, and it is therefore likely that there was a considerable rise in wealth in these vills, probably even greater than the assessments would indicate. The rise is most marked at West Ham where the amount of taxable property increased from £56 7s 6d to £173 15s 5d; the increase at East Ham was not so dramatic. In Barstable Hundred the biggest rises were at East Tilbury, Fobbing, Little Thurrock and Chadwell, and Horndon-on-the-Hill.

Taking the period 1066–1340 as a whole, it is possible to agree with Defoe that there was 'very good farming in the marshes.' It is also likely that the area was as unhealthy in the Middle Ages as it was later. However, Defoe's remarks are too limited to do justice to South Essex in the twelfth and thirteenth centuries. This was a time of vital and major change in the area, with the growth of population, the expansion of farming, an active land market, and the growth of towns and trade. By about 1340 the resources of the region were being far more fully exploited than they had been in the Norman period, and the area was more densely populated, and had a richer and more varied economy. Any visitors to South Essex in 1340 would be bound to notice the sheep on the marshes, just as Norden and Defoe did, but they would also be aware of the grain fields, the riverside ports and markets, and the traffic along the River Thames.

Notes and References

1. D. Defoe, *A Tour through the Whole Island of Great Britain* London, (1927), i, 8–9.

2. J. Norden, *Speculi Britanniae Pars: An Historical and Chorographical Description of the County of Essex* Camden Society, ix (1840), 8–9.

3. L. Dudley Stamp, *Fertility, Productivity and Classification of Land in England and Wales* Land Utilisation Survey of Britain, (1941).

4. *Domesday Book* (Subsequently *DB*), ed. A. Farley (1783), ii, 43b.

5. *Monasticon Anglicanum*, v (1846), 21.

6. *Feet of Fines for Essex* (Subsequently *FF*) (Essex Archaeological Society, Colchester, 1913–49), i, 134.

7. E.g. ibid. 50, 77, 201. B. Harvey, *Westminster Abbey and its Estates in the Middle Ages* Oxford, (1977), 420.

8. *FF*, i, 275; ii, 169, 172, 173, 175.

9. Ibid, iii, 15. *The Medieval Essex Community. The Lay Subsidy of 1327*, ed. Jennifer C. Ward, Essex Record Office Publication no. 88. (1983), 5.

10. *FF*, ii, 151. *Calendar of Inquisitions Post Mortem*, vi (1910), no. 210.

11. *DB*, ii, 11b.

12. Ibid. 12a.

13. Ibid. 17b–18a; 14b, 64a–b.

14. J. C. Russell, *British Medieval Population* Albuquerque, (1948), 38.

15. *DB*, ii, 18b, 43b, 45a; 26a; 1b, 4a, 14a, 43a; 12a, 26a–b, 42a–b, 93a, 93b, 99a; 24b, 66b, 91a, 96a; 63a. It is not always possible to distinguish between North and South Benfleet, and Grays and West Thurrock.

16. J. C. Russell, op. cit. 143–4. Russell also suggests making an allowance of 5% for those omitted from the poll tax return.

17. Public Record Office (Subsequently P.R.O.), E.179/107/50.

18. P.R.O. E.179/107/67.

19. The recorded figures for 1086 and 1377 are as follows, and in the text have been multiplied by 3.5 and 1.5 respectively: Horndon-on-the-Hill, 55, 129; Corringham, 30, 129; Fobbing, 54, 225; Mucking, 27, 155; East and West Tilbury, 16, and 161 and 80.

20. The ten vills in 1086 were Great Burstead, Fobbing, Wickford, Horndon-on-the-Hill, Bulphan, Ingrave, Orsett, Ramsden Bellhouse and Crays, Hutton and Mucking.

21. The ten vills in 1377 were Stanford-le-Hope (not mentioned in Domesday Book), Fobbing, Doddinghurst, East Tilbury, Great Burstead, Mucking, Downham, Horndon-on-the-Hill, South Benfleet, and Corringham.

22. *DB*, ii, 4a, 8b, 11b, 17b, 26a, 42a.

23. Ibid. 14b, 17b, 26a, 64a–b, 72b.

24. *Victoria County History, Essex*, i (1903), 369–73.

25. *DB*, ii, 12a, 26a.

26. Ibid. 17b.

27. Ibid. 64a–b, 72b.

28. Ibid. 44b.

29. Ibid. 17b–18a.

30. *Rotuli de Dominabus et Pueris et Puellis de XII Comitatibus* (1185), ed. J. H. Round, Pipe Roll Society, xxxv, (1913), 73–4. *The Great Roll of the Pipe, 31 Henry II* Pipe Roll Society, xxxiv, (1913), 43.

31. P.R.O. S.C.6/849/11.

32. Ibid. 840/17–21; 1089/7, 16–18.

33. Essex Record Office (Subsequently E.R.O.), D/DWt M18.

34. In addition to the figures tabled, the total receipts include £9 19s 7½d arrears for North Benfleet, and the items listed under the headings, Issues of the Manor, and Sold on Account.

35. The amounts were £2 11s 0d at North Benfleet, and £2 6s 2d at Eastwood. No item for rents or pleas was entered on the Westbury account.

36. P.R.O. S.C.6/840/18.

37. E.R.O. D/DMq M11.

38. P.R.O. S.C.6/1089/16.

39. Ibid. 847/26.

40. P.R.O. C.134, file 21 (7), m.5; C.135, file 60 (7), m.3. P.R.O. S.C.6/847/11; 849/36.

41. *Victoria County History, Essex*, i (1903), 369.

42. P.R.O. S.C.6/840/18.

43. *Statutes of the Realm*, ii, 267, c.8. According to a statute of 9 Henry VI, 1430–1, the wey of cheese should contain 32 cloves, and every clove 7 lbs.

44. P.R.O. C.135 file 60 (7), m.4.

45. *Literae Cantaurienses*, ed. J. B. Sheppard, Rolls Series, (1887), i, 243–6, 265–6.

46. *Close Rolls, 1254–6* (1931), 185.

47. E.g. *Calendar of Patent Rolls, 1330–4* (1893), 202; ibid. *1334–8* (1895), 147; ibid. *1338–40* (1898), 74.

48. R. H. Britnell, 'Essex Markets before 1350,' *Essex Archaeology and History, Transactions of the Essex Archaeological Society*, Third Series, xiii, (1981), 15–17.

49. P.R.O. S.C.6/840/17; 845/36; 1124/5 m.2.

50. *FF*, i, 51, 136. P.R.O. C.134, file 8 (20) and file 21 (7), m.5; C.135, file 60 (7), m.3.4.

51. *Patent Rolls, 1225–32* (1903), 18.

52. P.R.O. S.C.6/847/11.

53. *Calendar of Inquisitions Miscellaneous*, ii (1916), no. 106.

54. *The Great Roll of the Pipe, 5 John* Pipe Roll Society, New Series, xvi, (1938), 9. *Calendar of Patent Rolls, 1364–7* (1912), 377.

55. *Essex Sessions of the Peace*, ed. E.C. Furber (Essex Archaeological Society, Occasional Publications, no. 3, Colchester, (1953), 135–6.

56. *Curia Regis Rolls*, xiii (1959), no. 520. *FF*, i, 84.

57. *Calendar of Early Mayors' Court Rolls, 1298–1307*, ed. A. H. Thomas Cambridge, (1924), 246. *Calendar of Wills Proved and Enrolled in the Court of Husting, London, 1258–1688*, Part ii (1) London, (1890), 39.

58. H. T. Riley, *Memorials of London and London Life in the Thirteenth, Fourteenth and Fifteenth Centuries* (London, 1868), 179–80. *Victoria County History, Essex*, vi (1973), 76.

59. H. T. Riley, op. cit. 135, 244–5.

60. P.R.O. C.133, file 5 (8), m.7d. E.R.O. D/DMq M11.

61. *The Medieval Essex Community. The Lay Subsidy of 1327*, ed. Jennifer C. Ward, Essex Record Office Publication no. 88, (1983), iv.

62. P.R.O. E.179/107/1.

The Bounds of the Forest of Essex
'Man is preceded by forest, succeeded by desert.'*

WILLIAM LIDDELL

Conservation is a modern passion and yet it is possible to think of the medieval Forest Laws as an anticipation of modern concerns. Possibly our view of the effectiveness of the royal forest as a controller of change is determined in Essex by the irony that it was the disafforestation of Epping Forest which preserved the trees.[1] This is not to argue that William the Conqueror and his successors were men enamoured of trees but that in their concern for the joy of hunting the deer they created a system which could be used, and was used, to preserve tree cover for the deer and to control that nibbling at the boundaries which is so central to man's psyche. The very existence of the royal forests created a clash of interest between the king, whose private delight they were, and landholders, poachers and peasants whose own interests demanded less supervision and ever shrinking bounds.[2]

'. . . it is less well known that at one time the entire county of Essex lay under forest law. . .'[3] If that is so, how did it happen? Fisher, Round and Nisbet all agree with what might be called the 'traditional' story: the royal forest started in the south-west of the county and then was spread over the county by Henry I, decayed under Stephen as men ignored the laws, was revived and definitely included the whole of the county under Henry II, only to be partially disafforested by John so that given this encouragement the men of Essex strove throughout the 13th. century to restrict the forest to the south-west of the county, its only just bounds since that was where it started, and finally in 1301 it was so restricted and remained there without opposition until 1634 when Charles I made his unfortunate attempt to restore the royal forest to its widest bounds. Against this story one can only immediately respond that it smacks too much of the received story of the development and decline of the royal forests over the whole kingdom to satisfy one about the peculiarities of Essex. The evidence for a royal forest in Essex during the Conqueror's reign is quite unconvincing. Domesday Book merely records that Ranulph Gernon took a swineherd from the manor of Writtle and made him forester of the king's wood.[4] The argument that in 1224–5 and again in 1301 the men of Essex attempted to restrict the Forest of Essex to the south-west corner of the county does not help this hairline of evidence for they were speaking only about the situation before 1154 and anyhow, as I shall show, the statement reflects little more than their wishes and is not hard evidence. Indeed one might as well believe the statement of parliament of 1642 that Waltham Forest was the only forest in the county and always had been all evidence to the contrary notwithstanding, as believe anything said in the clash over the bounds of the forest in the 13th. century.

* a graffito during the French student revolt May 1968

There was certainly a royal forest in Essex by 1104 and it is possible that it spread over most, if not all of the county, but there is no solid evidence to support that. The forest jury in 1301 claimed that large areas had never been in the royal forest and, while one can discount that, there does seem to be no evidence that Rochford Hundred was in the Forest. It is true too that the Pipe Roll evidence for assarting presents a very patchy picture of the forest of Essex in the 12th. century. There is one date we can be sure of. In 1204 the men of Essex (presumably of the north of the county) purchased the disafforestation of the area north of Stanestreet for the enormous sum of 500 marks and two palfreys. This tells us more about the perceived oppression of the forest laws than it does about the particular boundary of the royal forest in the north of the county but it does give a boundary from 1204. No further part of the county left the forest until after the Charter of the Forest 1217 which declared that all forests created by Henry II should be reviewed by good and honest men and all unlawful afforestations revoked.[5] The earliest known perambulation of the forest of Essex under the Charter is that of 1224 though Fisher prints details of the perambulation he thought was earlier and which may be one of 1219. These perambulations left the south-west corner of the county within the bounds of the forest as the largest area of royal forest.[6] There are certain imponderables left by the perambulations. While mentioning 'a certain wood called Kingswood next Colchester as Forest, because Henry II took it from the common waste of Colchester and allowed the burgesses 40s. at the Exchequer in exchange', a piece of information given nowhere else, the bounds are not defined. Indeed the information given by the jurors is so impressionistic that the whole area between the great Essex Road and Stanestreet is omitted from their description, except in the south-west of the county. 'From the stream which runs from Tilty to Chelmsford and Maldon and so to the sea all to the east was outside the forest at the first coronation of Henry II.' Surely not all, for there is an area to the north of Stanestreet which was disafforested by John in 1204. 'By the road which leads from Chelmsford to Stratford except for the king's demesne manor of Havering all to the south was outside the forest in 1154.' What does this mean for half of Chelmsford and Barstable hundreds and the hundreds of Dengie and Rochford? It is difficult to put much trust in such a document, nor should one. Perambulations tell us about the desires of those making them, not what existed. Probably we can paraphrase the perambulations of 1225 as 'We know the king must have a hunting forest in Essex for we cannot deny the existence of the royal forest of Essex altogether but we would be happier if forest law oppressions were kept to the south-west corner of the county where they work with the intercommoning system the poor people have down there.' Henry III didn't see it that way at all. As soon as he was able, in 1227–8, he quashed the perambulation and ordered a new one.

These new bounds, which restored all those areas declared disafforested in 1225; were the ostensible bounds of the Forest of Essex, despite the fact that the writ ordering this new perambulation stated that the hundred of Tendring was afforested by Henry II and therefore outside the bounds of the forest. Those who have power do not worry about trivialities. In 1250

Henry III has foresters, verderers, regarders, the whole panoply of forest officials working in the Tendring hundred. Except for the period of the baronial revolt when the forest system throughout the county broke down most of Essex was in the Forest or was certainly so according to perambulations of 1277 and 1291. 'From the bridge at Stortford to Cattywad bridge and from the Thames to Stanestreet.' That certainly puts Rochford hundred into the Forest but what about Tendring? It is difficult not to blame our forebears for their imprecision.

In 1298, 1299 and 1300 Edward I, pushed for money because of his imperialistic adventures against the Scots, issued orders for new perambulations in the hope thereby of getting the money he needed for his war. The perambulations were unacceptable and so in 1301 in return for a tax on moveables a new perambulation was ordered and on this occasion the jurors gave detailed reasons for most of their statements. The result is fascinating. 'Tendring hundred has been outside the forest since time immemorial' – not in the reigns of Henry II and Henry III it wasn't. 'Clavering, East and West Freshwell and Uttlesford hundreds have been outside the forest since time immemorial' but Henry II amerced his steward of the forest of Essex for building a park at Stansted Mountfitchet and what were those men of Essex paying for in 1204 if all that area was never in the forest? The area disafforested by John is given a truncated size and is said to have been bought out of the Forest by Aubrey de Vere, earl of Oxford. If anything proves that oral evidence is still oral evidence and therefore no more to be believed because written down in 1301 that statement does. It is unhappily true that the written word carries authority but the Pipe Roll shows that the money paid in 1204 came from the men of Essex, no doubt Aubrey de Vere paying his share. Fisher, swallowing this story, went on to invent an explanation for de Vere's generosity based on the relationship between him and the nuns of Hedingham which says more for his innocence than it does for his critical intelligence. Even great historians are controlled by the values of their own age. This perambulation, which has been taken as so definitive of the 'true' bounds of the forest of Essex, is in truth no different from that of 1225, a statement of the passions of the men involved in making it. The south-west and nowhere but the south-west seems to be the cry. Of course, passionate but leavened with common sense. The abbess of Caen's manor of Felsted can stay in the Forest despite her claim to hold it as freely as it was held in the days of Edward the Confessor by grant of the Conqueror himself. Could this be an anticipation of the xenophobia which was to lead to the expulsion of the alien priories just over a century hence? The only other matter of real interest in this perambulation is that it restricted the royal forest to a slightly different area of the south-west of the county than in 1225, and left the king his own manors as forest, too.

This date, 1301, is usually accepted as that from which the forest of Essex ceased to cover most of the county. In 1305 Edward I removed his own manors from the forest system and held them as chaces and warrens, so Hatfield, Writtle and Havering ceased to be forest. Only the south-west corner of the county remained to suffer the oppressions of foresters. That is not so. In 1306 Edward I, having recovered his political position, had the

Pope quash the perambulation of 1301 and restored the situation to what it had been throughout the 13th. century. In 1317 Edward II had a number of responses drawn up to questions which the knights might ask about the perambulation of 1301 in preparation for a new perambulation. Most of the answers are based on claims of ancient demesne but the main argument lies in reference to the perambulation of 1228. So the main concern was with a document drawn up almost 100 years before, which put most of the county within the bounds of the Forest. Between 1305 and 1327 men ceased to talk regularly of the forest of Essex and began to speak of constituent parts like the forest of Witham, of Dunmow, of Harlow, of Ongar, of Waltham and of Becontree and yet not all of these were within the south-west quadrant of the county. If that were not sufficient to prove that the perambulation of 1301 was not at first worthy of the distinction it has been given as authoritative, the number and spread of places amerced for assarting during the forest eyre of 1323–4 would show the ineffectiveness of it in controlling the power of the King. Even Bentley, in Tendring hundred, is mentioned and there are few places, south of Stanestreet and outside Rochford hundred, which were not under the influence of royal forest officials.

The forest of Essex remained huge until in 1327 Edward III, seeking to consolidate his power, confirmed the Charter of the Forest and associated with this confirmation a repetition of the bounds laid down in 1301, thus giving them a posthumous reputation they did not at first have. Thereafter men referred increasingly to the Forest of Waltham: in the end the men of Essex had their way. Political pressure had been necessary to cut down the size of the Forest and restrict it to 'acceptable' bounds but the attack on the royal forest and the limitation of its useful area had been a continuous concern of Essex men. Conservation laws exist to be broken by individuals and when a sufficient number of individuals break the laws, those laws or the area over which they are applied are changed. This may be poor morality but I believe it to be true. In the forest of Essex throughout the 13th century woods were wasted, trees grubbed up, land cleared and planted, houses built and deer were hunted, most of them unlawfully but such was the pressure even the selfishness of England's monarchs could not prevent the erosion of their Forest. It is a telling coda to the story that by 1514 the existence of the great forest of Essex had been so far forgotten that men referred to the Forest of Essex or Waltham, as if they were the same.

Notes and References

1. There are three outstanding works on the Forest of Essex: W. R. Fisher, *The Forest of Essex*, (1887); J. H. Round, 'The Forest of Essex,' *Journal of the British Archaeological Society*, N.S. iii (1897); W. Nisbet, 'Forestry' in *V. C. H. Essex*, Vol. i (1903). Unfortunately we have no one word to distinguish the clearing of trees and the return of land held in the royal forest to normal land. This leads to problems of interpretation but OED makes disafforest and deforest synonyms.

2. Kings did not need to be interested in hunting in order to try to preserve their private perquisites. Edward VI complained that a rumoured disafforestation of Essex had led to a general anticipation of the never to be attempted deed.

3. A. L. Poole, *Domesday Book to Magna Carta*, (1951), p.30.

4. Round in *V. C. H. Essex*, ii (1907) translated *silva* as a plural rather than a singular noun and, as the first known steward of the Forest of Essex, Richard de Montfiquet, was Gernon's son-in-law he and Nisbet too proposed that Ralph Gernon was also the steward of the Forest of Essex and, for unknown reasons, that the forest was in the south-west of the county.

5. As the Forest existed by the King's will it is difficult to know what an 'unlawful' forest was. For the best discussion of this clash between different views of the proper organisation of the kingdom see J. C. Holt, *The Northerners*, (1961), pp. 159ff.

6. Fisher, *op. cit.*, p.21. The two perambulations are almost identical. Maps of the perambulations discussed in this essay are printed in Fisher's magisterial work.

Blackchapel, Great Waltham

ALAN DIBBEN

The ecclesiastical foundation, which is the subject of this essay, has flourished for over six centuries, and administers the charities of the neighbouring hamlet, yet has remained outside episcopal and parochial jurisdiction despite its adherence to the services of the Church of England. It has no printed history, possibly because it is so rarely mentioned in official records. Such a history will have to consider it in the general context of ecclesiastical building, and make appropriate comparison or contrast with examples elsewhere. This essay, which only incidentally refers to architecture and furnishings, merely presents, with the minimum of comment, those facts which can readily be discovered.

Blackchapel,[1] a late-medieval timber-framed building,[2] with house attached, lies in the north of the parish of Great Waltham, about four miles from the parish church,[3] at the junction of the Chelmsford-Dunmow road and the minor road through the hamlet of North End to Felsted.[4] Its situation, and even its name, have defied topographers: it has been placed in the wrong hundred and, by implication, in the wrong parish and archdeaconry:[5] the first two editions of Kelly's *Directory of Essex* (1845, 1851) revealed that 'At Black is a chapel': and the first edition of the Ordnance Survey 6″ map (1881) marked 'Black Church'![6] Local historians, explaining the chapel's name, have had equal difficulties. Coller, a century ago, connected it with 'Augustine monks [*sic*]' who 'sang masses in the olden times',[7] a view repeated in almost identical words in the 1960s.[8] More recently the name has been derived from the Augustinian (i.e. black) canons at Little Leighs Priory, some 2½ miles away, who used the chapel and house as a 'grange' when working on their estates,[9] but, alas, the priory had no property in the area of the chapel,[10] and Augustinians, a pastoral order, neither farmed their lands nor maintained granges.

Recent speculation has, in any case, been wholly misplaced for Reaney showed over fifty years ago that the chapel was originally Blecches or Blacches Chapel, the name being associated with a family of Bleche/Blacche (other spellings, but eventually Blatch(e)), and he gave references to Bleccheschapel (1377), Blaccheschapell (*c.*1500), and Black Chappell (1583).[11] Blache/Blatch, as Reaney explained elsewhere, is a palatal form of Black, and would originally have been given to a person of dark complexion or hair:[12] the transition to Black was, therefore, reasonable, but logically the genitive (Black's Chapel) should have been retained.

The story begins on 21 May 1376 (*die Mercurij in vigilia Assencionis . . . anno Edwardi tercij . . . quinquagesimo*) when the court roll of the manor of [Great] Waltham records the surrender by Robert Reignold to John Wrongy and his wife Joan of a croft of enclosed land lying over against Blecches Chapel in wording (*Robertus Reignold reddit in manus* [sic] *unam croftam terre incluse iacentem contra Bleccheschapel ad opus Johannis Wrongy et Alicie uxoris eius*) that suggests that the chapel was already a recognised topographical feature (it does not say, for example, a chapel newly-built).[13] That is surely confirmed by the next entry but one on the roll, a surrender by Reignold of land in Chapel Croft.

The Blatch(e) family was settled in Great Waltham by 1246.[14] It was prominent, and presumably wealthy, by the late 1370s when John Blecche was farmer (*firmarius*) of the manor,[15] but nothing connects him, or anyone else, with the chapel's foundation. The family must have flourished for the following places are found within the manor during the next century: Bleccheswayer (1404),[16] Bleccheswayer (1406),[17] Bleccheswayer (1416),[18] Bleccheshalfyarde (1442),[19] Bleccheswayer (1453),[20] Bleccheswayer (1454).[21] Even in 1616 four manorial properties were called Blat(c)hes/Bleches, and others were called Blache Meade and Kate Bleches.[22] Blatche's Wood, in the south-west of the parish, is named on current large-scale Ordnance Survey maps,[23] but the family disappears from the parish register after the burial of Phinea Blatch in March 1730.[24]

Authorities agree that the present building is late-fifteenth-century:[25] it cannot, therefore, be the chapel of the earliest reference. If that occupied the site of the present chapel (and there is no evidence), it could well have been erected on manorial roadside waste, but no grant has been found on the court roll and no foundation deed is known. Presumably the chapel was built either (a) for the convenience of travellers, subsequently becoming a recognised place of worship for the inhabitants of North End, the nearest settlement, some half mile away, or (b) directly to serve the hamlet of North End.[26] In either case the local people would have welcomed the opportunity to avoid the long journey to the parish church. The population of North End at the end of the fourteenth century is not known: the Great Waltham poll tax assessment of 1381, which lists three families named Bleche, is not arranged by hamlets.[27]

The manorial court was concerned in 1428 with the ownership of a cottage,[28] and in 1446 with an unscoured ditch,[29] both near (*prope*) Bleccheschapell. Nothing is known of the chapel as a place of worship or of its endowments until 1491 when five persons conveyed an acre of land in Felsted called Bridge Meadow for the maintenance of the chapel and of a parson to say service, and that is only known because over a century later Commissioners for Charitable Uses investigated the endowment (see below), but the vendors were almost certainly trustees transferring their interest to chosen successors.[30] In 1500 Thomas Wiseman of London, citizen and haberdasher, left in his will four shillings annually from unnamed lands in Great Waltham for the maintenance of the chapel and its services for 21 years.[31] About 1500 seventeen inhabitants of Great Waltham (so their surnames suggest) complained in the Court of Chancery that the legal estate in the manor of Dagnetts in Black Notley, left to them by one John Cowlond in his will in trust to help with the salary of a priest to say service in Blaccheschapell, had been withheld from them, but, this being the only surviving document in the suit, its accuracy, without a reply from the other side, or judgment of the court, cannot be assessed:[32] and there is no external help as Cowlond's will (if there was one) cannot be traced and the manor of Dagnetts awaits its historian.

One Thomas Tanner arranged in his will (dated 1530, proved 1531) for lands which he was leaving to his two sons to be sold should both die without issue, and the proceeds divided in unspecified proportions between the parish church and the chapel, but with the chapel having the greater part (no evidence that the chapel received any money).[33] In 1533 the manorial court granted four men, undoubtedly as trustees, a purpresture (i.e. an encroachment) next (*iuxta*) the chapel 3½ perches in length, three perches and seven feet in width at the chapel wall, and 1½ feet at the south end next the chapel, at an annual rent of one halfpenny (clearly a grant of land which the chapel was occupying illegally, though maybe inadvertently).[34]

Recent comments on the chapel's survival at the reformation have wrongly assumed that it belonged to a religious house.[35] There was nothing in the Acts of 1535 and 1539 (which respectively dissolved the lesser and greater houses) to justify the suppression of the chapel, and there was sufficient confidence in its future for John Wiseman to give in 1544 three acres of meadow in Felsted called Chappell Mead otherwise Butlers Meadow for its maintenance and for a parson to say service.[36] Nor were there grounds for suppressing the chapel under legislation of Edward VI: it was neither chantry (i.e. with a priest saying masses for the souls of the dead) nor 'free chapel' (i.e. of royal foundation),[37] nor one of the other institutions (colleges, hospitals, gilds, brotherhoods, fraternities) selected for dissolution. An endowment for a stipendiary priest should certainly have been confiscated but the Chantry Commissioners found nothing relevant in Great Waltham or elsewhere: indeed, none of the few endowments for obits and lamps discovered in Great Waltham specifically related to the chapel.[38] This suggests that the chapel was given a clean bill of health at the Reformation, but in April 1565 an exchequer commission found that Burgess Well Lands in Chelmsford (totalling sixteen acres) had supported a stipendiary priest to celebrate mass in the chapel and that those lands, instead of passing to the Crown, as the Act of Edward VI required, had been 'concealed':[39] next month the Crown granted the lands, which it did not physically possess, to Nicase Yetsweirt, the Queen's servant, on payment of twelve times their annual value.[40] This is an example of the 'third development' in the story of concealed lands, as identified by Dr. C. J. Kitching, i.e. the speculative purchase by private persons, often described as the Queen's servants, of allegedly-concealed lands 'at the very favourable rate of ten or twelve years' purchase', in the hope of enforcing their 'title'.[41] Nothing is known about the title to Burgess Well Lands between 1516 (when, according to a survey of the manor of Chelmsford made in 1591, Jeffrey Warren was owner)[42] and 1547 (the year of the relevant Act), but there is no evidence that the chapel received any income from them. But how remarkable that within six years of Yetsweirt's grant the chapel should have acquired a formal, albeit indirect, link with those lands (see below) which lasted for 400 years!

The form 'Black Chapel' is first recorded in the late 1550s. John Wiseman of Felsted (presumably the aforementioned), who died in 1559, left £3 6s 8d annually from the manor of Mucking Hall in Barling towards the finding of a priest to sing for his soul and for all Christian souls at 'Black Chappell' for twenty years (though the conditions could not have been fulfilled).[43] In 1561 the court of the Archdeacon of Essex ordered Robert Haris of 'Blake Chappell' to tear in pieces (*fringere*) in the presence of the people (*parochianos*) in the chapel on the following Sunday certain books of popery which he kept.[44] A survey of the manor in 1563 uses 'Black(e) Chappell' when referring to the chapel as such (it gives the rent of the purpresture, incorrectly, as one penny), but 'Blechischapell' when using it as a topographical feature.[45] The exchequer commission and crown grant of 1565 (see above) use 'Black(e) Chappell', and John Sanders, curate at 'Black Chappell' (the first whose name is known), was buried in April 1567, though the parish register is a later transcript and the entry, in respect of the chapel's name, is suspect.[46] A survey of the manor in 1577, made in a revised order and form, and after examination of the court rolls (it gives the rent of the purpresture, correctly, as one halfpenny), consistently uses 'Blatche Chappell' (a half-way version omitting the genitival *s*):[47] a survey in 1583 uses both 'Black' and 'Blache'.[48] Clearly 'Black Chapel' had become the regular form by the mid-century, although for some time thereafter the manorial officers felt constrained to follow the usage in their own records.[49]

The manorial survey of 1563 records another of the chapel's properties (a freehold tenement called Crouch House and garden platt).[50] It is not named in the surveys of 1577 and 1583, though both say that its issues are employed upon the maintenance of the chapel (and both say it is copyhold).[51]

In 1571 Thomas Wiseman of Great Waltham gave an annuity of £5 6s 8d from lands called Burgess Well in Chelmsford (see above) to be used in the most necessary or needful works of charity in North End: the trustees, a maximum of twelve, were all to be from Great Waltham, eight of them from North End.[52] Wiseman died in 1580, leaving the churchwardens of Great Waltham an annuity of £2 from lands in Great Baddow, half for the repair of the church and half for deeds of charity in North End at the discretion of six of its chiefest inhabitants.[53]

In 1589 the court of the Archdeacon of Essex ordered Silvester Dennis and his wife Margery to publicly confess their incontinence before marriage in the chapel immediately after public prayer on the following Sunday morning.[54] In 1603 the same court ordered Richard Cowland of North End, who had been accused of attending neither the parish church nor the chapel, though he claimed to attend the chapel, to go once a month to the parish church.[55]

In 1612 Commissioners for Charitable Uses found that Bridge Meadow (see above) was let for fourteen shillings a year, although worth twenty, but only 6s 8d was handed to the chapel, and that Chapel Mead or Butlers Meadow (see above) was let for three pounds a year, although worth four, but only twenty shillings was handed to the chapel. The Commissioners ordered John Wiseman of Stisted who had leased the properties, presumably as trustee, and received the rents, to pay four years' arrears of £9 9s 4d to John Johnson, chapelwarden.[56]

Jeffery Child of London, who died in 1620, left £100 for the purchase of lands to be held in trust for the relief of poor people living within North End where he was born: a house called Ellises in High Easter, and six acres of land, were purchased in 1625.[57]

The chapel seems to have had no difficulty during the Interregnum.[58] In 1650 the survey of church livings (or parochial survey), noted the chapel's topographical position and endowments (lands worth £14 a year) and that services were satisfactorily provided by John Jackson, an able, godly, painful preacher (routine wording, not to be taken literally), and found it useful and fit to be continued with an increased maintenance.[59] There is no evidence that the chapel received an 'augmentation'.

The title to the chapel and all the then charitable properties (except Ellises and the Burgess Well annuity) starts in January 1657 when the trustees transferred to successors a messuage (i.e. dwellinghouse) called 'Chappell'; an acre of meadow ground in Stebbing called Stebbing Mead, lying near a green or common in Felsted; five rods of land in Stock Croft Common Field in Great Waltham; one acre two rods of ground in North End called the Grove; and Crouch House, Bridge Mead and Butlers Mead (mentioned above): to be held for the benefit of the inhabitants of North End by gifts, works of Christian charity, the making or repairing of bridges, and the amending of the highways (no mention of the chapel, although Crouch House, Bridge Mead and Butlers Mead had been given for its maintenance). The deed is unusual: the title of the outgoing trustees is not recited, and the chapel, said to be in the occupation of George Oddyn and others, is merely described as a messuage.[60] There are two possible inferences: first, that the chapel's true function was omitted because of the uncertainty of the times: secondly, that earlier deeds have been lost (details of the Crouch House trust are known from manorial surveys, and those of the Bridge Mead and Butlers Mead trusts from proceedings of Commissioners for Charitable Uses) and a form of words was devised to cover all the bequests. The nineteenth-century Charity Commissioners, in the absence of any earlier evidence, described all the properties in the deed as the bequest of an 'Unknown Donor', a phrase still officially used. It is unfortunate that there is no earlier information about three of the properties (the land in Stebbing: the land in Stock Croft Common Field: and the Grove).

In 1664 the manorial court admitted trustees of the chapel to a small purpresture sometime (*aliquando*) parcel of the waste of the manor adjoining the back part (*parti posteriori*) of the chapel at an annual rent of 1½d.[61]

In 1682 Ann Wiseman left £60 to purchase lands for the maintenance of an honest and orthodox minister to preach in the chapel of North End (not named) every Sunday: if that was impossible, the poor of North End were to receive one-third of the rent, and poor children born within North End apprenticed with the remainder.[62] A house, now the Butchers Arms, in North End, and three acres of arable land, were bought in 1714.[63] This was the chapel's last landed endowment.

In 1686 Commissioners for Charitable Uses reviewed all the North End charities (i.e. those in the deed of 1657, Child's, and the Burgess Well

annuity), and found that the trustees, who had been appointed in or about
1672, had been negligent as some of the funds, which had been given for the
relief of the poor and other charitable purposes in North End (including the
repair of the chapel), had been paid to nonconformist preachers, and that
£79 14s 9d (i.e. more than 3½ times the annual income) remained unspent.
The Commissioners appointed new trustees, who included two baronets (Sir
George Alleyn of Little Leighs and Sir Thomas Luckyn of Little Waltham)
and the vicar of Great Waltham, presumably as natural leaders of the
community, and two of the existing trustees, presumably to retain
continuity: and ordered the existing trustees to surrender the £79 14s 9d,
and the new trustees to enter all receipts and payments in a book and submit
a statement of the accounts annually to the Chelmsford justices.[64] The
trustees took 'exceptions' (in effect, appealed) as (a) the Commissioners had
treated the charities as a single trust, whereas each of the three charities had
its own trustees, and those who were trustees only of Child's charity or of
the Burgess Well annuity should not be charged with the repayment of the
£79 14s 9d, which belonged solely to the other charity: (b) the Burgess Well
annuity had been properly applied: (c) the Commissioners had found the
accounts of Child's charity to be satisfactory: (d) trustees of the Burgess
Well annuity had to be of Great Waltham: and (e) John Oswald, the vicar of
Great Waltham, hoped to obtain the £79 14s 9d to pay his 'extravagant
charges' in prosecuting the decree, and to receive most of the future income
as he, and his curate, preached at the chapel.[65] The factual exceptions,
(a)–(d), were well-founded, and (although this point was not taken) there is
no evidence that trustees were appointed in or about 1672, or that the
charities were brought under one group of trustees.[66] Exceptions were
normally considered by the Court of Chancery, but no further action has
been traced: there was no conveyance to new trustees, and no record of the
alleged £79 14s 9d. The whole affair is not credible, and the Commissioners
were, surely, deceived by someone anxious to obstruct the administration of
the chapel and the charities. It would have been in character if Oswald was
the instigator.[67]

An account book for all the charities except Child's, effective from
November 1685, was opened by decree of the Commissioners for
Charitable Uses, who themselves authorised the first two 'disbursements'.[68]
All the North End charities were initially, or had become, attached to the
chapel, presumably as the religious and social centre of the hamlet, but the
income from Child's charity was, by the terms of its foundation, used for
routine payments to the poor, and with it was administered the annuity
from the Great Baddow lands (if and when received): the accounts of
Child's charity were kept separately (see below). The main account (i.e. that
started in 1685) covered, at its opening, the income from the properties in
the deed of 1657 and the Burgess Well annuity, a total of £16 18s 4d (and
from 1714–5 a further £4 5s from the Ann Wiseman charity): [69] it was
almost entirely spent on the upkeep of the chapel and the trust properties,
quit rents where appropriate, and payments to clergymen who officiated at
the Sunday service, though there were occasional emergency disbursements
(e.g. to surgeons for helping a woman in travail (1685–6) and healing a

hand (1702–3), and towards the loss by fire of a barn, full of corn, and a haycock (1704–5)), and the occasional gift to the poor (no named recipients) (e.g. £1 10s in 1688–9 and 1689–90, £2 4s in 1703–4, £2 in 1705–6 and 1708–9, £3 8s from a sale of wood in the Stebbing meadow in 1764 (paid without passing through the accounts), and £3 in 1771): there were payments for 'trophy money' or 'tax' (i.e. a levy for the militia) in 1686–7, 1696–7, and 1721–2. One John Steward was paid sixpence for singing on certain Sundays from 1726 to 1733: music is not mentioned again until 1750–1 when, and in most years thereafter to 1785, and again from 1820, there is a payment to the singers. There were payments for attending (or teaching at) a Sunday school in 1821–3 and from 1828. The earliest annual accounts were signed by some of the trustees, who appointed a collector (occasionally, chapelwarden, and sometimes, chapelwarden and rent reeve) for the next year, but this was not regularly done after 1736, was abandoned after 1769, and not resumed until 1808: there was then no annual appointment of collector, presumably because the chapel had a permanent treasurer.[70] In 1835 the income from the relevant charities was £55 19s 8d.[71]

The accounts of Child's charity, which survive from its foundation, were initially kept in a separate volume, but from 1808, though still administratively distinct, were entered in the main account book. The income, originally £5 a year, was spent on legal costs, taxes (including such occasional entries as coat for soldiers and for town (i.e. High Easter) arms (Michaelmas 1666) and for drums and culvers (Michaelmas 1675)), and the maintenance of the trust property, Ellises in High Easter (which could be a burden: the collapse of the kitchen in a great wind during the half year to Lady Day 1671 caused financial confusion for two years), with the remainder distributed in small sums (a few shillings each half year) to named persons (the statutory relief of North End being the responsibility of the Great Waltham parish officers). In 1797 £2 12s 6d was paid for teaching the poor children (an entry not repeated), and from 1835 the income, now £10 a year, was given in clothing or material (e.g. waistcoasts, calico, blankets) and no longer in cash, and sixteen girls who attended the Sunday school received a frock, tippet, bonnet and ribbon, and seventeen boys a smock, frock and cap (the number of children and the nature of the clothing varying slightly from year to year thereafter).[72]

The main account books name most of the clergymen invited by the trustees to take Sunday service. There was no formal contact with the parish church, and successive vicars of Great Waltham took little interest in, and knew little about, the chapel's affairs. Nicholas Tindal, the first historian of Essex, who was vicar of Great Waltham 1722–40, told the Bishop of London (Gibson) in 1723 that 'There is a Chapel', which he didn't name, 'in the Parish of some standing endew'd [sic] with certain Rents of Land, but how manag'd can't learn, for by the founder's order The Vicar is excluded from having the benefit of it' (i.e. prohibited from appointment as stipendiary curate),[73] but he took service at the chapel on 22 Sundays in 1724, being paid five shillings for each visit, as was his curate, Philip Morant, the future county historian, on 63 Sundays in 1724–5.[74] Over fifty years then passed before the vicar of Great Waltham next officiated there (see below).

The chapel, during most of the eighteenth century, was closely connected with Barnston. Henry Oborne, Oswald's successor as vicar of Great Waltham, took service at the chapel on three Sundays in 1706–7, but Samuel Adamson, rector of Barnston, then officiated until his death in 1724, and he was followed, after the intrusion of Tindal and Morant (which may have been an emergency arrangement), by successive curates, Mr. Herbert (1724–5),[75] William Wyatt (1725–6),[76], and (from 1727) Thomas Rayner, who served until 1750, though he became rector of Elsenham in 1731.[77] John Brett, rector of Barnston, then officiated until 1762, and, though he was followed by John Daniel Cotton, curate of High Easter and Aythorpe Roding (1763),[78] and Charles Clifton, who has not been identified (1765–8), Nicholas Toke, rector, took service in 1769 and 1772 (the accounts are defective at this period).[79] Indeed Gibson's 'diocese book' (1723–48) says that the parish's two Sunday services had been reduced to one, the inhabitants of Barnston and the chapel 'having agreed to frequent each, alternately.'[80]

The diocesan officers, who must have relied on information from the vicar of Great Waltham, had no knowledge of the chapel or of its services. The Bishop of London's Secretary noted in 1763 that it was 'seldom used'.[81] In 1766 the vicar (John Lovelace) told the Bishop (Terrick) that the chapel, which 'might be of great use' if 'properly endowed & served', 'has not the least Revenue', although, through the Ann Wiseman charity '& some other Contributions', 'some neighbouring Clergyman is now & then procured to preach, when the Trustess can afford to pay . . . for that Service':[82] the diocesan record of patrons and incubents solemnly recorded that the chapel was 'unendow'd – therefore not regularly serv'd'.[83] And Morant, going further than Tindal, wrote that the vicar is said to be 'excepted from being Preacher' at the chapel 'that he may not be induced to neglect the mother-church': he found the trustees 'very shy of shewing the feoffment' (i.e. trust deed), though that may reveal the exasperation of the historian rather than that of the clergyman.[84]

Lovelace tried to bring the chapel under his control, arguing (presumably incorrectly) that Walden Abbey, as appropriate rector of Great Waltham before the Reformation, must have been patron of the chapel, and that the patronage had passed to the abbey's then successor, Trinity College, Oxford. Lovelace, who had taken service at the chapel for the payment of six shillings a Sunday from at least 1780 (when the accounts, which call him 'Lovless', re-start), asked the college in 1782 to present him to the curacy of the chapel and enable him to apply for an augmentation from Queen Anne's Bounty (presumably arguing that the trustees, who may not have been consulted, had no right to invite clergymen to officiate): the college would have done so, but could not covenant to present future vicars to the curacy in case it was thereby held to have acquired an additional advowson, for a college was statutorily restricted in the number of advowsons it could hold. Lovelace, nevertheless, went ahead, but his application was rejected by the Governors of the Bounty in March 1784. He never again took service at the chapel, though he remained vicar of Great Waltham until 1797.[85]

The manorial officers remembered in 1760 that no trustees had been admitted 'to that Purpresture formerly parcel of the Waste . . . adjoining to the hinder part of Blackchapel yard' since 1664 (see above). First proclamation was duly made, and second proclamation a year later: no one sought admission, but the matter was not pursued.[86]

In 1798 John Pridden, the antiquary and, until the previous year, a beneficed Essex clergyman, sketched the chapel from the south-west, noting its 'very bad repair', and commenting particularly on the 'small decayed turret', although he acknowledged that service was held every Sunday.[87] Pridden's judgment seems to have been sound: £4 4s 8½d was spent on repairs to the chapel in 1800, though the account book gives no details. In 1825 the chapel bell was recast.[88]

Lovelace's successor at the chapel, a Mr. 'Burtfield', who took service 1784–93, must have beeen James Butterfield, who held curacies in the neighbourhood.[89] Then began the chapel's long, though not continuous, association with the staff of Felsted School.[90] The Mr. 'Comins', who officiated in 1794, was almost certainly William Collins Cumming, usher (or undermaster) of Felsted:[91] he was succeeded by Richard Houlditch (1795–9), also usher there, who was admitted to holy orders by the Bishop of London (Porteus) with the title of curate of the chapel.[92] The situation in 1800 is uncertain, but George Somers Clarke, Lovelace's successor as vicar of Great Waltham, took service 1801–4:[93] he was followed by John Simpson (1805–10, 1814–16), usher of Felsted, and William John Carless, headmaster (thirteen Sundays in 1812 and one in 1813). (The situation in 1811 is also uncertain). Butterfield returned in 1817–18.[94]

The first clerical directories were now being published. The three earliest editions of the Clerical Guide (1817, 1822, 1829) describe the chapel as a chapel to Great Waltham, and the Patroni Ecclesiarum (1831), a supplement to the Clerical Guide, calls the parish Great Waltham with Blackchapel. Clarke, the vicar, must have approved those entries (at least tacitly), though he had not officiated at the chapel since 1804! In 1823, when suspended (see note 93), he told the Bishop of London (Howley) to remember, in settling the stipend of the officiating curate, that there were two chapels in the parish, one 'now a barn': the identity of the other, though not named, is obvious.[95]

The chapel paid Edmund Squire, headmaster of Felsted, for taking service 1818–20, but both he and the chapelwarden (James Skill) subsequently acknowledged that James Foulkes Roberts, the usher, had officiated. When Roberts left Felsted in 1820, the chapelwarden invited Squire to suggest another Clergyman, clearly meaning Robert's successor at the school: the chapel would pay the 'usual' salary of £41 a year.[96] Squire sent the chapelwarden's letter to the Bishop and recommended William Wilkinson, 'second master' at Felsted, 'to perform the office of a Curate' at the chapel.[97] Wilkinson was made deacon in October 1820 by the Bishop of Chester (Law) by letters dimissory, apparently with the title of curate of the chapel: he was ordained priest in May 1822,[98] the chapelwarden certifying that he had satisfactorily performed duty there.[99]

Wilkinson died in 1824,[100] but the trustees' views had changed during the previous four years: they now believed (so Squire told the Bishop) that, by granting a written title and offering a yearly stipend, they might compromise the chapel's exemption from episcopal jurisdiction, though they were prepared to pay Wilkinson's successor at the school (Joseph Edwards) fifteen shillings a Sunday for taking service.[101] The Bishop would not accept Edwards's post at Felsted as a title to holy orders, though he had accepted Roberts's and was told by Squire that 'the neighbourhood' wanted the chapel 'regularly served', which might be impossible unless the 'undermaster' could do so, and that both Roberts and Wilkinson had 'performed the duty in a manner that pleased every body' and 'drew large congregations.'[102]

The chapel, therefore, looked elsewhere.[103] John Phillips Gurney, vicar of Great Canfield, took service 1824–7. Squire officiated (or at least was paid!) 1828–36. The chapel then turned again to Gurney, thereby involving the bishop of London (Blomfield) in the arrangements for its services. For the Bishop told Gurney in 1837 that the size of his parish (in terms of population) required him to hold two services every Sunday, unless he held 'the Curacy of an *adjoining* parish, the Church of which is near enough . . . to be resorted to by your parishioners': but the Bishop 'decidely' objected to his taking service six miles away, 'which is contrary to the . . . Act of Parliament', 'lays upon you the necessity of more travelling on the Lord's day than in . . . proper', and 'must . . . take you . . . from your parish . . . during those house which ought to be given to the superintendence of a Sunday School, or the catechising of the younger part of your flock'.[104]

The Bishop, however, took no immediate action, fortunately, because in January 1838 the trustees, recognising that 'great inconvenience was experienced from the want of more room to accomodate [sic] the Congregation during divine Service . . . and that many more persons would attend if they could have seats', resolved to enlarge the chapel with a north aisle (41ft × 12ft), to give about 100 extra seats, and a small vestry (12ft × 6ft), at a total estimated cost of £100. A public subscription was necessary as the chapel had only £3 13s 4½d in hand. The money was raised within two months, but the trustees then decided to repair the chapel and house, which were 'dilapidated', and improve them 'by Gothic Windows', estimated to cost £50. The final subscription list just failed to reach the £150, but collections at the two services on the re-opening Sunday in August 1838 (with sermons by Joseph Ridgeway, a rector of High Roding, and James Caporn, vicar of Takeley) brought the total to £173 6s, although the actual cost was a little more.[105]

Gurney took service during 1838, but next year the Bishop, having received two complaints about him from one of his parishioners,[106] again wrote about his duties. The Bishop now required Gurney to 'perform two full services' in his parish and 'relinquish the charge' of the chapel, though he did so 'with regret, believing your ministry to be very acceptable to the congregation'.[107] The trustees could not change the Bishop's mind, though he acknowledged that their 'request' was 'creditable' to Gurney,[108] who officiated at the chapel until Michaelmas 1839 and on two Sundays thereafter.

James Tweed, a clergyman living at Great Dunmow,[109] took service at the chapel on four of the remaining Sundays in 1839. James Thomas Johnson, curate of Writtle, officiated throughout 1840. William Tufnell, younger brother of the lord of the manor (John Joliffe Tufnell),[110] officiated on fourteen Sundays from Christmas 1840 to April 1841 'without making any charge', and Tweed took service on two further Sundays. The Bishop now told the trustees that 'no clergyman can lawfully officiate' at the chapel without his licence and that it was his 'duty to prevent an infraction of ecclesiastical discipline', though the trustees were entitled to nominate a clergyman who would be licensed 'upon his producing the customary Testimonials': if, however, the trustees refused to nominate, 'the responsibility of keeping the Chapel closed will rest upon *them*', and he hoped that they would 'conform to the law of the Church'.[111] The Bishop told Tufnell in June 1841 that, although there was no objection to his taking service at the chapel, he could not 'permit any Clergyman to officiate there permanently without my licence', and Tufnell must not perform duty there after the end of the month, the Bishop adding that he intended to 'bring the question to an issue', the trustees having 'not paid any attention to my former communications'.[112]

It is possible, of course, that the trustees and Tufnell parted for personal reasons, but Tufnell is known to have had reservations about the need for a testimonial,[113] and the trustees were unlikely to do anything that might affect the chapel's independence. That obvious inference may, however, be wrong for in July 1841 the Bishop understood that the Trustees were willing to nominate William Shepherd, rector of Margaret Roding, for his licence to serve the chapel, but, as he lived farther away than Gurney, the Bishop accepted the proposal without much enthusiasm ('too far for a clergyman to ride backwards & forwards every Sunday') and as a temporary measure only. Shepherd had agreed to take service at 6 o'clock, but that, as the Bishop realised, would only be possible during the summer, and he asked both the trustees and Shepherd if Tufnell would then take service at an earlier hour.[114] Shepherd's appointment seems to have upset Gurney, perhaps not unreasonably, but the Bishop would not 'dispense' with one of the services at Great Canfield.[115] In fact Shepherd officiated at the chapel throughout the second half of 1841 (but at what hour?), being paid travelling expenses in addition to his stipend, but was told by the Bishop in November that, for reasons previously given, he must stop at the end of the year.[116]

Gurney was remarkably persistent, and early in 1842 the Bishop suggested that he and Shepherd took service at the chapel '*alternately*'.[117] That was clearly an enforced retreat for the Bishop had previously said that both lived too far from the chapel, but the Bishop was in difficulty as he wanted two services in every parish: he was looking for, but presumably could not find, a neighbouring incumbent with a stipendiary curate, or an unbeneficed clergyman, who would serve the chapel regularly. The Bishop's suggestion was therefore adopted: in 1842 services were shared between Gurney and Tweed,[118] though not equally: in 1843 Gurney officiated on alternate Sundays for the whole year, Tweed for half the year, with the remainder divided between Shepherd[119] and Thomas Surridge, headmaster of Felsted. Gurney and Surridge then shared the duty for the last five years covered by the chapel's account book (1844–8), apart from one Sunday in 1846, though in January 1846 the chapel passed beyond the jurisdiction of the Bishop of London. Two points emerge from these manoeuvres. First, the Bishop approved of the services at the chapel, provided he knew what was happening, and there was no breach of ecclesiastical law or discipline: secondly, the Bishop did not consider the chapel to be a chapel of ease to Great Waltham for there was no consultation with the vicar, though the chapel (whatever its legal status) was in his parish and a good proportion of the congregation must have been his parishioners.

Unfortunately the chapel's own records (other than title deeds) between 1848 (the end of the account books) and 1895/6 (the opening of a combined accounts and minute book) are not available.[120] Moreover the diocese of Rochester did not share the diocese of London's close interest in the chapel. Our detailed knowledge of its affairs does not, therefore, continue into the second half of the century. Records, of course, survive elsewhere. The trustees reported at the census of religious worship in 1851, for example, that the chapel held 250 people: that a service was held each Sunday (morning and afternoon alternately): and that on 30 March 1851 there was an estimated attendance of 180 in the 'general' congregation and 27 at the Sunday school, the average attendance during the previous twelve months being 150 and 27.[121]

The chapel received three further endowments. Charles Skill, who died in 1857, left £500 on the trusts of the Ann Wiseman charity (see above) to support a second service.[122] In 1871 Sarah Jane Whimper Townsend gave £500 on trust to apply £3 of the annual income therefrom for the purposes of the Ann Wiseman charity, and distribute the remainder among the necessitous inhabitants of North End in clothing or relief in sickness:[123] and left a further £500 at her death in 1872 to augment the stipend of the minister of the chapel.[124] Two small, and presumably unwanted, pieces of land, allotted in the Felsted Inclosure Award (1867) in respect of Bridge and Butlers Meads, were sold.[125] The separate charities became a single trust in 1906.[126]

In 1871 the northern part of Great Waltham (including North End and the chapel) became the parish (technically, district chapelry) of Ford End.[127] The first vicar, Bartholomew Stephen Yolland, previously curate of Great Waltham and therefore familiar with the situation, was prepared, provided he had 'the help of another Parochial clergyman', to take services at the chapel, although he thought that such services were not required and alleged that James Hardwicke Dyer, vicar of Great Waltham when the parish was divided, 'was distinctly of opinion' that they should cease as soon as the new church was consecrated: neither the Bishop of Rochester (Claughton) nor the trustees 'favourably received' his proposal.[128] No action was taken, but the chapel's legal position was investigated, and the Registrar of the Archdeaconry of Essex (Augustus Charles Veley, a Braintree solicitor) claimed that at two episcopal visitations since the transfer to Rochester diocese in 1846 a clergyman had answered as 'Minister' of the chapel:[129]

unfortunately those records have not been traced.[130] Other comments by Veley must be treated with care.[131]

The story cannot, for reasons of space, be continued in detail after c.1875, but arrangements for services during the previous quarter-century (i.e. after the ending of the account book, with its detailed information, in 1848) must be considered. Clerical directories are woefully inaccurate, quite apart from the hazard of correct statements becoming out-of-date between compilation and publication, and the *Clergy List* often speaks with different voices in its separate lists of clergy and benefices. Moreover officiating clergymen are variously called, and describe themselves as, 'minister', 'curate', 'chaplain', 'lecturer' and 'morning lecturer'. For most of the quarter-century the chapel was served by Felsted masters. The arrangement in force in 1848 (Gurney and Surridge sharing duties: see above) must have ended by 1850 when Surridge resigned the headmastership of Felsted and left the district: it is not clear if that affected Gurney's position.[132] Cockburn Peel Marriott and Charles Bradford Wardale, both Felsted masters, were respectively 'morning lecturer' 1857–61 and 'minister' 1858–60,[133] but then comes a further gap in our knowledge though it was said in 1863 that 'the first and second masters of Felsted' officiated at the chapel.[134] Henry Charles Pryce Jones, assistant master, was 'minister' 1868–73,[135] apparently sharing duty 1869–72 with John Harris Backhouse, second master.[136] The Felsted connection then ended for the trustees next turned to Francis Burton Shepherd, son, and successor as rector of Margaret Roding, of the above-mentioned William, who seems to have been 'lecturer' until 1902.[137]

That concludes the detailed story of the chapel down to the allotted date, but a few topics (the legal status of the chapel, the reasons for its survival, its place in the local community, and the administration of the charities) need further examination. The chapel is often described as a chapel of ease, but chapel of ease, according to legal textbooks, is subordinate to the parish church and served by a clergyman appointed by the incumbent, which was not the position at Blackchapel:[138] vicars of Great Waltham (and, where appropriate, their curate) officiated there only at the invitation of, and at a stipend determined and paid by, the trustees: other clergymen officiated without the vicar's permission: and, as narrated above, the Bishop of London in the 1840s discussed the arrangements for services directly with the trustees without involving the vicar.[139] If the chapel was c.1875 (and is today) a chapel of ease, it could only be so described with an added proviso that it possessed special prescriptive privileges. It would, surely, be better described as a proprietary chapel (a view put forward in 1873),[140] even though that phrase is usually applied to a 19th-century building supplying the needs of a newly-built-up area. The writer, who is not a lawyer, prefers to accept that the chapel was (and is) a 'peculiar' of a very unusual nature lying outside the formal organisation of the Established Church, and not force it somehow within the strait-jacket of legal definition.

The chapel, having been founded after the parish boundaries of the area had been settled, could not become a parish church. It survived, with the support of the diocesan bishops and the neighbouring clergy, presumably,

by providing a nearby place of worship for people living at a distance from
the parish church, but, probably more importantly, because its endowments
provided a frequent (though not necessarily weekly) service. In addition, the
chapel was faithful to the Established Church: its worshippers, who no
doubt regularly paid the vicar his tithes, could not ignore the parish church:
the chapel was not licensed for marriages, it had no burial ground, and there
is no evidence that Holy Communion was celebrated[141] (though baptisms
took place).[142] Equally the visiting preacher in the chapel's pulpit on
Sunday did not relieve the vicar of Great Waltham of his responsibilities to
his parishioners at North End (e.g. the visiting of the sick) during the rest of
the week.

The trustees regarded the chapel as primarily a place of worship for the
residents of the local area, claiming 'the Power of allotting the Pews
amongst the Inhabitants of North End Quarter as they may think fit',
though others were, at the trustees' discretion, offered seats.[143] The Sunday
school, however rudimentary its teaching, must have been welcomed
locally, though its influence presumably declined after the national school at
Ford End opened in 1874. The chapel, as mentioned above, acquired
responsibility for all the North End charities: in 1835 twelve people (nine
from North End) were chosen when all the charities appointed fresh
trustees.[144] The charities were safely guarded[145] and well-conducted,[146]
despite a few hiccups – trustees not appointed at the correct time,[147]
ineligible persons appointed,[148] gaps in the accounts, and occasions when
they could have been more lucid. But such deficiences were, in context,
venial, and would certainly be found in charities administered by other
small farming communities with little or no professional supervision. The
working arrangements improved early in the 19th century when the Skill
family took charge and, significantly, the 19th-century Charity Commissioners
made no criticism or recommendations.[149]

The chapel seems to have been untroubled from c.1875 to the outbreak of
the Second World War, though a national newspaper accused the trustees of
financing it from the profits of beer![150] It suffered blast damage during an
air raid in September 1940, and was repaired after the war with funds from
the War Damage Commission. In 1952 the chapel and its charities were
regulated by a scheme of the Charity Commission.[151] The properties have
since been sold, and the Burgess Well annuity redeemed.[152] The chapel was
completely restored in 1975.[153]

Notes and References

1. This is the form now used by the chapel.
2. Royal Commission on Historical Monuments (hereafter RCHM), *Essex*, 2
(1921), 106, and illustration opposite p.186 (but the written account should have
included the commandments, Lord's prayer, belief and sentences, which, like the
royal arms, date from 1714 (see the chapel's account book, Essex Record Office
(hereafter ERO) D/Q 2/1), and, since the illustration was published, the seating on
the N side has been arranged to face inward, oak tie-beams have replaced the metal
braces, and the harmonium has been moved to the SW side of the screen: Nikolaus

Pevsner, *Essex* (2nd ed. rev. E. Ratcliffe, 1979), 307: Department of the Environment (hereafter DoE), *List of Buildings of Special Architectural or Historic Interest (Chelmsford Rural Area)*, 108.

3. Gt. Waltham (7457 acres, as given in OS *Book of Reference* (1876)) was the eighth largest of the (over 400) ancient Essex parishes, exceeded only (in descending order of size) by Barking, Waltham Holy Cross, St. Osyth, Hatfield Broad Oak, Writtle, Finchingfield, and Saffron Walden. Gt. Waltham church is in the extreme SE of the parish.

4. OS Map 1:50,000 sheet 167 (1983) ref 663179, which marks, but does not name, the chapel.

5. The whole of Gt. Waltham parish was in Chelmsford hundred and the ancient archdeaconry of Essex, but J. Adams, *Index Villaris* (1680) and N. Carlisle, *A Topographical Dictionary of England*, 1 (1808), both put the chapel in Dunmow hundred, and therefore in the archdeaconry of Middlesex: Thomas Cox, *Magna Britannia et Hibernia* (1720), puts it in both Chelmsford hundred (p.699) and Dunmow hundred (p.738).

6. There has been a recent error. Dr. Emmison (*Elizabethan Life: Wills of Essex Gentry & Merchants* (1978), vii) asks if 'Little Chapel' in Gt. Waltham, mentioned in 1585, is 'an otherwise unrecorded name for Black Chapel'. But 'Little Chapel' is the now-defunct Littley Chapel. Dr. Emmison agrees, and approves of this correction.

7. D. W. Coller, *The People's History of Essex* (1861), 252.

8. Winifred Eastment, *Ford End: The Story of an Essex Village* (new ed. 1968), 17.

9. E.g. *Essex Chronicle*, 16 Nov. 1984, which also mentions a local belief that the chapel is so-named 'because at one time the boards were tarred'.

10. Public Record Office (hereafter PRO) SC6/Hen.VIII/952, rott. 38–43 (accounts of the priory's possessions, 1535–6): PRO SC11/195 (valor of the priory's possessions, date missing, though clearly soon after the dissolution). But the necessary information is in *VCH Essex*, 2 (1907), 156.

11. P. H. Reaney, *The Place-Names of Essex* (English Place-Name Society 12, 1935), 272.

12. P. H. Reaney, *A Dictionary of British Surnames* (2nd ed. by R. M. Wilson. 1976), 38, and *The Origin of English Surnames* (1967), 237. A palatal sound is produced by 'the raising of the front of the tongue towards the hard palate' (R. H. Robins, *General Linguistics: An Introductory Survey* (3rd ed. 1980), 84).

13. PRO DL/30/66/829, rot. 12, which must be Reaney's earliest reference to the chapel, though he misdated it by a year. Court rolls of the manor of Gt. Waltham 1250–1398 are among the Duchy of Lancaster records in PRO: those for 1379–81, and from 1393 onwards (except for 1483–1509, 1546–1603, which are missing) are in ERO. Early this century Andrew Clark made detailed abstracts of some of the early court rolls and other documents now in ERO (D/DTu): Clark's notebooks are in the Bodleian Library (hereafter Bod. Lib.), Oxford (*A Summary Catalogue of Western Manuscripts . . .*, 6 (1924), 263–4). Clark does not mention the chapel in his articles, 'Gt. Waltham Five Centuries Ago', *Essex Review*, 13 (1904), 1–19, 65–80, 129–49, 197–214.

14. *Feet of Fine for Essex*, 1, 153: quoted by Reaney, Place-Names, 272.

15. He is first described as farmer at a court held on 19 Feb 1376 (PRO DL30/66/829, rot. 21), and last so described at a court held on 26 Jan 1383 (PRO DL30/66/833, rot. 18): a court held on 16 Apr 1383 refers to the time when John Blecche was farmer (PRO DL30/66/835, rot. 5). The lord of the manor, who was not resident, would have leased the demesne farm and the right to take some, or all, of

the profits of the manorial court to Blecche on payment of a fixed sum. (See L. R. Poos, 'Population and Resources in two Fourteenth-Century Essex Communities: Gt. Waltham and High Easter 1327–89' (unpublished Cambridge University PhD thesis, 1983: copy also in ERO), 31–3.) The manor was said to be worth £50 a year in 1373 (inquisition on the estates of Humphrey de Bohun, PRO DL/41/4/13) and 1389 (*Cal of Inquisitions Misc*, 6, 121).

16. ERO D/DTu 240, rot.30 (Clark's notebook, Bod. Lib. MS. Top. Essex e.5/1, f.93.)

17. ERO D/DTu 240, rot.38. (Clark's notebook, Bod. Lib. MS. Top. Essex e.5/1, f.94.)

18. ERO D/DTu 241, rot.23. (Clark's notebook, Bod. Lib. MS. Top. Essex e.5/1, f.106v.)

19. ERO D/DTu 242, rot.112. (Clark's notebook, Bod. Lib. MS. Top. Essex e.5/4, f.47.)

20. ERO D/DTu 243, rot.31. (Clark's notebook, Bod. Lib. MS. Top. Essex e.5/4, f.65v.)

21. ERO D/DTu 243, rot.35. (Clark's notebook, Bod. Lib. MS. Top. Essex e.5/5, f.15.)

22. Survey of the manor, ERO D/DTu 255, ff.16, 17v, 23v, 25, 26, 28.

23. E.g. 1:25000 sheet TL 61/71.

24. ERO D/P 121/1/1, f.145.

25. RCHM *loc. cit.* ('built probably late in the 15th century'): Laurence E. King, *Trans Essex Archaeol Soc* (n.s.) 24 (1944–9), 241 ('*c*.1500'): DoE *loc. cit.* ('dates from the late C15'). Pevsner *loc. cit.* does not attempt a date.

26. It was not uncommon in the middle ages for a chapel to be founded for the convenience of people living at a distance from their parish church, though it was more usual in the north of England where parishes were often larger and the terrain more difficult. There was a settlement at North End (Northande) by 1326 (PRO DL30/63/790, rot.10), that being a year earlier than the date given by Reaney, *Place-Names*, 273. North End was called a hamlet in 1369 (PRO DL30/65/825, rot.6).

27. PRO E179/107/63, m.17 (microfilm copy in ERO T/A 236).

28. ERO D/DTu 242, rot.36v. (Clark's notebook, Bod. Lib. MS. Top. Essex e.5/3, f.46v.)

29. ERO D/DTu 243, rot.11. (Clark's notebook, Bod. Lib. MS. Top. Essex e.5/4, f.52v.)

30. PRO C93/4/4, mm.6,7. In the nineteenth century the property was also known as Absol Mead. 'Trustees' has been used in preference to 'feoffees' throughout this essay.

31. PRO Prob11/12, ff.15–16 (formerly PCC 2 Moone). A summary in *Essex Review* 51 (1941), 30, prints 'Blackes Chapel' within inverted commas, implying an exact quotation, but the document reads 'Blaches'.

32. PRO C1/121/53, which was Reaney's earliest reference for the 'Blacche' form but, like other early chancery proceedings, is undated and addressed to an unnamed Archbishop of Canterbury: it could, therefore, date from Morton's appointment as Lord Chancellor in 1487 to Warham's resignation in 1515. Its text gives no date (not even of Cowlond's will or death). And the official endorsement that the matter was before the King in Chancery on the morrow of the feast of the Purification followed convention by giving neither calendar nor regnal year.

33. ERO D/AER 4, ff.94v–95v: recited in the court roll (ERO D/DHh M151, rot.20v).

34. ERO D/DHh M151, rot.17v.

35. E.g. 'The chapel that Henry VIII forgot' (*Essex Chronicle*, 9 Nov 1984).

36. Original deed not known to survive, but summarised in later proceedings before Commissioners for Charitable Uses (PRO C93/4/4).

37. The chapel is not mentioned in *Valor Ecclesiasticus*, though its compilers were required, under the relevant Act, to list both chantries and free chapels, and seem to have adopted a definition of free chapels wider than that in the text books (see vol. 1, pp. iv–v).

38. PRO E301/19 (entry 83) and E301/30 (entry 99).

39. PRO E178/797.

40. PRO C66/1012, mm.15–16: the entry in *Cal Pat Rolls 1563–6*, pp. 237–8, is not adequate for present purposes. Yetsweirt was one of the clerks of the signet, having been appointed, with effect from the next vacancy, in 1545 (*Letters & Papers, Henry VIII*, 20(1), 417).

41. C. J. Kitching, 'The Quest for Concealed Lands in the Reign of Elizabeth I', *Trans Roy Hist Soc, 5 ser*, 24(1972), 63–78 (esp. p.69).

42. ERO D/DGe M50, f.22. (The writer is very grateful to Miss H. E. P. Grieve for this reference, and for other help and encouragement generally.)

43. PRO Prob11/43, ff.55v–57 (formerly PCC 8 Mellershe): abstract in F. G. Emmison, *Elizabethan Life: Wills of Essex Gentry & Merchants* (1978), 145–7. Wiseman was buried at Felsted on 9 Jan 1559 (ERO D/P 99/1/1).

44. ERO D/DAEA 1A, f.33v. (The writer owes this reference to F. G. Emmison, *Elizabethan Life: Morals & the Church Courts* 180, but Dr. Emmison translates *fringere* as 'to deface'.)

45. ERO D/DTu 254, pp.21 (Blechis), 27 and 33 (Black(e)). (Clark's notebook, Bod. Lib. MS. Top. Essex e.5/7, ff.79v (Black), 94 (Bleche's [*sic*]): this was Reaney's earliest reference to the form 'Black Chappell', but he miscopied the date which Clark had transcribed correctly.)

46. ERO D/p 121/1/0. The transcript was made in 1628, and the transcriber may have used the then contemporary name of the chapel, irrespective of the form in the original version.

47. ERO D/DGe M273, pp.54, 59.

48. ERO D/DGe M274, ff. 21v (Black), 23 (Blache).

49. The forms 'Blechys' and 'Blatches' are used in a survey of the manor in 1622 (ERO D/DTu 256, ff. 6, 9v).

50. ERO D/DTu 254, p.27. (Clark's notebook, Bod. Lib. MS. Top. Essex e.5/7, f.79v).

51. ERO D/DGe M273, p.54, and M274, F.21v.

52. Original deed in ERO Acc 5373: abstract (but without details of the trusteeship) in *Report of the Commissioners Enquiring into Charities* (HC 1837–8), xxv, 684, (p.448 in the collected Essex volume).

53. PRO Prob11/62, ff.390–391v (formerly PCC 49 Arundell): copy (letters testimonial of the prerogative court) in ERO Acc 5373: abstract in Emmison, *Elizabethan Life: Wills*, 264–6. Wiseman must have died between 20 Nov 1580 (the date of the will) and 5 Dec 1580 (the date of probate), and, according to an entry in the Gt. Waltham booklet in the Holman MSS (ERO T/P 195/9 (no. 27), printed by Frederic Chancellor, *The Ancient Sepulchral Monuments of Essex* (1890), 278), the inscription on Wiseman's brass in Gt. Waltham church, gave the date of his death as 22 Nov 1580. But the parish register (ERO D/P 121/1/0), admittedly a transcript (see note 46 above), records his burial on 28 Nov 1581. (The date on the inscription is wrongly printed in *Memorials of Old Essex*, ed. A. Clifton Kelway (1908), 136.) The charitable bequest is abstracted in *Report of the Commissioners . . .*, 683 (p.447 in Essex edition): the lands in Gt. Baddow were part of Pond Land Farm in 1934 (deed in ERO Acc 5373).

54. ERO D/DAEA 14, f.153. (See *Trans Essex Archaeol Soc* (n.s.), 19 (1930), 17: Emmison, *Elizabethan Life: Morals*, 285.)

55. ERO D/DAEA 22, f.145. (The writer owes this reference to Emmison, *Elizabethan Life: Morals*, 86.)

56. PRO C93/4/4. (Commissioners for Charitable Uses were appointed, under Acts of Parliament of 1597 and 1601 to enquire into abuses of charitable gifts and rectify them by decree. It is not known how this matter was referred to the Commissioners.)

57. *Report of the Commissioners . . .*, 684–5 (pp. 448–9 in Essex volume). The will (dated 4 Aug 1620: proved 8 Nov 1620) is registered in PRO Prob11/136, ff.312v–314 (formerly PCC 102 Soane), and summarised in ERO D/Q 2/3. The deed of purchase, which recites the will, is ERO D/DU 905. The property is now called Ellis Farm.

58. Harold Smith, *The Eccles Hist of Essex under the Long Parliament and Commonwealth* (1931), 379, and A. G. Matthews, *Calamy Revised* (1934), 270–1, both say (apparently relying on Edmund Calamy) that Martin Holbeach, Headmaster of Felsted 1627–49, officiated at the chapel though neither gives dates. Calamy certainly said so in his first edition (*An Abridgment of Mr. Baxter's History of his Life and Times* (1702), 251), but he withdrew that statement in his second edition (*An Account of the Ministers . . .*, 2 (1713), 315), and in his third edition (*A Continuation of the Account . . .*, i (1727), 484), mentions Holbeach (whom he calls Holbitch) only as vicar of High Easter (which he calls High Easton). Neither of Samuel Palmer's 'corrected' versions of Calamy (*The Nonconformist's Memorial* (1777), 1, 504, and (1802), 2, 198) refers to the chapel in the entry for 'Holbitch'.

59. PRO C94/1, f.27 (but not in good condition and difficult to read: official copy in Lambeth Palace Library (hereafter Lamb. Pal. Lib.) COMM XIIA/8 (formerly MS.909), ff.208–10, and tabulated summary in British Library Lansdowne MS. 459, ff. 122v, 123: printed by Harold Smith, *Essex Review*, 33 (1924), 49 (though the name of the chapel appears as 'Clarke'), and in his *Eccles Hist*, 258, and noted by T. W. Davids, *Annals of Evangelical Nonconformity in . . . Essex* (1863), 246n. John Jackson was presumably the man of that name who was presented to the rectory of Leaden Roding by the Lord Protector and admitted by the Committee for the Approval of Public Preachers in 1654 (Lamb. Pal. Lib. COMM. II/417; COMM. III/3 (formerly MS. 997), i. p.210, and who was again presented to the rectory of Leaden Roding, a crown living, by letters patent (PRO C66/2916 (entry 367)) at the Restoration, having received episcopal ordination (Guildhall Lib MS 9537/16f.32).

60. Original deed in ERO Acc 5373: abstract in *Report of the Commissioners . . .*, 685 (p.449 in Essex volume), which ignored the change in the calendar and gave the date as 1656.

61. ERO D/DTu 247, rot.13: summarised in abstract of court rolls ERO D/DHh M173, p.2.

62. Registered copy ERO D/AER 24, ff. 102–110v: probate copy in ERO Acc 5373 (but why was the probate copy kept with the records of the chapel, and not with the records of the estate?): abstracted in *Report of the Commissioners . . .*, 686 (p.450 in the collected Essex volume). Anne Wisemen was buried at Gt. Waltham on 6 June 1682 (ERO D/P 121/1/0). She also left £3 to the poor of North End. The Wiseman family is said to have settled in North End about 1429–30 (Philip Morant, *The History and Antiquities of . . . Essex*, 2(1768), 88, and these were its fifth and sixth gifts to the chapel or to North End generally: at one time the family was believed to have built the chapel (that being positively stated in Gt. Waltham's return to the Ecclesiastical Revenues Commission in 1834: the writer is very grateful to Mr. D. A. Armstrong, Records Officer of the Church Commissioners, for this information and much other help).

63. Original deed in ERO Acc 5373. The income was never sufficient to pay a clergyman for every Sunday (see note 69 below). The property had become a public house by 1769 when the annual registers of Essex victuallers' recognisances start (ERO Q/RLv 24). (There was another property of the same name, which might cause confusion, because in 1753 the manorial court was concerned with a tenement formerly called Whites, but then the Butchers Arms (ERO D/DTu 253, rot.18v: abstract of court rolls D/DHh M173, p.204), which was found in 1786 to be ruinous and its seizure ordered (ERO D/DHh M159). This cannot be the chapel's Butchers Arms, and even the manorial officers were puzzled for there is a note in the abstract of court rolls 'NB ye Rent is £5 per Annum but this fine was taken it being a Charitable Affair'.)

64. PRO C93/42/30.

65. PRO C92/16, no.55 (copy in ERO Acc 5373).

66. Fresh trustees of Child's charity were appointed in 'March 1672' (i.e. 1673 by current reckoning) (one relevant deed in ERO Acc 5373, others on microfilm ERO T/B 252), but that did not involve the other charities.

67. Oswald, who was vicar 1684–1703, was a turbulent person: see, e.g., his *Some Memorandums of Matters of Fact . . .* (2nd ed., 1709). He was an 'enthusiastic tithe-collector, and opponent of dissenters' (*VCH Essex, Bibliography* (1959), 114).

68. These were payments for two sermons preached by William Hall, vicar of Good Easter, and an allowance of half a year's rent of Crouch House 'while it stood empty'. There was a payment of £6 15s 6d 'for charges and Fees in attending the Commissioners'. The book was not paid for until 1689–90. The Commissioners ordered the trustees to submit the accounts to the Chelmsford justices each Nov., so it was necessary to commence the first account from Nov. 1685 (almost eight months before the Commissioners' order).

69. Although the income of £4 5s from the Ann Wiseman charity was a return of over seven per cent on the capital sum of £60, it amounted to only about 1s 7½d each Sunday, less than one-third of the current rate (in 1713–4, for example, the chapel paid a clergyman £13 for taking service on 52 Sundays, i.e. five shillings each visit). The relative position remained unchanged: over a century later, the Charity Commissioners reported that the trustees paid 'the minister' £15 a year in addition to the £20 from the Ann Wiseman charity (*Report of the Commissioners . . .*, 685 (p.449 in the collected Essex edition).

70. The foregoing is based on the chapel's account books ERO D/Q 2/1 (1685–1773, the accounts for the final years are entered after those for 1708–9 and 1743–4) and D/Q 2/2 (1780–1848). There is a gap between 1773 and 1780. The Charity Commissioners reported that the Sunday school was attended by about thirty children who were 'taught the catechism, and to read, but not to write', and that some of the children attended the teacher on weekdays as well, 'for which the parents pay a small sum' (*Report of the Commissioners . . .*, 685 (p.449 in the collected Essex edition)).

71. The rents of the properties in the deed of 1657 totalled £27 13s, and the Butchers Arms was let for £23: details were entered in the account book (ERO D/Q 2/2) in Feb. 1835, with an increase in the rent of the Butchers Arms noted on the facing page, and printed in *Report of the Commissioners . . .*, 685–6 (pp.449–50 in the collected Essex edition): the Commissioners made no comment on the rent of the Butchers Arms, but thought that the rents of the other properties were 'in general fair . . . perhaps too high for the present time'. The income was completed by the Burgess Well annuity of £5 6s 8d.

72. This paragraph is based on the account books ERO D/Q 2/3 (1622–1799), the volume which satisfied the Commissioners for Charitable Uses, and D/Q 2/2 (1808–48). There is a gap between 1799 and 1808. The girls at the school had been

given a bonnet and ribbon in 1834. The trustees learned their lesson after the disaster of 1671 for the cost of repair after a fire in 1829 was covered by insurance. The Charity Commissioners thought that £10 was 'a high rent, considering the present price of agricultural produce' (*Report of the Commissioners . . .*, 685 (p.449 in the collected Essex edition)), and in 1833 the trustees allowed the tenant ten shillings because of his bad crop.

73. Guildhall Lib. MS. 25,750/2. (Essex was in the diocese of London until Jan. 1846 when all but nine metropolitan parishes was transferred to the diocese of Rochester (those parishes following in 1863). In 1877 the whole county was included in the new diocese of St. Albans. Essex became a separate diocese, called Chelmsford, in 1914.)

74. The entries referring to Morant are printed in *Essex Review*, 3 (1894), 28n. (though he preached on 44 Sundays (not 77!) in 1725). (*Alumni Cantabrigienses* incorrectly gives Morant as curate of Lit. Waltham.)

75. 'Harbert' in the account book (EDO D/Q 2/1). Identified in Guildhall Lib. MS. 9550.

76. Identified in Guildhall Lib. MSS. 9537/30, f.122, and 9550.

77. Identified in Guildhall Lib. MS. 9550 *sub. tit.* Barnston, Elsenham, and Gt. Waltham. Rayner did not remain curate of Barnston after his appointment to Elsenham.

78. Identified in Guildhall Lib. MS. 9537/39. Cotton became vicar of Good Easter and usher of Chelmsford Grammar School (*Essex Review*, 55 (1946), 113).

79. Dates in this paragraph are taken from the account book (ERO D/Q 2/1).

80. Guildhall Lib. MS. 9550 *sub tit.* Barnston.

81. Guildhall Lib. MS. 9557A (formerly No. 481), f.66. In fact Cotton was paid for taking service on 38 Sundays in 1763 (ERO D/Q 2/1).

82. Lambeth Pal. Lib. Fulham Papers (hereafter FP) Visitation Returns 1766, ff.1350v, 1352v. (The writer is very grateful to the staff of Lambeth Pal. Lib. for telling him of the Fulham Papers.)

83. Guildhall Lib. Ms. 9558, f.371. The chapel's accounts are confused, but either in 1765 or 1766 Clifton was paid seventeen guineas for taking service (ERO D/Q 2/1), which represents duty on almost sixty Sundays.

84. Morant, *op. cit.*, 2, 89.

85. For Lovelace's duties at the chapel, and for subsequent and comparable references to other clergymen, see the account book ERO D/Q 2/2. The rest of the paragraph is based on two letters from Lovelace to Trinity College, dated Jan. and Feb. 1782, annotated with the college's draft replies (both dated Feb. 1783), in the 'Gt. Waltham' volume in the college's archives: and on Lovelace's application to Queen Anne's Bounty. The writer is very grateful to Mrs. C. J. Hopkins, Archivist of Trinity College, and Mr. D. A. Armstrong, Records Officer of the Church Commissioners. In 1704 the Crown, by the Act 2 & 3 Anne c.20 (c.11 'in the common printed editions'), surrendered its right to first fruits (the notional first year's profits of a spiritual preferment) and tenths (the notional annual payment of the tenth part of the value of each preferment) to a corporation required to apply them (s.1) 'for the augmentation of the maintenance of . . . ministers . . . in any church or chapell . . . where the liturgy . . . of the Church of England . . . shall be used': the Queen Anne's Bounty, as the corporation was usually called, was united, by the Church commissioners Measure 1947, with the then Ecclesiastical Commissioners to form the present Church Commissioners. By s.4 of the Queen Anne's Bounty Act 1714 (1 Geo. I st.2 c.10), 'all churches, curacies, or chapels which shall . . . be augmented . . . shall be . . . perpetual cures and benefices', and s.5 of the Charitable Uses Act 1735 (9 Geo. II c.36), repealed in 1805 (45 Geo. III c.101), limited a college's advowsons to half the number of its fellowships. Lovelace told the

Bishop of London (Terrick) in 1766 that the college had 'promised to present' him to the curacy 'if the Queen's Bounty can be procured' (Lambeth Pal. Lib. FP Visitation Returns 1766, f.1352v).

86. ERO D/DHh M154.

87. DRO D/DU 3/139/1. For Pridden (1758–1825), 'Antiquary, amateur artist and architect' (*Alumni Cantabrigienses*), vicar of Heybridge 1783–97, and Lit. Wakering 1788–97, see *Dictionary of National Biography*.

88. ERO D/Q 2/2.

89. Could a genuine Mr. Burtfield have lived within, say, ten miles of the chapel for ten years without being mentioned elsewhere? No 'Burtfield' is named as incumbent or stipendiary curate of any Essex parish at the episcopal visitations of 1786 and 1790 (Guildhall Lib. MS. 9537/46), and no one of that name was admitted to holy orders by the Bishop of London, or licensed by him as a schoolmaster (though this last requirement had become obsolescent). Nor does 'Burtfield' appear in *Alumni Oxonienses* or *Cantabrigienses*. The chapel's accounts during the ten years are all in the same hand, so only one person was involved in the error (if error there was). James Butterfield (see note 94 below) was a curate in the vicinity of the chapel during those ten years.

90. During this period, the headmaster of Felsted usually appointed as usher a man who was about to graduate and who thereupon took holy orders. The school clearly gained if it could offer the successful applicant the experience of taking a regular service at the chapel and, perhaps more importantly, the additional stipend.

91. For a list of ushers (or undermasters), apparently compiled, for this period at least, from the Felsted churchwarden's accounts (ERO D/Q 11/33/2), see John Sargeaunt, *A History of Felsted School* (1889), 127–8. Neither the chapel's account book nor Sargeaunt gives Cumming's christian names, but William Collins Cumming officiated, as curate, at Felsted church 1792–4 (ERO D/P 99/1/6), and 'An adventitious *s* is freely added to surnames' (Edward Gepp, *A Contribution to an Essex Dialect Dictionary* (1920, 65). Cumming's position as usher supplements his entry in *Alumni Catabrigienses*.

92. Niether the chapel's account book (which calls him 'Houldich') nor Sargeaunt, *op. cit.*, gives his christian name. He thought, so he told the Bishop of London (Porteus), that the curacy of a church went with the appointment at the school, but later admitted that 'With reference to the Church which was to have been my Title, I cannot but fear that your Lordship will by no means accept it as such, as it is only a Chapel' (Guildhall Lib. MS. 10,326/126): the Bishop, however, did so, making Houlditch deacon in 1795 (Guildhall Lib. MS. 9532A/1, p.40). He was also curate of Gt. Waltham when ordained priest in the following year (Guildhall Lib. MSS. 9532A/1, pp.61–2, and 10, 326/127), but in 1797 Clarke, the new vicar (see note 93 below), resolved that 'Houlditch be never again permitted to officiate' in his church (ERO D/P 121/1/5, p.4). Houlditch had, as an undergraduate, migrated from Trinity College to All Souls, which presumably accounts for his meagre entry in *Alumni Oxonienses*.

93. He was vicar of Gt. Waltham 1797–1837, and a well-known eccentric. The chapel's account book merely says 'Mr. Clark', but his identity is confirmed by an entry in the parish register, 30 Nov. 1800, 'Commencing on this day the cure of the Chapel at North-end' (ERO D/P 121/1/4). His life is not yet written, but there are obituaries in *The Times*, 9 Feb. 1837, and (a longer one) *Chelmsford Chronicle*, 10 Feb. 1837. The Bishop of London's Secretary called him (*c.*1812) 'insane', with a gloss 'because he does not think as most Churchmen do, and gives utterance to his thoughts' (Guildhall Lib. MS. 9557A, f.66), and in 1817 the Archdeacon of Essex (Wollaston) found him 'strange, if not deranged' (Lambeth Pal. Lib. FP Howley vol. 52/3, f.18). In 1821 he was prosecuted in the consistory court by his churchwardens

for irregular conduct (Greater London Record Office (hereafter GLRO) DL/C/129, P.450): he was found guilty in May 1823, suspended for twelve months, and ordered to pay costs of £235 11s 9d (GLRO DL/C/130, pp.158, 249: *The Times*, 13 May 1823: *Chelmsford Chronicle*, 16 & 30 May 1823). Whilst suspended he again transgressed: in Jan 1825 he was suspended for a further two years, required to submit a certificate of good behaviour signed by three clergymen of the neighbourhood before resuming duty, and the living was sequestered because he would not pay the curate appointed by the Bishop of London (Howley) (GLRO DL/C/130, p.572: *The Times*, 27 Jan. 1825: *Chelmsford Chronicle*, 28 Jan. 1825). A certificate of good behaviour was sent to the Bishop, but not to the court, in Dec. 1826 (Lambeth Pal. Lib. FP Howley vol. 11, ff.145, 153), but Clarke had been imprisoned in May 1824 for debt (not having paid the costs of the case) (Lambeth Pal. Lib. FP Howley vol. 11, f.151v) and he remained there for the rest of his life, saying, as the vicar of Broomfield (Vincent Edwards) told the Bishop when sending the certificate, 'that nothing shoud [*sic*] induce him to pay the money . . . & that he found himself so comfortable as not even to wish to change his residence' (Lambeth Pal. Lib. FP Howley vol. ff.147). Comments made by Clarke (see, e.g., note 92 above) must, therefore, be treated with caution: he told the Bishop of London (Howley) in 1815 that the chapel would hold 300 people (Lambeth Pal. Lib. FP Visitation Returns 1815: and see note 121 below), and that totally absurd statement was duly entered in the diocesan record of patrons and incumbents (Guildhall Lib. MS. 9558, f.370v), so adding to the diocese's ignorance of the chapel's affairs. More importantly, Clarke told the consistory court in 1822 (*The Times*, 28 June 1822: *Chelmsford Chronicle*, 5 July 1822) and the Bishop in 1823 (Lambeth Pal. Lib. FP Howley vol. 11, f.136v) that he gave up duty at the chapel at the insistence of the Tufnell family (the largest landowners in the parish and lords of the manor) who wanted two services at the parish church, and promised him compensation (which he never received) for the £20 paid him annually by the chapel: the statements are vague, and without supporting evidence, but the trustees did pay him £20 a year! (For formal records of the consistory court proceedings (indexed under 'Office of the Judge promoted by Rust and Adams against Clarke' or 'Rust & Adams against . . '), see throughout GLRO DL/C/129–35 and relevant papers in DL/C/83; reports of the proceedings, in addition to those mentioned above, have been noticed in *The Times*, 26 Jan. & 6 July 1822, 21 & 28 May, 3 June 1823, 14 & 21 Feb. 1824, and *Chelmsford Chronicle*, 28 June & 5 July 1822, 25 Apr. & 2 May 1823, 20 & 27 Feb., 14 May, 4 June 1824, 25 Feb. 1825: for letters to the Bishop by, and about, Clarke 1815–28, see Lambeth Pal. Lib. FP Howley vol. 11, ff.5–138, 143–64: for copies of a letter from the Bishop to the churchwardens of Gt. Waltham 1815, and of three letters to Clarke 1822, see Lambeth Pal. Lib. FP Howley vol. 5, ff.21v–22v, 123–4.)

94. James Butterfield, youngest child of Thomas Butterfield, vicar of Boreham 1750–66 (Lambeth Pal. Lib. FP Porteus vol. 1, f.345), was baptised by his father at Wallington (Herts) in 1751: he served an apprenticeship to an apothecary, but entered Emmanuel College, Cambridge, in 1776, and next year (i.e. before graduation) asked the Bishop of London (Lowth) to admit him to holy orders, his title being the curacy of Radwinter (Guildhall Lib. MS. 10/326/108): the Bishop did so (Guildhall Lib. MS.9553, f.4). By 1780 he was curate of Writtle (ERO D/P 50/1/5), and in 1781 was ordained priest by the Archbishop of Canterbury (Cornwallis) by letters dimissory (Lambeth Pal. Lib. Vicar General Act Book vol. xi, p. 298: Guildhall Lib. MSS. 9553, f. 28, and 10, 326/112). He remained at Writtle to the end of 1781, but was curate of Gt. Dunmow 1782–4 (ERO D/P 11/1/5) and of Hatfield Broad Oak from at least 1785–91 (*VCH Essex*, 8 (1983), 179, relying on

ERO D/P 4/8/1). The above are the facts that have led the writer to identify Butterfield as the 'Burtfield' who took service at the chapel 1784–93 (see note 89 above). He became curate of Lit. Canfield in 1793 (ERO D/P 227/1/4), being allowed by the non-resident incumbent to reside in the parsonage house (Lambeth Pal. Lib. FP Porteus vol. 1, f.343). He was also curate of the adjoining parishes of Lit. Easton 1794–1800 (ERO D/P 180/1/4) and Gt. Canfield in 1810 (Guildhall Lib. Ms. 9537/50, p.312; ERO D/P 364/1/4). In 1795 he had become vicar of Norton (Herts) in the diocese of London (Guildhall Lib. MS. 9532A/1, p.45), but never resided, claiming that the living was too poor and the lath-and-plaster house, being 'only a very small Cottage', was 'wholly unfit for the residence of a Clergyman' (Lambeth Pal. Lib. FP Porteus vol. 1, ff.339, 341v, 346, and Howley vol. 9, ff.81–2). Successive Bishops of London granted him license for non-residence (see, e.g., Guildhall Lib. MS. 11,181, no.222). His curacy at Lit. Canfield ended in 1816 (ERO D/P 227/1/4) with the arrival of a resident incumbent, and he retired to Dunmow, but took service again at the chapel 1817–18 as he pointed out to the Bishop (Howley) in 1817 when asking for renewal of his licence for non-residence at Norton (Lambeth Pal. Lib. FP Howley, vol. 9, ff.81–2): he also assisted at Gt. Dunmow church 1817–9, when there was no stipendiary curate (ERO D/P 11/1/6,7,10,11). Butterfield died in 1819. His entry in *Alumni Cantabrigienses* needs expanding and the word 'Probably' deleted.

95. Lambeth Pal. Lib. FP Howley vol.11, f.136v. The barn must have been Littley Chapel (see note 6 above).

96. Guildhall Lib. MS. 10,326/156. Roberts had been licensed by the Bishop of London (Howley) as a schoolmaster in 1817 (Guildhall Lib. MS. 9532A/2, p.120): he was the only Felsted usher of the period to be licensed.

97. Guildhall Lib. MS. 10,326/156. See also a letter from Wilkinson's father to the Bishop in 1820 (Lambeth Pal. Lib. FP Howley vol.45, f.226).

98. Guildhall Lib. MS. 9532A/2, pp.163, 192.

99. Guildhall Lib. MS. 10,326/158.

100. He was buried at Felsted 21 Feb. 1824 (ERO D/CR 143). *Alumni Cantabrigienses* is defective and confuses him with someone else, although Sargeaunt, *op. cit.*, 128, gave the date of his death.

101. Lambeth Pal. Lib. FP Howley vol.40, f.239.

102. Lambeth Pal. Lib. FP Howley vol.40, ff.241–2.

103. Edwards was eventually made deacon by the Bishop of Bristol (Kaye), by letters dimissory, in March 1825 (Guildhall Lib. MS 9532A/2, pp.271–2).

104. Lambeth Pal. Lib. FP Blomfield vol.14, ff.33–4, 36. The population of Gt. Canfield in 1831 was 511. The Bishop told Gurney that he was referring to s.48 of the Act, 57 Geo. III c.99, which prohibited a curate from serving a church or chapel more than five miles from his residence, but he was bluffing: that section concerns the licensing of a curate to a parish with a non-resident incumbent!

105. ERO D/Q 2/2, but there was no separate account for the building and repair work, and it is necessary to decide which items in the payments list (for 1839) are relevant. There is a report of the services at the re-opening in *Chelmsford Chronicle*, 17 Aug. 1838. In 1851 the chapel held 250 people (see note 121 below), so it held 150 before the extension. The population of 'North End' was 549 (from 114 families) at the 1831 census but, as this was over a quarter of the whole parish of Gt. Waltham, and the remainder of the parish was divided between Church End and Howe Street (both in the south), 'North End' must be more than the hamlet and presumably included Ford End, which was nearer the chapel than the parish church (ERO D/P 121/18).

106. The complainant, a Mr. Wilson, presumably John Maryon Wilson (afterwards

7th bt.), patron of the living and lord of the manor of Gt. Canfield, alleged that on Good Friday 1838 (a) Gurney's men worked on his farm, for which he was rebuked by the Bishop ('probably the custom of the country, but .. a custom ... not to be followed by the servants of a Clergyman'), though the Bishop accepted that no work was done 'during the hours of divine Service', and (b) Gurney, when returning from the chapel, entered a shop in Dunmow 'belonging to a Quaker', the only one open, and 'passed some time there doing business', but this Gurney denied and the Bishop accepted his denial (Lambeth Pal. Lib. FP Blomfield vol.20, ff.21,47,77). (The Bishop's incoming letters do not survive, and the details of Gurney's denial are not known, but was there a service at the chapel on Good Friday (13 April) 1838, over six weeks after the decision to extend and repair, which was about a quarter of the time between that decision and the re-opening? The account book does not help as Gurney had a half-yearly stipend.)

107. Lambeth Pal. Lib. FP Blomfield vol.20, f.48.

108. Lambeth Pal. Lib. FP Blomfield vol.22, f.6.

109. He held 'no cure or preferment' (*Alumni Cantabrigienses*). His papers disclose no title on his admission to holy orders by the Bishop of London (Howley) in 1815 (Guildhall Lib. MS. 10,326/147).

110. At the chapel, 'his conversation and preaching was [*sic*] made ... the sanctified channel for the communication of heaven's favours to the saint's ('Josiah' [J. W. H. Collingridge], *Love's Tribute to the Memory of the Blessed; being Gleanings from the Life and Letters of the Late Excellent ... Wiliam Tufnell* (2nd ed., 1858), 32). Tufnell (1780–1855) held the family living of Wormingford 1805–25, and officiated at Pleshey church 1837–42 (ERO D/P 149/1/4), holding the living (a perpetual curacy, also owned by his family) March-Oct. 1842 (Guildhall Lib. MS. 9532A/4, pp.3, 18). He became an independent (or congregationalist) and in 1842 founded the Zoar chapel at Ford End in Gt. Waltham: 'To think that the first dissenting chapel ... in the parish ... should be built by one of the name of Tufnell!' ('Josiah', *op. cit.*, 35).

111. Letters from the Bishop to Charles Skill, chairman of the trustees, and Edward Swinborne Chalk of Chelmsford, the trustees' solicitor (Lambeth Pal. Lib. FP Blomfield vol.28, ff.12,75,98). Skill's sister had married Chalk, and, though later, his niece married Andrew Meggy, Chalk's partner (see Skill's will, PRO Prob 11/2252, ff.121–3).

112. Lambeth Pal. Lib. FP Blomfield vol.27, f.45.

113. In Feb. 1842 the Bishop had to explain to Tufnell the nature of a testimonial, 'which every Clergyman is required to produce before he is instituted to a Benefice or licensed to a Curacy', for 'I should almost infer ... that you had never read the form' (Lambeth Pal. Lib. FP Blomfield vol.32, ff.93–4). The Bishop was presumably referring to Tufnell's appointment to the living of Pleshey (see note 110 above), which, as a perpetual curacy, and not a rectory or vicarage, required his licence.

114. Lambeth Pal. Lib. FP Blomfield vol.29, ff.20–1.

115. Lambeth Pal. Lib. FP Blomfield vol.29, ff.21,34.

116. Lambeth Pal. Lib. FP Blomfield vol.31, f56.

117. Lambeth Pal. Lib. FP Blomfield vol.32, f.53.

118. Shepherd was presumably omitted because, to the Bishop's surprise, he was taking service at Aythorpe Roding (Lambeth Pal. Lib. FP Blomfield vol.32. f.61), where the incumbent was non-resident and the stipendiary curacy vacant.

119. Shepherd was no longer taking service at Aythorpe Roding (see note 118 above), but in June 1843 had been licensed to the living (a perpetual curacy) of Berners Roding, which adjoined Margaret Roding, the churches being only about two miles apart (Guildhall Lib. MS. 9532A/4, pp.34,36). (Reference books, e.g. *Crockford's Clerical Directory* and *Alumni Cantabrigienses*, give 1842, presumably

by error, as the starting date for Shepherd's incumbency at Berners Roding, although the parish register (ERO D/P 279/1/5) shows that he took service there that year.) The *Clergy List* of 1849 (list of benefices *sub tit* Waltham, Great) still shows Shepherd as officiating minister at the chapel, though there is no evidence that he took service after 1843.

120. The accounts and minute book and later records (except deeds) remain in the custody of the trustees.

121. PRO HO129/200, no.43: copy in ERO T/A 470/2.

122. PRO Prob 11/2252, ff.121–3; Skill lived at Northend Place, Gt. Waltham. The family had been involved in the affairs of the chapel since 1765 when Abraham and John Skill became trustees of the Burgess Well annuity: Alfred Skill, though no longer living in Essex, was reappointed trustee of the combined charities in 1919, but died before the next appointment in 1934 (deeds in ERO Acc 5373).

123. Deed, 7 Jan. 1871, in ERO Acc 5373. she was widow of William Townsend of Wall Farm, Gt. Waltham, who died in 1868. Her name, as given in the text, is that given in her husband's will (Principal Registry (Somerset House), 1868 ref. 143), in her own will (see note 124 below), and in the announcement of her death (*Chelmsford Chronicle*, 22 Nov. 1872, but official documents relating to her gifts spell her third name 'Whymper', and the deed appointing new trustees in 1934 (in ERO Acc 5373), gave her surname as 'Townend', which incorrect form is now regularly used. The Townsend family had been active in the chapel's affairs since 1808 when William Townsend of High Easter and his son Joseph were appointed trustees of the properties in the deed of 1657 (deed in ERO Acc 5373) and of Child's charity (deed on microfilm ERO T/B 252).

124. Principal Registry (Somerset House), 1872 ref. 790; recited (more accurately, paraphrased) in deed, 21 Dec. 1906, in ERO Acc 5373, as 'applied in like manner as the . . . income of' the Ann Wiseman charity.

125. The lands respectively contained 28 and 34 perches (ERO Q/RDc 67A). One piece was sold in 1871 (memorandum at foot of a copy of the Charity Commission's order for sale, 23 Dec. 1870, in ERO Acc 5373): the other had been sold by 1906 (schedule to deed, 21 Dec. 1906, in ERO Acc 5373, refers to the proceeds of the sale of both pieces).

126. Deed, 21 Dec. 1906, in ERO Acc 5373.

127. ERO D/CPc 32 (signed and sealed copy, with map, of Order in Council): text in *London Gazette*, 28 March 1871, 1618–9. Gt. Waltham and Ford End parishes are now re-united (*London Gazette*, 29 June 1979, 8230) as Gt. Waltham with Ford End.

128. Letter from Yolland to the Bishop of Rochester, 25 Aug. 1873, now among the records of the Archdeaconry of Essex (ERO D/AEM 1/7). Claughton became first Bishop of St. Albans in 1877, so the chapel had no problems at the change of diocese.

129. Letter from Veley (no address at the head, so probably an office copy), commencing 'My dear Sir', recipient unnamed (but not Yolland), 21 Aug. 1873, now among the records of the Archdeaconry of Essex (ERO D/AEM 1/7).

130. The writer is, however, very grateful to Mr. O. R. W Woodfield Registrar of the diocese of Rochester, for his interest, and to Rev. G. Lane, vicar of Hadlow, Kent, for accompanying him when he visited the diocesan registry.

131. In particular (a) that Hugh Chambres Jones, Archdeacon of Essex 1823–61, 'ascertained' that the chapel 'had been consecrated, and . . . would not have said so without being sure of the fact', but Jones is the only person to have so 'ascertained' and he left no record: and (b) that the chapel must have been 'recognized' (formally accepted as part of the ecclesiastical organisation) as John Ecton and John Bacon respectively included it in the *Thesaurus* and *Liber Regis*: the chapel is not

mentioned in Exton's first three editions (*Liber Valorum & Decimarum*, 1711, 1723, 1728), but was included in a list of ecclesiastical places 'not in charge' (i.e. exempt from payment of first fruits (see note 85 above)) in the next edition (*Thesaurus Rerum Ecclesiasticarum* (1742), 351). published after his death, and that was copied by Bacon in *Liber Regis* (1786), 593): both describe it as a chapel to Gt. Waltham of the certified value of £19 4s 4d, but who supplied and certified that figure?

132. Gurney described himself in *Crockford's* (repeated in *Alumni Cantabrigienses*) as formerly 'chaplain' of the chapel, but gave no dates.

133. *Crockford's*. Marriott and Wardale respectively left Felsted in 1861 and 1860. The *Clergy List* for 1862 seems to be wrong in describing Marriott as second master of the Grammar School, Chelmsford, and minister of the chapel: he was certainly at that school 1861–2 (though that was omitted from *Crockford's*, and therefore from Alumni Cantabrigienses), but the Governors gave him permission to act as curate of Springfield (ERO D/Q 12/4, pp.90,93,105). The *Clergy List* (in the list of benefices *sub tit* Waltham, Great, but not in the list of clergy) showed Marriott as officiating at the chapel until 1868!

134. William White, *History, Gazetteer, and Directory of . . . Essex* (2nd ed., 1863), 471. The first (i.e. head) and second masters were then William Stanford Grignon and John Harris Backhouse, but there is no evidence that Grignon took service at the chapel, and Backhouse only did so later (see note 136 below). But why did White say that?

135. The dates are taken from *Crockford's*, which in the earlier relevant volumes prints Blackpool Chapel! Jones left Felsted in 1873 (Michael Craze, *A History of Felsted School 1564–1947* (1955), 180–2), and moved from the district, although the *Clergy List* (in the list of benefices *sub tit* (Waltham Great) showed him as officiating at the chapel until 1875.

136. The *Clergy List* (in the list of benefices *sub tit* Waltham, Great) shows Backhouse as 'curate' of the chapel 1869–73, but he left Felsted, becaue of ill-health, in 1872, (Craze, *op. cit.*, 185), though he remained in the district. Craze, *op. cit* 157, implies that Backhouse succeeded Surridge at the chapel, but Surridge retired in 1850 and Backhouse arrived in 1852. Backhouse's entry in *Crockford's* does not include his service at the chapel.

137. *Crockford's*: *Essex Review*, 12(1903), 41.

138. The *Clergy List* (in the list of benefices *sub tit* Waltham, Great) down to 1868 called the chapel a 'perpetual curacy', but that must be wrong: a perpetual curacy is a living with cure of souls.

139. The chapel has its own entry (not under Waltham, Great) in *Report of the Commissioners . . . to Inquire into . . . Ecclesiastical Revenues . . .* (HC 1835), xxii, 636–7, so presumably it submitted a separate return, which was accepted.

140. 'Probably it is nothing more than a propriety Chapel' (in a draft letter by (?)Veley (see above), 23 Aug. 1873, among the records of the Archdeaconry of Essex (ERO D/AEM 1/7).

141. There are no entries in the chapel's account books (D/Q 2/1 & 2) for the purchase of sacramental bread and wine: and, after the repairs in 1838, Mrs Chalk (see note 111 above presented a chalice and salver 'In consequences of the Chancel . . . being made convenient for the Sacraments to be administer'd therein' (ERO D/Q 2/2).

142. Arrangements for the registration of baptisms are uncertain. The parish register has annual lists of baptisms at the chapel 1754–61 (57 entries: 59 names) (ERO D/P 121/1/: one baptism is entered in 1792 and eleven (in ten entries) in 1796, but in 1797 the new vicar (Clarke) 'Ordered, that no more Baptisms in the

Chapel be registered in this Book', though he changed his mind three years later when he officiated at the chapel as 'Baptisms there are from this time promiscuously registered in this Book with the Baptisms in the Church' (ERO D/P 121/1/4).

143. See e.g., a letter (copy) from Robert Tindal of Chelmsford, the trustees' solicitor, to Edward Livermore of Old Park, Gt. Waltham, 6 Oct. 1807, in ERO Acc 5373.

144. All twelve were appointed trustees of the Burgess Well annuity, though one did not execute the deed: ten of the twelve were appointed trustees of the properties in the deed of 1656, six of the Ann Wiseman charity (deeds in ERO Acc 5373), and ten of Child's charity (deeds on microfilm T/B 252).

145. The rent from the lands in Gt. Baddow may have been lost: if so, it was not the trustees' responsibility. The rent was (or should have been) paid to the churchwardens of Gt. Waltham and the relevant portion (£1) sent by them to the trustees.

146. In 1709 the parishioners of Gt. Waltham wanted a Commission of Charitable Uses to investigate the chapel's charities which (they alleged) were being misapplied by 'two Persons who have never given any account of their Trust' (Lambeth Pal. Lib. FP Compton vol.1, f.84), but the complaint was misconceived and inaccurate. They were not parochial charities, and (a) the main account Nov.1707 – Nov.1708 (the last to have been compiled) was approved by the signatures of four trustees, despite some arrears of income, including the Burgess Well annuity, which were subsequently received (ERO D/Q 2/1), and (b) the account of Childs charity shows that the annual rent of £5 from the trust property was received in two half-yearly instalments and duly distributed (ERO D/Q 2/3).

147. E.g. in 1677, 1731 and 1835 all the trustees of the Burgess Well annuity were dead and the eldest son of the last to die had to convey the annuity to fresh trustees (deeds in ERO Acc 5373): the Burgess Well annuity differed from the other charities, there being no property to administer and no tenant to choose and supervise, and there was no need for the trustess to do anything provided the owner of Burgess Well Lands paid the annuity to whomsoever was appointed to receive it, and that person disposed of it in accordance with instructions, but the same situation occured with Child's charity in 1775 (deed on microfilm ERO T/B 852). And also in 1775 the grandson of the survivor of the Ann Wiseman trustees had to convey to fresh trustees (deed in ERO Acc 5373)!

148. Sir George Alleyne, 6th bt., and his brother John, both of Lit. Leighs, were appointed trustees of the Burgess Well annuity in 1731, as was Sir Edmund Alleyne, 7th bt., nephew of Sir George, in 1745, although, as was pointed out in 1686, all trustees of the annuity had to be of Gt. Waltham.

149. *Report of the Commissioners . . . 684–6 (pp.448–50 in collected Essex edition)*.

150. *Sunday Express*, 15 Dec. 1929: a 'special correspondent' had been speaking to the landlady of the Butchers Arms. The trustees complained, and the paper said in its next number that 'The rent of the inn nearby is only part of the income of the trust, which maintains the chapel'.

151. References $\frac{H}{18,852}$ 5 Dec.1952.

152. A spring on Burgess Well Lands had for centuries supplied water to the town of Chelmsford. The property was purchased in 1844 on behalf of the inhabitants (ERO D/P 94/25/26), and was sold by the Chelmsford Borough Council, as trustees, to itself in 1966. The Council redeemed the annuity (now £5.33) for £37.51 (i.e. seven years' annual value) in 1974.

153. The writer acknowledges with gratitude the help given him by the various archive repositories that he has visited: they are mentioned in the above notes. For

printed sources, he is grateful to Guildhall Library and the Essex County Council's local studies libraries at Colchester and Chelmsford. Individuals who have helped with particular points are mentioned above, and thanks are due to friends who have read the whole or parts of the text. The writer is very grateful to Rev. G. L. Sanders, vicar of Great Waltham with Ford End, for his interest and help. In particular he must record his gratitude and thanks to the trustees of Blackchapel (in particular their chairman, Mr. Colin Priestman) and to the secretary Mrs V. Lanes) for willingly accepting his offer to write this essay (although he was a complete stranger), and for giving him all possible help and encouragement thereafter: they have certainly cast off the shyness which is said to have afflicted their 18th-century predecessors.

The Letter of the Law
Hatfield Peverel in the lay subsidy of 1524–5

JULIAN CORNWALL

Almost everything these days comes in 'handipaks' complete with directions for use; historical documents are the exception. Now that the professional dedication of generations of archivists has made them readily accessible in quantity, getting to grips with the records is imperative for anybody who wants to get to the bottom of a historical problem. As, unfortunately, deciphering old-time handwriting is only the first obstacle to be surmounted, the purpose of this essay is to put forward some constructive suggestions for avoiding unnecessary difficulties.

As every type of record poses problems peculiar to itself, the present paper discusses the interpretation of the lay subsidy of 1524–5, an important source for economic and social history, which is widely used, taking at the same time the opportunity of making up for the omission of guidance on its use which occasioned a mild complaint at the end of one otherwise indulgent review of my edition of the material relating to Rutland.[1]

Probing for the true meaning of the stark lists, which make up most fiscal records, can be a baffling process; unwarranted assumptions about their nature and unnecessary doubts about the accuracy and credibility of what are in essence quantitive statements serve only to deepen the confusion. Yet these difficulties can be avoided by reference to the rule book, which in fact means the Statute Book, for, in common with all lawful taxes, this subsidy was levied under the authority of an Act of Parliament which spelt out precisely who was to be assessed for it, and how.[2]

I

The best safeguard against the kind of over-simplification liable to accompany any attempt at generalization is to consider what the subsidy has to say about a single representative community. The parish of Hatfield Peverel, situated almost at the centre of Essex, well illustrates most of the salient features. As the subsidy was levied twice in successive years, there are two full returns,[3] but since it is frequently necessary to make do with a single list, we may concentrate on the one for 1524 which reads as follows, with changes to assessments made in 1525 given in parentheses:

William Studdynghe, sen.	in goods	£18	(land £10)
William Studdynghe, jun.	goods	40s	
Hughe Eton	goods	40s	
John Nobull	in wages	20s	
Alexander Wilmott	in goods	£12	

Thomas Haskyn	goods	£22	
Jamys Hawkyn	wages	20s	
John Hosyer, sen.	goods	£30	
John Hosyer, jun.	wages	20s	
William Hosyer	goods	100s	(wages 20s)
Andrew Wilmott	goods	£10	
Richard Harres	goods	£10	
John Hedich	goods	£ 8	
William Barwek	lands	66s8d	(goods £8)
Henry Holmested	goods	£ 8	
Thomas Osborne	goods	£ 8	
Robert Playne	goods	100s	
Thomas Beyll	lands	60s	(goods £5)
Alexander Osborne	goods	£ 4	
Robert Duke	goods	60s	
William Pycott	goods	100s	
Hughe Pycott	wages	20s	
Richard Boner	goods	£ 4	
Richard Hatchman	goods	100s	
John Hitchman	wages	20s	
Rauf Hitchman	goods	53s.4d	
John Hitchman	wages	20s	
William Fraunceys	lands	26s8d	(goods 53s.4d)
John Lugoe	goods	20s	
William Bedell	goods	£ 4	
Richard Bedell	wages	20s	
Thomas Blaknok	wages	20s	(goods 20s)
William Thomson	goods	20s	
Lawrence Baker	goods	20s	(goods 40s)
Robert Hitchman	goods	46s.8d	
John Tredgold	goods	53s.4d	(goods, 40s)
Hughe Lambe	goods	20s	
Thomas Childe	goods	£ 6	
Thomas Darsey	goods	40s	
John Dibnam	goods	66s.8d	
John Coke	goods	53s.4d	
John Heyward	goods	£ 6	
John Harres	goods	20s	
Thomas Brakley	goods	66s.8d	
Robert Davon	goods	20s	
Henry Ruddok	goods	20s	
Robert Betell	goods	20s	
William Dace	goods	20s	
Jamys Dace	goods	20s	
John Wardell	goods	20s	
Stephen Warner	goods	53s.4d	
Robert Hubbard	goods	£ 7	
Richard Hubbard	goods	20s	

Richard Austin	goods	£ 7	
John Husshe	goods	60s	
William Frynker	goods	20s	
Jamys Druk	goods	100s	
William Caton	goods	£ 4	
Robert Waterhouse	lands	£ 4	(wages 20s)

Laborers

William Hosyer, jun.	wages	20s
Richard fysshe, alien, maryner	wages	20s
John Morcok	wages	20s
Rauff Parker	wages	20s
Richard Talen	wages	20s
Richard Wardell	wages	20s
William Gayn	wages	20s
Robert Frank	wages	20s
John Auger	wages	20s
William Wryght	wages	20s
John Doughty	wages	20s

The Pryory Ther

Thomas Hedge	wages	20s
Thomas Bredge	wages	20s
John Hosyer	wages	20s
Roger Dey	wages	20s
Richard stephyn	wages	20s
John Leghe	wages	20s

Dame Margarete Reynesford	in goods	£200
Robert walle	wages	26s.8d.
John Hubard	wages	26s.8d.
Marten Couper	wages	20s
John North	wages	20s

The Stok of the trinyte guylde ther in the handes
of William Stoddynghe and Thomas Brakley wardeyns therof   £13

the total amount paid by the community was £20 9s 10d: it is unnecessary
to give the payments made by each individual, as they are easily computed
by reference to the official scale, and so are frequently omitted from printed
editions in order to save space.

The number of individual taxpayers in 1524 was 82, exclusive of the
Trinity Guild which was taxed on its stock, which, as the property of an
association of laymen, was taxable as such so long as it remained with the
guild wardens, and, being money, ranked as personalty. The clergy, both
secular and regular, were taxed separately, the former as individuals, the
latter as communities.

The first and most obvious question to ask is, how complete is this list?

Clearly it by no means included every inhabitant of the parish, for the 65 taxpayers returned in 1525 include 24 who were not in the first list, some of whom, though not necessarily all, might have been newcomers, and the balance of the two returns indicates that more had moved away in the interim. Where certificates of the musters held in 1522 are available, it is found that any single list from the years 1522–5 is likely to fall short of the combined aggregate by approximately one third, and, although the Essex return is no longer extant, it is reasonable to apply this rough yardstick to estimate the male population aged sixteen and above at 120, making some 400 souls all told.[4] One source of uncertainty is soon scotched: here and there the records of a manor yield a good many more names than the return for the eponymous township; however, not only were these units seldom co-terminous, but also the documents deal with entirely different types of people, manorial records being restricted to the tenants, many of whom might, and frequently did, live somewhere else, while taxpayers had to be residents, since the Act expressly stipulated that everybody was to be taxed at his usual place of residence.

II

Composition and completeness are the chief matters to be settled when these returns are used for computing population. We have seen in passing that 5 makes a practical multiplier for converting the number of men listed into total population, conveniently by-passing the problem of attempting separate estimates for the untaxed categories, men below the threshold, women and juveniles.[5] It is prudent to refrain from unwarranted assumptions like the unaccountable one that the assessments were made on families, or households,[6] which raises the unlooked-for complication – and largely unresolvable question – of average family size. The precise wording of the statute, which consistently stipulates the assessment of individuals, makes this quite unnecessary. The only (marginal) exception is that peers and the heads of religious houses were made responsible for their servants' taxes, and might deduct them from their wages; invariably, however, servants and their wages were listed individually, as were those of Lord Marney at Layer Marney.[7] the purpose of this provision would have been either to spare such dignified personages a visit by the common tax collector or to make sure that servants did not slip through the net by being in between jobs, for the assessments were made between Michaelmas and Martinmas, the very season when they were accustomed to change masters. It goes without saying that a good many taxpayers were in fact householders, the more affluent ones in particular, but this is too imprecise to distinguish with any certainty those who were.

The actual taxpayers – men aged sixteen and above – did not comprise the entire adult male population, but only those who reached the threshold of goods and chattels to the value of 40s (£2), although the taxing of labourers and servants on their wages reduced to a minimum the number who escaped assessment. Other than as widows, women seldom owned property in their own right on which they could be taxed. Only a comparatively well-off minority – the superior status of a good proportion of the few who were assessed being recognised by the style 'dame' – cared for this state: a farmer's relict would have been unable to manage without employing a man full-time, and, as this would have meant boarding him, marriage usually became inevitable.

III

Proceeding to consider the kind of community represented by this record, a start may be made by noting that

48 persons were assessed	on goods
3	on land
29	on wages

and even some trained scholars, who should be capable of making a more perceptive analysis, do not progress much beyond this strictly preliminary observation.[8] More significant, and not less obvious, is the division of the return into two main sections, each of which is similarly sub-divided. The longer one, which looks like the parish at large, is followed by another headed 'the Pryory', the first six lines of which corresponds to the sub-section immediately above headed 'Laborers', for all the men in it look like either workers on the home farm,[9] or the community's servants – unlike Cistercians and Augustinians, Benedictine monks did not do domestic chores, but led a gentlemanly existence in which scholarly pursuits filled the hours not set aside for worship. Vowed to poverty, none of the monks of course owned anything on which to be taxed, instead the house as a whole was rated on its income in the parallel clerical subsidy, while the prior settled with the village collectors for the dues of its lay dependents. When it was dissolved twelve years later, the priory's income totalled £83 19s 4d of which £37 14s 3d represented temporalities (land in the normal sense), consisting mainly of the manor of Hatfield itself; spiritualities comprised several rectories, the income of which accrued to the Priory which paid the vicar of Hatfield £10 per year: this and other charges reduced the net income to £60 14s 11½d.[10]

Following a space, left perhaps for the insertion of a sub-heading, the Priory section continued with Dame Margarete Reynesford. A woman in a community of celibate men comes as a surprise; the best explanation is that she was a corrodian, supported for life by the house in consideration of a substantial down-payment, or a contract to will her property to it.[11] the wage earners listed after her were probably her own servants, for, as a lady of rank, she would have continued to live in some state during retirement.

The profile of the village community would be much clearer if all its members, instead than just three fifths of them, were assessed on goods. Everyone, after all, must have owned something in the way of personal and domestic effects. Here fortunately, the 1525 return supplies the value of the goods of the three assessed on land, when one was changed to get more tax from him, although in fact it made no difference to William Frauncey's liability, while it actually cost Thomas Beyll sixpence less. the rule was that only the source of wealth that would yield the largest amount should be taxed, in consequence of which the returns almost invariably ignored untaxed assets, however great their value; an extreme example of this occurs in the 1525 when William Studdynghe, senior, paid ten shillings on £10 in land, while goods to the value of £18 were disregarded because only 9s was payable on them. Rates of tax were on a graduated scale: one shilling in the pound on all incomes from land and on the value of goods worth £20 and upwards, sixpence in the pound on goods less than £20 down to a minimum of £2. Anyone who did not own goods worth 40s, but received wages amounting to at least 20s (£1) in a year, paid a flat fourpence. This, it must be emphasised, was a sort of poll tax, certainly not a rate of 4d in £, as is sometimes supposed. What happened in practice was that some collectors, doubtless with the best of intentions, recorded wages of between 20s and 40s and charged a few pence more, as though pro rata, although most saw no point in entering more than the formal minimum of 20s; others made unauthorised assessments on goods of less than 40s, levying the standard 4d. Doubtless the labourer's goat was inserted in the Act to prevent the many persons who owned nothing at all, revealed by the assessments of 1522 escaping scot free. Nevertheless, in certain parts, notably the wood-pasture region of central Suffolk, the collectors on the ground corrected what they saw as a misapprehension, and made returns which emphasised that the smallholder reigned supreme in this country. Here as in many other parts, although it is tempting to conclude that cottagers, who owned a minimal quantity of goods, were carefully differentiated from men who literally had nothing but their wages, the apparently insouciant mixing of the two terms is more likely to mean a mechanical repitition of 'goods' which was allowed to stand because the amount of tax was not affected.[12]

Now that the rules have been settled, a start can be made on answering the central question, what kind of place was Hatfield Peverel at the time? The distribution of personal wealth promises the best all-round view of the community, not only were most people assessed on it, but there is also enough supplementary information tentatively to fill in the details relating to persons taxed on land or wages. Generally speaking the value of a man's goods and lands were much the same, though the former usually came to be recorded because it was somewhat greater, as a result of the differential rates of tax. As regards wages, it looks much as though no very fine distinction was drawn between them and goods at the bottom of the scale; in any case 20s is a realistic figure for the absolute minimum of moveables likely to have been owned by someone who technically had nothing but wages. Although not, like other assessments, the stock of the Trinity Guild was nonetheless very much part and parcel of the community's assets, for these instutitions, which flourished in very many parishes, were a characteristic expression of the religious aspirations of the laity towards the end of the middle Ages, associations of laymen who subscribed to funds to pay for Masses additional to the parish priest's regular daily quota.[13]

Forming a clear picture of the community requires first of all a semblance of order to be given to this mass of diverse assessments.

Mrs Reynsford's £200, which completely outclassed all others and comprised little short of half the grand total may be left for the moment, if only because an elderly lady living in seclusion in the monastery precincts can scarcely have counted as one of the community.

The principle and practice of the subsidy places everyone else in significant groupings. the primary demarcation can only be £20, the minimum for the higher rate, and clearly differentiating men able to pay a whole shilling in the pound from those of less wealth who paid only sixpence. as £40 was customarily regarded as a significant mark of superior status, and £40-men were called on to pay up in 'Anticipation' of the completion of the assessments, indeed £50-assessments on both land and goods were loaded with a one-shilling surtax in a later year, these should be distinguished, but here, in the absence of such people, the first group comprises the range £20–£39. Below this level the key point is £5, principally as the threshold for the forced loan of 1522–3. which was to all intents a tax sanctioned retrospectively by the next Parliament when it cancelled the Crown's obligation to honour the I.O.U.s given. It makes good sense to divide the long range £5–19 at the £10 point to get the next two groups, £10–19 and £5–9. below this point the loan was not levied, but there is surely some difference between, on the one hand £3–4 and, on the other, £2 which was the threshold for assessment on goods, as well as a very numerous bottom class in districts where there were few or no labourers. Finally, £1, normally on wages, was the assessment for men who owned next to no goods at all. Convenience (as well as realism) may take precedence over strict accuracy in disregarding fractions of a pound for purposes of classification in these two last groups, though of course counting them in group wealth. This simple classification gives a clear view of the distribution of personal wealth:

Group	Number of assessments	Total wealth of group	Percentage of wealth
£20–39	2	£52	17.3
£10–19	5	£63	20.9
£5–9	14	£88	29.2
£3–4	9	£33	11.0
£2	8	£19	6.3
£1	43	£46	15.3
Totals	81	£301	100.0

This of course is not exclusively a tally of individuals' assets, the stock of the Guild formed just over four percent of the community's wealth and a good fifth of the second group's holding, the absence of any of the better sort of gentry makes unnecessary the grouping £40–99, a prominent one in the rest of Essex, and deepens the gulf between Dame Margaret, as the lone representative of the topmost stratum of provincial society, and ordinary village folk. Three-figure assessments were manifestly in a class of their own, even though not subject to a special rate of tax, but Dame Margaret's was the only one in Witham half hundred and there were not fifty in the whole county. Looking beyond the subsidy roll, the valuation of £39 18s 4d made in 1536 justifies an estimate of £40 for the priory' goods; more than half of this represented the livestock on the home farm and corn brought the proportion up to five eights. Debts owed the house totalled £93 6s 8d making the grand total almost 200 marks (£133 6s 8d).[14]

IV

Verification of assessments lead only too easily to a fruitless search for controls; the subsidy act affords no assistance, the most it does is to stress the comprehensive range of property liable to be taxed – all income from land, irrespective of the tenure by which it was held, and every form of personal wealth, including clothing, domestic effects, plate and money, farm implements, livestock and harvested corn, as well as articles of trade; the only exemptions were for outstanding debts, and standing crops which were few because the assessments were made after the harvest.

It is misleading to assume that many assessments were necessarily fraudulent: dramatic allegations of derisory ones made at the turn of the century[15] cannot be considered relevant to 1524–5. In fact from an exhaustive study of early Tudor taxation Roger Schofield has concluded that direct evidence of under-assessment is not strong.[16] An achievement of the reign of Henry VIII, the Tudor subsidy, like most medieval taxes, reached its peak of efficiency at an early stage, and under this formidable monarch's successors became a wasting asset, degenerating to the point at which it had to be superseded. As imaginary difficulties serve only to confuse the real issue, the practical course is to assume, unless it can be demonstrated otherwise, that the assessments were the best obtainable at the time.

Independent checks have to be devised from records made for other purposes and, in most cases, some years before or after the subsidy. The scope for comparison varies with the basis of assessment. Landed property was often valued by an inquisition post mortem after the owner's decease, the short-term stability of land values serving to minimise the effect of the time lag; since, however, a separate inquisition had to be held in each county where he had property, reconstructing total income is no simple process. Feodary surveys, made when a minor became a ward of the Crown, are usually comprehensive and easier to use, besides being generally more reliable, but their provenance is of course contingent upon this accident. Inventories of personal estate, made for probate purposes, so far as they exist, look like the obvious check on goods, but since the value of these was governed by market prices – those of corn, which always formed much of a farmer's wealth, fluctuating widely – and in an age of accelerating inflation the value of a man's possessions when he died was certain to be more than an assessment made some years earlier. In such conditions it is noteworthy as well as reassuring how many assessments are broadly corroborated by inventories, and it is worth emphasising that any discrepancies between two kinds of record, made for entirely different purposes, cannot be held to discredit the whole subsidy: unless malpractice can be proved, the prudent course in general is accept the assessments for what they are.

Wages assessments are simpler. Almost certainly they were based not on actual earnings but on official rates. The regular 20s is in fact almost identical with the 16s 8d, plus 4s for clothing, laid down for a common servant in husbandry by an act of 1515, and higher assessments, up to 33s 4d correspond to the legal rates for senior servants and workmen possessing special skills.[17] These rates were no doubt based chiefly on the price of labour in the home counties, and the proviso that any lower ones operative in other shires should not be exceeded go as far towards accounting for the smaller proportions of wage earners in returns from the more remote regions. The statutory maxima for women were also low enough to keep them firmly below the threshold of taxation. Labourers were probably grouped together the better to distinguish them from servants, and, as in Southwest Essex, 'by the day' might well have been added to the heading,[18] indeed in parts of Sussex, day wages – the annual total of course – were distinguished from the yearly ones paid to servants.[19] This nonetheless made no difference to the regular 20s, even though the standard 4d a day must have aggregated at least £5 in a full year. As servants' money wages were over and above food and drink, labourers' assessments presumably allowed for basis subsistence costs, though 'wages . . . 20s' could easily have become mechanical repetition.

V

Early Tudor subsidy rolls have the advantage of being easy to read. Late medieval handwriting may not look particularly elegant, but at least it does not have to be painfully deciphered, almost all, moreover, are in English, Latin being confined to christian names, which are easily recognisable, and a very few formulae, such as *in bonis* for 'in goods', and so forth. Unstandardised spelling, complicated by the occasional ambiguous letter, may cause uncertainty as to some surnames. but since the persons in question were mostly unimportant this is not serious. Roman numerals are used for money which of course is in the old sterling system pointlessly abandoned in favour of the decimal one a few years ago. The long discontinued denomination the mark, two thirds of a pound, or 13s 4d cannot be precisely decimalised. Among the conventions of the period one shilling is always 12d, and amounts of less the £6 are usually stated as shillings, though with £3 and £5 the practice varied; marks appear expressed as such or in the equivalent £.s.d.[20]

There is nothing esoteric about these subsidy rolls; the only mysteries are those we create ourselves in making groundless assumptions, not least jumping to the conclusion that they misrepresent the facts, whether by accident or design. All that evidence of incorrect assessments on much later occasions can do is to warn us to be prepared to find imperfections in places.

Because taxpayers were not, as nowadays, required to file detailed declarations of their resources, back-checking of assessments is out of the question, and indeed was never envisaged in the first place. County commissioners discharged their duty in full on remitting to the Exchequer the moneys collected accompanied by schedules of taxpayers. If this was only the end-product, the subsidy act states the intention clearly and shows why the returns were cast in the form in which they have come down to us. Any problems arising from sixteenth-century taxes are soluble if only, like the officials who assessed and collected them, we abide by the letter of the law.

Notes and References

1. J. Cornwall, ed. *The County Community under Henry VIII*, Rutland Record Society, Record Series, vol. 1, Oakham (1980).

2. 14 & 15 Henry VIII, c.16, *Statutes of the Realm*, iii, 230–9.

3. PRO, E179/108154, 174.

4. J. Cornwall, 'English population in the Early Sixteenth Century', *Economic History Review*, 2nd ser.xxii (1970), 32-44.

5. Ibid.

6. L. M. Nicholls, 'The Lay Subsidy of 1523: The Reliability of the Subsidy Rolls as illustrated by Totnes and Dartmouth', *University of Birmingham Historical Journal*, ix (1964), 115–21; J. Patten, *English Towns, 1500–1700* (1978), p.99; C. Phythian-Adams, 'Urban Decay in late Medieval England', in P. Abrams & E. A. Wrigley, eds. *Towns in Societies*, Cambridge (1978), p.161.

7. PRO. E.179/108/154.

8. Cf. D. M. Palliser, *Tudor York*, Oxford (1979), p.136.

9. Similar cases are Butley Abbey, Suffs: *Suffolk in 1524*, ed. S. H. A. Hervey, Suffolk Green Books, x, Woodbridge (1910), 134 and Notley Abbey, Bucks: *Subsidy roll for the County of Buckingham, Anno 1524* ed. A. C. Chibnall & A. V. Woodman, Buckinghamshire Record Society, viii, Aylesbury (1950), 41.

10. *Victoria County History of Essex*, iii, 106.

11. M. D. Knowles, *The Religious Orders in England*, iii (1961), 266–7.

12. The most frustrating form of corner cutting is that which reduces entries to the sums paid, from which, except that 4d can only mean 20s on wages, or goods, it is generally impossible to reconstruct the actual assessments.

13. H. F. Westlake, *The Parish Gilds of Medieval England* (1919), *passim*.

14. *VCH Essex*, loc. cit.

15. Cf. J. E. Neale, *Elizabeth I and her Parliaments, 1584–1601* (1957), p. 415.

16. R. S. Schofield, 'Parliamentary Lay Taxation, 1485–1547', unpublished Ph.D. thesis, Cambridge University (1963), p.327.

17. 6 Henry VIII, c.3, *Statutes of the Realm*, iii, 124.

18. PRO, E.179/108/150.

19. PRO, E.179/189/126.

20. The numeral four was invariably iiij, never iv, though ix was never given as viiij. A final i is always written as j which is also the numeral one.

Those Greedy Hunters after Concealed Lands

HERBERT HOPE LOCKWOOD

'The finger of suspicion?'

Assiduous readers of the Rev. Philip Morant's *History of Essex* may occasionally have been a little surprised by the vigour of his denunciations of 'these men, Adams, Tipper and Dawes [who] were hunters after concealed lands'. The last two earn especial opprobrium from that normally urbane writer 'for they appear to have been fellows of insatiable greediness, without a grain of honesty'.[1]

In general, historians have paid little heed to their activities or to the question of concealed lands, although there was hardly a shire in the country that escaped their unwelcome attentions between 1560 and 1624.

But, to date, the only study specifically devoted to the question has been that written by Dr. C. J. Kitching, 'The Quest for Concealed Lands in the Reign of Elizabeth I' in the *Transactions of the Royal Historical Society* for 1974.[2]

It is not difficult to grasp the general meaning of 'concealed lands'. Unprecedented quantities of land changed hands as a result of the Dissolution of the Monasteries in 1536 and 1539, and of the Chantries in 1547. Some of this land was given away by its new owner, the Crown, as a reward for services rendered. A great deal more was sold, initially to those 'already well placed in the social or government hierarchy' who often resold through agents or middlemen. The remainder – perhaps a third of the total – was retained by the Crown and leased out, frequently to the sitting tenants at the same rents.[3] Such was the scale and complexity of these transactions that it is hardly surprising that some property went astray – whether by accident or design. 'Concealed lands' were those properties where the owner

153

or tenant had allegedly 'concealed' the Crown's title and so 'defrauded' the
Crown of revenue in the shape of purchase price, entry fines, rent, or
otherwise.[4]

It was not that the Court of Augmentations (absorbed into the Exchequer
as the Augmentations Office in 1554), which had been established to deal
with the property confiscated from Abbeys and Chantries, was particularly
inefficient or corrupt. But the administration was inadequate at lower levels
where the changes of ownership and the great expansion of Crown lands
had imposed new strains on creaking medieval machinery. Local officers of
the Crown – receivers, bailiffs and stewards of royal manors – owing their
position to patronage, were often inefficient and, to a greater or lesser
degree, corrupt. The Crown, hard pressed by inflation, tried repeatedly in
the late 16th and early 17th century to stir up its agents and to improve the
yield of Crown lands without increasing costs of administration; it failed in
the face of the combined inertia of officials unwilling to do more, and
tenants unwilling to pay more.[5]

Consider for example the situation on one large royal manor in Essex
when the takeover of the Treasury by Robert Cecil (1st Earl of Salisbury) in
May 1608 signalled a fresh and 'herculean' attempt to tighten up financial
administration.[6] The then Chief Steward of Royal Manors in Essex was Sir
Michael Hicks of Ruckholt (Leyton) who had been a private secretary to
William Cecil, Robert's father.[7] The deputy or under-steward, upon whom
the work fell, William Waldegrave, had held his office since 1580, or
thereabouts. His son Paul, who increasingly deputised for him, had
described him as 'very aged and impotent' in 1606.[8] In Barking, a former
Abbey Manor, where he himself lived, manor courts had not been held
regularly for several years and, reading between the lines of the correspondence,
he may have taken bribes from suitors in a hurry to secure a special court.
Almost certainly he had been taking advantage of the very low entry fines
inherited from the Abbey of Barking ('a yeres valew or very nere') to charge
extra to suitors requiring admission to copyholds, pocketing the difference
on the excuse that he was not allowed expenses. He obviously anticipates
the acquiescence of Hicks, 'I doubt the Awdyter will give me allowance for
dyett which yf it pruv trew, allowance must be taken while it lyes in our
power'.[9]

The following year, less than a month after the new Lord Treasurer had
taken office, they received his order to hold courts 'according to the true
custom of the said manor onely' but with one or more Justices of the Peace
present (an unprecedented step). And they were also supplied with a new
'schedule' of fines which was to be shown to the Justices beforehand.[10] And
these drastic measures were followed in 1609 by a new and more thorough
survey of the manor.[11] Yet though JPs attended the next three courts at
least, nothing particularly drastic seems to have happened: fines stuck at
two years annual quit-rent and Paul Waldegrave duly succeeded his father
in the job.[12] In 1612, Lord Treasurer Salisbury died and his office was 'put
in commission'.

The licence given to 'hunters after concealed lands' by the Crown must be
seen against such a background as another attempt – or series of attempts –

to regain lost revenue from Crown lands, by-passing the more official channels. It might be compared to the use of paid informers in a society without a professional police force. One can see why the idea appealed to the Crown and its ministers; public revenue would be increased without public expenditure; the 'hunter' would be spurred on by private greed to secure a public good.

The issue of such licences usually in the form of Letters Patent was well within the scope of the royal prerogative and not subject to parliamentary intervention. The 'hunter' paid the Crown for the privilege, and bore the legal costs of proving individual cases in the courts where necessary. When successful the Crown ultimately regained the land and the revenue, although the 'hunter' was allowed to compensate himself by various means such as a share in arrears of rent and a fee farm for perhaps 60 years (entitling him to a rent charge on the land). Alternatively the patentee might be allowed to lease or even buy the forfeited lands himself on favourable terms.[13]

The most serious drawback was the fear and resentment aroused amongst landholders in particular, by the activities of the 'hunters'. And virtually all ministers and officials were themselves landholders – hence their attitude towards the 'hunters' was often ambivalent. The government tried to meet some of the objections by offering protection to the lands of the church, of educational institutions, and of 'the poor'; but these did not go to the heart of the problem.[14] A constant probing into the titles by which private individuals held their lands when there was only a suspicion of concealment was an inevitable consequence of the process. Indeed by the 17th century the scope of commissions was widened to include any 'defective titles'.

In the case of charities in particular, Dr. Kitching points out that "much of the supposed 'concealment' was wholly inadvertent" in the first place.[15] Moreover as one 'hunter' admitted, 'most of the lands so drawn from the Crown are not in their nor their heirs' possession who committed the first offence, but are since transferred over to sundry persons, purchasers thereof – who albeit that they be faultless, yet must herein be punished . . .'.[16] Worse still, there is little doubt that many alleged 'concealments' were errors or fabrications where the 'hunter', armed with his Patent, threatened legal proceedings, 'thinking by this vexation to drive him to compound';[17] and the victim paid up and bought himself 'a good title' rather than face the uncertainties and legal costs of defending himself.

One of Sir Robert Cecil's correspondents wrote in 1602, 'The chief foundation of mischiefs has been the want of authentic surveys and the preservation of court rolls'.[18] This was of course connected with the shortcomings of local officials already discussed. Here the Barking example was above average. Barking was lucky in having a Court House which had been built in 1567–8 'at the charge of Her Majesty', and the Court Rolls and most of the Surveys were stored in the Record Loft there in a chest with three locks.[19]

But even when the records were properly kept there remained a difficulty; measured surveys accompanied by 'plots' (ie. estate plans keyed to terriers) were a new creation of this period (the Walker surveys in the E.R.O. are excellent examples, but 1586 is the earliest) and still infrequent. So it could be very difficult in disputed cases to decide precisely which existing lands and buildings ('the corporeal hereditaments') were covered by the documentary titles or described by the purely verbal formulae of earlier surveys. These difficulties could prove at least as daunting to the hunter as to the hunted.[20]

Dr. Kitching has illuminated the initial role of courtiers and royal officials – 'by the end of the 1560s licences to seek concealments as a reward for service were well established'.[21] This present article tries to throw more light upon the professional 'hunters' who came into their own in the 1580s. Of these, William Tipper was undoubtedly the most notorious, but the earlier success of the brothers, Theophilus and Robert Adams, in holding the Corporation and Companies of the City of London to ransom created a climate of apprehension and capitulation which Tipper exploited.

Theophilus Adams was born in his parents' house 'near the Weighouse' on the north side of Cornhill and baptised at 'St Peters upon Cornhill' on 12th February 1550. His father was a Mercer but he leased his house from the Grocers' Company who owned the Weighouse, 'where merchandises brought from beyond the seas are to be weighed at the king's beam', together with what Stow called 'a fair front of tenements towards the street'.[22]

I have not traced the baptism of Robert, but he was probably the elder brother; he became a member of the Grocers' Company. There were at least two other brothers, Edward and Alexander. The latter was the youngest; he was rector of East Clandon in Surrey from 1590 to 1620.[23] As Mercers went, their father does not appear to have been particularly wealthy; in 1575, his widow, 'Goodwife Adams', asked the Grocers to assist Alexander as a 'poor scholar' at Cambridge, and back in the 1560s, her husband had been ordered by the Company to repair his house.[24]

It was then that the elder boys had made their first contact with a concealment hunter, when Peter Osborne demanded from the Grocer's Company a lease on their family home which was granted on condition that Adams and his wife continue as occupiers.[25]

The initial task of a 'hunter' was to search the royal records in London – particularly those of the Augmentation Office of the Exchequer – and prepare a list of possible concealments with their annual values, known as a 'Book of Concealments'. But even when the necessary access had been obtained, the costs could be formidable – half a mark (6s 8d) for a search and 4d per line copied – and familiarity with records and procedures was required.[26]

But Peter Osborne as Lord Treasurer's Remembrancer was a senior officer of the Exchequer and their leading expert on procedure. He submitted one Book of Concealments in 1571 and was authorised to produce another in 1574 with a third of the arrears recovered as his reward.[27]

In April 1580 Edward, Theophilus and Robert Adams petitioned to have a lease on reversion of the house on Cornhill 'which their late Mother had', supporting their plea with letters from Secretary of State Walsingham and Sir Christopher Hatton, Captain of the Yeoman of the Guard. Though 'well considered' by the Grocers' Court, it was turned down because the reversion had already been given to another Grocer provided he came to an agreement with Peter Osborne.[28]

It is probable that this request for the family house was connected with the marriage of Robert Adams to Elizabeth Thurland, the widow of Gervase (or, Jerveys) Thurland, in December 1580, since the marriage licence had been applied for during the preceeding year. Gervase, a prominent fellow Grocer, had died in 1577, leaving his wife to bring up an infant son born the previous year.[29]

We do not know how far this incident may have influenced them, but during the next two years it emerges that the brothers had themselves entered the ranks of concealment hunters. Probably their initial involvement was as agents of Hatton, or of Lord Wentworth, or both. Thomas, Lord Wentworth had obtained an extensive grant of concealed lands in fee-farm in 1570.[30] With items scattered throughout the country, a patentee unable to give his full time to the task of pursuing the individual tenants was virtually compelled to use agents, or to sell off parts of his grant to others.

In April 1582 Theophilus linked up with one James Woodshawe to obtain a Patent of Concealments[31] – the latter had had previous experience of such business since, back in 1577, he had presented a claim for a tenement in Shoreditch to the Grocers – bought from an earlier 'hunter', John Farnham, another member of Hatton's corps of 'Gentleman Pensioners'.[32]

The next move must have been concerted with Hatton – now Vice-Chamberlain of the Queen's Household and a Privy Councillor – because within a month (May 1582) the City Companies were subjected to a barrage of claims. Most of these alleged concealments were purely technical and based upon some hitherto unsuspected loopholes in the Chantries Act of 1547.[33] The Companies appealed to the City Corporation for help, and it quickly became clear that the broker through whom they must negotiate in dealing with the patentees or in seeking relief from the Queen and her Council was Hatton himself. He proposed a scheme of arbitration involving two judges and three Privy Councillors to decide the claims. He demanded that the Companies made up their minds quickly 'with as good secrecy . . . as may be', or even this offer might be withdrawn.

Effectively cornered, the Companies agreed to the scheme, acknowledging 'with one consent' Hatton's 'accustomed goodness to the City'![34] By the end of 1583 the two judges had rejected their case; negotiations over the amount of the composition dragged on until 1586 when the City finally settled for the then large sum of £4000. This charge was divided, in proportion to their holdings, amongst the eleven companies chiefly affected; the Grocers for example paid £600, the Drapers £584 and the Clothworkers just under £227.[35]

In the case of the Grocers there was a last minute hitch. Patentee Theophilus Adams, backed by Hatton, now demanded the *freehold* of the former family house in Cornhill as a final condition of settlement. The Company refused, and bought off Hatton by giving him the entry fine of their next tenant – £100.[36] Perhaps Theophilus wanted to revenge his family on the Grocers for previous slights, and perhaps he wanted to live there himself, for in June, 1583 he had married Susanna Coppinger and now had an infant son.[37]

The Grocers for their part had no cause to love the Adams brothers. The minutes of their Court for 11 July 1586 lament, 'This year it fell out by reason this house was put to great and excessive charges in clearing their lands from the pretended title of Adams and Woodshawe no dinner was kept' and they ordered the 16 yeomanry admitted to the livery that year to pay '40s apiece over and above the sum of 23s 4d usually heretofore paid'.[38]

It is not to be supposed that he and his partner were able to share out the £4,000 between them. Apart from 'research' and legal fees, we may be sure that Hatton paid himself well for his part: his biographer E. St. J. Brooks has shown that he had been £10,000 in debt in 1574.[39]

But whilst the City Companies stood at bay, the Adams pack were already flushing out other game. In July 1583 a new patent was obtained on the petition of Lord Wentworth, but in the names of Theophilus and Robert Adams. This grant covered 40 membranes of parchment (i.e. the roll is around 80′ in length), and the properties were scattered over 34 counties.[40] More will be said later about certain Essex items. After a pause, two more Letters Patent were secured. That of 30th April 1587 in the names of Theophilus Adams and Thomas Butler was issued the day after Hatton became Lord Chancellor! That of March 1589 was in the names of Walter Coppinger and Thomas Butler. But there is little doubt that they were all in the same syndicate since Theophilus himself collected an extra £600 from the City in 1589 on the strength of all three grants.[41]

Their favourite procedure when dealing with individual tenants was to convey a new title to those willing to pay and enrol the conveyance in Chancery (on the back of the Close Rolls). The sums paid are never detailed in the agreements, of which about 20 per year were being entered in the name of Adams by 1585. By 1589 a number were enrolled on the day after the Patent was issued showing that many tenants had been investigated and coerced into compounding before the Letters Patent were issued.[42]

Judging from the Patent and Close Rolls, Theophilus and his associates were still busy in the 1590s although leadership in the concealment racket was passing to William Tipper. Hatton died in 1591. Theophilus died in 1608 and one clause in his will speaks eloquently of his cash-flow problems. 'Most humbly I desiring all my creditors . . . to deal mercifully with my said Executors [wife and son] and to have such patience with them as they may have reasonable time to make up moneys to pay my said debts . . . for that the greatest part of my substance remaineth in other men's hands . . .'.[43] Did Theophilus, one wonders, ever heed similar pleas from his victims?

William Tipper (born c.1543), like Robert Adams, was a member of the Grocers' Company. When he served his first writ for concealment upon his own fellowship in 1585 he was already well known, even notorious, for previous ventures.[44] He had also (like Gervase Thurland) been a member of the Fellowship of Merchants trading in Spain and Portugal when they received their charter of incorporation in 1577.[45] But relations with Spain were strained, the once lucrative trade was increasingly hazardous, it virtually ceased in 1585, three years before the Armada, when the Spanish authorities tried to seize all English ships in their ports.[46]

In 1576, with the assistance of Hatton, Tipper had obtained a patent for 'hosting' or compulsory lodging of foreign merchants visiting the realm. This revival of an obsolete medieval practice provoked reaction both at home and abroad. Tipper surrendered it in 1582 and, claiming to have lost thereby, ultimately received another controversial patent for the import of cochineal.[47]

Tipper now entered into a series of negotiations which would lead him into a share in a patent for concealed lands. This had been issued in October 1581 to yet another Gentleman Pensioner, Edward Stafford, who, being in debt, had sold it within a month. Through a series of arrangements it ultimately passed between 1583 and 1585 into the hands of Sir Edward Dyer, courtier poet and diplomatist, with Tipper as his financial adviser and agent. Further patents were obtained in Dyer's name, and Tipper underwrote part of his debts.[48]

In 1588 Tipper also obtained the first of a series of patents in the names of himself and Robert Dawes, and a new flood of enrolments in Chancery began under Tipper's name.[49] Amongst others, the City Companies found themselves in the firing line again; but this time they were anxious to come to terms.

The Grocers in 1591, whilst assenting to a contribution to the City's common fund for the purpose, decided to 'purchase their own peace with Mr Typper'. And they now sought his advice on obtaining a new charter from the Crown which might strengthen them against similar demands in the future; shortly afterwards they announced that Tipper was 'chosen to be added to the new Livery'.[50] In the same year, the Clothworkers agreed to pay him £70 'in consideration of his friendship'. The Drapers only invited him to dinner in 1590 – in 1591 and 1596 they couldn't afford a dinner.[51]

Tipper's star was in the ascendant but by 1597–8 he was running into new problems. The old Queen had grown impatient with Dyer whose debt to the Crown had run into several thousands of pounds and she was threatening to have his lands seized. She had also been provoked by the latest 'Book of Concealments' prepared by an indefatigable researcher, Edward Wymarke. Apparently she suspected the 'concealment hunters' were defrauding her as well as robbing her subjects. So her ministers decided to set up a supervisory body of Commissioners for Defective Titles.[52]

But the powerful Cecil family had a soft spot for Dyer, so Tipper was able to use their influence to turn the situation to advantage.[53] The Commission was appointed in 1600, but Tipper and Dyer were granted a new licence to search for defective titles. And they bought Wymarke's Book of Concealments – on credit of course.[54] The accession of James I in 1603 had little practical effect; Tipper's influence was at its zenith. A substantial part of his income from compositions was now paid through the Exchequer; he could now enjoy the prestige and power of a royal agent.

The Lansdowne MSS contain examples of his long and carefully-penned lists arranged under counties, like that of 2nd Nov., 1607, 'Tipper's note of those who are to appear this Michaelmas term about his business and to compound with the said Commission'. To use Essex examples, it includes aristocrats like Lord Riche and gentry like Humphrey Mildmay.[55]

Sometimes the victims got an unexpected shock, like Sir Gawen Harvey of Marks in 1608 whose title to lands – formerly demesne of Barking Abbey – which his father Sir George had bought in 1582 from Lord Buckhurst, the Lord Treasurer before Robert Cecil, with a warranty of a thousand pounds an acre, was challenged by Tipper (immediately after the Treasurer's death!).[56] Yet we cannot assume that all who compounded saw themselves as 'victims' of the system or of Tipper: some may have regarded the process as a relatively convenient method of assuring titles which they suspected were open to challenge.

It was a lucrative business for Tipper. After the death of Sir Edward Dyer in 1607, still up to his ears in debt, his cousin and heir, Edward Dyer, sued Tipper in the Court of Exchequer for an alleged debt to Sir Edward. The accounts placed before this court throw some light upon the sums involved.[57] The original patents in the name of Stafford and Dyer had provided a gross yield of £7,184 from 1585 to 1606, split equally between them. The composition for defective titles had amounted to £22,136 since 1600, though a large part of this was retained by the Treasury. Legal fees and research had to be paid for – Edward Wymarke had been promised £1,200 in instalments (though none had been paid at the opening of 1602).[58]

Tipper had other sources of income, his 'professional' and social standing was high, he had influence at Court. His progress in the heriarchy of the Grocers was now rapid. He was made an Assistant in 1602, and in 1605 he and his wife were granted precedence at dinners as if he were a past Warden. The next year he presented a grateful company with their new charter, and promised new safeguards for their lands; 'poacher turned gamekeeper' indeed.[59]

So no doubt he claimed part of the credit when in 1607 the first parliament of James I passed an Act for 'scuringe and confirminge . . . the Landes Tenementes and Rentes heretofore graunted' to the Companies and the City of London.[60]

One can deduce from his will in 1613 that William Tipper was enjoying a more comfortable life-style than Theophilus Adams had done.[61] There are legacies to eleven servants, mention of his wife's jewels, and bequests of silver, gilt and crystal tableware.

William died later in the year at his house in 'the parishe of St Andrews in holborne within the Suburbes of London with the little garden next adjoyninge'. His son Robert carried on the family business. With the appointment of Thomas Tipper in 1624 to the post of 'Commissioner for enquiry into defective titles' that business ran into the third generation.[62] But the game was up. That same year which saw Parliament pass the important Act regulating Patents of Monopoly also saw an Act 'agaynst all pretences of Concealments'.[63]

No professional 'hunters' were as successful as the Tippers, or even the Adams – Robert Dawes seems only to have worked in tandem with Tipper and remains a name on legal documents.[64] Their nearest rival was Nicholas Geffe (or Jeff) whom we find in the 1580s and 90s purchasing claims from the Adams syndicate or perhaps acting as their agent.[65] Later he worked for Tipper and Dyer and, claiming that he had been rewarded with £66 instead of the £1500 which was his due, he took action against them in Chancery.[66] He hoped to emulate them by seeking the patronage of Robert Cecil for his own schemes. But in 1604 he was unexpectedly arrested by the Sheriff of Middlesex as a surety for debt. Unable to raise £600 he was held in prison claiming that his adversaries were contriving to keep him there. But whether he meant his rivals, Tipper and Dyer, or some victim who had rounded on his 'hunter' is not apparent.[67]

No doubt there were other concealment hunters who got more than they bargained for. To illustrate this point we must endeavour to follow in sufficient detail a particular hunt in its local context.

The large grant of the 27th July 1583 in the names of Theophilus and Robert Adams has already been mentioned. Amongst a number of Essex items in the Patent, there occurs the following: ' – all lands, tenements and hereditaments whatsoever situated . . . in the vills and parishes of Barkynge, Daggenham, Estham and Westham in . . . Essex once given and appointed for the maintenance of the anniversary of the lady Matilda of Monte Acuto and the lady Joan de Felton . . . within the monastery of Barkynge . . . '.[68]

This seemed to promise rich pickings but to threaten difficulties of identification. Sin in 1584, the Adams brothers sold it to Geffe partnered by an Essex man, Robert Pease of Springfield.[69]

Their appetites may have been whetted by the Patent Rolls from which they, like us, could learn that Joan de Felton had licence in 1398 to alienate to the Abbey 'll messuages, 219 acre of land, 2s 3½d rent'.[70] The Abbey's Office of Pension paid for her, and other anniversaries, so we might look for those properties in the Rental of that office in the 1540 Minister's Account.[71] But they could not be identified without more local information; nor do the 'hunters' seem to have followed that trail anyway.

But between 1586 and 1588 there occurs a complicated series of transactions[72] by which one Peter Palmer of Lincolns Inn (who had it from George Harvey in 1585) conveyed the title of the site and precinct of the Abbey of Barking itself, together with some 41 acres in scattered portions of demesne, to Mark and Thomas Steward. Geffe and Pease, (now 'of Writtle') are made party to these on the premise that their grant had given them an interest in the lands conveyed. In respect of the Abbey site this is plainly false since the Abbey had been there long before the 14th century. And it is dubious in respect of the other lands which were abbey demesne not administered by the Office of Pensions. Significantly this is the same estate that Tipper was to claim against Sir Gawen Harvey in 1608 as noticed above – so the title was still 'defective'.[73]

The interest which Robert Pease had derived from the 1583 grant now passed on to Anne Pease, his wife or daughter (Geffe seems to have withdrawn). By 1607 she had commenced an action against William Nutbrowne in Chancery.[74] William, his father, had been Bailiff and Collector of the Manor of Barking and had built himself a fine new house in

Barking, later known as Wakering Place, which he furnished lavishly.[75] He claimed a freehold title for his house and associated land; but there were doubts about this – the estate was said to be built up partly of freehold and partly of copyhold lands.[76] It was a tempting target for concealment hunting, but the court dismissed Anne's case with costs.[77]

However in 1608 Wakering Place was bought by William Dawes, a London Clothworker, to whom it had been mortgaged. Dawes, doubtful about his title, tried to compound a further claim by Anne by yielding possession of a portion of the estate called the Still House.[78] But by 1609, Anne Pease had married a William Clarke who was determined, or persuaded, to press his wife's claim.[79]

The suit was now revived in the name of the Attorney-General before the Court of Exchequer, and widened to include two other defendants, William Cowper and John Inche. The former, and probably the latter, held some lands which had been part of the Manor of Fulkes and which had passed through the hands of William Nutbrowne senior.[80] This could well be the key to both actions.

Of all the manors of Barking, of which the Abbess was once Lady Paramount, Fulkes is the most elusive. It seems to have begun disintegrating in the 15th century and by the 17th century, the title was like the grin on the Cheshire Cat with only a few fragments of body still visible.[81]

There is no obvious link with the Montague or Felton families or with Clarke's claim. But we know that from the death of Thomas Sampkyn in 1398 until 1539 the manor was held by 'the feofees of Thomas Sampkyn'; although we are ignorant of what properties were included because these were listed on a separate rental kept by the Abbey of which no copies have survived.[82] We also know that Thomas Sampkyn was squire to Abbess Sibyl de Felton (1393–1419), daughter of Joan de Felton, and successor to Maud de Montague.[83] And we know that a chantry in the Abbey with two priests was named after him, but very little else about it.[84] It looks very much as though he may have created a special trust to endow his chantry with the manor of Fulkes – and the failure of documents to survive may be no accident.

The Court of the Exchequer got off to a good start by immediately appointing Commissioners to question local witnesses.[85] The depositions in the case of Wakering Place are far more informative than those in relation to Fulkes – perhaps that interrogatory was inadequate. Most witnesses had heard of a manor called Fulkes, none knew where it was, many remembered Fulkes Barn (which had stood near the junction of Axe Street and Ripple Road). The denial by 80 year old John Sparkes to having even heard of a manor called Fulkes is peculiarly interesting since he had formerly lived in the Old Vicarage in North Street (later called Northbury House) which more recent opinion has been inclined to think was Fulkes manor house.[86] For a man who had been deputy-steward of the manor for over 25 years, William Waldegrave's answers were singularly uninformative – perhaps because he was fearful of implicating himself in anything, perhaps because he was just old and infirm. But his unsolicited comment on Fulkes, 'the same was given for poor maides mariadges (as he hath heard)' strikes one as disingenuous.[87]

The case now began to turn on the issue of access to the manorial records. In June, 1609, the court gave orders that the Manor Court Rolls should be made available for examination by counsel for Clarke and the Crown, and for production in court when required. Specific reference was made to rolls in the custody of Thomas and William Fanshawe esquires.[88]

Nevertheless, in October and November, 1610, the case was twice brought before a jury to try the title by Common Law before the bar of the court, and twice stopped because the prosecution claimed that they could only produce some copies and not the original records they required to prove their case.[89] Following this the Attorney General lodged a Bill of Complaint that records had been concealed or disposed of by Thomas and William Fanshawe, Paul Waldegrave, Thomas Carter and William Dawes. The enquiry that followed in January and February, 1611, produced a sheaf of detailed depositions repudiating the charges.[90] Apart from Dawes (who was not actually accused of holding official records) the persons named claimed to have been legitimately handling the documents in connection with manorial surveys taking place. Clarke was not satisfied for in April, 1611, he obtained leave of the court to examine witnesses in the case of Attorney-General v. Thomas Fanshawe and others, before any one Baron (judge) of the Exchequer. One wonders if this were an attempt to exclude those he thought partial to the Fanshawes.[91]

For what does emerge is the importance in all this of the Fanshawe connection. Thomas Fanshawe of Jenkins was a prominent Barking landowner; he was also Clerk of the Crown on the Kings Bench, and had been appointed a commissioner for surveying the manor of Barking. William was his unmarried younger brother. Their father had been Thomas Fanshawe (d. 1601), Queen's Remembrancer of the Exchequer and the leading authority on the procedures of that court. Their mother had inherited the title to Fulkes and some associated properties. Their half-brother, Sir Henry Fanshawe of Ware Park, Hertfordshire, was the present Remembrancer of the Exchequer (the third of the family in succession to hold that post). So the family combined position in the top ranks of the civil service with strong local interests.[92]

It is plain from the depositions that most, if not all, the original records in question which had not already been returned to the Record Loft were in the possession of Thomas Fanshawe at Jenkins, and Sir Henry at the Exchequer. What are we to make of the Attorney-General's complaint since some of the documents in dispute were being held by a top official of the court in which he was prosecuting his case? Were the Fanshawes really under attack for obstruction or corruption? Or was it chiefly a masquerade put on for the benefit of William Clarke?

Anyway the original case seemed to be running out of steam. It was November, 1611, when the court got around to publishing the last depositions and when, on 20th May, 1612, William Dawes was ready to 'pleade the general yssue', Mr Attorney-General informed the court that he was too busy to attend.[93] This was probably a genuine excuse since it was only four days before the death of Robert Cecil, 1st Earl of Salisbury, the pillar of James 1st's government. But again the case had to be postponed for another term – it was now in its fourth year.

We do not, unfortunately, know the outcome: by 1616 Wakering Place had passed to Sir Charles Cornewallis. But it is certain that later tenants had to abandon the freehold title which Dawes claimed in the 1609 Survey (and which presumably had been invented by the Nutbrownes) for a combination of copyholds.[94] But whether Clarke was able to show that any part of these were encompassed by his patent claims is open to question.

But Clarke appears to have been undaunted by whatever setbacks he received; the prospect was now dangled before him of a 'perfect survey' which could reveal all.[95] True, there had been surveys recently of the manor of Barking, in 1605–6 and in 1609. The former is referred to repeatedly in the 1611 Enquiry; the latter is not, but it was perhaps a revision of the former, and it is still extant.[96] With that proviso, much of the 1609 Survey was based on up-to-date and first-hand information clearly set out. Yet it was still dependent upon verbal description and abuttments. Moreover there were some 23 tenants who failed to come before the jury to show their evidences of title, including several with large estates such as Cranbrook, Clayhall, Porters and Malmaynes. And at least one substantial tenant does not even appear on the 'defaulters' list, whilst Crown leases and fee-farms are mainly unrecorded.[97]

The solution would be a measured survey on the new pattern where each parcel of land with its area would be recorded under its owner, with his tenure ascertained and a valuation made. Theoretically concealment would become impossible and the Crown surveyors could decide how rents and fines could be 'improved'. But the Manor of Barking was thirty square miles in extent – including Ilford and Dagenham. An expensive undertaking. Who would pay? Clarke was informed that he would have to bear half the charge. But Mr Treswell, Surveyor-General of Woods, assured him, 'there wanted £30 of ould rent and two or three woods and lands that he did know which now would come to light'.[98]

A warrant for £60 for Tresswell was issued from the Exchequer in July 1616.[99] The survey was to consist of a 'plot' [a plan] in two parts – North and South – keyed to a 'rental'. The sequel is best told in Clarke's own words in the Petition which he addressed to the King early in 1619, 'which plott being ruffe made by the Surveyors was ready this tyme two yeares and a halfe past and many sittings since by the Commissioners and by reason the officers of ye mannor produced no materiall rentall nor records concerninge ye tennaunts holdings nor no certain rent nor tennure to distinguish Freehould from Copiehould nor Lease have longe delayed and put your Ma'tie to a greate charge of £87 16s and yo'r peticoner £243 4s' which charge ought to be paid by the tenants 'for theire Contemptes to y'or Ma'tie'. He pleads for a new court of survey, and a lease to himself 'before any other' of 'that which shal be found'.

The 'plot' has long since vanished – a pity, because it was the first large-scale plan of this area. But a draft rental, still incomplete, survives as a witness to Clarke's despair.[100] The tenants' names are there with the measured and numbered parcels that they held – even some field names have been filled in – all very useful to the local historian. But the column headed

'Rental' is blank, and the column for the type of tenure is nearly so (there are preliminary notes on this against names in the Index).

Against one item only, on fo.41, of this lengthy terrier a hand emerges from a frilled cuff to point an accusing index finger at a large wood, a grove called Frith hayes of 45 3/4 acres belonging to William Finch. (*see Illustration* p. 153)[101] The view halloa? Game in sight at last? Perhaps.

In the 1609 Survey, William Finch's freeholdings had included Great and Little Frith Heyes totalling 32 acres, but also Cadworth grove and Threefields grove which adjoined, and totalled 14 acres.[102] Suppression of internal boundaries and modification of names being within the rights of a freeholder, there is no obvious concealment. However, another survey appeared in 1617 in which 12.5 acres of 'Frithaies' is revealed as Crown land with Finch as tenant.[103] So it looks as if Clarke scored a hit here; Finch did not lose his tenancy, but he may have had to compound. But that would have been a poor return on an outlay of £247 or more. And one wonders if Clarke realised that not only Cadworth and Threefield groves had originally been bought as fee-farm, but Frith Heyes as well — for such is revealed by the Inquisition Post Mortem on Thomas Fanshawe, their former tenant, in 1601.[104]

The relationship between the 1616 survey and that of 1617 just mentioned is curious. The latter is entitled 'The Surveigh and Admeasurement of that part of the Parish of Barking w'ch lyeth in ye Forrest of Waltham taken by Vertue of his Ma'tyes Commission — AD 1617'.[105] That part of Barking 'within the Forest' was Ilford and Chadwell Heath north of the Romford Road. From internal evidence it was made late in 1617, but still close upon the heels of the 1616 survey. The format is quite different and it is not keyed to a map; but the measurements seems similar though not identical. Presumably it was supervised by Tresswell in his official capacity and he must have found the previous survey greatly simplified his task. As to its purpose — there is evidence to suggest that the information provided was used over the next few years in conjunction with a scheme by the Crown to raise revenue by accusing landowners within the Forest of encroachments by themselves and their ancestors since Domesday, which culminated in the notorious Court of Justice Seat at Stratford in 1634–35.[106]

But all these labours of searching old records and taking new surveys of Barking Manor which took place during the reign of James I were to prove valuable in another quarter. In 1628, Charles I, desperate for money, sold the great Manor to Sir Thomas Fanshawe, to whom it was already mortgaged, for £3,000. In the following years local rumour had it that this was only two-and-a-half years purchase at its true valuation and that the Fanshawes had made certain that they were better informed upon this than the King.[107]

Doubtless the Act of 1624 had put an end to any further hopes that William Clarke may have had left. Throughout one suspects that he had been 'played for a sucker'; victim of the ambivalent attitude of a landowning bureaucracy towards concealment hunters. At least in his case, and that of Nicholas Geffe, their prey might quote the words of the 9th

Psalm 'In the net which they hid is their own foot caught' and moralise on 'God's secret judgement'.[108]

Notes and References

1. P. Morant, *The History and Antiquities of the County of Essex*, 1763 (1816), I, 8, 33; II, 343; Other refs. I, 120, 137; II, 213, 454.

2. C. J. Kitching, 'The Quest for Concealed Lands in the Reign of Elizabeth I', *Trans. Royal Hist. Socy.*, 5th ser., xxiv (1974), 63–78. Henceforth cited as Kitching (1974).

3. C. J. Kitching 'The Disposal of Monastic and Chantry Lands', *Church and Society in England: Henry VIII to James I* (1977), Chap 6., 122 and passim. Henceforth cited as Kitching (1977).

4. Ibid. 125, 132–134; Kitching (1974) 63–66.

5. Kitching (1977) 124–126; Kitching (1974) 65–66; E. Kerridge 'The Movement of rent 1540–1640', *Economic History Review*, 2nd ser. vi (1953); C. Russell 'Parliament and the King's Finances', *The Origins of the English Civil War* (1973), 95–6.

6. E. Kerridge (1953); Russell (1973), 99.

7. *DNB*; J. Kennedy, *A History of Leyton* (1894), 348–349; Mrs Wm. Hicks Beach, *A Cotswold Family* (1909) – she says Sir Michael Hicks (d.1612) is known to have taken bribes; BM Lansdowne MSS 90/63.

8. E 178/841; F. G. Emmison, *Elizabethan Life – Home, Work and Life* (1976), 222; E 112/80/81 (Answer of Paul Waldegrave); BM Lansdowne MSS 91/8.

9. BM Lansdowne MSS, 90/9; 90/60.

10. Ibid. 90/60.

11. LR 2/214; SP 14/37/103; SP 14/37/102 – suggests discovery of concealed lands as well as re-assessment of fines was purpose; BM Lansdowne MSS 91/8.

12. BM Lansdowne MSS, 90/63, 91/61, 91/63; E 112/80/81. An entry fine of two years quit rent was stated to be the true custom of the manor by the jury of survey in May 1609, *Essex Review* LIX, 233 (1950), p.6.

13. Kitching (1974), 67–70; and see below for further examples.

14. Kitching (1974), 70–71, 73, 75, 77: the present essay does not attempt to deal with the various orders and proclamations imposing restriction – most of them proved only a temporary application of the brake.

15. Kitching (1974), 65.

16. 'N. G.' [Nicholas Geffe] to Sir Robert Cecil, *Hist. MSS. Com., Cecil* V, 24.

17. Earl of Pembroke complaining about Tipper, *Hist. MSS. Com. Cecil* XX, 159.

18. Sir Robert Johnson, *Cal. S. P. Dom., 1601–3*, 176.

19. *Trans. Barking Arch. Soc.* 1935–6, 3ff.; E 112/80/81; *Essex Review* LIX, 233, p.5.

20. S. Tyacke and J. Huddy *Christopher Saxton and Tudor map-making* (1980), 46–60; J. B. Harley, *Maps for the Local Historian* (1972), 23–24; F. G. Emmison (ed.) *Catalogue of Maps in the Essex Record Office* (1947), Introduction.

21. Kitching (1974), 68.

22. J. Stow, *Survey of London*, ed. H. Morley (1899), 201, 202; Calendar to the Court Minute Books of the Grocers Company, ed. W. Le Hardy (typescript, c.1930) (henceforth cited as Cal. Grocers) I, 155, 166, 686.

23. Ibid. 546; Edward d.1610 at Reigate and the children of his brother Theophilus were his administrators, *PCC Admins*, ed. M. Fitch (1968) V.s.v.; *Alumni Cantab.* comp. J. and J. A. Venn (1922), 4.

24. Cal. Grocers, I, 434, 150.

25. Ibid. I, 155, 166, 539.

26. Kitching (1974), 70; c.f. Edward Wymarke's Book, Cecil MSS. 53/91, P391.

27. Kitching (1974), 70; *DNB*; Peter Osborne in 1572 wrote a treatise for Lord Burghley which, revised by Thomas Fanshawe, the Queen's Remebrancer, was eventually published in 1658 as *The Practice of the Exchequer Court*, J. Howson, *Fanshawe Family and other Portraits* (1983), 3.

28. Cal Grocers, I, 536, 543, 546.

29. *Registers of Christ Church, Newgate St.*, Tr. W. A. Littledale (1895) – Marriages, 1580, 1575, Christenings, 1576 (Edward, son of Jarvens Thurland); *Allegations for Marriage Licences, Bpc. of London, Harleian Soc.* XXV (1887) 88; *Harleian Soc.* xliii, 190, 1x, 114.

30. *DNB*; Kitching (1974) 68; *Cal. Pat. Rolls 1569–72*, 15 (14 Jly, 12 Eliz.)

31. C 66/1219 m. 28.

32. Cal. Grocers I, 476; Kitching (1974), 68; Gentleman Pensioners were the predecessors of the Gentlemen-at-Arms – Hatton had been enlisted in this corps of royal guards in 1564: he was made Captain of the Yeomen of the Guard – the other corps – in 1572, E. St. J. Brooks, *Sir Christopher Hatton* (1946), 42–43, 58–59.

33. Cal. Grocers I, 576–7, 580, 588, 590–1, 611; Rev A. H. Johnson, *History of the .... Drapers of London* (1915), 202–4; T. Girton, *The Golden Ram* [History of the Clothworkers] (1958), 61–2.

34. Johnson (1915), 204–5; *Remembrancia of the City of London, Analytical Guide*, comp. W. H. and H. C. Overall (1878) (henceforth cited as *C. of L. Rem.*), I, 339, 348, 349, 418, 512; C. of L. Repertories of the Court of Aldermen, (henceforth cited as *C. of L. Rep.*), xx, 325v., 415, 463; Cal. Grocers, I, 611, 623, 656–7.

35. C. of L. Rep. XXI, 1, 249v, 502, 529v,; Cal. Grocers, I, 683; Johnson (1915), 205; Girton (1958), 62.

36. Cal. Grocers, I, 684, 685, 686, 687, 693.

37. Marriage register, St. Stephens, Coleman St., trans. W. H. Challen (typescript, 1932) – 25 June 1583; a son, Theophilus, was baptised on 31 Aug. 1585, and another Theophilus on 25 Oct. 1589 (both at St. Stephens) – so he must have lost his firstborn son, IGI – London and Midd'x.

38. Cal. Grocers, I, 695, 703.

39. Brooks (1946), 221.

40. C 66/1266.

41. C 66/1287; C 66/1328; C. of L. Rep., XXII, 76v. Walter Coppinger was obviously a relation of his wife.

42. H91 – MS Index to Close Rolls; e.g. C 54/1327.

43. PROB 112/103, fo. 346a. One of Theophilus's executors was his cousin, Francis Fuller, whose first wife was a widow, Margaret Redmore, nee Adams. As Clerk of the Estreats in the Court of Exchequer one wonders if he had been a source of useful information. Susanna, widow of Theophilus, died at his home, the Beehive, Ilford, in 1621. (PROB. 11/138; PROB. ACT BOOK 8/19).

44. Feb. 1585, Cal. Grocers, 658; (the claim was to land in Dagnams and Cockerells, a Romford manor v. VCH Essex VII, 66); for Tipper's age, v. C. J. Sissons, *Thomas Lodge* (1977), 47.

45. *Cal. Pat. Rolls, 1575–78*, 317.

46. E. Lipson, *The Economic History of England* (1956), II, 365–6.

47. *Cal. Pat. Rolls, 1575–78*, 71; Brooks (1946) 223–8; *Cal S. P. Dom., 1598–1601*, 368.

48. Kitching (1974), 71–2; C 66/1208 m.26; Cecil MSS (Hatfield Ho.) 186/34, p.415; *Cal. S. P. Dom. 1581–1590*, 48, 101–3, 119.

49. C 66/1319; MS Index H91 shows many Chancery enrolments in name of Tipper from C 54/1288 of 15 July 1588: Kitching (1974), 72.

50. Cal. Grocers, I, 766, 770, 772, 779, II 7, 12.

51. Girton (1958), 65; Johnson (1915), 206, 207, – Tipper even challenged the Drapers' title to their Hall, 209.

52. Cecil MSS 49/46, 53/91, p.391, 186/34; C 66/1310; Kitching (1974), 77.

53. *Cal. S. P. Dom. 1598–1601*, 22, 23; *Hist. MSS. Com., Cecil*, IX, 55, X, 79.

54. *Cal. S. P. Dom. 1598–1601*, 470, 537; *Hist. MSS. Com, Cecil*, XII, 16. Some record material seems to have been paid for by the Commission for Tipper's use, Cecil MSS 123/69, and c.f. that purchased from Susan, widow of Theophilus Adams, in 1610, *Issues of the Exchequer, James I*, ed. F. Devon (1836), 126.

55. B. M. Lansdowne MSS, 169/7. various inducements such as reduced fines and future guarantees seem to have been offered for voluntary admissions of 'concealments', *Cal. S. P. Dom. 1603–10*, 460, 505.

56. Articles by J. E. H. Spaul, *Romford Record*, 4 (1971), 36 and 6 (1974), 33–35.

57. E 126/1, 253; E 124/16, 132; Cecil MSS, P2415.

58. *Hist. MSS. Com., Cecil*, XII, 16 – Up to 1600, Tipper and Dyer spent £2335 on research, legal fees, etc. Cecil MSS, 186/34.

59. Cal. Grocers, II, 272, 280, 295, 307–8, 437.

60. *Statutes of the Realm*, Record Commis. (1819) IV, pt 2, 1133 – Private Act, 4 James I, cap. 10. Larger companies, such as the Grocers and Drapers paid £300 towards the costs, Cal. Grocers, II, 342; Johnson (1915), 85. But even after this fines for defective titles were levied on them, ibid. 85, *C. of L. Rem.* IV, 115.

61. PROB 11/122.

62. *Cal. S. P. Dom. 1611–1618*, 173, 203, 590; MS Abstract of Registration and Appointments, Exchequer of Receipts.

63. *Statutes of the Realm*, (1819) IV pt. 2, 1210–11 – 21 James I, cap. 2.

64. It is just possible that he is to be identified with the Robert Dawes who was father to the William who occurs later in this essay v. below, note (78).

65. e.g. C 54/1174, C 54/1199, C 54/1324, C 54/1530.

66. *Hist. MSS. Com., Cecil* XXIII, 207–8.

67. Ibid. V 25 (a curiously insinuating letter to Sir Robert Cecil signed 'N. G.'), V, 84; *Cal. S. P. Dom. 1598–1601*, 470, Ibid. *1603–1610*, 42, 43, 73; *Hist. MSS. Com., Cecil, XVI, 187, 217, 324*.

68. *C 66/1226 m.3*.

69. *C 54/1199*.

70. *Cal. Pat. Rolls, 1396–99*, 340, 353.

71. *Trans. Barking A. S.*, 1958, passim; SC 6/964 [Item 901 and ff. in the MS transcript, Barking and Dagenham P. L., Valence]; H. H. Lockwood, 'Where was the first Barking Abbey?' *Trans. Barking H. S.*, 1986, pp.12–13.

72. *Romford Record 4* (1971), 36; C 66/1261; E.R.O., D/DU 297/1; E.R.O., D/DB T539.

73. See above p. 160 and note 56.

74. C 33/111. fo.513; C 33/113, fo.336; E 124/11 fo.242 v.

75. E 718/815 – this enquiry of 1580 into 'misdemeanours' in office of Wm. Nutbrowne Snr. shows that he was Bailiff from 1562, had full access to earlier manorial records, and showed a special interest in 'decayed properties'; E 134/7, James I, Eas. 29; P. C. C. Leicester 38. – He died in March 1589. Wakering Place stood on N. side of East Street and is shown on manorial map of 1653 (E.R.O., D/DSa.146) as 'Coblers Hall'.

76. L. R. 2/214 fo.262 [B. and D. P. L. transcript, item 224], Dawes claimed only one (unidentified) acre as copyhold, viz. fo.333 [560]; E 134/7. Jas. I, Eas.29, see esp. the answers to Q.3, Q.5, and Q.9 on Wakering Place.

77. E 124/11 fo.242 v.

78. E 134/7 Jas. I, Eas. 29 Q.13 and Q.15 on Wakering Place and answers. According to the Visitation of London 1633–35 (*Harleian Soc.* XV, 222) the father of William Dawes was Robert Dawes of Long Stratton. I can find no evidence to identify him with Tipper's partner but the possibility is intriguing.

79. E 112/80/81; answer of Thos. Fanshawe; E 124/11 fo.242 v.

80. Ibid.; E 124/8 fo.77 v. – Wm Clarke now had the technical status of 'relator', i.e. informant, with the A. G. as 'complainant'; C2 Eliz. N1/51; E 134/7. Jas. I., Eas. 29. esp. Q.3 and Q.4 and answers on Fulkes.

81. Ibid. and *V.C.H. Essex* V, 203 record most of what is know about the disintegration of this manor after the King had granted it to Lord Chancellor Audley in 1539. Henry Fanshawe acquired the title with his 'moiety' in 1563. The difficulty is to identify the core of the manor before the Dissolution of the Abbey – the Ministers Account includes the enigmatic 'rent of certain lands and tenements in Barking called Fulkes' (SC 6/964, item 856 in the B. and D. P. L. transcript) in the tenure of 'the feofees of Thomas Samkyn'.

82. C 1/8/25, refers to the appointment of feofees to perform the will of Thomas Sampkyn in March 1398. (This vital clue not noticed by V. C. H. or earlier historians); *Trans. Bark. Arch. Socy.* 1937, 32, Abbey rental of 1456; SC6 848/9; SC6/964.

83. E. A. Loftus and H. F. Chettle, *A History of Barking Abbey* (1954), 44, 45.

84. *V. C. H. Essex* V 223, 225, note connection with Sybil de Felton.

85. E 134/7, Jas. I, Eas. 29.

86. Ibid. answers to Fulkes Q.1, Wakering Pl. Qs. 1, 4 *V. C. H. Essex* V, 203.

87. E 134/7, Jas. I, Eas. 29. Fulkes Q.1. note also William Waldegrave's surprising failure to answer Wakering Place, Q.2., 'Whether had the said William [Nutbrowne] ever paid fine for his copyhold lands?' His witness – or lack of it – must be suspect. If Nutbrowne as bailiff had snapped up 'decayed properties' and manufactured a new title, as he seems to have done, the connivance of the deputy-steward would have been indispensable. The answer of John Atkinson to Q.3 adds to the suspicion, 'it [Nutbrowne's great house] was builded where certain tenements did stand which William Waldegrave did pull down'. William died 15 Oct. 1610 – his monument is in Little Ilford Parish Church.

88. E 124/7 fo.251.

89. E 124/10 fo.228; E 124/11 fo.242.

90. E 124/9 fo.191; E 112/80/81.

91. E 124/12.

92. H. C. Fanshawe, *History of the Fanshawe Family*, (1927) passim. On (Sir) Thomas of Jenkins (d. 1631), William of Jenkins and Parsloes (d. 1634), and Joan, their mother, see also C 142/273/104 (but H. C. Fanshawe's statement that Mrs Joan Fanshawe actually lived at Fulkes must be an error). For surveys see E 112/80/81 and LR 2/214. For Thomas, their father (d. 1601) see *D.N.B.* and note (27) above. For Sir Henry Fanshawe of Ware (d. 1616) see *D.N.B.*. Alice, sister to William, m. (1601/2) Sir Christopher Hatton, nephew and heir of the Chancellor of the same name.

93. E 124/13. fo. 161; E 124/14, fo. 141.

94. E.R.O. D/DHS M29 fo.190; C2 Chas. I, 012/48. This shows that James Oyles (alias Jacques Oeiles) was admitted to the house and lands on 15th April 1636 as several copyholds. He made an agreement in 1637 with Sir Thomas Fanshawe, then Lord of the Manor, for fixed fines in future. (The house was demolished before 1680).

95. I have borrowed the phraseology of SP 14/7/102.

96. The 1609 survey, LR2/214 fo.210–351, began on the 25th May and must have

been authorised by SP14/37/103 of 29 Nov. 1608 which commissioned surveys of crown lands in 48 counties. The depositions in E 112/80/81 were taken in Feb. 1611 and three witnesses refer specifically to a survey made in 1605–6. One witness, Thomas Carter, was on the jury of this survey, but not on that of 1609. Two others, Thomas Fanshawe and John Harvey, were Commissioners for both surveys. Yet, very curiously, no witness mentions the 1609 survey. Was there a conspiracy to prevent Clarke from obtaining access to this second survey?

97. LR 2/214, fo.345 [615]. Some missing names and estates can be worked out from later surveys of 1616 and 1617 mentioned below. But the 1609 jury of survey states that commissioner John Harvey took note of the 'farme rents' due to the King out of the manor at a recent survey [1605–6?] 'and the said notes hath carried away with him' – *Essex Review* LIX, 233 (1950), p.3.

98. SP 14/104/49.

99. SP 39/6.

100. SP 14/104/49; E.R.O. D/DHS M29. The ending suggests that Clarke was no longer restricting his search within the limits of the claim obtained through his wife, but was looking for any concealment or defective title.

101. Ibid. fo.41. 'Frith Hayes' lay along the NW side of Blind Lane (now Ashurst Drive) and stretched towards Great Gearies.

102. LR2/214 fo.222 [47], fo.263 [229, 230].

103. E.R.O. D/P 81/3/110 Rear, fo.8. Remainder included in Finch's Gearies freeholding.

104. C 142/273/104.

105. E.R.O., D/P 81/3/110 Rear fo.1. (another copy is E.R.O. D/DHS M29A).

106. SP14/202/17; SP14/202/25; and see *Cal. S. P. Dom. Addenda, 1603–25* 584–91 for similar cases from other forest manors; W. R. Fisher, *The Forest of Essex* (1887), 37–47.

107. H. C. Fanshawe (1927), 233–34. Thomas Fanshawe was knighted in 1624.

108. *Psalms* 9, 15; *Cal. S. P. Dom. 1591–94*, 325–6, 'The small success it brings to the dealers therein, who, but for God's secret judgement, might have been greatly enriched by such grants'.

New College, Oxford and Its Hornchurch Estate, 1391–1675[1]

MARJORIE McINTOSH

Like all absentee landlords in the medieval and early modern periods, New College, Oxford found it difficult to supervise its estates effectively. In order to maintain its landed income, the college had to fight constantly against the efforts of local people to profit at its expense. It had to keep detailed records and be willing to take legal action against it tenants and leaseholders when necessary. It needed also to display its presence within estates scattered among ten counties. College officials travelled to the properties once each year, but the rest of the time local bailiffs represented the college's interests. Gaining an appropriate income from its property was a particularly severe problem in Hornchurch, Essex. There the college's tenants enjoyed unusual enonomic privileges as residents of the royal manor of Havering, within which the Hornchurch lands lay.

In this paper we shall examine the relation between New College and its Hornchurch estate from the acquisition of the property in 1391 until 1675. We may first define the components of the estate and consider how the college oversaw its lands and esslesiastical rights between 1391 and 1659. We draw here upon the documents preserved in William of Wykeham's Muniment Tower at the college.[2] The second part of our discussion is based upon a more personal source – the detailed notes kept by Michael Woodward, warden of the college from 1658 through 1675. Woodward's account of his annual 'progresses' to Hornchurch and his searches through the college's old records make vividly clear the obstacles which New College faced.

A. The Hornchurch Estate and the College, 1391–1659

The formation of the Hornchurch estate began in 1158/9, when King Henry II gave *c.* 1500 acres near the village of Hornchurch to the Augustinian hospital of St Nicholas and St Bernard at Montjoux in Savoy.[3] This land henceforth supported a small religious community called Hornchurch Priory. Hornchurch lay within the royal manor and later Liberty of Havering (-atte-Bower).[4] The church of St Andrew's in Hornchurch village was the mother church for the parish of Hornchurch, coterminous with the manor of Havering. The parish also included a chapel in the market town of Romford and a tiny chapel in the smaller village of Havering-atte-Bower. The church of St Andrew's with its tithes and other income was given to the priory by Henry in 1163, joined in 1177 by the chapel in Romford. A century later the priory agreed to provide a priest for the chapel in Havering-atte-Bower. Hornchurch Priory remained in possession of the

Hornchurch estate, both the land and the ecclesiastical rights, until 1385. The property was then confiscated by the crown. During the later 1380s William of Wykeham, Bishop of Winchester, made arrangements to purchase the estate. With the completion of the transaction in 1391, Hornchurch became part of the original endowment of Wykeham's College of St. Mary at Oxford, better known as New College.

New College was the lord of *c.* 1860 acres in Hornchurch. Although this land was located within easy reach of the lucrative London consumer market, the college found it impossible to collect a suitable profit from it. Most of the property (*c.* 1130 acres) was held in 1391 by tenants who gave a fixed, customary payment to the college for their rents and commuted labour services. Because the tenants were protected through Havering's status as a manor of the ancient royal demesne, the college was allowed neither to raise their rents nor to demand new services.[5] The most which the college could hope to gain was the full worth of their traditional payments, valued in 1391 at £19 17s ½d. Nor was it an easy matter to gather in this sum. The tenants worked assiduously to withhold or obscure their obligations, and if they managed to avoid a payment for a period of years, the college had little chance of recovering it. In the very first annual account, the Hornchurch bailiff reported to the college that he was unable to collect 15s 5½d in rent payments and 68s 4d from commuted services.[6] By 1481 a backlog of £280 18s ½d had accumulated.[7]

In theory New College had more opportunity to benefit from the remaining 730 acres.[8] These were the demesne lands, held in the college's own hands. Hornchurch Priory had used the demesne for direct farming, hiring servants to work the arable fields and tend the animals. For the first generation after Wykeham's purchase, the college continued this practice.[9] Soon, however, the drawbacks of demesne farming became apparent. It was difficult to supervise the operation from a distance, and the crop yields from the badly depleted Hornchurch fields were low whereas wages were high during the century after the 1349 plague. The alternative was to lease out the demesne, a decision made by the college in the early 1420s. Most of the land was granted in three large units rather than in smaller batches. This reduced the number of people from whom the college had to collect rents and created holdings attractive to substantial local people.

Leasing the demesne could have been financially advantageous if the college had raised its rents to keep up with inflation and the growing demand for land within London's vicinity. It did not, however, do so. The rectory or parsonage of Hornchurch was leased initially in 1421 for a term of three years at an annual rent of £24 6s 8d.[10] Although the rent was later increased slightly through the addition of extra land, the base value remained permanently unchanged.[11] The rent of the (sub)manor of Suttons likewise became fixed almost immediately at a value of £22.[12] The rent of £22 13s 4d for Risebridge, a holding in northern Havering, followed a similar course.[13] New College was in fact legally free to adjust its rents upwards. Yet when it did not do so, both local people and the college itself came to believe that the leasehold payments were frozen as a result of Havering's ancient demesne status.

In addition to its role as landlord, New College had a series of religious rights and duties as proprietor of the parish of Hornchurch. The college collected the tithes from the entire manor of Havering, covering 16,000 acres.[14] While the Hornchurch demesne was being farmed directly, the college took in the tithes itself.[15] Once leasing of the demesne began, the great tithes were granted out together with specified holdings of land – those from the southern part of the parish along with the rectory of Hornchurch and those from the northern section with Risebridge.[16] The small tithes of southern Havering were at various times divided between the farmer of the rectory and the vicar of Hornchurch, while those of the northern region went to the farmer of Risebridge and/or the chaplain in Romford. The college also received 'the profits of the altar', the gifts and oblations of the faithful. Ecclesiastical income was of considerable value: tithes and oblations accounted for more than half of the yield from the estate in the mid-fourteenth century.[17] But, because the college included the religious income within its leases, this profit went entirely into the hands of the college's lay leaseholders and clerical appointees.

As proprietor, the college had to provide a vicar for the church in Hornchurch village plus chaplains to serve in Romford and Havering-atte-Bower. For the vicarage at Hornchurch, the college signed a formal contract with a priest or minister, specifying that he was to hold office on good behaviour for a stated number of years in return for some combination of a salary, allowances of grain and cloth, and part of the small tithes.[18] The vicar normally named a secondary priest and a clerk to assist him in Hornchurch. During the first few generations after 1391, the college hired a chaplain for Romford, using a contract similar to that with the vicar but less generous in its provisions.[19] Thereafter the Romford chaplain was named by the vicar, the college having the right of removal. His support came originally through tithes, but by the seventeenth century the parishioners of Romford chapel were supplementing the salary of their minister in return for a strong voice in his selection.[20] The college was supposed to maintain a curate for Havering-atte-Bower, named by the vicar.[21] In some periods, however, there was no resident chaplain, and services were conducted instead by a lay reader or the minister of another church within the parish.

The clergy of Hornchurch parish were seldom men of distinction. Prior to the 1490s, most of the vicars were men about whom nothing is known.[22] Thereafter the college commonly named one of its own graduates. Although some of these men had distinguished careers, many were either nonresident in Hornchurch or pluralists with commitments outside the parish.[23] Until the later sixteenth century, the secondary priest at Hornchurch and the chaplains at Romford and Havering-atte-Bower were poorly educated and poorly paid men. Nor did the college do much to make places available to Hornchurch boys who wished to have university training. Between 1396 and 1696, only eight boys from the parish entered the college, all between 1428 and 1530, and just two of them received degrees.[24]

New College tried to protect its ecclesiastical jurisdiction and rights within Hornchurch. Several disputes arose over the relation between the three churches. The earliest concerned the supremacy of St. Andrew's,

Hornchurch over the chapel at Romford. Here New College was concerned to maintain the dominance of the mother church because it wanted to ensure that people living in the northern part of the parish continued to render their tithes and oblations and to contribute toward repair of St Andrew's church.[25] By the late fifteenth century, those who attended Romford's chapel of St Edward were behaving like an independent unit, electing their own chapelwardens and collecting rates for repair of the church and to support a parish clerk.[26] In the late 1520s, Romford's wardens refused to pay the sums demanded of them by Hornchurch, arguing that they supported their own services and building. Both sides agreed to submit to the arbitration of six men, including the warden of New College, who ruled that henceforth the parishioners of the northern section of the manor were to pay the set sum of 26s 8d annually to the churchwardens of Hornchurch, unless St Andrew's suffered catastrophic damage.[27] In the 1590s a parallel dispute erupted between Romford and Havering-atte-Bower. The people who worshipped in the chapel of St Mary began to choose chapelwardens of their own and refused to pay rates to Romford.[28] Romford took the matter before the church courts in 1603, finally obtaining a favourable verdict. Havering-atte-Bower people were ordered to pay rates to Romford and to receive communion there at Easter.

New College also became involved in several legal controversies concerning the right of ecclesiastical supervision over the parish. It has traditionally been stated that the college enjoyed full legal control over Hornchurch, which was said to be a 'peculiar' jurisdiction belonging first to Hornchurch Priory and then to the college.[29] However, the medieval evidence from Hornchurch does not accord with this account. Early records show that the parish was supervised in normal fashion by church authorities. The bishop of London acted within Hornchurch prior to 1391, and after New College's acquisition of the estate the archdeacon of Essex held an annual visitation of the parish and proved local wills.[30] Yet the legal situation was not entirely clear, for as early as 1427 there was a complaint from Hornchurch to the court of Canterbury against jurisdiction wrongly claimed by the archdeacon.[31] In the mid-1520s, the college and its farmer of the rectory of Hornchurch refused to pay fees owed to the archdeacon for his visitations, on the grounds that he did not have the right to oversee the parish. This led to an exceptionally complicated series of legal suits which extended until 1532.[32] The matter eventually went to arbitration: two canon lawyers granted the right of ecclesiastical jurisdiction and visitation of Hornchurch to the archdeacon. The archdeacon agreed to respect the rights of New College as proprietor of the parish. This decree was soon forgotten by both parties, and in Elizabeth's reign the college began once more to claim rights of supervision.[33] By 1610 the archdeacon said that he acted within Hornchurch on behalf of the college.

In attempting to maintain its income and rights in Hornchurch, New College used several modes of control. Once each year the warden and several other college officials visited the estate in person to meet with local leaseholders, inspect the college's possessions, and hold a session of the Hornchurch manor court.[34] During the rest of the year the college was represented by its bailiff or rent collector, chosen from among the prosperous tenants and leaseholders on the estate.[35] The chronic inability of the bailiffs to collect all the rents nominally due to the college suggests that they were unwilling to scrutinize the rent-rolls too closely or to push their neighbours too hard. Another vehicle by which the college might have been able to force compliance was the manor court, convened by the college's steward and attended by all the tenants. In practice, however, the Hornchurch court was of minimal use to the college. Unlike the powerful court of the royal manor of Havering, held in Romford every three weeks, the college's court met infrequently – not more than three times per year in the fifteenth century and just once per year from the 1490s onward.[36] The uncooperative tenants sworn as jurors at the Hornchurch court provided little useful information to the college about land transfers or matters of public interest, and the court generated little financial profit.

New College thus failed to tap the true wealth of its Hornchurch estate. Against its effectively stagnant income it had to set expenses for salaries, repair of buildings, and such obligations as maintaining 500 feet of the wooden pale around the royal hunting park at Havering-atte-Bower and 1000 feet of the great wall which separated Hornchurch marsh from the Thames.[37] The 'valors' prepared by the college reflect the virtually static yield from Hornchurch. An account made before Wykeham's purchase of the estate showed a net annual profit of £89 7s 3d.[38] In 1487 the net profit was £91 2s 9d, and a century later it was still only £94 2s 11d.[39] Since the college held 840 acres in its demesne by the mid-seventeenth century and possessed tithes valued at £800, this income constituted a pitifully small share of the actual value of the estate.[40] Local people, on the other hand, were in a position to reap abundant reward from the land which they held from the college as tenants or leasees.[41]

B. Warden Woodward's Progresses, 1659–1675

We gain a more lively sense of the administrative problems faced by New College from the progress notes of Warden Michael Woodward. Woodward was born in Salford, Beds. in 1602 and entered Winchester College in 1613.[42] Matriculating at New College in 1621, he took his degrees of B.A. in 1625, M.A. in 1628, and D.D. in 1660. After his election to the wardenship in 1658, Woodward worked to restore discipline within the college and to improve its financial situation after the difficulties of the Civil War period. He was described by a contemporary as a 'dull and heavy man'; a more politically committed witness scorned him because he 'cringed to the late times and was a man of no spirit'.[43] Modern historians of the college prefer to speak of his personal dignity and his diligence in supervising the college's estates. He died of 'apoplexy' in 1675.

Woodward maintained the tradition of making annual progresses through all the estates of the college. Unlike his predecessors, he kept extremely detailed notes of everything he did and learned while on his progresses.[44] Between his travels he searched through the college's records for information which he could use during the following year's progresses: comments in his distinctive handwriting are found in the margins of many of the documents today. Woodward's visits to the Hornchurch estate occurred usually in April or May and lasted from two to four days. He was accompanied each year by a fellow of the college who served as outrider, by the steward of the college's estates, and by several servants. The company normally came to Hornchurch from Writtle, travelling next to London. While in Hornchurch, Woodward stayed in a room in the parsonage, reserved to the college's use.

Woodward entered into his administrative role with vigour, demonstrating immediately a businesslike, hardheaded approach. He demanded that the college's leaseholders in Hornchurch prepare for him a detailed 'terrar' describing each subunit of land. He inspected in person the buildings belonging to the leaseholds. If they were in poor condition, he refused to approve renewal of the lease until they had been repaired. After hearing that one of the leasees planned to make over his lease to his son-in-law, Woodward jotted a memorandum that this was 'a cunning fellow, & must bee fast bownd or otherwise some way or other, hee will deceive us. Bee carefull of it in the renewall of the Lease.'[45] Woodward had to operate largely on his own, for neither the bailiff of Hornchurch nor the manor court provided much assistance. Woodward regarded each of the three men who served as bailiff during his wardenship as untrustworthy, more concerned to make a profit from the lease of land which accompanied the office than to represent the college's interests. The manor court, convened by the steward in Woodward's presence, was not much better. Few tenants attended – just three men in 1665 – and Woodward was seldom able to use the court to enhance the college's authority.

Woodward examined each aspect of the Hornchurch estate. In trying to enforce full payment of the customary rents, Woodward took several recalcitrant tenants to court, but none of these suits ever came to trial. Woodward was hampered by lack of clear information about what rents were actually due. Although the college's records were safely preserved in the Muniment Tower, they were not indexed or even well listed. Consequently, both the college and the current tenant of a holding might be unsure of what the original rent had been. In 1661, for instance, Thomas Legatt and the bailiff came before Woodward and the steward with a disagreement over rent. Legatt claimed that he owed only 7s annually, while the bailiff said 12s 8d. When the steward looked into the 'old Booke of Court rolls', he found an entry from the eighth year of James I showing that the tenant had paid just 7s. There the matter would have ended under most wardens. Woodward, however, began to search for information about this holding in the college's records when he returned to Oxford. In 1665 he discovered an entry stating that although the simple customary rent for Legatt's holding was indeed only 7s, it owed a further sum of 5s 8d for commuted labour services. Unfortunately, the latest reference to this sum which he could find was 1623, and any payment which had lapsed for more than 40 years was virtually impossible to reinstate. As late as 1673

Woodward was still trying to collect the full rent of 12s 8d, but his effort was in vain.

The leaseholds presented different problems. Because their rents had become fixed, the tenants (and the college) found it easy to forget that they were not freeholds. In 1665, after a productive winter of digging through the records, Woodward brought to the attention of John Lenthall, the bailiff, 'some Lands, that were ancyently in Lease for yeares but now pay only Quitrents, as freeholds'. Lenthall pointed out 'that much of our Lease hold Land is lost, & now they, after soe long discontinuance cannot bee recovered'. When a tenant held a piece of leasehold which adjoined his own land, he might be tempted to shift the boundaries of his unit over onto the leased land. In one case the tenant of an alehouse extended the end wall of his building by about 8 feet, encroaching upon his leasehold from the college in order 'to widen his roome, to entertaine the bowlers'. Woodward was particularly annoyed when he learned that Lenthall himself had taken in some of the college's ground. Woodward rode out to the land and observed that the bailiff had indeed placed his fence hedge a foot or two onto the college's property. Woodward gave a curt order 'to sett his hedge where it should bee, . . . my Selfe being sworne to maintaine what is ours, though Mr Lenthall bee not'. Lenthall was soon replaced as bailiff.

With respect to the college's ecclesiastical position, Woodward first addressed the question of tithes. Here he found great confusion and loss of income. After several years of working through the college's records, he noted in 1664: 'Memorandum to aske at Hornechurch, God willing, at our next Court there, who hathe the Tyth Hay ancyently . . . demised to the vicars of Rumford'. After citing descriptions of tithes from northern Havering mentioned in documents from 1369–70 and 1384–5, he continued, 'Our farmer of the Rectory hath only the Tythes of the Southend, our vicar only the small Tythes, & in Risbrigg Lease what was anciently demised to the vicar of Rumford is excepted, who therefore enioyes them?' Inquiry revealed that although some of the tithes were given to the minister at Romford, others were no longer being rendered. Woodward encouraged the farmers of the rectory and Risebridge to consult with the college's legal counsel, Master Sergeant Richard Holloway, about going to court to recover the tithes. Two years later Woodward delivered an abstract of the records concerning Romford's tithes to the farmer of the rectory, but nothing more is heard of the matter. Presumably Holloway advised that their suit was impossible.

Woodward had also to deal with the appointment of clergy for the parish. Hornchurch was not an issue. The vicar throughout his wardenship was Michael Well, M.A., fellow of New College from 1649 to 1658, incumbent in Hornchurch from 1658 to 1685, and a man acceptable to Woodward. Romford, however, posed problems. Here a long dispute over the selection and payment of the curate challenged the rights of the college and the vicar. In 1659 the inhabitants of Romford, 'weary of standing to the courtesie of the Vicar of Hornchurch or of the College it selfe for provision of their Minister', tried to obtain independent status.[46] When their appeal to the

Committee for Plundered Ministers failed, they decided to proceed through an act of Parliament which would have established Romford as a distinct parish. New College was, of course, bitterly opposed to the proposal, and its legal counsel worked to accomplish its defeat. In 1663 Woodward himself became involved. He had just finished his dinner in Hornchurch when 'there came some Rumford men unto mee, with one Mr Pecke their Minister, & did desire, that I would confirme him in his place. I told them, that without Mr Wells, I should doe nothing'. Woodward then had a series of conversations with the vicar about why he refused to name Pecke to Romford chapel for more than one year at a time. Wells initially justified his uncooperative stance by complaining that Romford people paid to him only £10 annually, whereas they gave nearly £90 to their own minister. After a night's thought he added that (1) he was afraid that if the parishioners of Romford paid Pecke a stipend only, rather than tithes in kind, the tithes would be lost to the college, and (2) if the curate at Romford had an ongoing appointment, he would be dependent only upon the college, not upon the vicar.

In responding to this controversy, Woodward began with a strong defense of the rights of the college and its vicar. He told the Romford men that he would maintain both 'to the uttermost', adding that 'a Chappell of Ease should not have a greater allowance then the mother Church. The Salary of a Curate is £50 per Annum, & more then most Parsons can make of all the rest, & why should a Curate (because it is a Market Towne) have more then the Vicar?' After this opening, however, Woodward proposed a compromise. He agreed to approve the regular appointment of a minister for Romford if the parishioners would prepare and accept a detailed record of the tithes due from their region, and if the curate of Romford and the parishioners would acknowledge that the curate was under the vicar. In addition, Woodward took the opportunity to clarify a further set of issues involving the relative positions of Hornchurch, Romford, and Havering-atte-Bower. He stipulated that Romford should agree not to make themselves 'a Parish distinct from Hornechurch, as they seem to have done by their late perambulations, & marks in Trees that were never there before'. Romford was also to cease infringing upon the rights of Hornchurch by auditing the churchwardens' accounts of Havering-atte-Bower and allowing the burial of Havering-atte-Bower people in its churchyard. Although these conditions were accepted at the time, in the long run Woodward's attempt to halt the growing religious independence of Romford and Havering-atte-Bower proved unsuccessful.

Woodward also entered into a tempest in a teapot concerning secular jurisdiction. This conflict set the authority of the Hornchurch manor court against the court of the manor of Havering. The episode began in 1668 at a session of the Havering court, when those living in the Hornchurch region asked that a cage, stocks, and whipping post be installed in their village. At present, such facilities were available only in Romford, and the Hornchurch constables 'knew not what to doe with Vagrants or Fellons . . . till they could bring them to the Justice [of the Peace]'.[47] The following year the high constable of Havering was ordered to set up this equipment speedily in

Hornchurch; in 1670 the jurors reported that the cage, stocks, and whipping post had been erected in Hornchurch street 'in the most convenient place as is thought fitt by the officers & inhabitantes'. Unfortunately, the cage was situated in an awkward location. At the Havering court held in the spring of 1672, Edward Thorowgood, New College's bailiff acting here in a private capacity, led a complaint 'that the said Cagge stood not in a conveneint Place & that it hindred the passings & carts (the place being soe narrow)'. The Havering court ordered that a group of men should view the cage and try to find a better place to set it.

Now Woodward became involved, for reasons which are not entirely clear. Apparently he felt that the Hornchurch court at its View of Frankpledge should have control over all public matters within the village. In any case, he decided that the cage was an affront to the jurisdiction of the college's court and should come down. In his notes for 1672, Woodward commented, 'Mr Thorowgood had gott an Order to pull downe the Pillory-house in the Street, but none of the Parishioners would ioyne with him: & besides some other were ready there with Holbeards [halberds] to oppose any that should pull the house downe'. In each of the next two years, Woodward instructed the steward to tell the Hornchurch manor court that the cage, pillory, and stocks must be removed.

The issue came to a head in 1675. Woodward and his company arrived in Hornchurch at 5:00 in the afternoon of Friday, April 30. Woodward noted at once that the pillory and stocks were still standing in the highway. The next morning the steward convened the Hornchurch court. He complained to those present 'that the Kage, where the Stocks are, was not pulled downe, not withstanding that hee had often warned them of it'. The jury evidently excused itself by saying that the Havering manor court had decided to leave the cage where it stood. Woodward was outraged at the suggestion that the Havering court had greater authority than did the college': 'I told the Homage that our Customes & Priviledges here were equall with the Kings, by an Evidence out of Doomesday Booke: for the reading of which, & turening it into English, I sent for Mr Wells, who read it to them in English'. One would like to know exactly which section of Domesday Book the vicar read, for there is no mention of the Hornchurch estate in that document, nor does it speak of any special rights pertaining to Havering. The next afternoon, after the Sunday sermon, the college's outrider and steward met with Robert Prujean, William Rame, and other leading figures in Hornchurch. The latter promised that they would hire a carpenter to take down the cage the following day.

Monday morning began ominously. Several of the college's leaseholders came to the parsonage to warn Woodward and the steward that a group of people opposed to the removal of the cage had gathered outside. The steward ignored this, sending orders that the cage should come down. When there was no response, 'Mr Outrider ... & Mr Steward went downe themselves & caused some part of the Kage to be taken downe'. A crowd of at least forty people looked on as the outrider, his servant, and the hired carpenter tackled the cage. As soon as the demolition began, several Hornchurch men rode to Romford to alert Carew Hervey *alias* Mildmay, one of the Justices of the Peace for the Liberty of Havering. They obtained a warrant from him 'to bring all such as riotously endeavord to pull downe the Kage before either him, or some other Justice of the Peace'. Mildmay was clearly frightened by the report of violence, describing it as 'a great Brech of the Peace, *ad Terrorem Popula*' and writing himself notes about the punishment stipulated for rioters.[48] The warrant was delivered to the high constable of Havering, who promptly arrested those at work on the cage. The outrider and his servant, accompanied by the steward and several of the college's leaseholders, were taken to the home of Captain Thomas Cheeke, another of the Havering Justices. Cheeke 'used them very Civilly', agreeing that he would himself inspect the cage, '& if it stood soe inconveniently in the high way, as they sayd, & might stand in another with more convenience, hee wold Order the pulling of it downe'. Woodward died six weeks later, and our detailed information ends. We know that the cage was replaced but whether on its original site or in a less inconvenient place remains obscure.[49]

By the end of his life, Warden Woodward's attitude toward the supervision of the Hornchurch estate had lost its crusading edge. In part this was a purely personal change, due probably to his increasing age. In his early progresses he focused entirely upon the business at hand, mentioning no interludes with congenial people or other diversions. By 1670, however, Woodward had come to enjoy the non-working aspects of his progresses. Since he was now in his late 60s, he was surely entitled to a less demanding schedule and to such welcome luxuries as travelling to London by 'the Hornechurch Stage Coach' rather than by horseback. With Vicar Wells, Woodward shared some moments of intellectual companionship. In 1671 they discussed the origins of the name Hornchurch. Wells reported that he had seen a seal of 'the Monasterie of Mount Joy in France' which displayed an ox- or bulls-head with horns, suggesting that 'the said armes were putt upon the church (or the Chancell at lest, as belonging unto them) & soe called Hornechurch'. The following year Woodward paid a call on Wells at the vicarage, as he 'was troubled with Piles, & could not ride'. There the vicar showed Woodward the scholarly project on which he was engaged, a translation of 'the Historie of Tamberlen', arranged 'in 2 Columes in each page, the Arabique in One, & Latine in another'.

Woodward also took increasing pleasure in the 'entertainments' provided for his company along the way. He described with enthusiasm a repast in Greenwich after leaving Hornchurch in 1670: 'wee were treated with Cherry from the Grape, with Ale, Claret, a faire Westphalia hamme, & some Pickled Oysters sent from Scotland.' In 1673 he recorded with pride that he had dined at Writtle with Lord and Lady Petre. Woodward likewise became more tolerant of recreations. In 1671 the outrider and a companion stopped off during the ride from Writtle to Hornchurch to bowl with Lord Petre and Sir John Bramston at Ingatestone. Although they were late in arriving in Hornchurch because the game lasted longer than they had expected, Woodward did not seem annoyed. In his final progress, he received an unexpected visit from Mr Barret *alias* Lennard, an old friend who 'used at Winton College to walke with mee to long Hills'. After they had dined together, some fiddlers came to the parsonage, and Barret asked 'whether I would suffer the young people to daunce, & whether it would not displease mee'. Evidently to everyone's surprise, Woodward approved the request, 'and soe for the afternoone they fell to daunceing'.

Woodward's changing attitude must also have been affected by the scant success of his labours. The college had not recovered any customary rents or tithes, the leaseholders were still enriching themselves at the expense of the college, and the current bailiff was just as unsatisfactory as his predecessors. Woodward may well have concluded that his initial zeal and those long, cold hours spent pouring over the records of the college had not been worth the effort. In retrospect, it seems clear that no warden could have overcome the obstacles which prevented the college from profiting fully from its Hornchurch estate. The difficulties which confronted any absentee landlord, magnified here by the unusual privileges of the tenants, prevented even the most determined and knowledgeable administrator from enlarging the college's income and rights. Woodward's final stance was perhaps the most sensible approach: to make an honorable effort to sustain the college's position but to seek satisfaction in pleasant entertainments.

Notes and References

1. The author is grateful to the Warden and Fellows of New College and to the County Archivist of Essex for permission to cite records in their collections.

2. The records are admirably catalogued in F. W. Steer, *The Archives of New College, Oxford*, Oxford, (1974).

3. M. K. McIntosh, 'Hornchurch Priory, Essex, 1158/9–1391', *Revue Bénédictine*, XCV (1985), 111–129. Another 360 acres were later given to the priory by the local laity.

4. M. K. McIntosh, *Autonomy and Community: The Royal Manor of Havering, 1200–1500*, Cambridge, (1986), *Victoria County History of Essex* (henceforth *VCH Essex*), VII ed. W. R. Powell, Oxford, (1978), and A. V. Worsley, *Hornchurch Parish Church: A History* Colchester, (1964).

5. M. K. McIntosh, 'The Privileged Villeins of the English Ancient Demesne', *Viator*, VII (1976), 295–328. For below, see New College, Oxford (henceforth NCO) MS 9744, fol. 186r–v.

6. NCO MS 6386.

7. NCO MS 6476.

8. The size of the demesne grew gradually after 1391 through addition of customary holdings which escheated to the lord.

9. McIntosh, *Autonomy and Community*, ch. 4.

10. NCO MS 9654, fol. 205r. The lease included a house and *c*. 250 acres, a stock of 22 horses, cows, and pigs, some farming equipment, and the great tithes from southern Havering.

11. Later leases are in NCO MSS 9654 and 9757–67, *passim*.

12. NCO MS 9654, fol. 247r–v, and MSS 9757–67, *passim*. The Suttons lease included *c*. 350 acres plus a house, barns, dairy house, and 191 horses, cows, and ewes.

13. Risebridge comprised a barn, *c*. 70 acres, 63 cows and sheep, and the tithe of grain and hay from much of the northern half of Havering (NCO MS 9654, fols. 53v–54r, and MSS 9757–67, *passim*).

14. The original papal bull approving Wykeham's purchase of the estate from Hornchurch Priory had specified that the college must appoint a perpetual vicar to serve at St. Andrew's; he would necessarily have received the small tithes (*Hornchurch Priory: A Kalendar of Documents in the Possession of the Warden and Fellows of New College Oxford*, ed. H. F. Westlake, London, (1923) [henceforth *Hornch. Pr. Kal.*], #311–12). In 1398, however, the college obtained a revised bull freeing it from this obligation (*ibid.*, #315b, misdated as 1498).

15. E.g., NCO MSS 6386, 6399, and 6421.

16. Leases of land from 1400 through 1675 are recorded in the college's White Book and the *Registri Demissiones ad Firmam*, vols. 2–12, NCO MSS 9654 and 9757–67.

17. NCO MS 9744, fol. 186r–v.

18. Contracts with clerics are recorded in the *Registri*, note 16 above.

19. E.g., NCO MS 9654, fol. 46v, and *VCH Essex*, VII, 83.

20. Public Record Office (hereafter PRO) E 317/Essex/13; Essex Record Office (hereafter ERO) D/DXa 31 and ERO T/A 521/1, p. 71.

21. *VCH Essex*, VII, 23, and NCO MS 2551. For the absence of a curate, see M. K. McIntosh, *The Liberty of Havering-att-e-Bower, 1500–1620* (forthcoming), ch. 4.

22. A list of the clerics for each of the three churches/chapels is given in App. D. of McIntosh, *Autonomy and Community*.

23. McIntosh, *Liberty of Havering*, ch. 4, and the list of clergy in App. E.

24. Andrew Clark, 'Early Essex Wykehamists', *Essex Review*, XVI (1907), 173–5.

25. When the original chapel in Romford was replaced in 1410 by a larger building adjacent to the market, the new chapel had its own burial ground but the parishioners were still required to support St Andrew's (*VCH Essex*, VII, 82).

26. ERO T/A 521/1, reverse folios, PRO C 1/1146/43–9, PRO SC 2/172/40, m. 25, and ERO D/AER 2, 26.

27. Their award is NCO MS 4592. By the early seventeenth century Romford had given to Hornchurch a piece of land, the income from which replaced the cash payment.

28. McIntosh, *Liberty of Havering*, ch. 4.

29. Worsley, *Hornchurch Parish Church*, p. 12, and *VCH Essex*, VII, 46.

30. For the bishop's role, see *Hornch. Pr. Kal.*, #237, 142, 137, and 21, and NCO MS 9744, fol. 153r; for the archdeacon's visitations, see, e.g., NCO MSS 6400, 6449, and 6476, and *Hornch. Pr. Kal.*, #366; wills are ERO D/AER 1 and D/AEW 1, *passim*.

31. NCO MS 10880 (= *Hornch. Pr. Kal.*, #231).

32. NCO MS 4593 (= *Hornch. Pr. Kal.*, #212–26), PRO C 1/624/15, and C 1/642/41; McIntosh, *Liberty of Havering*, ch. 1.

33. NCO MS 3425 (from 1574). For below, see PRO KB 29/252, m. 36.

34. NCO MSS 6386, 6421, 6449, and 6476.

35. McIntosh, *Autonomy and Community*, ch. 4, and NCO MSS 2548 and 2577.

36. The rolls covering 1391–1675 are NCO MSS 3732–9, 3746, and 936; a microfilm copy of the first set is available at the ERO, T/A 168/2 and 3. For the Havering court, see McIntosh, *Autonomy and Community*, ch. 5.

37. For the pale and wall, see McIntosh, *Autonomy and Community*, chs. 4–5, and *Liberty of Havering*, ch. 2.

38. NCO MS 9744, fol. 186r–v.

39. NCO MSS 2577 and 2551.

40. *VCH Essex*, VII, 32, and PRO E 317/Essex/13. In 1650, the vicar of Hornchurch received £55 from the small tithes, the minister of Romford £45, the minister of Havering-atte-Bower £20, and lay leasees the rest.

41. For Havering's prosperity, see McIntosh, *Autonomy and Community*, chs. 4 and 6, and *Liberty of Havering*, ch. 2.

42. For biographical material, see R. L. Rickard's introductions to *Progress Notes of Warden Woodward for the Wiltshire Estates of New College, Oxford, 1659–1675* ed. Rickard, Wilts, Archaeol. and Natl. Hist. Soc., XIII, (1957) and *The Progress Notes of Warden Woodward Round the Oxfordshire Estates of New College, Oxford, 1659–1675* ed. Rickard, Oxfords. Rec. Soc., (1949). Rickard also edited 'The Progress Notes of Warden Woodward, 1659–1675, and Other 17th Century Documents Relating to the Norfolk Property of New College, Oxford', in *A Miscellany*, Norfolk Rec. Soc., XXII, (1951), pp. 85–115.

43. See Rickard's introductions, note 42 above; for below, see *ibid.* and *New College, Oxford, 1379–1979* ed. John Buxton and Penry Williams, Oxford, (1979), pp. 57–8.

44. In 1949 R. L. Rickard transcribed Woodward's notes concerning Hornchurch from the original copy at New College (NCO MS 3548, pp. 3–127). Rickard's transcription, now at the Essex Record Office (T/A 92/1), has been compared by this author against the original and found to be accurate. Woodward did not go to Hornchurch in 1666, 1668, or 1674.

45. NCO MS 3548, p. 9 = ERO T/A 92/1, p. 8. Woodward's abbreviations have been extended here. Subsequent quotations from his notes will not be individually referenced.

46. NCO MS 2936.

47. ERO D/DMs 037, sheet 3. The following account is based upon D/DMs 036–7 and Woodward's notes.

48. ERO D/DMs 037.

49. *VCH Essex*, VII, 8.

'Dear Betsey': Reflections on two letters from the First Carlist War

IAN ROBERTSON

Of all the kinds of documents in our archives, surely the most familiar is the personal letter. From the eighteenth century onwards the number surviving is substantial, written on every conceivable subject – business letters, love letters, begging letters, threatening letters, letters of condolence, and so on.

While collections of letters have attracted the interest of the historian and have been published in full or in summary, the individual letter, especially of the nineteenth century, has been somewhat neglected, very often being collected for its postal or philatelic interest rather than for any other purpose, unless, of course, the author has been famous, or the contents particularly exciting.

However every letter is a product of its times and the local historian may seek by analysis of form and content to use it as evidence. Before the introduction of the 'Penny Post' in 1840[1] the carriage of letters could be expensive (depending upon distance travelled) relative to other costs, including both wages and prices; therefore correspondents, however brief their letters, wrote for a purpose and the local historian should seek to determine what that purpose was. The question should also be asked as to whether the letter relates to any national or international event or is in response to a statutory requirement. If the letter is simply the exchange of family news, then does the latter throw any light upon the social position or particular circumstances of the group in question?

The way in which the letter has been carried is worthy of consideration; postal history is not simply a matter for the specialist but is part of the social life of the times and may provide information of use to the local historian. Finally the question has to be asked as to why the letter has survived – is there anything about it which has caused it to be preserved? Often letters have been retained because they have acquired a quasi-legal significance as evidence or justification of a claim, or, at the other end of the scale, simply because they remind one person of the love of another. Frequently some of the most helpful information to the local and family historian is not contained in the body of the letter, but rather in the notes that someone else has made on it by way of elucidation or comment.

To demonstrate the argument let us take, for example, two letters, dated 26th March and 16th September 1836, signed by 'Your Loving Husband Geo McKay, Bugle Major, Queen's Own Rifles B(ritish) A(uxiliary) Legion St. Sebastian, Spain'. Both letters[2] were addressed to his wife Elizabeth McKay – 'My dear wife' or 'Dear Betsey' – who was then living 'Care of Mr. Jas. Harridance, Boot and Shoe Maker, High Street, Maldon, Essex'. Both letters give graphic accounts of life during the First Carlist War, but before quoting them, it is helpful to ask what Trumpet Major McKay was doing there in the first place.

The answer lies in that recurrent theme of modern European history, the problem of the succession to the throne of Spain.[3] The particular cause of the fighting which broke out in 1833, and which George McKay describes in his letters to his wife in Maldon was the fact that King Ferdinand VII (born in 1784 and King since 1808) on his death in 1833 left a daughter Isabella (1830–1904), a Queen aged three, by his fourth marriage in 1829 – the only union which produced any children – to Maria Christina of Naples, who was Queen Regent on behalf of her daughter from 1833 until 1840.

The right of Queen Isabella to the throne was challenged by Don Carlos (1788–1855), the elder of the two surviving brothers of Ferdinand VII, on the grounds that the Salic Law, barring the succession of females, introduced in 1713 by Philip V, was in force at the time of his birth in 1788, and therefore, the Pragmatic Sanction of 1789, in which Charles IV restored the medieval rights of women to succeed, post-dated his birth and could not cancel his claim. The matter was further complicated by the fact that the Pragmatic Sanction of 1789 abolishing the provisions of Salic Law was kept secret and the terms not fully published until March 1830 by King Ferdinand under the influence of his wife, the effect of which was, of course, to prevent Don Carlos from ever becoming king even if the expected child of the Queen was a daughter, as indeed proved to be the case with the Infanta Isabella being born on 10th October 1830.

Apart from the purely legalistic arguments of the matter the First Carlist War[4] demonstrated a certain polarisation in Spanish politics which was to be evident well into the twentieth century. In very broad terms the cause of Queen Isabella had the support of the populace, the proponents of parliamentary liberalism and anti-clericalism, while Carlism can be associated with absolutism, the assertion of the rights of the Catholic Church and the royal interest. In particular Carlism was strong in northern Spain, especially in the Basque Provinces and Navarre where the maintenance of traditional rights of autonomy was perceived as being threatened by a liberal centralising government in Madrid.

The attitude of the British Government to events in Spain was very much determined by Palmerston, the Foreign Secretary in Grey's, and Melbourne's First and Second, Administrations, indeed for the whole period of this Carlist War except for Peel's First Government of December 1834 to August 1835. Given that there were Pretenders to both the thrones of Portugal and Spain threatening instability in Western Europe, Palmerston promoted the concept of a Quadruple Alliance, signed in London on 22 April 1834 between the constitutionally governed states of Great Britain, France, Spain and Portugal, under the terms of which the Regents of Portugal and Spain were compelled to remove the Pretenders from their Countries. Palmerston's tactic was to commit France to working with Great Britain in support of Spain and also to draw her into an alliance in the west which would serve as a counterpoise to the 'Holy Alliance' of the absolutist East European states of Russia, Austria and Prussia.

While the problem of Don Miguel in Portugal was speedily settled to enable the Queen Regent to carry out the terms of the Quadruple Alliance, a British Naval force, including Royal Marines was sent to Northern Spain and under the terms of the Foreign Enlistment Act of 1819 permission was given by King William IV for the formation of a volunteer British Legion to fight against the Carlists in Spain.

It was General Alava, the Spanish Ambassador in London, strongly supporting the Queen Regent, who raised with Palmerston in June 1835 the feasibility of the raising of a force of ten thousand British volunteers to fight in Spain against Don Carlos and it is he who offered the command to Colonel George de Lacy Evans, the Peninsular War veteran and radical M. P. for Westminster. Great speed was made with the arrangements for on the 10th July the first detachment of the British Auxiliary Legion had arrived in San Sebastian in Northern Spain. Although supporting the liberal constitutional allies of the Queen Regent had obvious attractions for the Whig establishment, there was considerable opposition especially from the Tory Press and the personal attitude of King William IV appears to have been ambivalent, as indeed was that of the Duke of Wellington. While some of his Tory colleagues declared for Don Carlos, Wellington was not enamoured of the prospect of a Spanish Government based on a fanatical Catholicism nor indeed for Don Carlos himself whom Wellington was later to describe as 'one of the silliest devils I ever knew'.

As Palmerston made clear the British Auxiliary Legion was not part of the British Army, and could not drill in England; although weapons and other material were drawn from the Tower of London, pay was a matter for the Spanish Government. The full strength of four hundred officers and 9,600 men were on one or two year contracts.

While this background information may seem the most complicated reason why any man has ever written to his wife in Maldon from Spain, its recapitulation establishes the important point, not self-evident from the contents of the letters, that George McKay was a mercenary, although by enlisting in the service of the Queen Regent he was not acting illegally as a British subject in that under the terms of the Foreign Enlistment Act of 1819 service in a foreign army was permissible provided it was sanctioned by the Crown.

As we are concerned with George McKay and his family in Maldon it is not part of our task to retrace the course of the First Carlist War which ended in victory for the Government forces, although not in the defeat of Carlism.[5] Nor is it part of our task to expatiate upon the problems of the British volunteers fighting in Spain, including illness and indiscipline. For our purposes it is sufficient to note the verdict of a recent historian: 'In spite of its obvious deficiencies the Legion was a useful reinforcement for the Cristinos at a time when their own armies were discontented and under strength. Though the 'filthy and ragged' legionaries had no great victories to their credit they at least helped to prevent the Basque Provinces from falling entirely into Carlist hands, and apart from their unhappy experiences at Oriamendi and in the first attempt to take Fuenterrabia they appear to have fought reasonably well. Their two years' service in Spain may be regarded as having made a small contribution to the success of the Queen Regent's armies.'[6]

Turning now to the contents of George McKay's two letters to his wife, it is worth noting that although correspondence from members of the British Auxiliary Legion has been published before, the letters have always been those of officers;[7] because he does not belong to this class, and because, so far, he is the only mercenary in the First Carlist War known positively to have been domiciled in Essex, George McKay's account of his small part in the campaigns is of interest.[8]

Although the first detachment of the British Auxiliary Legion had landed on the 10th July 1835, McKay's first letter is dated the 26th March 1836 and written in San Sebastian. After having noted that he had received his wife's last letter when in Vitoria, which he left on the 12th March, he arrived in San Sebastian on the 24th. While on the ship *Donna Isabella*, on the 23rd March 'on our Voyage here we had one man of our Regt. killed and likewise one Sailor likewise a Nother Sailor wounded . . .'. This happened because ' we fell in with some of the Carlist boots having troops on bord when we gave them four shots from too 24 punders and then manned the Boots when that these cowardly Rascals took to the mountains and played at our Boots when the above whare Killed we Captured too of the Boots I can assure you that since we have been in this Country we have been very much Harried about and doing nothing I have been extended in the front of the Regt. with the Advance but never properly engaged I have had one Narrow Escape A Shot fell about a yard from me we have had the misfortune to lose a few of our men.' The above is typical of McKay's breathless unpunctuated style with idiosyncratic spelling and use of words. He continues: 'I must noe Decline for a few moments as my Ration of Wine is just come in only one pint. I just now commence again after eating of a piece of Irish Pork as it Salt provision that we have had these 2 days one pound of salt beef yesterday and a pound of pork today with ½lb of Bread.'

McKay then harks backs to the serious problems encountered in Vitoria, to which the British started their march from Bilbao on the 29th October of the previous year. Aggravated by the poor weather, inadequate quarters, bad food and wine, what came to be known as Vitoria fever[9] set in; this was a variety of typhus, which frequently began with dysentery, and which took a substantial toll of the British troops, encouraging others to desert.

Of this period McKay notes: 'During the stay of the English in Vittoria we lost a great many English as their was not the least chance of a man when he whent into Hospital of ever coming out again where 2 Bakers executed in Vittoria just before we commenced our march for putting in Poison into the Bread that they made for the troops so you must not be surprised at us losing so maney men.'

Returning to the present, having noted that his inkstand had been knocked over the thereby caused the 'Blauch' still visible on the notepaper, McKay continues: 'Whilst wrighting to you our Guns are playing on the Enemy, as this place is fortified something like Portsmouth so I will leave you to guess . . . I am almost stunned with Cannon Drums and Bugles as the(y) are almost continuously going . . . I have not seen anything of Cox lately But he is not marching with the Regt. . . . my Dear Betsey you Ask me in your letter when that I think of comeing home that is more nor I can tell you As I do not See any more likelihood now nor their was the first day we landed tell the Children if the Almighty thinks propper that I should return again to old England that I shall bring them something home, their is plenty of Everything in this Town But money is scarce with the British Legion.'

Coming now to George McKay's second letter which is written from 'Outpost Alza Near Sebastian 16 Septr. 1836', we find him writing: 'I have seen maney ups and Downs and most heavy marches and have felt the Clemency of the Weather and likewise I have been in Action with the Enemy and have Been Continually in front of the Regt. and thanks be to god not a Hair of my head has been hurt. The time that i am writing the Great Guns are firing on the Left at the Carlists and the(y) are making Brest works Quite Close to us, we are very familiar and too much so as maney a Rascal deserts his ranks in the Supposition that they will be sent through france to England I have had 2 Buglers Deserted to them one took my Bugle with him and is now in Hinani (Hernani), for my own part i Converse with them But Never goes amongst them when our men goes a foraging. But I am General Interpreter as i speak the french and Spanish Language. I have Just Come of from a Brigade parade on the Sands Near St. Sebastian we was there 2 Hours since then I have drunk my wine and eat some Cold pork and Bred I Love Plenty to eat and more than I Can make use of as I Allways draw from the Stores my Selfe having that Priviledge as Bugle Major . . . I dare say you would grin if you was too see me in front of 3 Regts. with a Notorious Large Pair of Whiscars and Mustachos But Hold Age is creeping on Grey Hairs they say is Honourable and the Bald Head . . .'.

It is often the case that correspondents frequently tell us inadvertently as much about themselves as the events they endeavour to describe. For instance it would not be difficult to guess that McKay was a former member of the Regular Forces of the British Crown; he has a clear belief in discipline, including self-discipline; he is proud of his bearing and appearance; and like the old soldier he is he eats well and makes sure that he has plenty in hand; he appears to enjoy his soldiering, although he is aware that he runs the risk of death and is grateful to be alive.

However, McKay feels he is getting old and the second theme of these letters is the degree to which he misses Betsey and his family. One way in which this concern was expressed was his fervent desire for letters from home. George begins his letter of the 16th September to Betsey in this way: 'I embrace this Oppertunity of wrighting to you hoping you and my dear Children Vidz Daniel Harriett is well as this leaves me in most Excellent Health Dear Betsy I can Assure you that i feel very uneasy and have felt for a Long While in my not Receiving a Letter from you your Last was dated on the 21st. Ja'y, and I Did not Receive it untill the Latter end of Feby and that Whilst i was at Vittoria which I Answered. . .' He had indeed — he is referring to his letter of the 26th March; in other words when he wrote on the 16th September he had not heard from his wife since the end of February.

Because George McKay was so concerned about the length of time it took for him to hear from his family, it is worth considering the ways in which the two letters travelled from Spain to Maldon, Essex.[10] The first was written in San Sebastian, being dated 26th March 1836, and bears a handstamp of 'S. SEBASTIAN' in a red oval. The handstamp 'ESPAGNE PAR/ST. JEAN-DE-LUZ', unframed, was subsequently applied also to the front, indicating that the letter had been transferred from Spain and into France via St. Jean-de-Luz on the coast road. A small handstruck '2' was received in Bayonne indicating a two 'decimes' charge, a 'decime' being a standard French charge.[11]

The final addition to the front is a manuscript '2/7' from the British Post Office of which two shillings was Foreign Postage, namely the sum which after the French Post Office had taken its share, (ie the 2 'decimes') would be accounted for by the French to the Spanish Post Office. It is probable that the letter would have travelled in a closed bag from Spain to Paris and on to one of the Channel Ports, from thence it would have been transported to England arriving in the Foreign Post Office, as the circular transit stamp shows, on 13th May 1836.

The letter was then transferred to the General Inland Post Office on the same day, as the second circular transit stamp proves. The F.P.O. and the G.P.O. were two separate organisations but were located within the same building in Lombard Street at this date. Finally came the journey from London to Maldon, for which the final 7d of the 2/7 was charged, the receipt of the letter by Mrs. McKay some forty-eight days after her husband had dated it in San Sebastian.

However, that is not the end of the story because it was the recipient, in this case Mrs. McKay, who had to pay the two shillings and seven pence. It was to be another four years before the prepaid adhesive stamps came into use – the 'Penny Black' 'Twopenny Blue', and Mulready envelopes and letter sheets came into use on 6th May 1840 – although the use of prepaid stamps did not become compulsory until 1853. To pay 2/7 on receipt of a letter was to find a substantial sum, when it is considered that Charles Hicks, farmer of Great Holland in the Tendring Hundred of Essex, noted in his Diary[12] that in 1830 one of the convicts sentenced to transportation at Chelmsford for rioting came from Great Holland, had had all the best work at the Hall for some years and was then earning 15s per week and beer'. Hicks also noted that the 'Average of flour for the year 3s. per peck Wages 11s. per week and beer'. However, pay the postage required, Mrs. McKay did indeed do.

The method of travel of the second of Trumpet Major McKay's letters to Maldon was different; whereas the first one had gone from San Sebastian to Maldon entirely through the postal services of the Countries concerned, the markings on the second letter demonstrate that it was handled differently. Headed in McKay's hand: 'Outpost Alza Near Sebastian 16th Sept. 1836', the letter has only two stamps, a step-type 'PORTSMOUTH/SHIP LETTER' which would have been applied when the captain of whatever vessel carried the letter, (probably directly from San Sebastian as there are no San Sebastian or French hand stamps) handed it into Portsmouth Post Office. The vessel was not a Post Office Packet as that would have been indicated by a different handstamp, but would have been a private sailing vessel outside the Post Office's direct control. It was subsequently stamped again when the letter was received by the G.P.O. in London on 27th

September, only eleven days later, for onward transmission to Maldon, substantially faster than the previous time taken. There are two manuscript rate marks, a '1/4' deleted and a correctly calculated '1/5'; ie 8d. 'ship letter charge', (4d. was taken by the Post Office and 4d. went to the private ship's captain who delivered the letter to Portsmouth Post Office); the remaining 9d. was for the inland postage, computed by the mile, for the carriage of the letter from Portsmouth to Maldon via London. The one shilling and five pence would, of course, have had to be paid by Mrs. McKay, but this letter was both cheaper and arrived faster than the earlier one.

George McKay was obviously concerned about the cost of the postage, not least to himself, as he would have had to pay on receipt also in Spain and in his letter of 16th September he writes to his wife: 'When you write your letters to me Direct them to Colonel Weathershole No 5 Freemasons Court London and post them under Cover and they are sure to Come free.' Under this arrangement it would have still have been necessary for the Colonel to pay the postage on the letter to him from Mrs. McKay, but no doubt he had arranged a bulk shipment of letters to the soldiers in Spain which would represent a great saving in cost. It is interesting that the Soldiers' Penny Concessionary Rate introduced in 1795[13] and used by troops in the Peninsular War[14] did not apply because the Carlist Wars were not ones in which the United Kingdom was officially involved; in other words the troops serving were not part of the British Army and were paid by the Queen Regent's Government. Sailors and Marines on British naval vessels did however get the benefit of the concession.

Apart from urging his wife 'to let me have a letter in return', or 'write directly', the other way in which George McKay indicated his concern for his family and friends was to list them in some detail. In his first letter he hopes that his wife and children are well, and from the second letter we learn that the latter are called Daniel and Harriett. Then also in the first letter are those people to whom he wishes to be remembered: 'When you write to London give my love to Elizabeth and I trust she is well and in good health and tell her I shall write to her when opportunity admits. . . give my love to Lucy and I hope and trust that she is a good Girl and I hope that I shall have the pleasure to hear at my return to old England which I hope will not be long that she is a good girl. Give my love. . . to George and I trust he is well, at the same time give my respects to John Saward likewise Hannah and hope they are well. . . My respects to Mr. and Mrs. Spurgin Harris, Likewise Mr. and Mrs. Brown likewise Geo. Joseph Wm. and James and to Hannah Cracknell and to her Intended perhaps they are married by this time if so their Wedding Cake whas not good enough as I never Cooked it. Give my love to your Brother James and Wife and I hope they are Well likewise the children and i am glad that your Brother Henry as Being to Kind. . . I had forgott Wm. Wheeler hope he is Well Give my Respects to Mr. Br-br-ge likewise Mrs. B. and family and to all Enquiring friends and the Blessings of the Almighty rest upon you and family so no more from your loving Husband Geo. McKay Bugle Major The Queen's Own Rifles B. A. Legion St. Sebastian Spain. Give my love to my dear Children and Accept the same yourself. Adieu, Adieu, farewell let me have a letter'.

It may well be that McKay had not long left Maldon when he wrote the letter in March for he is clearly at pains to mention everyone; by September, however, apart from hoping Betsey and the Children are well, the long list of relations or friends has been reduced to: 'Give my Respects to All Enquiring friends not forgetting Sayward my love to your Brother Jas. and family Likewise Mrs. Ross and I hope they are all well So no more at Present from Your Loving Husband Geo. McKay. . .'

The expressing of 'love' and the paying of 'respects' are not uncommonly found in letters of the period, but the listing of names in the manner of George McKay may seem of no particular significance to the reader a century or so hence. But it is worth looking more closely; at first sight it seems odd that the one person omitted would seem to be James Harridance, the Boot and Shoe Maker in Maldon High Street to whom McKay sends his letters for his wife.

However the only person specifically mentioned in both letters is his wife's 'Brother James and family'. We may infer that Elizabeth McKay was born a Harridance. From this it follows that her 'Brother Henry as Being so Kind' is Henry Harridance, who is clearly a man of some importance in Maldon by the time of the publication of the first edition of William White's *Directory*[15] in 1848. Indeed while no James Harridance appears at that latter date, the family is clearly part of the Maldon bourgeoisie: Samuel Harridance is a Baker in the High Street, while Henry Harridance appears as a Corn Merchant also in the High Street, with Harridance and Wright as a company following the same trade at Fullbridge in addition to being Ship Owners; Henry is the representative of the Essex Economic Fire and Life Office and an Alderman of the Borough.

Some credence is given to the suggestion that George McKay had married into the Harridance family of Maldon by a perusal of the Parish Registers of the Borough.[16] From these may be established a chronology of the relevant part of the Harridance family, who are given as residing in St. Mary's Parish, as follows:-

a. Samuel, son of William and Mary, was baptised on the 6th February 1780.

b. Elizabeth, daughter of William and Mary, was baptised on the 4th February 1787.

c. James, son of William and Mary, was baptised on 18th April 1790.

d. Henry, son of William and Mary, was baptised on the 17th January 1796.

Unfortunately no record of the presumed marriage between George McKay and Elizabeth Harridance has yet been found, but it is possible to trace the growth of their family from the All Saint's Parish Register, thus:-

a. George, baptised on the 9th September 1818: father's occupation given as labourer.

b. John, baptised on the 1st June 1821: father's trade given as tanner.

c. Daniel, baptised on the 28th May 1825: father's trade given as tanner.

d. John, baptised on the 16th February 1830: father's trade given as tanner. John, buried on the 21st November 1830.

Also in this Register is the baptism on the 16th March 1831 of Anne, daughter of James and Mary Harridance, which confirms the father's trade as shoe maker as indicated on George McKay's letter to his wife. It would be possible in addition to check through the Parish Registers for other friends mentioned in the lettes such as the Saward family.

The conclusion to be drawn seems to be that George McKay having married Elizabeth Harridance, settled in Maldon and bettered himself by rising from being a labourer in 1818 to becoming a tanner from, at the latest, 1821 onwards. An improvement no doubt noted with approbation by the Harridances who were themselves becoming important as a family in the craft and commercial life of Maldon. As to what happened thereafter, the record is not clear; Harriet's birth has not been traced and the ultimate fate of the McKay family is unknown; certainly in 1848 there was no mention of any McKay in the Maldon *Directory*.

This might have been as far as the story could be taken were it not for endorsements on each of the letters. On the one dated 26th March 1836 is written under the hand of George Choate, Overseer of All Saints Parish:- 'I have also inclosed that you might see that George McKay the Pensioner wishes and says he has Ordered his Pension to be paid for the Benifit of his Wife and Family'. George McKay had indeed stated as much for in the same letter, amongst his accounts of his campaigning and sending his regards to all and sundry, he wrote to his wife: 'You mention in your letter that you received on the 22nd for the first time my Pension I beg Betsy that you will be very particular in what you Receive and Gett it Set Down in a Book so that I might know What you Receive as I have sent my permission for you to receive the same and you ought to have received it Before'. This statement has been underlined in a colour of ink very close to that used for George Choate's declaration and we may infer that the letter owes it survival to the fact that it was essential evidence with which Betsey could claim George's pension.

But pension for what? The sworn declaration written in another hand at the end of George McKay's second letter of 16th September 1836 runs as follows: 'Elizabeth McKay wife of George McKay late a Soldier in the 95th Regiment Rifle Brigade and now an Out Pensioner of the Hospital at Chelsea maketh Oath and saith that the annexed letter is the handwriting of the said George McKay and that the same was received by this Deponent in the regular course of post at the end of September last.' It is signed by Elizabeth McKay and sworn on 6th December 1836 before 'two of His Majesty's Justices of the Peace for the Borough of Maldon', namely John Payne, Mayor, and Edward Bright, both of whom are, incidentally, in 1848 Justices and Aldermen of the Borough.

This declaration was not only vital to the preservation of the second letter also, but it provides a lead to a very important archive, the records of former members of the Regular Forces.[17]

First it is perhaps helpful to explain the term 'out-pensioner'.[18] The Royal Hospital of Chelsea was originally planned by Charles II to accomodate all the old soldiers then known, namely four hundred and seventy-two; however, despite additional buildings authorised by James II it became clear as a result of casualties sustained in Monmouth's Rebellion that some other arrangements for the care of old soldiers would have to be made. Accordingly on the 21st July 1685 James II gave verbal instructions that all soldiers who had become unserviceable as a result of wounds or after twenty years with the Colours, should be paid pensions from the following 1st August; this was confirmed by a Royal Warrant five months later. The rate varied according to rank, starting with five pence per day for a private soldier. In other words, unlike the inmates of Chelsea Hospital, the 'out-pensioners' were paid pensions to enable them to live at home. These pensions were computed and controlled by the Commissioners of the Royal Hospital and this arrangement continued until 1955 when responsibility for Army Pensions was taken over the Army Pensions Office at Stanmore and subsequently Glasgow. Clearly the Admission Books for Chelsea Hospital are an important source of information, and perhaps the importance of the 'out-pensioner' in local economic and social life is overlooked.

Now knowing also that George McKay had served in the 95th Regiment, it is possible to consult his record of service[19] which we find adds considerably to our information about the man. We learn that McKay enlisted on the 12th June 1806 at Woodbridge in Suffolk at the age of fifteen for unlimited service having been born in Portsmouth, Hants, in 1791. He proceeded to serve in the 95th Regt. as a Bugler for a total of eleven years and thirteen days between the 12th June 1806 and the 24th June 1817, from which service prior to the age of eighteen had to be deducted; therefore McKay's pension was calculated on the basis of eight years and thirteen days service. In this record it is noted that his general conduct had been good and that he had served in the Peninsular War and at Waterloo. At the time of his discharge on the 24th June 1817 from the 1st Battalion, the Rifle Brigade McKay was serving at Bourlon-en-Artois near Cambrai in France, being paid at the rate of 7¾d. per day, and described as being about twenty-five years of age, five feet six inches tall with fair hair, grey eyes, fair complexion, and with his occupation given as a labourer. McKay was discharged by the Army because he was 'ruptured' and on the 18th April he was invalided back to England with twelve other private soldiers.

From his service record certain aspects of McKay's character and personality may be inferred. In the first place the 95th (Rifle) Regiment[20] was an elite unit formed to gain the maximum advantage from fire-power coupled with movement and it recruited men of initiative and intelligence; clearly McKay had these qualities. By using cover and mounting a steady stream of fire Riflemen were effective against field artillery as was demonstrated when the 1st Battalion, McKay's unit, 'holding the sunken lane on the ridge at Waterloo, were able to prevent Napoleon's gunners at the crisis of the battle, from blasting a decisive hole through Wellington's crumbling centre.'[21] The 95th was the first Regiment to be armed with the rifle – the Baker, a muzzle-loading, three-grooved weapon issued in the Peninsular[22] – and in 1816 by Order in Council it became the Rifle Brigade and was, therefore, not a Regiment of the Line.

Major General Sir John Moore, who was to die so famously at Corunna, trained Riflemen in Kent in 1803 as a defence against invasion. Moore was also sent to survey the Essex coast so that it might be defended against an expected French attack. Thus is was that the 95th Regiment found itself at Woodbridge in Suffolk, in 1806 and it was here that George McKay enlisted having clearly made a conscious effort to join this particular Regiment. Although different companies of the Regiment undertook various missions at home and abroad, they were concentrated in Essex in 1808 being quartered at Colchester, Warley and Woodbridge in Suffolk with the intention of providing defensive cover for London in the event of a French invasion. Incidentally it was in April 1808 at Harwich that Captain Brodie Grant of the 95th was shot by Lieutenant Jonathan Layton of the same Regiment, the former being buried in Ardleigh Churchyard, and the latter indicted for murder but subsequently acquitted.[23]

It is not part of our task to chronicle the history of the 95th Regiment, but it is clear that its service in Essex preparing against the threat of a French invasion provided the context in which George McKay, the young lad enlisted as a Rifleman, could meet Elizabeth Harridance. It also explains, by way of his training and military service, how McKay could maintain his self discipline and military bearing during the hardships experienced by the British Auxiliary Legion in Spain in 1836.

We are also permitted to reflect upon the circumstances of McKay's rupture – the reason for his being invalided out of the British Army in 1817. It is well known that many of those who joined the British Auxiliary Legion were not physically fit and had not been medically examined before acceptance. A British medical board sitting in Bilbao in the early stages of the Carlist War learned that 'upon an average a hundred men in each regiment of infantry were either too young or too old for service, deformed, diseased or crippled.'[24] McKay, who was medically unfit for further service with the British Army, was probably in better shape than many, which may have accounted for his ability to survive the disease-ridden conditions at Vitoria, of which he writes.

One question remains: why did McKay re-enlist to serve as a mercenary in the Carlist Wars. There is no evidence that he shared the radicalism of that other ex-soldier, who died in 1835, William Cobbett, nor was he one of the disaffected agricultural workers about whom Charles Hicks complained in his Diary in 1830: 'In Essex the labourers were paid better than in any other Eastern county; particularly all round by the coast one shilling per week was generally paid more than 10 miles inland. Where best paid, the men behaved the worst.'[25]

Comparatively well-paid the Essex agricultural labourers might have been, but George McKay did better than that in his adopted County; he became a tanner – a skilled craftsman – and married into a respectable Maldon family to be of significance both in the trade and local government of the Borough. Articulate, literate, numerate, able to speak French and Spanish, a devoted family man, it seems most unlikely that he would be found fighting in Spain at the age of forty-five. Unless further correspondence or diaries come to light, we shall never know the reasons for his joining the British Auxiliary Legion for sure. It may be that he was opposed to Carlism by conviction, but far more likely is the explanation that he was a born soldier and had it not been for his being invalided out of the British Army he would have been content to serve on. Like many Scots and men of Scottish descent the Army was a way of life and the chance to serve again, in a Regiment which if not part of the British Army had the approval of the British Government, was simply too tempting to reject.

Having looked in detail at the circumstances of George McKay and his family, it is not unreasonable to consider whether any general conclusions may be drawn from this exercise. In the first place it is possible by the careful analysis of the contents of a letter and the way in which it is addressed not only to set it in its historical context, but also by linking the evidence deduced to other archival sources, to extend the range of permissible interpretation. Secondly, if the main focus of attention had been the Harridance family, George McKay would probably have been dismissed as an in-law of no particular importance and indeed perhaps of some eccentricity. But by highlighting his particular family, even though he was not Essex-born, we are forced to realise that George McKay contributed to the life of the County and also that his wife and dependants had their own history too.

Thirdly it is appropriate to reflect upon the influence that soldiers stationed in the County have had not just on its social life, but also on the composition of the population. George McKay first came to Essex because he was posted here; thousands of other men likewise came to Essex during the Napoleonic Wars, many spending several years in the County; some of these must have married and returned to settle in Essex after the wars with France had ended. Of these a substantial number would be out-pensioners of the Royal Hospital at Chelsea and as such at least marginally better off than those labourers who had no regular income. Little research has been done on the numbers, distribution, social impact and economic significance of Army pensioners in Essex in the decades after 1815. After all, if nationwide some 25,650 ex-soldiers applied for their Military General Service Medal when it was issued in 1848,[26] some thirty-three years after the last battle it commemorated, there must have been considerable numbers of old soldiers scattered throughout the Essex parishes.

If nothing else this approach steers the local historian back to considering people as individuals in all their variety and is a useful counterbalance to the conventional local histories which concentrate on institutions and are in danger of becoming increasingly stereotyped.

Notes and References

1. R. M. Willcocks, *England's Postal History To 1840*, (1975), 136.

2. Purchased by the Passmore Edwards Museum from Messrs. Argyll Etkin Ltd; Museum reference numbers: LDPEM: AE24830(1) and AE24830(2).

3. For a detailed discussion of the historical background see Raymond Carr, *Spain 1808–1939*, OUP (1966), on which these paragraphs are based.

4. The most accessible history of the War may be found in Edgar Holt, *The Carlist Wars in Spain*, London (1967).

5. Despite the Carlist Wars of 1833–40 and 1870–5, the First and Second Republics of 1873 and 1931, and the Civil War of 1936–39, it was the descendant of

Ferdinand VII and not Don Carlos who ultimately ascended the Spanish throne when the monarchy was restored. On the 22nd July 1969 General Franco nominated Prince Juan Carlos of Bourbon (1938–) as his successor and was supported by the Cortes. Following Franco's death Juan Carlos I acceded to the throne on the 22nd November 1975.

6. Holt, op. cit., 166–7.

7. As in Ronald G. Shelley, *The British Legion in Spain During the First Carlist War 1832–1839*, Spanish Philatelic Society Book Club No. 4. (1975).

8. In studying these letters the author wishes to acknowledge with gratitude the assistance provided by the staff of the British Library, Essex Record Office, the National Army Museum, and the Public Record Office; in addition he is particularly indebted for help in tracing sources to Dr. Jane Feltham and Bernadette Gillow.

9. Holt, op. cit., 111.

10. The author is greatly indebted to James Grimwood-Taylor and Arthur Brown of Messrs. Argyll Etkin Ltd. for their courtesy in discussing the postal history aspects of this paper.

11. For similar examples of these stamps and marks see Shelley, op. cit., passim, but especially, 61.

12. A. F. J. Brown, *Essex People 1750–1900*, E.R.O. Pub. 59 (1972), inc. 'Charles Hicks, Farmer of Great Holland 1778–1865.'

13. Willcocks, op. cit., 110–111.

14. P. B. Boyden, *Tommy Atkin's Letters*: 'The Postal Service of Wellington's Army in the Peninsula and France 1809–1818,' National Army Museum Report (1983).

15. William White, *History, Gazetteer, and Directory of the County of Essex* (1848), 514–520.

16. E.R.O. T/R 149/1–8(1), and T/R 149/9–14(2).

17. The Records of Servicemen are preserved in the Public Record Office in Kew.

18. The author is indebted to Lieut.–Colonel J. J. Kelly, O.B.E., (Retired), the Curator of the Museum at the Royal Hospital Chelsea, London, SW3 4SL, for providing the contents of this paragraph.

19. P.R.O. WO 97 1083.

20. The most accessible history of the Rifle Brigade is Arthur Bryant, *Jackets of Green* (1972).

21. Bryant, op. cit., 39.

22. Bryant, op. cit., 299.

23. G. O. Rickword, 'Fatal Duel Near Harwich in 1808, Essex Review, vol. xliv (1935), 200–1.

24. Holt, op. cit, 86–87.

25. Hicks in Brown, op. cit., 74.

26. Major L. L. Gordon, *British Battles and Medals*, 5th edition revised by Edward C. Joslin (1979), 22.

Four Colchester Elections: Voting Behaviour in a Victorian Market Town

ANDREW PHILLIPS

(This research was based on computer programmes devised and written by Mr KEITH ENFIELD for the Amstrad CPC464 Personal Computer. Without his inventive contribution this essay would not have been possible.)

On the eve of the introduction of the secret ballot Colchester experienced four Parliamentary elections in quick succession: general elections in 1865 and 1868 and by-elections in 1867 and 1870. Printed contemporary pollbooks have survived for all four elections, listing the voters and the candidate or candidates they voted for. Together they represent a last detailed glimpse of the voting behaviour of an average two-member English borough, typical of what has been called 'the Provincial Backwaters',[1] but crucial to any understanding of mid-Victorian politics. Spanning the Second Reform Act of August 1867, the four pollbooks also shed interesting light on that event and the changes effected in the electorate.

This essay represents some summary findings of a computer-based analysis of the 3,716 electors who featured in one or more of these elections. A search of the 1871 Census, taken five months after the 1870 by-election provided, in conjunction with a contemporary directory, the age and occupation of 2,323 surviving electors.

The Elections (see also Appendix A)

Date	Interval	Electors (From Pollbooks)
13 July 1865		1361
15 February 1867	19 Months	1387
18 November 1868	21 Months	3060
30 October 1870	23 Months	2810

In the 1859 general election Colchester returned two Conservatives: Taverner Miller, a successful London merchant and a sitting member, and Philip O. Papillon, the youthful and resident Lord of the Manor of Lexden. Papillon displaced the other sitting member, John Gurdon Rebow of Wivenhoe House, a Whiggish Liberal and another local squire. Rebow was the only Liberal candidate.

In 1865 the same three candidates stood for office. Rebow headed the poll, followed by Miller: a reversion to the situation prior to 1859. Papillon was displaced, at 39, never to stand for Parliament again, though he remained active in Colchester's affairs for the next 20 years.

In 1867 Miller, now a sick man, took the Chiltern Hundreds and at the subsequent by-election E. Kent Karslake, Conservative, brother to the Solicitor General but a total stranger to the borough, defeated another carpet-bagger, Dr William Brewer, a Liberal and close friend of John Stuart Mill.

In the 1868 general election two Liberals faced two Conservatives: Rebow and Brewer against Karslake and Colonel Learmonth of Edinburgh, formerly of the 17th Lancers, a son of a former Lord Provost. The election was significant for a 124% increase in the electorate as a result of the Second Reform Act. The Liberals won both seats.

In October 1870 Rebow suddenly died. The government sought to use a snap by-election to secure a Parliamentary seat for General Sir Henry Storks, Cardwell's chief assistant at the War Office. A former colonial governor, Storks had been a strong supporter of the Contagious Diseases Acts (C. D. Acts). These provided for compulsory inspection and, if necessary, compulsory medical treatment of prostitutes in garrison towns, of which Colchester was one. Opponents of the Acts, including the feminist, Josephine Butler, descended on Colchester and put up a rival Liberal candidate, Dr. Baxter Langley, a well-known London Radical, as part of their campaign to secure the repeal of the C. D. Acts. Only on election day did Langley withdraw his candidacy. The Conservative, Learmonth, won comfortably over Storks. There was a large abstention vote.

Reliability

How accurate are the findings of this survey? Errors – even falsifications – occurred in recording 19th century votes. Voters, alive or dead, were impersonated. There were inaccuracies in the compilation of pollbooks. The four in question possess mathematical contradictions. That for the 1870 by-election (published by two Conservative newspapers) prompted indignant correspondence in a Liberal newspaper. One example will suffice:

Candidate	Official Return	Total Printed at Conclusion of Pollbook	Actual Votes in Pollbook
Learmonth	1363	1353	1373
Storks	853	841	853

These are not large errors.

There are errors in the 1871 Census and (mea culpa) errors in the transcription of all this data to a computer. Even so the author is satisfied that no error exceeds 5% and few exceed 1%. The problem lies in dealing with voting consistency. Few voters switched party. There must be the probability that error has exaggerated this. The author's own contribution has been to eschew decimal points and retain pollbook data even where it does not quite add up.

The Electorate

Who were the electors of Colchester? Before 1868 they represented two broad categories: the resident, hereditary Freemen (residence extending to seven miles from the borough) and the £10 Householders. According to the 1868 Boundary Commission the numbers were as follows:

£10 occupiers	1000
Freemen	405
Total	1405

Traditionally the Freemen were regarded as a separate body, but their occupational profile considerably overlapped that of £10 householders:

Category	£10 Householders %	Freemen %
Agriculture/Horticulture	11	14
Professional/White Collar	19	10
Business	11	13
Retail	24	15
Publicans/Beersellers	7	2
Craftsmen	24	30
Labour	3	12
	100	100

(Figures based on Appendix B)

Since they represented at this stage a wider cross-section of the community, the Freemen ranks included a significant but not overwhelming proportion of labourers and poorer craftsmen. On this basis it was calculated that the Colchester electorate was from 25% to 28% working class. The 87 non-Colchester Freemen also boosted the representation of agriculture.

Before 1868 the Freemen vote was vital. Generally it produced a Conservative majority, a result achieved, according to Liberal dogma, by bribery and treating. This was an oversimplification; not just because both parties treated (though the Conservatives apparently more so) but because treating coincided with or paled before ties of occupation and social allegiance. Freemen farmers were overwhelmingly Tory, Freemen shoe-makers predominantly Liberal. The same pattern was true of £10 householders and their successors, the household voters of 1868, who were widely expected to be yet more subject to corruption. However there is evidence for the 1868 election that crude bribery could become counter-productive. Certainly treating was always less significant than influence and those persuasive pressures traditionally applied to the socially and economically dependent.

Could this sway an election? Could attention to the Freemen deliver a Parliamentary seat? Evidence is provided by the 1867 by-election won by Karslake with a majority of 77 (83 from the pollbook). The by-election was caused by the progressive deterioration of the health of the senior M.P., Taverner Miller. This gave the Conservatives an initial advantage which they exploited well. Aware of the true state of their member's health they could prepare in advance. Anticipating a future general election the Conservatives had two candidates duly adopted and introduced to the faithful in October 1866. Party workers became active. Not till December did the Liberals produce a candidate, their first choice, a Maldon barrister, having turned them down. In January the Conservatives stepped up their campaign. On Friday February 8th Miller took the Chiltern Hundreds. The by-election was called for the following Friday.

Colchester had a natural Conservative majority. This had been upset in 1865 by the unpopularity of Papillon and the popularity of Rebow, a local squire. Karslake now faced a stranger to the borough, Dr Brewer, who lacked the common touch, adopted a high moral tone and talked of Parliamentary reform.

January was bitterly cold. Years later the Liberals referred to this as the blanket election, when Conservative ladies distributed blankets and coals among the poor in large quantities. Karslake courted the Freeman vote more directly. A True Blue banquet was held to which they were all invited. If the Radicals got their way, he warned, Freemen would lose their franchise. One convert to this view was the erratic W. R. Havens, brother of the Lord of the Manor of East Donyland, an erstwhile Chartist, who had twice stood for Parliament himself with derisory consequences. Havens was an egocentric as well as a buffoon. To lose his status as a Freeman would deny him any further right to continue in Colchester politics.

After the True Blue banquet 600 gallons of soup were distributed to the deserving poor. The Liberals held a similar feast for the Freemen, but at the poll Karslake made a net gain of 72 on Freemen votes, outvoting Brewer 26 to 12 among those newly enfranchised. This represented 89% of his majority. Of the 15 Freemen who switched to Conservative, having voted Liberal in 1865, ten (including Havens and his brother) were from Wivenhoe or East Donyland. This concentration is so remarkable that it is hard not to see in this the hand of Havens and the scaremongering of Karslake. Add three former abstainers from Wivenhoe who voted Conservative and Havens effectively delivered 23 extra votes to Karslake, 28% of his majority. On such slender actions could a Colchester election be won before the 1867 Reform Act.

The contribution of Havens was but an extreme example of the pressures and persuasions that characterised the system. The point is this: Karslake had fought a traditional campaign, courting the constituency, showing the common touch, playing the Freeman card. But any claim that armies of potential Liberals were hustled into Tory votes should be tempered by the thought that the Conservatives won both Colchester seats in the first election (1874) conducted under the secret ballot.

The Reform Act of 1867, extending the franchise to all householders, effected a fundamental change in the Colchester electorate. The number of registered voters rose from 1,405 to 3,060, over 55% of the eligible male population. Even if garrison numbers are added, this is far higher than a national percentage of around 33%.[2] Contemporaries regarded attention to the register as fundamental to electoral success. It is a measure of the energy and thoroughness of local party organisation that such a figure was achieved. In some parishes the electorate rose by over 300%.

The key to registration was not the initial action of the Overseers of the Poor in drawing up a parish list, but the energies of local activists in seeking out those of their own persuasion who had been overlooked, while challenging the qualifications of supporters of the other side at the annual registration court, a contest which was traditionally pursued more effectively by the Conservatives who had more time and more solicitors at their command. In 1868 it was pursued so thoroughly by both sides that claims that

> '. . . the election (of 1868) cannot be seen as a trial of strength between 'old' and 'new'.'

because

> '. . . the process of getting the newly enfranchised on to the register had hardly begun in some constituencies and was far from complete in any . . .'[3]

will not do for Colchester. Proof lies in subsequent contests.

In the general election of 1874 when the population had significantly grown, there were only 123 more electors (4%) than in 1868,[4] while in the snap by-election of 1870 held less than three weeks after the death of the sitting member, the inability of the political parties to conduct any registration campaign produced a register of only 2,810 electors, a fall of 8% on that held two years earlier.

The 1871 Census, taken five months after this, shows clearly that the bulk of the lost electors were still alive and resident. The census also underlines how selective even a household register remained, coupled as it was with a one-year residence qualification. The Colchester garrison of 2,650 adult men made virtually no impact on the electorate. Even a proportion of the middle class remained disfranchised. In, for example, the parish of St Mary's at the Walls non-electors included not only such luminaries as the head of the grammar school, the rector of the parish, the owner of a large clothing factory and a leading borough solicitor, but 28 assorted merchants, retailers and representatives of the professions as well as numerous craftsmen and skilled workers.

Another consequence of a household franchise was the maturity of the electorate. The average age of the 2,323 voters identified was 48, at a date when less than a quarter of the population were over 45. Among 80 enfranchised agricultural labourers in the parishes of Lexden and Mile End the average age was 50. Only two were under 30, only two were over 70. A not unusual labouring household in the poorer parts of Colchester extended over three generations. Invariably the vote was exercised by a grandfather in his 60's rather than his more active son in his 30's. This was an electorate of patriarchs.

Working from the 1871 Census the pre and post 1868 electorate breaks down as shown overleaf.

The new voters were numerous in three areas:

a) An influx of agricultural labourers and 'gardeners', increasing the stake of agriculture in the electorate.

Category	Pre 1868 %	Numbers	Post 1868 %	Numbers
Agriculture/Horticulture	11	94	15	340
Professionals	13	125	8	179
Other white collar	4	34	3	66
Publicans/Beersellers	5	52	4	86
Business	10	100	6	141
Petty Business	1	10	2	40
Retailers	22	207	14	329
Craftsmen	26	246	31	722
Labourers	4	37	12	280
The Railway	0	1	1	36
The River	2	15	2	50
Others	2	21	2	53
TOTAL	100	941	100	2323

b) A similar influx of urban labourers, including railway and quayside workers.

c) A major increase in the number of traditional craftsmen, equal in size to the combined increases in agricultural and urban labourers (a and b above).

These new voters substantially changed the role of the Freemen. Firstly the Freemen vote fell from 29% to 13% of the electorate, no longer the vital element it had been. Secondly, since almost two thirds of the Colchester-resident freemen were also householders, their social profile was now little different from the rest of the electorate. In a sense Karslake's warnings had been realised.

A more detailed breakdown of occupations is given in Appendix B. This table follows, with minor adjustments, a similar breakdown of electors for the borough of Cambridge in 1868 which appears on pp.92–93 of Professor Vincent's study of pollbooks.[5] As with that study, and indeed all Victorian censuses, it has not been possible to distinguish between master and man in the host of crafts that still dominated an old market town, which Colchester still was in 1871. It is however clear from the census and elsewhere that in Colchester the small workshop was everywhere the norm and the number of large employers very few. Indeed the characteristic relationship of most Colchester electors to one another was of buyers and sellers, not employers and employees. This highlights another difficulty with the general categories used. It is clear that many of those listed as craftsmen were retailers too, albeit often in a small way or to specialist tradesmen. Likewise some retailers were wholesalers and some businessmen, retailers. These factors must be accepted as the blurred edges of an imprecise science. By the same score some voters pursued two different occupations and others undoubtedly changed their occupation during the period covered by the four pollbooks. None of this renders nugatory the information in Appendix B.

The occupational pattern revealed is typical of that host of medium-size boroughs that lay at the heart of the mid-Victorian political process. It is almost wholly pre-industrial. It is dominated by an electorate crammed into a densely-populated historic town which barely extended outside its medieval limits. Beyond this, however, the constituency embraced an area of 15 square miles, mostly devoted to traditional agriculture. This and the non-Colchester Freemen provided a significant body of farmers and agricultural labourers. The importance of farming to Colchester, particularly to shopkeepers and agriculture-related businesses, was frequently cited for the predominantly Conservative behaviour of the electorate between 1832 and 1868. Equally interesting is the role of horticulture, market-gardening, flower and soft fruit cultivation. The occupational category 'gardener' is the most unsatisfactory of the study: it ranges from a market gardener employing 25 men to an under gardener at the rectory. Efforts to detail out purely domestic gardeners (categorised as domestic servants) may not have been totally successful. The even division of 'gardeners' between the two political parties may mask important differences by status.

Voting Behaviour

The voting behaviour covered by this survey appears consistent and partisan. Of the 3,716 voters involved, 906 were concerned with one election only. Of the remainder, 61% recorded a 'full party vote', that is to say they voted to the fullest extent for one party on all occasions. This figure rises to 76% if we include those Liberals who only baulked at the candidature of Sir Henry Storks in 1870. For a detailed analysis we shall concentrate on those 887 voters who feature in all four elections. Of these, 233 (a disproportionate number) were Freemen. This table summarises their voting behaviour:

1. Full Party Vote (F.P.V.)	63%	(£10 Householders 64% (Freemen 60%)
2. F.P.V. with one Abstention (mostly 1870 Liberals)	12%	
3. F.P.V. with one Plump for same party	2%	
4. F.P.V. with one Split (mostly Miller/Rebow in 1865)	5%	
5. Changed party once, voting consistently thereafter	4%	
6. Abstained more than once, but did not switch party	5%	
7. Abstained at all four elections	2%	
8. 'Floating Voters' – those not listed above	7%	
TOTAL	100	

From this it can be argued that over 70% of the old electorate voted consistently for the same party. This is based on three reasonable assumptions: that those Liberals who abstained in 1870 did so under exceptional circumstances, that Liberals who voted for Miller in 1865 would not have done so had there been a second Liberal candidate and that those who abstained once may well have done so through absence or sickness (or death) rather than political apathy. Beyond this one can claim that over 85% (groups 1–4 and some of 6 and 8) demonstrated a clear partisan allegiance, suggesting in turn a partisan self-image, to borrow a phrase from contemporary psephology. A further 4% held firm views but changed them. This leaves only consistent abstainers and the erratic. These were remarkably few. If Colchester electors were venal, they were consistently so: only 1% of four-time voters switched party twice; not one voter voted for the successful candidates at each election and only two voters, William Jones and John Chamberlain, both Wivenhoe shipowners with a Freeman franchise, alternated between the parties at each election. Perhaps they made an alehouse wager; perhaps they were at the beck of Havens. The undecided, pendulum voter did not otherwise exist.

All this underlines what is clear from the Colchester press: that politics was an activity passionately pursued, a tribal allegiance or a sacred trust; that so long as the franchise was neither secret nor universal, few were neutral or easily moved from their belief.

A caution is however needed. Our four elections cover a period of only five years. Modern studies of voting behaviour suggest that many of those with a strong partisan allegiance can stray occasionally from their allegiance over a sufficient period of time. The previous election to 1865 was in April 1859. Working from the Freemen only (the most volatile group) 109 voters can be certainly identified who recorded a full party vote between 1865 and 1870. Of these, 8% cast a different vote in 1859, four of them for the opposite party. On this basis, over an extended period and including upsets like the Storks candidature, perhaps little more than half the electorate were totally immovable from a permanent partisan commitment. If so, such a figure is very similar to studies made in the 1960s.[6] The difference lies in the far greater number of abstentions recorded today.

Electoral Change

With so much potential shifting, can any conclusions be drawn about the processes of electoral change, the 'swings' of contemporary psephology? In the age of two-member constituencies the individual voter had a greater range of choices. Assuming two candidates from each party (as in 1868 but not 1865) he could cast a full party vote, he could split his vote between two candidates from opposite parties, he could plump for one candidate and not cast his second vote or he could abstain. This gave him eleven possible voting choices. The by-elections of 1867 and 1870, with only one seat at stake, presented but three choices. Nevertheless over the four elections our 887 voters faced 693 possible voting combinations (4,851 if we add the election of 1859) viz:

$$1865 \quad 1867 \quad 1868 \quad 1870$$
$$7 \text{ choices} \times 3 \times 11 \times 3 = 693$$

On top of this, at each election some previous voters had died, left the area or not been re-registered, while new voters had been added – dramatically in 1868. For our four elections the figures are as shown opposite:

To show how this worked out in detail we will take the easiest of all cases, the 1867 by-election.

		1865 (Freemen Only)				1867		
Voters from 1859	:	269	67%	Voters from 1865	:	1129	81½%
New Voters	:	129	33%	New Voters	:	258	18½%

		1868				1870		
Voters from 1867	:	1186	39%	Voters from 1868	:	2520	90%
Voters from 1865,				Voters from 1865/67	:	19	½%
Missing in 1867	:	46	1%	New Voters	:	271	10%
New Voters	:	1828	60%				

Movements of Votes 1865–1867

1. LIBERAL
LOSSES FROM 1865

Lost from Register	
Splits with Miller	12
Splits with Papillon	5
Rebow Plumps	88
Sub Total	105

Lost to Abstention	
Splits with Miller	17
Splits with Papillon	1
Rebow Plumps	28
Sub Total	46

Lost to Conservatives	
Splits with Miller	33
Splits with Papillon	7
Rebow Plumps	26
Sub Total	66

1865 Rebow Votes	689
Total Losses (105+46+66)	217
Carried Forward	472

GAINS IN 1867	
Carried Forward	472
Gains from Abstention	7
Gains from Conservatives	11
New Voters	102
TOTAL FOR BREWER	592

2. CONSERVATIVE
LOSSES FROM 1865

Lost from Register	
Splits with Rebow	12
Miller Plumps	4
Splits with Papillon	81
Sub Total	97

Lost to Abstention	
Splits with Rebow	17
Miller Plumps	2
Splits with Papillon	8
Sub Total	27

Lost to Liberals	
Splits with Rebow	32
Splits with Papillon	11
Sub Total	43

1865 Miller Votes	647
Total Losses (97+27+43)	167
Carried Forward	480

GAINS IN 1867	
Carried Forward	480
Gains from Abstention	35
Gains from Liberals	26
Gains from Papillon Plumps	1
Gains from Rebow/Papillon Splits	7
New Voters	126
TOTAL FOR KARSLAKE	675

From this mass of detail three points should be stressed that illustrate general patterns. Firstly, the number of 1865 voters switching party is 37, compared to 115 moving in and out of abstention. These proportions are generally true of all elections. Secondly, although each switcher carries a total weight of two votes to the opposite party this is offset by movements in both directions. Although 26 previous Liberals voted for Karslake, 11 previous Conservatives voted for Brewer. There is a similar pattern at each election, even the Conservative landslide of 1870. Thirdly, although 114 voters who gave a split party vote in 1865 might disappear, abstain or opt for one party in 1867, these three actions tended to cancel one another out, leaving a net gain to Karslake of only three votes.

In conclusion, there was in 1867 a broad 'swing' to Conservative based on three sources: old voters changing sides, previous abstainers voting Conservative and new voters showing a Conservative preference. As we have already seen this was most marked among the Freeman. Briefer analyses of the other elections are as follows:

In 1865 Rebow headed the poll for three broad reasons: firstly more former Conservatives switched to Liberal than vice versa, secondly more Liberals survived from the old register (figures are too uncertain to quantify), thirdly, and crucially, some former Conservatives and some new voters were persuaded to split between Miller and Rebow.

In 1868 the Liberals won by a massive majority among the new household voters (59% to 41%). Among old voters not only was there a Conservative majority (55% to 45%) but a net swing to the Conservatives, despite the fact that more Conservative than Liberal voters disappeared from the register.

In 1870 the Conservatives won by a landslide among both new and old voters. The figures for those who cast a full party vote in 1868 tell their own story.

	Stayed Loyal	Switched Party	Abstained	Left the Register	
Liberals	52%	13	19	16	100%
Conservatives	77%	2	6	15	100%

Two broad statements follow. With the possible exception of 1865 (after a six-year break) losses from the register were not significant. Victory was gained by converting the existing electorate. Secondly, at all four elections there was a continuous erosion of Liberal compared to Conservative votes:

	After Two Elections (1867, 1868)	
	Lib.	Con.
Number of surviving 1865 full party voters	445	401
Percentage still loyal	76%	92%

No great philosophical evidence need be seen in this of disappointed expectation. Some were Liberals who had voted Conservative in 1859, others happy with the Whiggish Rebow were less confident of Dr Brewer in 1867 or alarmed by democracy in 1868.

Plumpers, Splitters and Abstainers

Some general observations can be made on these three options to straight party voting. As we have seen they were a far more frequent practice than the Draconian step of switching to the opposite party.

Plumpers are only found at general elections, and in 1859 and 1865 only among Conservatives, since to plump for Rebow was a full party vote. Plumping was not common (3% of voters in 1868), and is best described as an abstention against a member of your own party, presumably on personal grounds. Of the 126 plumps recorded there are only 7 examples of a plumper subsequently or previously voting for the opposite party and 5 of these are Rebow voters in 1870 when there was so strong a Conservative swing. There are also only 14 examples of a plumper finding their unacceptable candidate acceptable at the next election (Miller or Papillon in 1865, Learmonth in 1870).

Splitting your votes between the two parties is a more frequent practice and open to several interpretations. It can be the action of a rational voter judging a candidate on his individual merit (or status) regardless of party label. George Errington, banker and landowner, one of Colchester's most respected figures, split for his friends the gentry: Rebow and Papillon in 1865, Rebow and Karslake in 1868. Splitting is also a device for the even handed, for opponents of political partisanship or seekers of a quiet life. Such voters, however, would surely split in both 1865 and 1868. Yet of the 887 voters who featured in all four elections of whom 76 split in 1865 (9% of total) and 25 in 1868, only 12 split on both occasions. A similar pattern exists between splitters in 1859 and 1865. Splitting is thus largely the resort of the undecided and the least partisan. Of the 64 most unpredictable four-times voters 42 split at least once.

The infrequency of abstention in these elections is the most marked divergence from modern electoral behaviour. At the five general elections between 1970 and 1983 the abstention rate ranged between 22% and 28%. The figures for our four elections are:

1865	8.5%	1868	10.5%
1867	8.4%	1870	20.8%

Of all voters recorded, 24% abstained at least once. This figure is however inflated by the high abstention rate in 1870. Of all those who voted in the first three elections only 14% abstained at least once.

Why did Victorians abstain? Some were dead. The 1867 pollbook obligingly records that 19 had died (1.4%) since the register had been made up four months previously. Others were sick; we cannot know how many. Others abstained because their vote was no longer needed. With public voting, on election day figures were issued each hour of the state of the poll. There is probably a genuine basis to Rebow's claim in 1868:

'The numbers polled do not indicate the strength of our party as a great many who promised to vote if necessary did not do so, considering early in the day that triumph was complete. . .'[7]

This may have been a factor in the high abstention rate of 1870 when the Liberals had clearly lost after the first hour or so.

Some voters were absent: away from home or moved from the district. The mobility of Colchester's population is reflected in the movements of voters from pollbook to pollbook. Of the 2,373 household voters who appear in more than one pollbook at least 180 (8%) move from one parish and reappear in another. Some individuals managed three moves. These numbers do not include those who moved within the same parish or the far larger number who left the district. With oft-repeated local surnames, a remarkably small range of forenames and the common practice of naming son after father, the difficulty of identifying these mobile individuals is another minor source of error.

It is also significant how many of the 1870 voters cannot be found in the 1871 census, taken five months later. In the stable rural parishes of Lexden and Mile End 14% of them cannot be found. In the more mobile 'outer urban' parishes of Greenstead and St James the figure is 21%. It is inconceivable that they had all moved or died. Greenstead abutted the Hythe where the abstention rate among mariners as an occupational group is dramatic. It is easy to envisage why members of other occupational groups could also be absent from Colchester for a day or more.

The incidence of deliberate abstention can be better gauged by looking at those who abstained more than once. Of all four-time voters this is 9%. Of these, 15 individuals (1.7%) abstained at all four elections. This is a remarkably small number. In terms of occupations and age these 15 men are not distinctive. Not one of them however was a Freeman. This suggests that they represented a determined minority who voted firmly against politics.

Other multiple abstainers deliberately chose neutrality. Victorian policemen were expected to be non-partisan. Of three with the vote, two habitually abstained. So did the Borough Surveyor and his assistant. Farmers abstained, perhaps because of distance; shopkeepers wished to appear even-handed; mariners were at sea. Four solicitors, acting as Party Agents for the elections, abstained, although among the most active political protagonists in Colchester. Was this a legal obligation?

Mainly, however, casual abstention was the common response of the least committed. In this consistent Victorian electorate 64 individuals, 7% of all four-time voters, split, abstained, switched party, or any combination of these three, on more than one occasion. They include such 'rational' splitters as George Errington, cited above. They form a hard core of 'floating voters' even though many (Errington, for example) had a clear partisan affiliation. Over 70% of them abstained at least once.

Indecision and erratic voting nonetheless occur in a context. Adding the cumulative votes of these 64 individuals produces this result:

Preference	1865	1867	1868	1870
Liberal	23	23	11½	2
Conservative	4	22	6½	39
Abstention	6	19	19	23
Split Party	31		22	

Note: To achieve uniformity between all elections, a full party or Split party vote counts as 1, a plump as ½.

The extent to which these are undecided voters is shown by the popularity of splitting and abstaining. As indecision (or apathy) mounts, the number of abstentions rises. Yet when a party preference is made (except in 1867) disproportionate support is given to the winning party. Floating voters drift with the tide.

Among four-time voters the floating vote had no clear social location. It was however twice as frequent (12% to 6%) among Freemen compared to £10 householders. Among occupational groups it was low among professionals and high among beersellers/publicans, fishmongers/butchers and pipe makers (though numbers are small). Among Freemen there is a significant number of mariners who handsomely win an occupational prize for maverick voting.

Candidates and Issues

Splitters and plumpers are traditionally used to estimate the personal vote of a candidate. This was a product of three factors: whether the candidate had local connections, whether he had been a candidate at a previous election (better still, a sitting member) and whether he was free from extreme views likely to offend a part of the electorate.

John Gurdon Rebow scored high on all three counts. He was a considerable local landowner and a popular squire. Besides the customary funding of soup kitchens and charities he seems to have put up a full purse at election time. He was a candidate in 1857 (twice) 1859, 1865 and 1868. His social status and moderate stance rendered him acceptable to a wider electorate, especially when the Liberals followed the familiar minority party device of offering but one candidate. An appropriate contrast lies with Philip O. Papillon. The youthful squire of Lexden was elected in 1859 on the Conservative ticket, though with fewer splits and plumps than Miller and Rebow, the sitting members. At Easter 1865, under pressure from his High Church uncle, now rector of Lexden, Papillon banned the traditional Easter Fair on Lexden Green. Rightly fearful that this ban might be ignored, Papillon arranged on the morning of the event to smear the stiles and fences with tar and cover the ground and bushes with soot. Popular indignation was considerable and 'Three groans for POP and the soot of Lexden' became an effective Liberal slogan in the election that year. Papillon came bottom of the poll with 13% less votes than his fellow Conservative, Miller. Rebow secured 94 votes (14% of his total) from splits with Miller and headed the poll by 51 votes. Papillon had given him the seat. Led by the Town Clerk (a political appointee) determined efforts were made to remove Papillon as a future candidate. In compensation he was made chairman of the Bench and mayor of Colchester, but in 1868 the lack-lustre Colonel Learmonth was drafted in as the second Conservative candidate.

In 1868 Rebow again headed the poll, but not the personal vote which was topped by Karslake, the other sitting member. The two junior candidates lagged some way behind:

'Personal' Votes 1868			
Karslake	82	Brewer	27
Rebow	63	Learmonth	22

This time however there was a dramatic concentration on straight party voting:

	Liberal	Conservative	Total
All Votes	2884	2501	5385
Straight Party Vote	2724	2380	5104
Percentage	94%	95%	95%

As such, 1868 represents a turning point. Rebow was the last of the truly local candidates. Henceforth outsiders contended for Colchester and general elections became increasingly preocccupied with party rather than personal votes, national rather than local issues – even with ideology.

This can be seen from the detailed record of the election campaigns recorded in the Colchester press. Local newspapers were an essential part of the political process, unashamedly partisan, with two Liberal and two Conservative weeklies produced in Colchester at this date. It is often claimed that reform of Parliament and the extension of the franchise were not issues at the 1868 general election. This was not so in Colchester. Indeed they were issues in 1865, 1867 and 1868. In 1865 the Liberal cry was

'if we want Parliamentary Reform we must strengthen Lord Palmerston's hand'.[8]

though with Rebow cautious over the extent of reform that was desirable and John Bright a possible source of lost votes, it was not high on the Liberal agenda. The Conservative candidates openly opposed reform.

The by-election of February 1867 came at a sensitive time, during the frantic preparation in Cabinet of Derby's own Reform Bill. The Conservatives of Colchester handled the issue skilfully, by parading their own likely role as reformers while embarrassing Dr Brewer over the extent of reform he favoured. Karslake's victory, as we have seen, depended on more traditional methods. This neutralisation of reform in 1867 renders more interesting the contest of 1868.

The run-up to the 1868 election was exceptionally long, stretching over six months. During that period both parties worked hard on the new register. The Liberals however went further. Following a visit from the National Reform Union, in February a Colchester Workingmen's Liberal Association was formed to woo, educate and protect the new voters. An early resolution was passed to hold no meetings in public houses. Led by Brewer, the more active candidate (and a Vice-President of the Reform Union), a long campaign was launched against blankets, soup and political intimidation. The Liberals themselves boasted of a 'pure' campaign and ostentatiously met in the theatre to organise protection of working men. They also mounted a series of eight open air meetings in different parts of the borough, attendance at which, even allowing for the optimism of the Liberal press, was impressive. It is clear that the Liberals themselves were delighted, even intoxicated by the outcome. The deferential tone of the first meeting in March is in marked contrast to the popularism of the final rally at St John's Green, attended by over 2,000.

At these meetings the current national issues received an airing: the need to disestablish the Irish Church, the growing cult of Mr. Gladstone.

Increasingly however a second theme – a liturgy – developed thus: The Tories are the enemy of the Working Classes; for years they have oppressed you. Now you have the vote. It is a sacred trust. Stand firm. Be men. Resist bribery and soup. Reform comes only from the Liberals. They gave you the act of 1832, the cheap press, the abolition of church rates – and now your enfranchisement is due to Liberal pressure.

It was the rhetoric of class. It secured for the Liberals a decisive majority among the new voters and a swing to the Conservatives among the old. The Liberals won both Colchester seats for the first time since 1832 (no real comparison). Once more the hapless Papillon provided political ammunition for his opponents. Chairing the Conservative rally to adopt their new candidates, one hand went up against the proposal. 'It is a dirty hand', he said, 'I consider a dirty hand no hand at all.' Immediately 'dirty hands' became a Liberal slogan. According to a Conservative newspaper Papillon's comment cost them the election. The opinion of the Liberal *Essex Telegraph* is worth quoting more fully.

> 'Hitherto almost all governments have been administered for the oppression of the many and the benefit of the few. The governing classes have persistently fought for the retention of class privilege, class legislation . . .
>
> As the masses have become more educated and their social status improved . . . the more bitterly do they resent interference which . . . humiliates and degrades them in their own esteem: workmen coerced, tradesmen intimidated . . . bribery in the form of blankets . . .
>
> The intellectual commotions of the last 20 years have in ever widening circles passed over Essex and our county, once the Boetia of England, despised alike for its political serfdom and intellectual gloom, is gradually taking a fair stand among the educated counties of England.'[9]

In 1868 the Colchester Liberal Party stood ready to assume a leadership of the masses against the classes, of light against darkness. It did not succeed. Why?

The Sources of Political Persuasion

A glance at the occupational voting patterns in Appendix B shows clearly that electoral Colchester was at war with itself. No occupational group of more than 10 individuals gave unanimous support to one party, no social stratum was too high, no neighbourhood too low that both parties might not find there political adherents. What factors then fashioned a voter's political persuasion?

All modern studies are agreed on the crucial role of family and upbringing in fixing initial political affiliation. In Victorian times a prevailing domestic authoritarianism and emphasis on the wisdom of maturity would have reinforced the role of family, not least because two other key determinants, religious denomination and occupation, were closely related. It is of course necessary to remind ourselves that most of the electors in this study did not cast a vote until they reached early middle age. Only 7% of the 1870 voters were under 30. The household franchise also meant that relatively few cases of fathers and sons occur in the total.

The role of family can however be examined among the Freemen. Membership at this stage was confined to the sons of existing Freemen. There are 35 surnames that boast 5 or more individuals, 299 voters in all. It is almost certain that blood relationships were fairly distant within some of these surnames. Nonetheless an aggregation of all the votes they cast – including abstentions – and a weighting of two for those who plumped for Rebow in 1865, produces only four surnames where there is less than 60% support for one party. In 16 cases there is over 80% support, a figure that would be far higher if abstentions were discounted.

A pattern of one-party preference becomes more marked if we attribute a partisan identity to each individual, ignoring occasional abstentions or cross-party votes. With all but six 'mixed' surnames there is an overwhelming pattern of one-party allegiance, with one or two individuals showing an opposite allegiance. Of the six 'mixed' surnames two are known to contain separate families while a third, the Greens, shows strong internal evidence for two families, one full party Conservatives, the other abstainers with occasional Liberal votes. There are other family-specific patterns. The Newtons begin Liberal and mostly switch to Conservative (a rare practice). The volatile Prestneys, champions of the Freemen cause, are classic floaters, ringing the changes of splitting, switching and abstaining. Six of the ten Johnsons split for Rebow and Miller in 1865. Nor should the political significance of the larger families be ignored. The Bacons, the Bromleys, the Halls and Heweses cast 228 votes for the Conservatives over our four elections. Others were stalwarts of the town's political structure. The Wires had been Liberals for 100 years; the Daniells were to provide six Town Councillors. The total picture is as follows:

	No. of Individuals	%
Problem 'Mixed' Families	56	19
Loyal to Surname	215	72
Disloyal to Surname	28	9
TOTAL	299	100

Unless the Freemen were a people apart, family tradition was a dominant factor in electoral predisposition. This was also true in mid-Victorian times of religious denomination. The rise of political nonconformity is well charted, and few commentators doubt that by 1868 most nonconformists were committed to the Liberal Party. This was clearly so in Colchester which had a lively and considerable nonconformist presence. By common account the only Liberal doubtfuls were the Wesleyans which, as we shall see, was to be significant in 1870.

Defence of the established church was made a key Conservative principle in 1865, 1867 and 1868 and Gurdon Rebow, otherwise universally respected in the borough, was pointedly attacked because he, a churchman, was a Liberal candidate. Though Rebow and Brewer were both Anglicans, attacks on establishment were notable in Liberal speeches in 1867 and 1868. Of 19 Anglican clergy only 3 voted Liberal. Two Roman Catholic priests voted Conservative in 1867; one then abstained, the other voted

Liberal. Nine nonconformist ministers, missioners or lay preachers all voted Liberal. Led by the Rev. Thomas Davids, minister of Lion Walk Congregational Church, practically all the active Liberal leadership was nonconformist. But how far did denominational affiliation embrace the wider community?

There is evidence from the 1851 Religious Census that perhaps 70% of Colchester's adult population attended church on Census Sunday, with a 5:4 preponderance to nonconformity. This however did not extend to active church membership. In 1874, on the Rev. Davids retirement, Lion Walk, the town's most important nonconformist congregation had only 63 male members. At the same date Headgate Chapel had 173 members, male and female.[10] It is unlikely that the other four leading nonconformist chapels had a larger membership. For a great many Liberal voters, nonconformity was increasingly only a cultural tradition, based on Sunday School, marriage and death. With no statistics as yet to offer, it is arguable that among the crucial artisan community, and notably among unskilled labour, passive nonconformity was a bridgehead not only into religious apathy but electoral Conservatism too. By claiming the moral high ground in 1868 the Liberals thrust upon the Conservatives the moral low ground. There is a lot of mileage there. Even before Gladstone upset the drink interest and drowned in a torrent of gin, the publicans and beersellers of Colchester voted 70% to 30% Conservative, one of the highest occupational biases in Appendix B. The town's influential temperance lobby was of course firmly lodged in the Liberal Party. The first response of the Colchester Conservatives to their defeat in 1880 was to establish a Conservative Workingmen's Club, licensed and offering convivial comforts, which was widely seen as a factor in their recapture of Colchester in 1885, secret ballot notwithstanding, even, perhaps, secret ballot assisted.

How far then was respectability, in a more secular, if not a Marxist, sense, a determinant of political preference? The occupational voting patterns in Appendix B show that while Colchester's electoral divide was vertical, not horizontal, there was still a greater propensity for the wealthy and educated and those who waited on them to be Conservative (those that waited on horses were notably Conservative). Liberalism owed most to artisan radicalism and a marginal majority among shopkeepers and businessmen, categories which, as we have seen, overlapped.

Even here there are subtle variables of social standing, even of assumed social standing. Booksellers and chemists have some education, but there is none so questionable as a 'general dealer' (often in cheap furniture) or marine store dealer (a euphemism for a second-hand shop). Booksellers/chemists are 12 to 3 Conservative, dealers are 15 to 1 Liberal. Is there significance in the fact that while shoemakers per se, the most Liberal of occupational groups, are 88–26 Liberal, those describing themselves as cordwainers are only 10–7 Liberal?

With few large employers and a host of small masters and the self employed, occupation tended to be a family affair. Solicitors' sons were solicitors, shoemakers' sons, shoemakers. This can be seen among the Freemen. What however happens when an inherited political affiliation conflicts with social standing? There cannot be a single answer, but the presence of Liberal voters among professionals, farmers and large business-men is frequently a triumph of inheritance over social mobility. One example must suffice. Of the five Francis cousins, one was a solicitor, one an Anglican clergyman, one a surgeon and two corn merchants. Here surely is a recipe for Conservatism. Not so; offspring of a nonconformist family that provided 17 Liberal freemen over four generations, they voted full party Liberal at all four elections.[11]

This however is to consider only those voters of independent action. How were men placed who called a man their master? Following his visit to Colchester in 1868, George Davis, the representative of the National Reform League, wrote a confidential report on the prospects for the Liberal Party among the working class. He said

> 'The Conservative interest is very strong, as they have 16 parish churches . . . Most of the house property is in the hands of the Conservatives . . . The Countess Cowper has a large property here, and although she is considered Liberal, all her Agents are said to be bigoted Tories, who will use their influence in the most unscrupulous manner. . .'[12]

This is not the rhetoric of Liberal newspapers but a serious report by an experienced working class political activist. How far did landlord pressure secure the Conservative majority among both urban and agricultural labourers? The Countess Cowper, an absentee landlord, held the manors of Mile End and Greenstead. Mile End was always Conservative, but Greenstead, where the very resident Gurdon Rebow was equally influential, registered one of the largest swings to Liberal in 1868, swinging sharply back to Conservative in 1870. By then, of course, Gurdon Rebow was dead.

Greenstead is also significant for the number of enfranchised agricultural labourers it acquired in 1868. As well as Gurdon Rebow, the parish boasted several influential Liberal farmers and the charismatic Dr Meshach Seaman, the only Liberal Anglican incumbent in the borough. Lying on the outskirts of built-up Colchester, Greenstead can be contrasted with the rural parishes of Mile End and Lexden, the latter traditionally dominated by P. O. Papillon. The figures show a dramatic correlation between the voting patterns of masters and men:

Agricultural Labourers	Total	Full Party Con.	Variable Con.	% Con.	Full Party Lib.	Variable Lib.	% Lib.
Greenstead	26	6	1	27	10	9	73
Mile End	46	16	8	52	3	11	30
Lexden	38	30	0	79	2	5	18
Farmers	Total	Full Party Con.	Variable Con.	% Con.	Full Party Lib.	Variable Lib.	% Lib.
Greenstead	7	3	0	43	3	1	57
Mile End	15	5	1	40	4	1	33
Lexden	10	7	1	80	0	0	0

Note: Those of no clear party persuasion are omitted.

The question remains whether the labourers of Lexden voted Conservative because their employers or their squire required it or whether the political culture of Lexden was wholly Conservative. This is the same as asking whether so many Greenstead agricultural labourers voted Liberal because their employer required it or because Greenstead Road and the Bucks Horns inn were centres of Radicalism.

The consistent electorate included the Old Heath agricultural labourer who told Dr Brewer, 'Master says I must vote blue: it is my bread'. This is not the same view as that of Mr Bones of the Wormingford Branch of the National Agricultural Labourers Union who recalled in 1880:

> '. . . before the union started we labourers were as ignorant as the cattle we attended. Not one in a thousand of us knew the meaning of politics. . . . .'[13]

What of urban labourers? Brewery and wine merchants' labourers were 12 to 7 Conservative (though most brewers were Liberal). Mill labourers were all Liberal – so were most millers. The clearest case is with porters. Porters as a body were 29 to 21 Conservative, but grocers' and millers' porters were 4 to 1 Liberal and coal porters and coal meters were 20 to 6 Conservative. These were nearly all employed at the Hythe by the Conservative coal merchant, Thomas Moy, and formed the core of his storm troopers, the Colchester 'lambs'. (Three Liberal coal porters were confined to adjacent houses on Hythe Quay.) Another employed group of new voters were railway workers. In 1868 they voted 27 to 7 Liberal. In 1870 warnings appeared in the Liberal press that they were subject to 'undue influence'. In the event they voted 15 to 8 Conservative with 10 abstentions.

From such statistics the Liberal campaign of 1868 can be understood. A social and intellectual gulf distanced the shoemaker, the tailor and the basket maker from the beer-swilling Hythe labourer. For skilled artisans the franchise was an assertion of their independence and Liberalism the glory of the thinking man. Appropriately superior, and shocked by Dr Brewer's craven labourer, they missed the note of perceived self interest in his response. With craftsmen too there was an hereditary dimension. Weavers (an almost dead trade in Colchester) had been Liberal for a century, iron and foundry workers (not above beer-swilling) were linear descendants of millwrights and machine makers, though, significantly, they had Liberal employers too.

Craftsmen, small town business and to a lesser extent shopkeepers brought in a Liberal majority, but not too large a majority. At all points of the electorate the Liberal vote is lower than it is for the equivalent Cambridge poll of 1868. The superficial distinction is that Cambridge had more craftsmen than Colchester which had a larger agriculture/horticulture electorate; but the significant distinction is that while business, retail and the professions form the same approximate percentage in both electorates, those at Colchester were more Conservative inclined. So were tailors, painters, printers and carpenters. Indeed the Conservatism of Colchester carpenters is interesting, given their pioneer trade union activity in the borough.

Modern studies of voting behaviour suggest that working class voters are less likely to vote Labour in predominantly Conservative areas and vice

| Categories | CAMBRIDGE 1868 | | COLCHESTER 1868/70 | |
	% of Electorate	% Liberal	% of Electorate	% Liberal
Gentry and Farmers	5	41	3	36
Professionals	10	40	9	38
Publicans, etc.	3	50	4	30
Labour	23	51	14⎱	
Ag. Lab./Gardeners			11⎰	45
Business	6	64	6	60
Craftsmen	37	67	31	63
Retail	13	58	14	56
TOTAL ELECTORATE	100	57	100	52

Total Electors: Cambridge 3225, Colchester 2323.

Note: Although the Colchester figures are for voters identified in the 1871 Census, their
Liberal: Conservative proportions coincide with the 1868 election result. The
Cambridge figures do not include abstentions or split votes. The Colchester figures do
not include abstentions.[14]

versa. Colchester in 1868 was still regarded as a Conservative town. The
besieging armies of rural Conservatism and the inner forces of Hythe
Toryism left urban Liberalism less secure. There was however a reciprocal
process. Horticulture returned a Liberal majority, and traditional agriculture
was only 3:2 Conservative with, as we have seen, dramatically different
patterns at Greenstead and Lexden. If Colchester elections were a simple
contest between town and country, the constituency was riddled with
turncoats and fifth columnists.

This brings us to the by-election of 1870. The unusual circumstances of
this election and its effect upon the Liberal vote throw further light upon
electoral processes. The simple pattern of what happened is clear. The
intervention of Langley's candidature resulted in a big swing to Conservative
among previous abstainers and previous Liberals. More interesting was a
large abstention vote among previous Liberals. Their identity is revealing:

Previous full party Liberals	Stay Loyal	Abstain	Vote Conservative	
New Voters of 1868	55%	25	20	100
Old Voters	82%	14	4	100

Of the 4% of old voters who switched to Conservative nearly half were
Freemen.

There is also a strikingly different desertion rate between 'inner' and
'outer' Colchester, as represented by the three parishes of Greenstead,
Lexden and Mile End:

Full Party 1868 'New Liberals'	Stay Loyal	Abstain	Vote Conservative	
Outer Colchester	38%	33%	29%	100
Inner Colchester	59%	23%	18%	100

Finally, an occupational analysis of full party Liberals who switched to Conservative shows an overwhelming bias towards those who could be considered least politically informed and from the lower social strata:

OCCUPATION	%	% OF ACTUAL ELECTORATE
Agricultural Labourers	17	6
Gardeners	7	4
Farm Servants/Under Gardeners	5	1
Labourers, Porters, Railway Workers, Mariners, Hawkers, Costermongers, Rat Catcher	27	12
TOTAL LABOUR	56	23
Bricklayers	10	3
Shoemakers, Carpenters, Sawyers	10	11
Other Craftsmen	9	17
TOTAL CRAFTSMEN	29	31
Beerseller/Publican	6	3
'Shopkeeper', Dealer	3	2
Butcher	2	1
TOTAL RETAIL	5	14
Businessmen	2	6
Farmers + Professionals	2	10
	100	90

When we look at the far larger number of Liberals who abstained, there is a wider cross-section of the electorate and a far greater proportion of craftsmen, though the professions, business and retail, the leaders of the community, are disproportionately few. This is particularly true of the leadership of the Liberal Party. Of 82 prominent citizens named as present at the first public meeting for Storks, five cannot be certainly identified in the pollbook, but of the rest all but six were to vote for him. These six abstainers included the Party Agent (Philbrick), the impossible W. R. Havens, and two voters whose Liberalism must be in doubt since they had both abstained in 1868.

What are we to make of this? Firstly it is clear what did not happen in 1870. Faced with a Liberal candidate who supported prostitution (an oversimplification of course, but prior to his candidature Storks had said 'prostitution is a necessity') godly and respectable Liberalism did not vote Conservative or abstain in droves. Nor did their leadership. Of seven nonconformist clergy with the franchise only one abstained. The Catholic priest and the three Anglican clergy who were Liberals all voted for Storks. The Rev. Thomas Davids, an outspoken critic of the extent of prostitution in the town, was an active Storks campaigner. It is also clear that Langley's candidature won no support from local Liberals. Not one appeared on the platform at his two rallies, both of which were shouted down by an organised Liberal presence. Indeed according to Josephine Butler's account, organised violence was directed against these London interlopers.[15]

They did however find one local supporter. The newly established Wesleyan minister, the Rev. Ellis, was moved to write a letter, a printed copy of which was mailed to every elector. It gave very explicit information about the C. D. Acts and urged against voting for Storks. Though not a voter himself, Ellis was named by the Liberal *Essex Telegraph* as a Conservative and his motive as political. His long letter of self defence is our sole means of knowing the significant part he played in the election.

There was of course a moral answer to Langley, which had been carefully spelt out in a recent letter to *The Times* by the late Gurdon Rebow: that the alternative to the C. D. Acts was 'widespread and harmful infection'. This pragmatism was suitably summed up by the Liberal banner displayed at Langley's meeting, 'Sir Henry Storks & No Humbug'. But the moral equivocation this implied must have sat uneasily with the deacons of Lion Walk. It is difficult to deny that, faced with a strain between its political and moral loyalties, political nonconformity clung firmly to the former.

This was not so with the wider electorate. Liberal abstentions and, more particularly, Liberal defections were greatest among those voters least likely to harbour a nonconformist sensitivity and least likely to attend a Liberal political rally. Realising what was coming, J. S. Barnes, Colchester's Liberal godfather, urged his hearers to stand firm, stick to their beliefs and not betray their trust. Appreciating the impact of the Rev. Ellis's letter he said,

> "conciliate your wives, gentlemen . . . I know the ladies influence is very strong indeed."

In earnest tones the Rev. Davids warned "Don't go back to the Tories", much as he would urge in the pulpit against reversion to irreligion.

It may be argued that the lower orders, fearful that their own wives might be 'inspected', voted (or abstained) against interference by authority, except that Colonel Learmonth was equally supportive of the C. D. Acts. In point of fact the tendency of the humble to stray from party allegiance and of the educated and employing classes to register a higher degree of full party voting is true over all four elections. This is why the Freemen, who represented 26% of all four-time voters, provided 40% of those who switched party or voted erratically.

Appendix B distinguishes between partisan voters who voted full party and those who did not – even to the extent of a single abstention. They are labelled 'variables' and provide the basis for assessing disloyalty by broad categories. The table opposite seeks to offset statistical factors which would distort categories with a high proportion of 'old' voters or Liberal voters (both of which tend to increase a disloyalty ratio).

Here is a scenario to fit these facts. Parliamentary elections were dramatic civic events embracing the whole community. The detailed newspaper accounts are evidence of this. Elections were conducted by the middle classes – it was their windows that were broken afterwards. Partisan political allegiance based on inheritance, self-interest and religious affiliation

Partisan Disloyalty

Category	% of Liberal Deserters 1870	Rank Order	% of Conservative Variables	Rank Order
Professions & White Collar	14	1	13	2
Business and Farmers	20	2	16	3
Retail	21	3	9	1
Craftsmen	25	4	17	4
Labourers	26	5	17	4
Publicans/Beersellers	50	6	23	7
Agricultural Labourers	57	8	19	6
Mariners	56	7	43	8

was almost universal. Few were undecided, fewer still turned their backs upon events. There was however a dichotomy between persuaders and persuaded. It was a blurred line dividing them, but not very different from another line between middle and working class, clean and dirty hands. For the latter an election was one of those rare occasions when 'they' were dependent on 'us'. Hence a greater readiness among those below to withhold a party vote and a greater public expectation that those above would maintain theirs. In the event it is remarkable how few voters below proved fickle. It needed a crisis like 1870 to render more manifest the blurred line. What was evident in 1870 was not a moral dilemma but a Liberal Party machine in disarray. Even their own paper admitted that after the first few hours' polling, the Conservative bandwaggon took over: Head Street and High Street were a sea of blue.

In this election scenario the skilled craftsmen stood uneasily in the middle. Chief beneficiaries of the 1867 franchise, and the largest element in the electorate, they were encouraged to join the political persuaders with token membership on the party platform. With heroes like Cromwell and Bunyan, political nonconformity had only scorn for those who betrayed their trust. After the 1870 result a broadsheet was distributed in Colchester listing all those who had voted Liberal in 1868 and Conservative in 1870. It contained not many craftsmen, few of the respectable and no political activists. Peculiar odium rested on those who changed sides. The appearance of Havens on the hustings was a signal for pandemonium. In 1865 Thomas Rouse, ironmonger and former Liberal, became an active Conservative canvasser. His presence on the hustings brought events to a standstill. A newspaper commented:

> 'It was a strange sight to see several hundred men pointing their hands of scorn at him and groaning their discontent and determination that he should be turned out.'[16]

In 1872 the curtain fell for ever on the hustings. How far the secret ballot changed the Victorian political process lies beyond the scope of this study.

APPENDIX A: OFFICIAL ELECTION RETURNS FOR COLCHESTER[17]

1859	Taverner J. Miller	Con.	651		1868	J. Gurdon Rebow	Lib.	1467
	Philip O. Papillon	Con.	598			Dr. William Brewer	Lib.	1417
	J Gurdon Rebow	Lib.	518			E. Kent Karslake	Con.	1284
						Col. A. Learmonth	Con.	1217
1865	J. Gurdon Rebow	Lib.	691					
	Taverner J. Miller	Con.	640		1870	Col. A. Learmonth	Con.	1363
	Philip O. Papillon	Con.	561			Sir Henry Storks	Lib.	853
1867	E. Kent Karslake	Con.	675					
	Dr William Brewer	Lib.	598					

APPENDIX B: OCCUPATIONAL DISTRIBUTION OF ELECTORS

OCCUPATION	OLD VOTERS	NEW VOTERS (1870 ONLY)	CONSERVATIVE VARIABLE	CONSERVATIVE FULL PARTY	TOTAL CONSERVATIVE	TOTAL LIBERAL	LIBERAL FULL PARTY	LIBERAL VARIABLE	PREDOMINANTLY ABSTAIN	1870 ONLY ABSTAIN	SWITCH PARTY OR ERRATIC
Landowner	14	3(1)	2	7	9	8	5	3			
Farmer	47	16(2)	3	32	35	17	11	6	7	2	3
Bailiff	0	4	1	3	4	0	0	0			
Gardener or Seedsman	35	72(8)	10	34	44	56	36	20	1	1	5
Agricultural Labourer	4	130(14)	14	59	73	51	21	30	6	1	2
'Skilled' Agricultural Labs.	3	15(2)	2	9	11	7	2	5			
Livestock Dealer/Keeper	5	3	1	4	5	2	2	0			1
TOTAL AGRICULTURE/ HORTICULTURE	94	246	31	141	172	139	77	62	14	4	11
Artist/Architect	5	0	0	4	4	1	1	0			
Auctioneer/Estate Agent	10	1	0	5	5	6	5	1			1
Accountant	6	0	1	5	6	0	0	0			
Banker	7	3(1)	1	9	10	0	0	0			
Clergy C of E	18	2(1)	2	14	16	3	3	0	1		
Clergy Nonconformist	3	5(1)	0	0	0	8	6	2			
Clergy Roman Catholic	2	0	1	0	1	0	0	0			1
Doctor	21	1	1	13	14	8	5	3	1		1
Dentist	3	1(1)	0	0	0	2	1	1	1	1	
Vet./Medical Botanist	3	1	0	2	2	2	2	0			
Lunatic Asylum Staff	0	3	0	0	0	3	3	0			
Army Officers	1	4(2)	1	2	3	0	0	0		1	1
Lawyer	21	2(1)	3	12	15	7	6	1	1		
Musician/Music Teacher	2	3	1	3	4	1	1	0			
School Teacher	8	3(1)	1	5	6	5	4	1			
Customs/Coast Guard/ Harbour Master	2	4(2)	0	4	4	2	1	1			
Government/Municipal Officers	8	9	1	6	7	5	2	3	3		
Agents/Brokers	5	10(1)	1	7	8	7	5	2			
Gas Engineer/Newspaper Editor	0	2(1)	0	0	0	2	1	1			
TOTAL PROFESSIONAL	125	54	14	91	105	63	46	17	6	3	4

OCCUPATION	OLD VOTERS	NEW VOTERS (1870 ONLY)	CONSERVATIVE VARIABLE	CONSERVATIVE FULL PARTY	TOTAL CONSERVATIVE	TOTAL LIBERAL	LIBERAL FULL PARTY	LIBERAL VARIABLE	PREDOMINANTLY ABSTAIN	1870 ONLY ABSTAIN	SWITCH PARTY OR ERRATIC
Clerk	18	16(2)	3	18	21	7	7	0	3	1	2
Commercial Traveller	4	2(1)	1	3	4	2	2	0			
Shop Assistant	6	8(2)	2	3	5	8	8	0	1		
'Manager'	4	3(1)	0	3	3	3	3	0	1		
Railway – Administrative	2	3(1)	0	2	2	3	3	0			
TOTAL 'WHITE COLLAR'	34	32	6	29	35	23	23	0	5	1	2
Licensed Victualler	6	1	2	2	4	0	0	0	1		1
Publican/Innkeeper	38	19(1)	8	27	35	14	5	9	3		5
Beerhouse/Beerseller	8	12(3)	2	9	11	8	3	5			1
Temperance Hotel/Billiard Room	0	2	0	2	2	0	0	0			
TOTAL 'DRINK'	52	34	12	40	52	22	14	8	4	0	7
Warehouseman	4	4	1	3	4	4	4	0			
Army Non Commissioned	2	8	2	4	6	4	2	2			
Policeman	0	3	0	0	0	1	1	0	2		
'Foreman'	2	1	0	2	2	1	1	0			
TOTAL 'RESPONSIBLE' LABOUR	8	16	3	9	12	10	8	2	2		
Labourer	11	77(10)	10	26	36	44	33	11	4	1	2
'Drink' Labourer	1	18(2)	1	11	12	7	6	1			
Bricklayers Labourer	0	6(1)	0	3	3	3	1	2			
Mill Worker/Labourer	0	6(2)	0	0	0	6	5	1			
(TOTAL LABOURER)	12	107	11	40	51	54	40	14	4	1	2
Porters (Other)	3	22	1	12	13	11	8	3			1
Grocers/Millers Porter	0	6(2)	0	1	1	4	2	2		1	
Coal Porter/Meter	5	23(1)	2	18	20	6	6	0	2		2
Messenger/Waiter	1	3	0	2	2	2	2	0			
Carter	5	14	3	6	9	7	6	1	1		2
Carman/Driver	1	14(3)	1	4	5	9	4	5	1		
Cab Driver	0	6(1)	2	4	6	0	0	0			
Coachman	3	6(2)	0	7	7	2	2	0			
Ostler	2	4(1)	1	3	4	2	2	0			
Groom	3	23(4)	3	14	17	7	4	3	2		
Machinist	1	5(1)	1	1	2	3	2	1		1	
Domestic/Farm Servant/Gardener	1	16(1)	0	8	8	10	4	6			
TOTAL LABOUR	37	249	25	120	145	117	82	35	10	4	7
Mariner/Fisherman	13	28(5)	6	5	11	7	0	7	14	3	6
Ferryman/Lighterman	2	7	1	4	5	2	1	1	2		
TOTAL QUAYSIDE	15	35	7	9	16	9	1	8	16	3	6
TOTAL RAILWAY MANUAL	1	35	0	7	7	27	8	19		2	

OCCUPATION	OLD VOTERS	NEW VOTERS (1870 ONLY)	CONSERVATIVE VARIABLE	CONSERVATIVE FULL PARTY	TOTAL CONSERVATIVE	TOTAL LIBERAL	LIBERAL FULL PARTY	LIBERAL VARIABLE	PREDOMINANTLY ABSTAIN	1870 ONLY ABSTAIN	SWITCH PARTY OR ERRATIC
Sweep	0	6(3)	1	2	3	3	2	1			
Hawker, Pedlar, Tinker, Costermonger	2	15	0	4	4	11	3	8	1		1
Well Sinker, Excavator	5	1	0	1	1	5	2	3			
'Petty' Business	3	8(1)	2	3	5	5	2	3		1	
TOTAL PETTY BUSINESS	10	30	3	10	13	24	9	15	1	1	1
Brick Maker	5	3	3	3	6	2	1	1			
Builder	17	4(1)	1	10	11	7	7	0	1	2	
Brewer	10	1	0	2	2	8	7	1			1
Cab Proprietor	4	2	3	0	3	1	0	1	2		
Clothier	5	1(1)	1	2	3	4	2	2			
Coal Merchant	5	1	0	5	5	1	0	1			
Corn Merchant/Dealer	6	2(2)	0	1	1	4	3	1	1	1	1
Engineer (Manufacturer)	1	3(1)	0	1	1	2	2	0		1	
Hay/Straw Dealer	3	2	0	2	2	1	1	0	1		1
Miller	20	11(3)	1	5	6	23	15	8			1
Maltster	0	5	0	4	4	1	1	0			
Shipowner	8	0	0	1	1	5	5	0			2
Timber/Wood Merchant	3	1	0	3	3	1	1	0			
Woolstapler/Leather Merchant	5	3(1)	0	0	0	8	0	0			
Others	8	2(1)	0	2	2	5	3	2	1		2
TOTAL BUSINESS	100	41	11	39	50	73	56	17	6	4	8
Basket/Mat Maker	2	5	1	1	2	5	5	0			
Blacksmith	4	11	1	1	2	9	7	2	2		2
Bricklayer	11	56(5)	4	16	20	40	14	26	4	1	2
Broom/Brush Maker	6	3	0	2	2	5	3	2	1		1
Cabinet Maker	14	15(3)	2	9	11	17	9	8		1	
Carpenter/Joiner	22	70(7)	3	42	45	35	17	18	4	1	6
Coach Builder	5	4	0	2	2	7	3	4			
Coachbuilding (Other skills)	5	14(1)	1	8	9	8	5	3		1	
Cooper	5	3	1	2	3	5	5	0			
Engine Driver (not Railway)	0	7(2)	0	2	2	4	3	1		1	
Farrier	3	2	0	1	1	4	3	1			
Foundry Work	6	22(2)	1	3	4	22	19	3	1	1	
Harness/Saddle Maker	7	6(1)	2	5	7	6	6	0			
Leather Work	3	4	0	1	1	6	4	2			
Millwright	2	3	0	0	0	5	3	2			
Pipe Maker	5	1	1	2	3	1	1	0			2
Printer	10	2(1)	1	7	8	3	3	0		1	
Painter, Plumber, Glazier, Plasterer	15	23(2)	2	15	17	16	9	7	3	1	2
Sawyer	0	15	1	4	5	9	6	3			
Silk Weaver/Throwster	2	6	0	1	1	6	5	1			1
Shoemaker	47	79(14)	5	21	26	88	71	17	2	1	8

OCCUPATION	OLD VOTERS	NEW VOTERS (1870 ONLY)	CONSERVATIVE VARIABLE	CONSERVATIVE FULL PARTY	TOTAL CONSERVATIVE	TOTAL LIBERAL	LIBERAL FULL PARTY	LIBERAL VARIABLE	PREDOMINANTLY ABSTAIN	1870 ONLY ABSTAIN	SWITCH PARTY OR ERRATIC
'Cordwainer'	1	16(1)	1	6	7	10	7	3			
Stone Mason	4	4	0	5	5	2	1	1			1
Tailor	25	45(7)	5	18	23	41	34	7	3	1	2
Upholsterer	10	5	0	7	7	8	6	2			
Umbrella Maker	1	5	0	1	1	4	3	1	1		
Watchmaker	5	7(1)	2	3	5	5	4	1			2
Wheelwright	2	9(1)	2	2	4	6	3	3	1		
Others	24	35	6	13	19	31	21	10	5		4
TOTAL CRAFTSMEN	246	476	42	200	242	407	279	128	27	10	33
Baker	31	15(2)	3	13	16	23	15	8	4	1	2
Butcher	18	14(5)	1	11	12	13	4	9	4		3
Bookseller/stationer	5	2	0	5	5	1	1	0	1		
Chemist	8	2(1)	0	7	7	2	2	0	1		
Confectioner	8	5(1)	0	2	2	10	8	2			1
Draper	20	7	0	14	14	13	10	3			
'Dealer'	3	10(1)	0	1	1	12	4	8			
Fishmonger	8	4	1	4	5	4	0	4	1		2
Greengrocer/fruiterer	5	7(1)	0	8	8	1	1	0		1	2
Grocer	25	9(2)	1	11	12	17	15	2	3	1	1
Haberdasher/Glover/Hosier	10	2(1)	1	4	5	6	5	1	1		
Hairdresser	3	6(1)	0	3	3	3	2	1	1	1	1
Ironmonger	16	5(5)	0	8	8	12	12	0		1	
Milkman/Dairyman	2	8(1)	1	0	1	7	5	2			2
Photographer	5	0	0	1	1	4	1	3			
Wine Merchant	15	0	1	10	11	3	3	0	1		
'Shopkeeper'	11	12(1)	3	6	9	13	8	5			2
Others	14	14(1)	10	7	7	17	11	6	3		1
TOTAL RETAIL	207	122	12	115	127	161	107	54	20	5	17
Ex-Army	1	10(2)	1	7	8	3	3	0			
Annuitant, Pensioner, Income from Property	9	4(1)	0	2	2	7	5	2	2		2
Unemployed/No Occupation	2	3(1)	0	1	1	4	2	2			
TOTAL OTHERS	12	17	1	10	11	14	10	4	2	0	2
GRAND TOTAL	941	1382	167	820	987	1089	720	369	113	36	98

NOTES All categories are those used of voters who were traced in the 1871 census. Although far short of the total 1868/70 electorate, these 'census' voters closely reflect the party vote in the 1868 election:

	Liberal	Conservative	
'Census' Voters	52%	48%	100%
1868 Rebow/Karslake	53%	47%	100%

Where a census occupation is preceded by 'former', 'retired' or 'unemployed', such individuals are nonetheless included in the main occupation groups. (Only two individuals termed themselves just 'unemployed').

All of the following numbered less than five individuals: Skilled agricultural labourers were shepherd, ploughman, thatcher, woodman, gamekeeper, hop cutter, binder, drover.

Government officers included Inland Revenue staff; Municipal Officers were public health and workhouse personnel.

Petty business included lodging house keeper, coffee house keeper, boat letter, carrier, lime burner, rat catcher, travelling draper. 'Other' businessmen were fish, tea, silk and potato merchants, soda water and ginger beer makers, laundry owner and newspaper proprietor. 'Other' craftsmen were cutler, carver, gilder, engraver, pattern maker, chair maker, boxmaker, bookbinder, cork cutter, blacking maker, coppersmith, brazier, tinman, dyer, French polisher, gas fitter, gun maker, piano maker, scales maker, rope maker, shipwright, sack and cloth maker, sail maker, whip maker, whitesmith, wood turner, last maker, candle maker.

'Other' retailers were china dealer, hatter, jeweller, newsagent, 'Marine Store dealer', oil and colourman, tea retailer, outfitter, tallow chandler, tobacconist.

Notes and References

The Pollbooks used for this research and microfilms of the 1871 census, the *Essex Standard* and the *Essex & West Suffolk Gazette* (both Conservative) are held by Essex Libraries, Local Studies Section, Colchester. The *Essex Telegraph* (Liberal) is only fully available in the British Library, Colingdale.

I have not provided detailed references for local newspaper sources which relate solely to the four election campaigns.

I am grateful to Mr RICHARD WILSON for his help with the 1871 census.

1. H. J. Hanham, *Elections & Party Management: Politics in the Time of Disraeli and Gladstone* (1959) Chapter 4.

2. 3060 is the 1868 pollbook figure; but what is the official figure? *McColmont's Parliamentary Pollbook* (the 19th century authority) says 3145; Craig: *British Parliamentary Results* (the current authority) says 2970 (clearly wrong) and has 3145 for 1870 (also wrong).

Non-Colchester Freemen (87) need to be excluded. The male population in 1871 was 13,295. Of these from 46% to 50% were under 21, while the garrison and workhouse housed 3057. This leaves a maximum-minimum eligible male figure from 5425 to 5150. Registered Colchester voters would form 55% or 58% of these totals. For a discussion of garrison totals see A. Phillips, *Ten Men and Colchester* (1985) pp.134–137.

3. E. J. Evans, *The Forging of the Modern State: Early Industrial Britain* 1783–1870 (1983) p.354.

4. Based on pollbook figures for 1868 and 1870 and Craig (op.cit) for 1874.

5. J. R. Vincent, *Pollbooks: How Victorians Voted* (1967).

6. D. Butler & D. Stokes, *Political Change in Britain* (1971) Chapter 12.

7. *Essex Telegraph* 24.11.1868.

8. Ibid. 11.7.1865.

9. Ibid. 20.11.1868.

10. A. Phillips, 'Mormons in Essex 1850–1870' in *Essex Journal* Vol. 18 No. 3; *Essex Standard* 26.6.1874; J. W. Newby, *The Story of Headgate 1843–1944* (1944) p.29.

11. I am indebted to Mr. J. Bensusan-Butt for help with the Francis family.

12. Original in Howell Collection, Bishopsgate Institute, London. See also R. Harrison, "The British Working Class at the General Election of 1868" in *International Review of Social History* No. 5 (1960).

13. I am indebted to Dr. Arthur Brown for this reference from the *English Labourers' Chronicle*, 24.9. 1881.
14. Vincent, *Pollbooks* (op.cit.) pp.92–93.
15. J. Butler, *An Autobiographical Memoir* (1928) pp.80–85; H. J. Hanham, *Election & Party Management* (op.cit.) pp.219–220.
16. *Essex Telegraph* 18.7.1865.
17. Taken from F. W. S. Craig, *British Parliamentary Results 1832–1885* (1977).

Essex and the 1871 Fairs Act.

'Because Solon is virtuous shall there be no cream cakes and ale!'

JOHN BOYES

Because of their importance in the economic life of local communities much research has been undertaken on the origins and development of markets and fairs. Their presence was regarded as a valuable asset by the manorial lords and the acquisition and renewal of charters setting out the rights and benefits for the owners are a recurring theme in the progressive growth of market towns. Research on the decay and eventual demise of many local fairs has been much more limited and generally confined to specific decisions by Quarter Sessions to suppress fairs. But, as in other fields of administrative progress, that which starts as a local action often leads eventually to national legislation. So with fairs, the local manifestations of concern for the welfare of the community by the suppression of gatherings allegedly accompanied by drunkenness and dissipation duly led to the passing of Acts which gave a framework for the abolition of fairs. The principal Act concerned was the Fairs Act 1871 but little research has been done on its operation and success in the local scene.

This essay examines the impact of the Act in Essex using material of the kind which Dr Emmison has so consistently recommended in local historical research.

Fairs by their charter and constitution were invariably annual events primarily undertaken for trade. When first instituted they served a general purpose but over the years many became specialised either as stock fairs where livestock were traded or as hiring fairs where servants offered their labour on an annual basis. Usually, whatever the specialised content, there would be some form of entertainment provided. The fair would thus have social implications in that it furnished a day's relief from the monotonous routine of daily labour being a welcome break to be anticipated and then enjoyed in retrospect and when travel beyond walking distance from a village was virtually impossible the fair offered an emotional safety valve.

In the 18th century many of the smaller village fairs declined as trading centres while the entertainment and freedom evoked by the fair degenerated, according to those in authority, into licence and dissipation. They were thus regarded by the gentry as disagreeable events profitless to the community. The logical solution to eliminate the annoyance was to make representation to Quarter Sessions for abolition. This was the fate of fairs such as Pebmarsh, Boxted and Ardleigh as early as 1761. This decline, creeping in the 18th century, steadily gathered momentum in the 19th consequential on national economic development. Many of the traditional fairs became pale ghosts of their former selves with little trading and only a few toy and gingerbread stalls, swings and a coconut shy. Nevertheless as annual events they were still an anticipated pleasure by the agricultural labourers and their families as a change from routine. On the other hand the gentry and better class residents – all who had previously patronised the fair – were now finding alternative outlets for their amusement. This, with the growing moral rectitude of the early 19th century, reinforced their opinion of the worthlessness of fairs. In 1837 a group of Essex clergymen wrote to the Colchester Gazette deploring the jingling matches, jumping in sacks, grinning through collars, bobbing for oranges and various other useless activities as remnants of bygone ages of moral darkness. They urged people to indulge in more refined pursuits such as archery societies for the fair sex and for the male cricket clubs and grounds for the practice of gymnastic exercises. A remote hope for those with one day's holiday a year! Whether any encouragement was given to this ideal is hard to say but even had it been one wonders what the reaction would have been from the agricultural labourers and their wives when they were looking for an escape from the regimentation of work.

With this background of the widening gulf between those who enjoyed fairs and those who regarded them as outmoded, and even in typical popular exaggeration as places of drunkenness and debauchery, it is not surprising that pressure was brought to bear on Parliament to control this evil. As a result the Fairs Act 1868 was passed to allow alterations in the dates of fairs but the direct power of abolition was contained in the Act passed in 1871 and this became for the next 30 years an effective tool in the hands of those enthusiasts seeking to suppress the fairs.

The Fairs Act 1871 was very short having only four sections and its purpose, and incidentally the views of authority, is adequately described in the preamble. 'Whereas certain of the fairs held in England and Wales are unnecessary, are the cause of grievous immorality and are very injurious to the inhabitants of the towns in which such fairs are held and it is therefore expedient to make provision to facilitate the abolition of such fairs be it enacted . . .' Of the four sections the first announced the title of the Act and the second defined the owner of a fair so that the meat really came in the third section.

'Where the magistrates of a Petty Sessional Division within which a fair is held or the owner of any fair represent to the Home Secretary that it would be for the convenience and advantage of the public that the fair should be abolished the Home Secretary, with the consent of the owner of the fair or of the tolls, can abolish the fair provided it shall be advertised once in the London Gazette and three times in the local papers before the Home Secretary will consider the representation.'

Finally the fourth section required that the order of abolition should be published in the London Gazette and a local paper. It received the Royal Assent on 25 May 1871. (34 Vic Ch 12).

This clearly gave the opportunity some authorities had been anticipating and soon applications were being received at the Home Office from Essex magistrates. By December 1872 32 fairs in the county had been abolished.

Only one application was refused (Chipping Ongar). Invariably there was a certificate from the magistrates couched in the actual wording of the preamble of the Act or something very similar; e g Good Easter, 'It appears that a considerable amount of drunkenness and debauchery prevails . . . . a great nuisance to the inhabitants of the village and neighbourhood'.

In the initial months following the passing of the Act there was little opposition and most of the orders went through without question. In Essex the first sustained opposition came not from a village community but from a market town and it is interesting to see the reactions where there was less monolithic control.

In Chipping Ongar the prime mover for the abolition of the fair held annually on 12/13 October under a charter granted by King John was H Gibson, a member of a committee formed in April 1872 to promote the fair's abolition. The non-resident owner of the tolls, Philip Chaplin of Harlow, gave written consent on 22 June 1872 and an application was sent to the Home Office on 12 August signed by four justices. On 19 August the Home Secretary gave notice that there would be a formal consideration on 19 September for the fair's abolition. This sequence of stages was the standard pattern in promoting an abolition.

At Ongar the pattern was distorted by the very vocal opposition which arose in the town, in the press and in correspondence with the Home Office. The April meeting was apparently attended by 14 people – some from outside Ongar – and it 'was asserted again and again that the fair led to drunkenness, riot and immorality'. An opposition letter of 25 July signed by, among others, the Rector's churchwarden pointed out '. . . .that statements relating to drunkenness etc are not only easily made but, if true, easily proved. For the drunkenness and riot we beg to call your attention to the proveable fact that on the mornings after the fair the police cells are unusually empty. For the immorality a reference to the return of illegitimate births will prove at all events that seduction finds no place at our little town.'

The very wet weather on the day selected for the opposition meeting did not deter a large crowd and the meeting had to adjourn from the Town Hall to the schoolroom and even that was inadequate to hold the crowd. On 30 August another letter signed inter alia by the churchwardens stated that at least half the freeholders and ratepayers desired the retention of the fair; while a further letter on 11 September protested against an abolition on three grounds. First, the fair was a boon to the town and a source of innocent amusement; second, the fair was and always had been extremely well-conducted and respectable; and third, that any form of interference would cause ill-feeling and bad blood which would take years to allay. The letter also alleged that the whole movement for abolition was the work of 'a few amiable busybodies who after bringing random accusations of drunkenness and immorality' had after five months failed to show a single case.

Because of the volume of opposition the Home Office sought police opinion and Supt. Simpson reported on 6 September that he had been in the Division 4 years and 8 months and 'I have attended the Ongar fair annually and I never saw it attended with any disorder or immorality. I find. . . .that there has not been any conviction at Ongar arising from the Fair for the last ten years and I [think] the reasonable enjoyment of the agricultural labourers would be interfered with by its abolition'.

The protests had their effect and on 23 September abolition was formally refused. There was evident jubilation in Ongar for on 21 October the Home Office received a letter pointing out the success of the fair and 'you will be glad to know that your decision has contributed to the happiness and welfare of the people.' The fair had been accompanied by a 'Programme of Athletic Sports' including Pony race, High Jump, Mile Flat race, Bicycle race, Throwing the Cricket Ball, Hurdle race with River Jump etc. and the day concluded with a firework display with Rockets with drooping rains, Large Shell of Comets, Mines of Snakes, Flight of Parachute Rockets etc.

A good time was not had by all for on 23 October the Chairman of the Abolition Committee asked for information on the grounds for refusal and requested that a deputation be received to reconsider the case. The Home Office reply was unequivocal concluding 'the present application has failed and the Secretary of State cannot reconsider his decision. If he did so, the account of the fair since held would not lead him to alter it.' The civil servant writing the final minute penned the words at the head of this essay 'Because Solon is virtuous shall there be no cream cakes and ale'.

Over the next 20 years declining interest in the fair and diminished opposition rewarded Gibson's pertinacity when a further application resulted in the fair's abolition on 1 July 1892. But the saga was still not finished. In October 1893 Gibson complained to the Home Office that 'in defiance of the order a number of stall holders have this year held the Fair in a private field adjacent to the town but beyond the Parish Boundary. Bills were circulated several days before the Fair – 'Ongar: Look out for the Old Fair which will be held etc etc'.' A convoy of caravans, steam engines, etc arrived on Tuesday, 10 October, and stayed several days. Gibson asked what action he should take. This problem had, however, arisen elsewhere and in connection with Wantage in Berkshire the Home Office had sought the Law Officers' opinion. Although the matter was not free from difficulty the view was held that 'it appears that the power conferred on the Secretary of State is to abolish the right to hold a fair and not to prohibit the holding of it'. The Home Secretary therefore refused to advise on the matter.

This case has been dealt with at length as three points emerge from it. Firstly, effective opposition could influence the Home Office; secondly, the ultimate impact of the Act could be relatively negligible particularly as there were no penal sanctions against disobeying the prohibition (though naturally the Home Office did not publicise this loophole). At Clavering, for instance, prohibition took place in 1877 but the fair continued to be held on 18 June into the 20th century. Thirdly, consultation with the police instead of being occasional became almost routine, but it is significant that in the villages the police tended to confirm the establishment view more than in the towns.

This was evident in Barking where in 1874 the Ilford Justices' Clerk forwarded a petition for abolition signed by approximately 380 inhabitants.

There was also a counter-petition from some 450 people. The police were consulted and reported, 'The fair is frequented by a large number of persons during the evening but it is an exaggeration of the petitioners to state that it is a cause of great disorder in the town as during the past five years only the following charges have been taken during the days of the fair.

1870. Two persons drunk and disorderly.

1871. One person for assault. One for wilful damage.

1872. One person drunk.

1873. One felony. Two drunk. One discharging fireworks.

(Shades of Ongar's organised firework display).

1874. None.

There seems to have been a certain amount of ambivalence in the Home Office decisions as this is minuted, '. . . The . . . . police reports that no evidence can be obtained as to the allegedly disorderly practices at the fair but as the memorial for abolition appears to be far more powerfully supported than that for continuation an order should be made'. Powerfully in this connection appears to equate more with important people than with numbers!

Two examples may be taken of early police reports in rural areas, both in 1872. Belchamp St Paul. '. . . the parties who attended the fair for the most part were of the very lowest class of horse and donkey dealers, prostitutes and thieves. Drunkenness and disorder was the result.' but there is no mention of arrests. Tollesbury. The police clearly wished to be helpful 'No one can point to any particular act of disorder or immorality (the counter-petition signed by over 300 said it was absent) but the fair brings a large number of youth of both sexes together and there is noise and foul language. Farmers have their standing crops damaged by people running into them.'

Twenty years later the police view at Stebbing still reflects the difference between the rural and urban areas though the comment of one officer may cause a lifted eyebrow. Dunmow magistrates applied for abolition on 2 January 1893, supported on 19 January by written consent from the Lord of the Manor. The next day a petition from many inhabitants was sent saying, inter alia, that nine tenths of the population supported the continuance of the fair. On 6 March the police superintendent reported '. . . . I walked through the street which was lined on both sides with the usual class of stalls . . . . . and the street being narrow it struck me as very dangerous for anyone with a spirited horse attempting to drive through and the noise of the stall people is quite enough to frighten any horse. With reference to the enjoyment of any class of people being interfered with this place is only attended by young people of the labouring class of both sexes from the immediate neighbourhood and in consequence of the filthy language and conduct of the stall people . . . . attending the fair I do not think it likely to improve the morals of the rising generation.' Another officer commented 'The fairs have been fairly well-conducted. There have been several scrimmages but nothing serious and I don't think there has been much immorality. I myself have patrolled the lanes and outskirts frequently when I have thought immoral conduct would be likely to take place but I never caught any person committing an immoral act. But as to the stall keepers this seems to be a fair for them to fight out all their grievances both men and women. I believe [that at] every fair there have been rows and fights between them. At two fairs the stall women fought desperately.' Stebbing fair was abolished on 10 March 1893.

Section 3 of the Act laid down that the abolition of the fair 'is for the convenience and advantage of the public'; a requirement very properly regarded by the Home Office as important. Though it is virtually impossible to quantify such a condition the Home Office wanted to be satisfied that it had been considered. Even as early as April 1872 when a memorial by 14 St Osyth people including the vicar was endorsed by the Tendring Hundred magistrates to the Home Office the file minute notes the abolition for the convenience and advantage of the public was not answered in either the memorial or the magistrates' submission. 'For aught that appears it might only be for the convenience and advantage of the persons signing the memorial. [It probably was!] The Secretary of State must have some assurance that the public will be benefitted before he can act'. The magistrates on receipt of this view paternalistically replied that it was for the good of the public. Effectively there was no control over the statement and the fair was abolished on 29 April 1872. The same magistrates avoided making the same error again for on 20 April 1872 they forwarded a similar application from Little Clacton containing the required assurance, and this time there was no riposte from the Home Office.

The reservation regarding Solon in the Ongar case suggests an apprehension in the Home Office that the Act was not always being used as originally intended. For Berden a counter-petition stated 'the fair is held annually on the grass by the roadside on 1 June and when such day falls in Whitsun week there is generally but one woman with a small stall to sell cakes and nuts, together with small toys, mostly penny articles; at other times (when not falling in Whitsun week) two or three such stalls, and once in the last seven years a man with a swing boat besides which have been annually a booth in the stable yard of the public house for country dancing to the music of a violin, drum and dulcimer.' This was minuted 'I don't see what there is to abolish.' The later police view was strikingly different. '. . . considerable amount of disorder and immorality going on arising from the excessive drinking indulged in and the presence of those females attracted there from other places and whose conduct after nightfall in leaving the dancing booth with men at frequent intervals leaves no room for doubts as to their object in being there'.

Opposition produced some interesting examples of the bitter divide which existed in politics and other affairs in the last quarter of the 19th century. A particularly striking letter is one concerning the abolition of Billericay fair in 1878 written by George Ward of Burstead House, Billericay.

Sir,

I am a retired London Merchant, became a Capt. of the 6th Tower Hamlets Rifle Volunteers November 26th 1861. Have for 50 years as man and boy been an ardent supporter of Lord Russell and other Whigs.

I am shocked and disgusted at the doings of Mr Gladstone and other semi-traitors.

I am as loyal as man can be to my gracious Queen and the Government of Lord Beaconsfield.

I intreat you not to abolish the fair here.

The petition to abolish it was got up mostly by the Dissenters.

Yr obdt servant

George Ward.

Associated with the opposition were appeals to the abolitionists to provide an alternative activity. This was clearly demonstrated at Abridge. A counter-petition contradicted the alleged drunkenness and disorder and then added, 'that with the exception of the annual fair Abridge possesses no amusement of any kind having neither a lecture hall, reading room or cricket club, and that while it sought to abolish this annual fair the only festival the villagers possess it must be mentioned that there is at present no school in the district and the children of the poor are growing up in ignorance'. It is obvious that the petition is not implying a fair and a school are substitutes but it does emphasise the isolation which the villagers must have felt.

This concern was also expressed by the Rev Henry Elwell of St Mary Magdalene, Harlow. He opposed the abolition of Harlow Bush Fair in 1879 to the annoyance of Sir Henry Ibbetson, Chairman of the Magistrates, who apparently was given improper access to the Home Office reports. Mr Elwell went on to become a strong advocate for the retention of fairs elsewhere and for the provision of alternative activities.

A very different problem arose at Chelmsford which had it roots earlier in Chelmsford's history. Section 3 of the Act required that there must be consent by the owner of the tolls before abolition was granted. Generally this presented no difficulty. Either there were no tolls or the tolls were in the hands of the Lord of the Manor who had little interest in bothering with their diminished value. But Chelmsford was different. An application was made by the Chelmsford Local Board and signed by 47 ratepayers on 25 June 1879 giving the usual reasons for abolition of both the May and November fairs. The memorial was returned by the Home Office as the ownership of the tolls was unclear. It was not resubmitted until 24 November 1880 and stated that on 7 December 1875 'the Local Board purchased and now are owners of all and singular rents tolls duties and profits arising from the markets and fairs in Chelmsford together with all rights of pickage, stallage, and all rights customs etc. The fair comprises a cattle fair lasting one day and a pleasure fair lasting two days; that the cattle fair was until February 1880 held in a meadow near the town; that the Board has constructed a new market place opened 13 February 1880 and the market which was formerly held in the public streets is now held there. The pleasure fair is still in the public street.'

Then comes the sentence which was to cause the difficulty 'that the Lord of the Manor has from time to time granted to the owners of several houses in the High Street small strips of land in the street in front of their houses to set moveable stalls upon on Market and Fair days'. The Home Office could not reconcile the purchase of all rights by the Board with the grants made by the Lord of the Manor and queried it. The Clerk to the Board later conceded that there some part owners who had not given written consent and he promised to obtain the necessary signatures. Some were very reluctant to sign and it was not until 20 June 1883 that the consents allowed the application to proceed.

Some of the grants were not too difficult to clear as in the case of the oldest made on 4 November 1834 of a strip 40 ft by 8 ft to Sally Archer. She had sold her property about 1860 but no one had been admitted in her stead to her strip of land and no rights had been exercised for 20 years so consent was deemed to be unnecessary. Others who were persuaded to give consent were Joseph Watts who, on 27 April 1865, was granted stallage rights belonging to the Half Moon Inn and the shop adjoining and for two spaces 15ft by 6ft and 21ft by 6ft in front of the Bell Inn for hog pens and movable stalls; and Mark Cottes who was granted a space 22ft by 15ft for movable stalls. The art of persuasion finally successful Chelmsford fairs were formally abolished on 20 July 1883.

But all the problems and allegations of riotous behaviour pale into insignificance before the Mistley outburst of 1893. A fair had been held on the green at Mistley on 10 and 11 August from 'time immemorial' but for some reason in 1893 the local people wanted it to run a third day. The accepted claimant as owner of the fair was the Revd Canon Charles F Norman of Mistley Place. He was apparently a very unpopular clergyman and when he refused to allow the fair on the third day hostility grew and reached fever pitch on the Thursday night. Let the police report speak for itself.

'On Thursday 10 August last at 9pm I was on duty on Mistley Green when I saw an effigy brought out of the back yard of the Thorn Inn, which premises back on to the Green, carried by two men with their faces blacked and several more following, one was ringing a large bell, the effigy was carried over the Green into the road and up Mistley Street through the Thorn Inn yard and on to the Green again when it was set fire to and the fire was kept burning until about 1am the following morning by placing a tar barrel and paraffin casks; and paraffin by the gallons was thrown onto it. At 12 midnight when a paraffin cask was being brought to put on the fire I took possession of it to prevent any more fire being made or any damage being done; the stalls and steam circus were standing on the Green at the same time. PCs 210 Everard, 274 Judd, and 278 Ridgewell were with me and took charge of the paraffin cask, in a short time after this a pail of water was thrown on to the constables and the cask taken away from the police by the people who numbered near two hundred and placed on the fire. No damage was done to any property beyond the grass on the green.

On Friday, 11 August, during the evening another demonstration took place when an effigy which was said to represent the Rev Canon Norman was placed on a bier and carried through the streets of Mistley and Manningtree on the shoulders of three men with their faces blacked; a large body of people followed. It was afterwards taken on to Mistley Green where a fire had been made and the effigy burned in the presence of several hundred people who all returned home about 10pm. No damage was done to any property.'

Canon Norman was furious and notified the local magistrates who signed an application for the abolition of the fair which was forwarded on 25 September 1893. The accompanying letter from the Clerk to the Justices indicates Canon Norman's anger. '.... a number of persons of bad character most of whom had been convicted for all sorts of crimes and offences burnt Canon Norman in effigy in his canonicals amidst a violent scene of cursing and swearing amounting to a riot and in the midst of which they went through the form of throwing the Bible into the Fire they had made. I am directed to enclose you herewith an original anonymous communication which Canon Norman received on that occasion to justify these facts and I also am directed to send you a very influentially signed memorial Canon Norman received entreating him to stop this Fair if possible for the future.'

The petition in favour of abolition was signed by 14 influential people most of whom did not live in Mistley. This produced a counter-petition signed by nearly 800 denying the allegations of immorality etc and added that the Rev Canon Norman succeeded to land in Mistley and was very unpopular. There is little doubt that the application for abolition was a direct consequence of the demonstration. The Home Office must have accepted this because after a fortnight's deliberation they refused to abolish the fair.

As a final quotation let the protest against abolition at Berden reflect the brighter side of the debate prior to the onset of violent change heralded by the 20th century. 'The inhabitants purely agricultural look forward to the fair as a great annual treat when they meet the young people who have left home (the girls mostly for domestic service and the young men for London where they obtain more remunerative employment) and make it a point if possible of coming home to visit their parents and see their old school mates at the same time, and the other inhabitants, more particularly the children, of the village anticipate their annual fair as a sort of recreation they have been accustomed to and the only one granted them from one year to another.'

When set against the comprehensive 19th century public statutes the Fairs Act 1871 was a very minor piece of legislation. It passed through Parliament virtually on the nod. It was not even good legislation as it was in many ways a bluff – a kind of grandmotherly treatment. With hindsight we can see that many of the fairs would have faded away from natural causes within a few years. But at the grass roots some 70 Essex communities were violently agitated during little more than a quarter of a century emphasising the divisions between those in authority and those whose 'daily round and common task' was enlivened on only one or two days a year. The bias reflected in petitions and counter-petitions reinforces the fact that contemporary statements demonstrate that there are three sides to every question – my view, your view, and, if it can be found, the truth.

Essex Fairs for which Application for Abolition was made to the Home Office under
the Fairs Act 1871.

Fair	Date of Abolition or Refusal	Public Record Office File No. HO 45 series.
Abridge	25 July 1878	9461/74248
Great Baddow	14 June 1878	9460/73598
Barking	12 June 1875	9359/32112
Baythorne End	17 June 1872	9309/12747
Belchamp St Paul	14 Dec 1872	9322/17272
Great Bentley	16 May 1872	9306/12113
Berden	28 Jan 1873	9325/18052
Billericay	4 June 1878	9460/73377
Bradwell on Sea	16 Apr 1872	9303/11272
Brentwood	26 May 1877	9422/59477
Burnham	25 Apr 1872	9297/9887
Canvey Island	6 Aug 1872	9313/14051
Castle Hedingham	16 May 1872	9302/11077
Chelmsford	30 July 1883	9603/A38
Great Clacton	22 Mar 1872	9300/10621
Little Clacton	31 May 1872	9307/12313
Clavering	26 Dec 1877	9450/69113
Colchester St John's Grn	28 May 1872	9307/12356
Colchester	12 Apr 1873	9335/20369
Cressing	19 Dec 1872	9321/17214
Danbury	21 Jan 1880	9587/89747
Dunmow	18 Mar 1872	9300/10406
Earls Colne	28 Sept 1871	10231/B37093
Fiddlers Hamlet	6 July 1872	9311/13440
Foulness	12 June 1883	9633/A26880
Good Easter	12 Sept 1872	9315/14960
Grays Thurrock	14 Nov 1876	9420/58954
Halstead	4 Mar 1872	9297/9664
Harlow Bush	22 Mar 1879	9571/77833
Hatfield Broad Oak	22 Mar 1872	9298/10102
Havering atte Bower	27 Aug 1877	9434/63659
High Roothing	11 July 1872	9309/12721
Hornchurch	28 Mar 1878	9455/71591
Horndon-on-the-Hill	3 June 1873	9340/22129
Kelvedon	25 Oct 1872	9316/15435
Mistley	1 Dec 1893 (refused)	9876/B15186
Newport	19 July 1872	9311/13428
Great Oakley	8 Apr 1873	9335/20444
Ongar	23 Sept 1872 (refused)	9315/15117
Ongar (2nd Application)	1 July 1892	9857/B12458
Orsett	23 May 1872	9305/12069
Prittlewell	28 Aug 1872	9310/13389
Purfleet	10 May 1910	10598/188530
Rainham	12 Feb 1878	9452/69944
Rayleigh	8 Aug 1899	9906/B20611
Romford	27 Aug 1877	9434/63658
Roydon	26 Mar 1891 (refused)	9834/B9997

Fair	Date of Abolition or Refusal	Public Record Office File No. HO 45 series.
Saffron Walden	11 Dec 1871	10231/B37100
Saffron Walden (2nd fair)	25 Jan 1902 (refused)	9666/A45846
St Osyth	29 Apr 1872	9300/10554
Sandon	14 Jan 1879	9574/79654
South Benfleet	6 Aug 1872	9313/14051
South Ockenden	12 Nov 1873	9351/27346
Southend	13 May 1893	9864/B13787
Southminster	5 Apr 1872	9301/10894
Stanford-le-Hope	6 Oct 1875	9390/47757
Stansted Mountfitchet	15 Jan 1872	10231/B37103
Stebbing	10 Mar 1893	9863/B13617
Thorpe	24 May 1872	9307/12321
Tillingham	16 Apr 1872	9297/9887
Tollesbury	1 July 1872	9309/12657
Toppesfield	26 May 1873	9338/21569
Ugley	26 Mar 1873	9335/20176
Great Wakering	2 June 1874	9361/32984
Walton	15 June 1872	9310/12906
White Roothing	1 July 1878	9461/74161
Willingdale Doe	25 Apr 1878	9457/72259
Witham	10 Apr 1891	9835/B10169
Woodham Ferris	19 July 1872	9313/13764
Woodside Green	17 Feb 1881	9604/A1040
Writtle	8 Jan 1907 (refused)	10243/B37892

Aspects of Local Cartography in Kent and Essex, 1585–1700

FELIX HULL

It seems probable that more examples of local map-making have survived in Kent and Essex, especially for the sixteenth and seventeenth centuries, than for any other part of England and Wales.[1] It is justifiable, therefore, to enquire why this should be so and in what ways the two counties differed both from the rest of the country and from one another. Any consideration of this kind, however, presents formidable problems which, by the very nature of the material to be examined, may prove impossible to answer satisfactorily, even though trends may be suggested.

Some of these problems are immediately apparent: first, that despite a basic assumption of fecundity, the actual numbers of maps are small and are virtually impossible to use in any sound statistical manner; second, that we are dealing with survivals which are now stored in particular repositories or are recorded by those repositories – we have no means of knowing what has been lost or destroyed over the years and any assessment made must therefore be incomplete; third, maps are the individual expression of individual surveyors. We may be able to associate family or business groups, but there is no way in which we can qualify cartographic skill on a geographical basis. The maps which survive for one particular surveyor may vary according to his experience, needs of the occasion, or client's purse, but to compare the works of Essex surveyors with those of their colleagues in Kent on a basis of quality of work is impractical. Moreover, because of the small numbers involved, the existence of a single book of maps for one man, while it will enhance our knowledge of his work, can only throw into imbalance the results of any analysis. This is particularly noticeable in Kent where a volume of some forty maps by John Pattenden of Lamberhurst and Brenchley made between 1640 and 1645 has to be taken into consideration.

Having said that, the basis for what follows rests on the published lists of maps issued by the two County Councils: in the case of Essex the *Catalogue of Maps in the Essex Record Office* (1947), together with the *1st., 2nd., and 3rd. Supplements* (1952, 1964 and 1968), but excluding those entries for maps held only in reduced photographic form; and in the case of Kent, the *Catalogue of Estate Maps in the Kent Archives Office* (1973) together with the contents of an unpublished Supplement prepared by the writer in 1980, but excluding for some purposes those maps prepared for the Commissioners of Sewers and kindred bodies, because of the lack of corresponding early maps for Essex. For initial purposes, therefore, we have a corpus of estate maps about 130 for Essex and 190 for Kent, surviving for the period 1585 to 1700.

ii

It is a matter of fact that Kent and Essex together form the south-eastern corner of this land and that they are separated by the Thames. The word 'separated' is used advisedly for it would appear that the water-way created a more formidable boundary so far as cartographers were concerned, than one might have expected. There is, however, one similarity which had a significant effect upon local map-making, the fact that both counties were 'old enclosed'. This convenient label implies four kinds of land pattern within the areas under consideration: (a) survivals of open-field husbandry particularly in north-west Essex and in the extreme east of Kent, around Deal; (b) areas in which there is some evidence for communal husbandry, often in the last stages of decay, such as northern Essex and the Lea Valley and in northern Kent, between the ragstone ridge bordering the Weald and the Thames: (c) areas of assart from the forest, essentially the core of each county: and (d) coastal marshlands.

The significance of this fact is shown in that during the period 1585–1700, no maps apparently exist for those parts of the two counties in which open-field survived, the earliest example, known to the writer, being a map of Ringwould near Deal dated 1709.[2] It is also noteworthy that excluding a very fine series of maps prepated for parts of the Kent marshes in the seventeenth century, there are few surviving maps for the coastal areas, but that the core of each county is well covered by the work of local surveyors. Understandably the vast majority of these maps were prepared as proof of ownership, though some – e.g. Sewers Maps – were associated with aspects of taxation and occasionally some other purpose lay behind the survey. For example, the finest early maps in Kent are of Dover and its environs including the harbour and castle.[3] Whether these were prepared primarily in connection with rents for the Harbour Board lands or were concerned with the defence of the Narrow Seas is uncertain, but there is evidence that the coast of Kent, in particular, attracted the attention of those involved in defence matters and the care of the harbour was a constant theme. These survivals, although outside the immediate terms of this examination, suggest that possibly there is a wider application of surveying skills in Kent than in Essex which was less vulnerable. In other ways, however, there were peculiarities which affect the main stream of estate maps and the first to be considered is the use of scales. It had been noted, many years ago, when the present writer was listing the maps in the Petre MSS. that early surveyors in Essex appeared to have a predeliction for a scale of 4 chains to one inch, or 20 inches to a mile. Equally, in Kent, the impression grew that scales of a larger size were common practice, but was this more than an impression and had it any relevance other than individual idiosyncrasy? An analysis of the relatively small number of maps examined for the 1585 to 1700 period produced a suggestive result when it was found that 36 *per cent.* of the Essex maps were, indeed, on the scale of 20 inches to 1 mile, while only 18 *per cent.* were of that scale in Kent. It must be said that scales are somewhat difficult to assess because surveyors used so many, sometimes of extraordinary complexity, and one feels at times that the size of the parchment skin or sheet of paper was the determining factor. Nevertheless a rough comparison of those in use in Kent and Essex is informative.

Percentages of maps	less than 13ins to 1m.	13.3	16	20	26.6	more than 26.6 ins. to 1m*
Essex	8	9	11	36	11	10
Kent	5	17	7	18	13	32

* A few scales in between these points have been omitted.

From these admittedly inadequate figures it would appear that the impressions already gained had some validity although scales of 13.3 ins. to 1 mile and 16 ins. to 1 mile were also in common use. The question remained, however, as to why there should be this difference in usage: was it simply individual preference or was there a social or economic factor behind the variation? Fortunately the majority of maps provide some indication of the acreage covered and an analysis of areas once again provided an interesting comparison.

Percentages of maps	under 250a	251–500	501–750	751–1000	over 1000a
Essex	37	24	15	3	15
Kent	68	13	4	3	5

The preponderance of maps for areas of less than 250 acres in Kent is striking and if we analyse further we find that no fewer than 31 *per cent.* of the Kent maps were for properties with no more than 50 acres. It is clear from the evidence of these maps, even if it were not also known from other sources, that the typical Kentish estate was relatively smaller than that in Essex and that there is a correlation of scale in use and size of estate in each county and it can be added that this kind of picture can also be found in the eighteenth and nineteenth centuries, though the emphasis in Essex on the 20 inch scale becomes less marked and maps of farms with a smaller acreage also become more common

But did Essex surveyors really have a preference for the 20 inch scale? In all only 47 maps of those examined were drawn on this scale and for 13 of them the name of the surveyor is lacking, so that numbers have very little meaning. One can say that of the thirty-four maps drawn by known surveyors ten were by John Walker, father and son, and one by Samuel Walker; five were by John Coffyn and four by William Stane(s), all Essex cartographers. No evidence appears as to why they chose this scale on many occasions, it does not seem to relate to patronage and on other occasions other scales were chosen. It can also be added that in Essex the use of 20 ins. to 1 inch is found from estates of 20 acres to those of 2,700 acres; the size does not seem to be the determining factor. One is left with a feeling of an interesting trend, but whether there is more than that cannot be said.

iii

The suggestive figures found for the size of holdings require further examination and one must ask for what purpose the maps examined were drawn and of what kind of property. It is usually possible to analyse not just the acreage but the economic or social unit represented, i.e. one can determine in most cases whether the map is of a parish, manor, farm or just land, and in that last case whether it is of arable, pasture or meadow, or of woods or marshland. Excluding those maps drawn for other specific purposes (e.g. Sewers maps), such an analysis once again presents a striking difference between the two counties.

Percentages of maps	Manors	Farms	Land	Marsh*	Woods
Essex	50	17	19	6	–
Kent	17	30	31	5	6

* Excluding 23 Sewers maps for the period.

The essential difference revealed lies in the high percentage of Essex maps drawn for manors and the comparatively high figures for farms and land in Kent. This is, in fact, a close reflection of the social structure of the two counties. Essex was highly manorialised. In the sixteenth century there may well have been over eleven hundred such units varying significantly in size but normally comprising demesne, a small number of freeholds and leaseholds and a large number of customary tenancies.[4] In contrast, Kent, although apparently well covered by manors, in fact presents a very different picture. There the manor has the appearance of a foreign body superimposed upon a different agrarian pattern. It has far less strength as an institution and there is virtually no copyhold land.[5] Again, in Essex, the manor is frequently coterminous with the parish, although there may be a number of maneriola in addition to the principal lordship. Such a pattern is a rarity in Kent: the manor there hardly ever relates to the parish and a major lordship, e.g. Wrotham or Folkestone, is much more likely to be associated with the hundredal system (there were some sixty-three hundreds in Kent compared with twenty in Essex). In addition the Kentish holding, whether of manorial status or not, is usually discrete: there will be small units in various areas of a parish, there may be 'dens' in the Weald some miles away and marshland elements in the Romney marshes or possibly on the Isle of Sheppey. This has the result that whereas John Walker, father and son, mapped the manor of Ingatestone in 1601[6] and by so doing also mapped the parish of the same name, the estate of Thomas Plummer, when mapped mainly by John Pattenden of Lamberhurst and Brenchley, in the 1640's, comprised forty-three properties in some twenty-one parishes.[7] In thirty cases these properties were of units less than fifty acres in extent, though two of the holdings exceeded 250 acres. This picture is emphasised by the fact that there are eleven maps of this early period in Essex which are for entire or almost entire parishes, while in Kent not one estate map covers a whole parish.

In some ways, of course, the situation thus outlined, creates further problems for only parts of each county are to be found in these estate maps and what was done depended to a degree upon the wishes of the individual landowners and upon the nature of the estates held by them. Late sixteenth century Essex can be seen as a land of a number of considerable magnates of whom Rich, De Vere, Darcy and Petre were only four of the chief. These families alone held very considerable estates, much of the land being monastic in origin. In contrast Kent is a county of the lesser gentry with few great estates and even those held by courtiers such as Sidney (later Earls of Leicester) or Tufton (later Earls of Thanet) are small compared with the major Essex estates. It becomes necessary, therefore, to consider who the clients were who requested maps to be drawn and their influence upon the sudden output of cartography in south-east England.

iv

The principal difficulty arising from this determination, however, is the relatively small number of maps surviving which actually record the name of the owner for whom the work was done. In fact, in Essex we find 73 maps drawn for 41 patrons and in Kent (including the Sewers maps), 177 maps drawn for 75 patrons. Once again it would seem that there is a significant variation between the two counties for, in Essex, a mere 10 *per cent.* of the maps were drawn for other than private individuals, whereas in Kent the figure is 20 *per cent.* This difference might be ignored but for the fact that a similar difference continues into subsequent centuries. In other words, throughout the period when local cartography flourished – say 1585 to 1840 – the proportion of maps prepared for corporate or statutory bodies in Kent was very much higher than in Essex.

To explain this difference it is not really necessary to point to the very fine seventeenth century surveys prepared for the Lords, Bailiff and Jurats of Romney Marsh or for the North Kent Commissioners for Sewers, although in this early period these maps create the wide difference noted.[8] The fundamental difference lies in the effects of the Reformation settlement in the two counties, as well as in the fact that Kent contained more corporate bodies within its borders. It has been estimated that in Kent, whereas ecclesiastical and charitable holdings before 1539 may have covered as much as forty *per cent.* of the land, the existence after that date of two dioceses and two capitular establishments resulted in as much as ten *per cent.* remaining in the hands of the church.[9] In contrast monastic holdings in Essex vanished into the new estates of the gentry – Petre being perhaps the prime example – and only one or two holdings of the Dean and Chapter of St. Paul's survived the changes.

The importance of this distinction in terms of local cartography cannot be overstressed for the establishments of the Dean and Chapter of Canterbury and Rochester; the corporation of the Lords, Bailiff and Jurats of Romney Marsh; the Commissioners of Sewers for the extensive marshes along the Thames shore and between the mainland and Thanet, together with the marshlands of the Rother basin in Kent and Sussex; the Wardens of Rochester Bridge, who also administered Cobham College; and the Dover Harbour Board together present a significant corpus of continuing corporations requiring periodic surveys of their estates and therefore offering continuous employment to a number of surveyors. While principal landowners in both counties might likewise provide considerable and periodic opportunities for map-making, only occasionally, as with Petre in Essex or Filmer in Kent, is there evidence of the kind of continuing employment offered by those bodies which were unaffected by the natural events of death and dispersal.

During the period 1585–1700, despite the very small figures involved, the difference between Kent and Essex is emphasised and if one considers which corporate bodies were patrons at that time and where they were based. Only six such institutions are noted in Essex and of these, four, St. Thomas's Hospital, Christ's Hospital, Rochester Bridge Trust and the Duchy of Lancaster were administered from outside the county, while two, the Free Schools of Dedham and Earls Colne were within. In contrast fourteen such bodies are found in Kent (and this excludes the Dean and Chapter of Canterbury whose maps are not considered in this survey), and only one of these, Magdalen College, Oxford, is an institution external to Kent. The like difference is found in later centuries when the two capitular establishments, in particular, carry out extensive surveys of their properties and when, despite the presence of Sewers maps in Essex the balance is still towards Kent with its high proportion of indigenous corporations.

Of course, if one excludes this special factor there is a much greater comparability: eight landowners in Essex, including Petre, Abdy and Tyrell, account for thirty-one *per cent.* of the maps drawn in this period, while in Kent five gentlemen, including Filmer and Twisden account for forty-one *per cent.*, though it must be added that this figure is suspect because of the survival of two books of maps making up a total of 59 surveys or about a third of all those bearing the name of a patron in Kent.[10]

v

This discussion inevitably leads to a consideration of the surveyors themselves. Were they indeed local men or figures of national standing who happened to work in a particular locality and what, if indeed it can be established, is their relationship with the patrons served. Unfortunately, once again, it is seldom that the map-makers record either their place of work or their domicile and seldom, too, that they leave Wills or other records of identity, so that there is a measure of guesswork in what can be assessed. The *Dictionary of Surveyors*[11] provides much valuable information, but inevitably it is neither complete nor can it establish an unknown. There is a *prima facie* case, however, for suggesting that when a surveyor is only recorded as working in one county area he is probably a local man and this must be the basis upon which to work in the present imperfect state of knowledge.

For the period 1585–1700, therefore, there are fifty named surveyors in Essex and sixty in Kent, but that closeness of numbers hides a wide difference in other respects. Less than half of the Essex cartographers are either known to be local or are probably local, whereas three-quarters of the Kentish map-makers fall into that category. Even if we exclude half a dozen who might equally well be from Sussex that still leaves two-thirds who can be regarded as local. In contrast to these figures as many as thirty *per cent.* of the cartographers at work in Essex are known to be from other counties, whereas in Kent the figure is only twelve *per cent.* This still leaves a large number in each county whose arrivance cannot be determined or suggested with any degree of certainty. It appears, therefore, that Essex patrons were more ready to employ men from without the county than were those in Kent and evidence from later centuries continues to bear out this suggestion with an emphasis on London and East Anglia as sources of surveyors. There is far less apparent use of Londoners in Kent, though, understandably, both Surrey and Sussex provide a quota of map-makers.

Perhaps the most unexpected fact is the apparent barrier of the Thames from the Essex side. Only one Essex surveyor seems to have crossed the river to work in Kent, Thomas Peachye or Petchye of Romford; but at least six Kentish cartographers are found at work in Essex.[12] Of these six, some prove to be of special interest. The Lennard family of Chevening were linked with the Barrets of Belhus in Aveley, Essex and when the representative of that family sought the services of Samuel Peirse of Maidstone to map his Essex estates in 1619, the question immediately arises as to whether the Kentish connection was at work.[13] Similarly, in 1675, Robert Felgate of Gravesend mapped properties in Great Wigborough and also in Aldham, Stanway and Chapel.[14] The latter estate belonged to John Marsham, the *caput* of whose property lay in the Lower Medway valley not far from Gravesend.[15] These associations are, alas, tentative, but in the case of Philip Symonson and George Russell, of Rochester, there is no such doubt, for both were surveyors to the Rochester Bridge Trust and it was for those patrons that they crossed the Thames and worked in East Tilbury, West Thurrock and Stifford in 1594 and 1699 respectively.[16] So, once again, the significance of the Kentish corporation is apparent as a means of spreading Kentish skills and this pattern is found again in later years when Henry Hogben and James Gouge likewise work in Essex for Kentish patrons. Nevertheless this evidence, although of interest, provides no indication of true cross-fertilisation. The Walkers of West Hanningfield or Symonson of Rochester do not apparently provide the neighbouring county with newly trained surveyors ready to establish an Essex school at Maidstone or a Kentish school at Colchester. In that sense the craft remains essentially local and one can only say that individual patrons call upon the services of individual surveyors because of local associations, family links, or the desire to obtain the best service available.

It is of interest that the great Christopher Saxton worked in both counties[17] but he had no close association with either and similarly Nicholas Lane, probably from the London area of Surrey is known for his work in Cambridge, Northants and Londonderry as well as Kent and

Essex.[18] Among the surveyors found in Essex who have a wide reputation is Ralph Agas, rector of Gressenhall in Norfolk, while Kent was fortunate to be able to call upon a fine Sussex cartographer in John de Ward.[19]

vi

The conclusion of this brief examination must be that although many surveyors worked in various counties at different times, the great majority were essentially local and that in the case of Kent and Essex the Thames proved a greater barrier than one might have anticipated, unless the needs of patrons or some other very good, though unknown reason, inclined the map-maker to make the crossing. This is somewhat strange for the cross ferry was active and the journey could hardly be regarded as unduly hazardous despite the occasional loss of a ferryboat with its passengers.[20] But this overall assumption does little to identify the men who worked from town and village on either side of the river. Some were schoolmasters: George Russell worked at the Sir Joseph Williamson School at Rochester and William Cosin at the Free School at Earls Colne. The Symonson family, too, may have had scholastic connections – Philip and Edward are known as surveyors, but there was also Thomas Symonson who was headmaster of Maidstone Grammar School in 1585.[21] Many others were linked in some way with mathematics and referred to themselves as 'philomath', or, in one case as 'welwiller unto the Mathematticks', and one, R. Burley, stated that he was 'reader in mathematics at Chatham'. Others simply referred to themselves as surveyors or, perhaps, as 'curators', or else simply gave their status, i.e. yeomen, gentlemen, etc., but by far the greater number chose to make no such claim either relating to position in society or to profession. One man, Marke La Pla from Lincolnshire, who drew maps in Kent for the Commissioners of the Rother Levels, had no inhibitions and referred to himself as 'a very able engineer'.[22]

It is one thing to claim that between forty and seventy *per cent.* of the surveyors were local, but what evidence is there of their place of work or residence, how were they related to one another either by blood or by training, and were there centres of activity which may indicate one or more firms with a continuing life? With the very limited research possible for this paper no satisfactory answer can be given, especially for Essex, where surveyors seem to have been particularly coy when it came to mentioning their place of activity. Of the twenty-two Essex surveyors whose names we know and who were working between 1585 and 1700, only two actually refer to their place of work – William Cosin, as noted above from Earls Colne, and Thomas Peachye from Romford. Other evidence links John Walker, senior, with West Hanningfield and with him can be associated his son, John, junior, and also Samuel Walker, but by 1640 this brilliant trio had finished work and apparently without any direct successors. In the eighteenth century Colchester was certainly a centre of cartographic skill, but although one may postulate the probability of certain people having a Colchester connection, no direct shred of evidence is provided by the maps they left.

Once again there is a marked contrast with Kent for in that county at least twelve places are recorded as homes or work centres of local surveyors and the list suggests that, apart from some of the coastal towns, few places of any size or significance lacked a person capable of producing maps. Canterbury, the Medway Towns, Maidstone, Tonbridge, Ashford and Gravesend all figure before 1700. More significant still, William and Thomas Boycot, both of Fordwich,[24] established a practice in Canterbury which on the basis of style was carried on by Thomas Wrake in a map of 1679 and, more important, were the forerunners of the family of Hill of Canterbury, Thomas, Francis and Jared who were notable surveyors of the late seventeenth and early eighteenth century.[25] Jared, although outside our immediate period, was a most individualistic and distinctive cartographer who also worked in Essex.[26] It is possible, too, that Marke Peirse of Sandhurst (on the Sussex border) and Samuel Peirse of Maidstone were related and that there was a continuing group of surveyors at Tonbridge, represented by Henry Allen in early years and by Robert Spillett at the end of the period. The towns of Rochester and Chatham, with their Royal Dockyards, capitular establishment and the Bridge Trust undestandably had their share of competent surveyors.

It is of course probable that if we had all the relevant information to hand the Essex picture would be more comparable with that in Kent and that few Essex towns and villages of any size would lack surveyors. Size of township is not necessarily the determining factor and sometimes places with very small populations produced major figures in this field. The Walkers of Hanningfield are a good case in point and so too, was John Pattenden of Lamberhurst and later Brenchley or John Watts of Thurnham near Maidstone.

vii

In general terms the kind of picture revealed continues throughout the ensuing two centuries. There is still evidence of a link between the use of scale and size of estate; maps of manors and parishes continue to be more common in Essex than in Kent: the use of extraneous surveyors by Essex patrons and the significance of corporate bodies in Kentish patronage remain important factors in the overall growth of the profession; and the wide dispersal of local surveyors over both counties is modified only by the greater tendency for groups and firms to arise in larger urban areas. Of the quality of workmanship little can be said for, as noted earlier, this is a matter of human individuality, but one can state that Essex has good reason to be proud of the work of the Walkers, both beautiful and accurate. A map such as that of Chelmsford in 1591 or of Ingatestone in 1601, is a complete statement in itself of the township as it was that day and, indeed, for many years to come.[27] In Kent the Boycots present something of a comparable duo though without the detailed accuracy of the Essex pair, though they, too, tend to use both blue and red pigment from time to time. In each county many magnificent maps survive often of great interest, such as that of West Thurrock in 1645/6 which reveals a pattern of open-field husbandry having an affinity to the rare survivals in Kent rather than to that found in the rest of Essex.[28] Maps of Kent are often for smaller areas, as already noted, but the very fine series of the Waterings controlled by the Lords, Bailiff and Jurats of Romney Marsh drawn in the mid-seventeenth century are oustanding and mention must also be made of an exceptional map of the entire marshland area from Rye to Hythe by Matthew Poker in 1617.[29] No Essex surveyor of the period seems to have been tempted to map the entire county: Philip Symonson did just that for Kent in 1596, and in so doing improved upon the work already done by Saxton.[30] One could continue to list outstanding work in each county, but one surveyor who worked in both was George Russell of Rochester, a cartographer in tune with the future who, while capable of drawing some beautiful vessels on the Thames and outstanding compass-roses, basically drew maps which were both clear and essentially scientific in approach.[31]

If indeed, as seems probable, these two counties produced more maps than most, this fact may be linked with their relative wealth during the period, for each was highly favoured by the topographers of the day; by reason of their early enclosure which encouraged individual landowners to record their estates as a practical element in their proper management; and also because each county had coastal areas, subject to flood, and, indeed, to invasion. One particularly fine survey was produced for the Harbour Board at Dover in 1641, by William Eldred, comprising both a plan of the entire town with harbour and castle and also detailed surveys of every street.[32]

The value of this great series of maps and plans for research and for the detailed study of each county cannot be overestimated for they form both a source of information, economic, social and at times political and military, but, in addition, are a source of artistic joy. Much of this last feature is idiosyncratic, according to the individual and although one may occasionally meet with a surveyor, like Henry Allen of Tonbridge,[33] who uses sepia alone, in general the blaze of colour and the fashion of cartouche, border or heraldic achievement provide a delight to the eye supplementing any information of a more mundane nature.

One final point: it is interesting to see the distribution of maps over the period, for, subject to the comment on survival, it would seem that Essex is peculiarly rich in maps produced between 1585 and 1620, but that there is a relative drop in output until the last quarter of the century. In Kent, very few maps antedate 1620, but there is a burst of map-making between 1620 and 1640 which, unexpectedly, is continued throughout the Civil War and Interregnum – especially in the work of John Pattenden – and that there is then a drop until 1680, after which a considerable output is apparent. Perhaps one should not argue overmuch from these apparent trends, but it is clear in each county that the twenty years between 1660 and 1680 are relatively less active than any other twenty year period during the time covered by this paper. So, too, those difficult years 1640–1660 are unexpectedly active, especially in Kent.[34] Two thoughts occur, one that each county was relatively stable, despite the incident of the Second Civil War; and two, in each case it was the period 1660–1680 which saw a time of radical adjustment in areas where Parliament had been dominant. The burst of activity after 1680 suggests that each county had been taking a breathing space and that landlords were once again ready to assess their position and their estates. The early difference is less easy to explain, although the Essex magnates may well have become involved in this element of estate management before the smaller landowners of Kent and the corporate bodies had really come to terms with the newer methods.

Emmison in the Introduction to the *Catalogue of Maps in the Essex Record Office* wrote of the value of maps to the historian, topographer, economist antiquary and philologist for the evidence they provide of the changing face of the landscape and of features long since vanished from our sight;[35] in this brief article an attempt had been made to examine some aspects which lay behind this outpouring of an artistic and scientific skill as they affected the maps in two counties. Doubtless there are other features which would come to light if a wider cross-section of local cartography were to be analysed.

There is much still unknown or only guessed at and work of the kind which has recently been published on the Walkers of Hanningfield is eagerly awaited for other surveyors of the period across the country. Only then will it be possible to prepare definitive studies of the background and activities of these remarkable craftsmen, whose work still delights and enlightens both scholar and casual observer.

Notes and References

1. This proposition is based on a recent survey of early maps held in local record offices. The information was received from V. W. Gray, County Archivist of Essex.

2. K.A.O., De/P33. Illustrated in *Catalogue of Estate Maps*, plate 8.

3. K.A.O., DHB/P141–5. The originals are in the British Library but facsimile copies were made in the late nineteenth century when the originals were transferred to London. See *British Museum Catalogue of Maps*, pp.93–5.

4. Based on an examination of the descent of manors and other estates given in Morant. *History of Essex* (1768) and discussed in *Agriculture and Rural Society in Essex, 1560–1640*, an unpublished thesis by F. Hull (1950), a copy of which is in the Essex Record Office.

5. Lambarde in his *Perambulation of Kent* (1576), referred to Kent as having no copyhold land. This is not strictly accurate, there were small areas on the Sussex and Surrey borders and at Ashford.

6. E.R.O., D/DP. P8.

7. K.A.O., U1506.

8. See K.A.O., S/Rm and S/NK. The earliest Essex 'sewers' map noted is for Havering Level in 1735. (E.R.O., D/SH25).

9. This thesis is based on an examination of the descent of manors, etc., as given in Hasted, *History of Kent* (1st. edtn., 1778–99).

10. These two books are K.A.O., U1506 and U49 P4. The latter includes a map of Larkfield, near Maidstone, which shows the surveyor's house at the cross roads. This house still exists.

11. P. Eden ed., *Dictionary of Surveyors* (3 vols., 1975–6).

12. Peachey or Petchye is known by two maps, one of Dartford in 1617 and one of Kelvedon in 1634.

13. E.R.O., D/DLP1. Samuel Peirse also mapped the Godinton estate in Great Chart for the Toke family in 1621 (K.A.O., U967).

14. E.R.O., D/DWeP2 and D/DQal. No example of Felgate's work had been found in Kent.

15. Whornes Place, Cuxton near Rochester, was the Marsham home until the acquisition of The Mote, Maidstone in the late seventeenth century.

16. E.R.O., T/M409 and T/M203.

17. E.R.O., D/DTh 18; K.A.O., U390 P2.

18. E.R.O., D/DNeP1 and D/DGeP3; K.A.O., U312 P2, U908 P78.

19. K.A.O., U31 P3, U814 P1, 2.

20. The earliest parish register for Milton next Gravesend refers to the loss of ferries and their passengers. (K.A.O., P252/1/1).

21. *Maidstone Grammar School, a record* (1965 edtn.), p.6.

22. K.A.O., U455 P4.

23. A work on the family of Walker of West Hanningfield by Augustus Edwards, formerly Education Officer in the Essex Record Office and the late Ken Newton formerly County Archivist was published during 1985, entitled *The Walkers of Hanningfield, surveyors, map-makers extraordinary.*

24. *Calendar of the White and Black Books of the Cinque Ports*, ed. Hull (1966), pp.461–535 *passim.*

25. A brief note on this important Caterbury family has been prepared by Miss A. M. Oakley, archivist to the City and Dean and Chapter of Canterbury.

26. Kenneth Neale has written on Jared Hill in respect of an example of his work in Essex, for the Chingford Historical Society; and maps by him of Bolingbroke, Lincs., are held in the Public Record Office. His style is not unlike that of James Birmingham, surveyor of the Havering Levels in 1735–41. (E.R.O., D/SH25).

27. E.R.O., D/DMP1 and D/DPP8.

28. E.R.O., D/DU15. This unexpected survival of open field is also noted in surveys of the Thames shore parishes in Essex and shown on some Tithe Maps also. See, Hull, Thesis *cit.*, pp.35–7.

29. K.A.O., U1823 P2. See also *Archaelogia Cantiana*, vol. 30, pp.219–24, for an article on this map and its later copies by the late Dr. F. W. Cock.

30. K.A.O., PP121, Symonson's special feature was the inclusion of roads on his map.

31. See K.A.O., S/NK in particular.

32. K.A.O., TR1380. The original has been retained by the Dover Harbour Board.

33. K.A.O., U840 P6. Illustrated in the *Catalogue of Estate Maps*, plate 3.

34. The volume of maps, K.A.O., U1506, may perhaps create a false impression of output, but nevertheless there was a surprisingly constant map-making activity, not least by the surveyors to the Lords, Bailiff and Jurats of Romney Marsh.

35. See *Catalogue of Maps in the Essex Record Office*, p.ix.

Essex: An Appreciation
'full of profitable thinges'

KENNETH NEALE

The essays in this volume range over a wide field of Essex history and archives. There are new and interesting insights into the governance of the ancient East Saxon kingdom; a study of the complexities of the socio-economic patterns that defined the life of Essex in the Middle Ages; the archives of Tudor Essex have yielded more and further endowed an already rich period for Essex historiography; new light has been shed on aspects of Essex life in the Victorian period which, as time and circumstances recede, is attracting more attention and, thankfully more rational perspectives than seem to have been possible in the immediate aftermath of Empire and commercial affluence. The book has also been enhanced by essays on specific topics of wider application. The whole has been compiled in a mood inspired by scholarly appreciation of the work of Derick Emmison.

In offering their tributes the authors have also, with warmth and sincerity, pronounced their own interest in and devotion to county history. As editor I am thus encouraged, by way of a postscript, to close these essays with a tribute to Essex itself. That seems apposite and consistent with the common commitment to Essex and its history shared by the recipient, the essayists and the readership. The wealth of scholarship and research in this volume allows me, for the purpose of this appreciation, to forsake the academic themes and to indulge my own devotion to the county in prose that springs as much from the heart as from the mind. I shall do no more than allude broadly to some of the more conspicuous aspects of the Essex scene and history without, I hope, impugning the integrity of the subject. In doing so I seek to establish a tangible Essex context in which readers may reflect on the essays and their place in the corpus of county history and experience. The emphasis will be on contemplating Essex in terms of its textures, human and physical, and the harmonies that they inspire in the fundamentals of life in the county.

Essex, everyone agrees, is a county of contrasts. Whether this mildly condescending platitude is uttered by way of a muted apology, or to emphasise those still considerable aspects of beauty and tranquility in a county much of which is now sullied by the legacy of the industrial revolution and the inexorable encroachment of the London sprawl on the ancient marshlands and forests does not matter. Hemmed in by the boundary rivers, the over-flowing capital and the incoming tides where it 'encountreth the mayne Ocean'[1] Essex has been decisively constrained by definitive natural barriers. The rivers, though not large, have been enough to define the administrative limits and recognisable cultural idioms. The confrontation with London has imposed massive change in most dimensions of life in the metropolitan areas. The sea has been similarly significant in determining the character and orientation of much of the life of the Essex littoral. All that has been fundamental. Now, the superficial image is of a dichotomous county bisected at the interface between the burgeoning urban and industrial conglomerations and the comely fertile arable.

In contrasting reference to the awesome magnificence of the pass at Killiecrankie in Perthshire, Alison Cockburn wrote that 'Plain corn counties look as if men had made them'.[2] That, of course, is because they did. It is important to bear that in mind when contemplating the equally awesome and awful product of the hand and mind of man in the age of technology that has scarred the southern reaches of Essex for ever. The contrasts between the sullen profiles of industrial Essex, the high-density residential areas, the corn and copse country and the lonely estuarine tracts could hardly be more palpable. So we may ask, in what terms does Essex now find its unity? What are the common strands of experience and perception that can envisage the county as a discrete entity and generate a common image that leads people in Becontree, Walthamstow and Southend, or equally demanding, in Belchamp Walter, Tillingham and Pleshey to think of themselves as Essex folk along with those in Saffron Walden, Thaxted, Dedham and Colchester? Primarily, it is the historical dimension, the shared inheritance. It is also that Essex, although serenely beautiful in some areas, has not, in general, the countenance of an English pleasance; it is a working county. It is not, as are extensive areas of some of the southern counties, country parkland. Nor yet does it exhibit the glorious scenic drama of the Scottish hills and the English uplands. It and its people are largely devoted to work, manufacturing, servicing and farming. It is thus the underlying themes of unity, the heritage and the purpose, that give contemporary Essex its authenticity as a logical successor to the old East Saxon kingdom, its boundaries now rationalised by geography and the vicissitudes of political evolution. It is distinct, discrete and has deservedly attracted the loyalty of its people. To acknowledge that is essential to the understanding and appreciation of Essex.

There are many influences, too numerous to rehearse here, that determine the ultimate character of the landscape. Soils, climate, ecology, geography and (often the most significance of all) the ways in which people use it for subsistence and leisure are the principal factors. It is necessary when describing the Essex landscapes – the plural is deliberate to acknowledge the variations that characterise the farmlands, the urban territories and the marshland archipelago – to note that they are always changing. Landscapes change over unimaginably long periods as a consequence of natural phenomena; in the shorter, historical timescale, under the impact of human enterprise. The Essex landscapes have evolved over aeons of time from the arctic tundras of pre-history to the grass and crops in the tidily-hedged fields of the enclosures. It could be argued that one of the Essex landscapes, the industrial, has come a comparable distance in a mere century or so of time in its modern phase of development. Even in the brief term of a human generation there has been marked change. The rural landscape has recently had to absorb the loss of the hedges and elms that has impoverished the roadsides and the headlands, the massive spread of cereal growing that has transformed the arable and the arrival of fields no longer golden with buttercups but splashed with the yellow phosphorescence of May-flowering oil-seed rape. In the urban manifestation recent change has been characterised by tower-blocks, super-markets, shopping-precincts, car-parks and industrial dereliction. Change, it is apparent, is continuous, threatening and inevitable.

What then, is Essex like today? Or rather, what characterises the definable areas of the county and what is it that still retains them within the ambit of an authentic Essex heritage? As has been implied already, Essex is virtually an island, geographically, but in no other sense is it insular. The relationship with London and the commercial intercourse that has been facilitated by the river and sea communications, as well as cultural factors, have precluded that. It is helpful, however, to refer briefly at this point to the physical attributes of the county. It is, on the whole, low-lying land, sloping south-eastwards from the chalk-based uplands of the north-west and drifting down to the forest ridges and beyond to the central plain and the coastal reaches. Exposed to the cold winds and relieved of the high rainfall that has created the pastures and tree-filled slopes in the west country, it is made for corn. The riverine and coastal dimensions and the proximity of the capital have assured the commercial and industrial resources of the county. There is not, however, a simple division, cornfields and townscape. Out to the east, in the old Dengie and Rochford hundreds is the flower-strewn marshland mosaic that S. L. Bensusan called the 'Back of Beyond' and where, he insisted, one walked 'with shadows',[3] redolent of the past and the nebulous relationships of these remote areas with the hinterland. In the same context there are numerous islands, havens for flocks of restless birds – Foulness got its name from them – and inseparable like the creeks and saltings from mud, silt and the overflowing tides that ripple and glitter to reveal a territorial texture as assertive as that of the Essex clays.

It is in the lands where corn and copse, in tidy fugal undulations, dominate the horizons that the essential qualities and vagrant charms of Essex are most assimilable. Those who reproach Essex for a flat, dull or colourless landscape are, quite simply, wrong. Much is certainly flat, but not generally dull and certainly not colourless. Indeed, the rolling landscape of the northern vistas is colourful beyond anything to be seen in the rain-drenched pasturelands in the shires. Here one may stand on the wind-swept slopes of flint-strewn fields, under the towering clear skies typical of the eastern counties, in silent contemplation of a land at rest but vibrant in its promise. After the harvest the stubble is often burnt and ploughed in, turning the fustian fields into a patchwork of varying brown pigments flecked with chalk and flint. Shortly after it is drilled, the winter corn spreads an emergent filmy viridescent mist across the fields. In the wake of a bleak winter night we may glory in the beauty of the frost steaming off the deep furrows in the soft early sunshine as the light morning breezes fan the ploughlands into life. The sinuous streams – in Drayton's alliterative references[4] 'little Roding', 'choice Chelmer', 'clear Can' and Blackwater which 'Pant was called of yore' – contribute colour and movement to the delightful scenes over the cornfields that flank the Essex rivers. Soon, as winter reluctantly recedes and springtime steals in, the corn grows on. The land becomes bright green and alive. Preceded by the effulgent, some would say garish, yellow of the rape and relieved, here and there, by crops of varying green textures or the blue haze of borage, the corn ripens through to its golden maturity. It is breathtakingly beautiful and the corn-country villages seem to float in an arable ocean of foaming gilded crops that shimmer in the summer airs in elusive rippling rhythms. Radwinter, Finchingfield, the Bardfields and the Sampfords are typical of these corn-girt villages which, seen across the glowing grain, nestle, like those of Normandy, on undulant horizons in pleasing profiles that artists find irresistible. The vernacular charm of their cottages, the prim, immensely relevant styles of the village churches and the ancient geometry of their furtive lanes evince an image of Essex at its best. Here, plaster and thatch pronounce a regional accent that, to the east of the county is emphasised more by weatherboarding, a pleasant texture that was taken by the settlers to the eastern seaboard states of North America in the seventeenth century and has endured to the delight of their posterity. The land in east Essex tends to flatten into hedge-trimmed fields without the generous rise and fall of the contours that elevate the Essex scene to the west. Humble in its pretensions, this countryside is pleasant enough and in the river valleys exudes a special quality that is at once relaxing and pretty. It does not seem to have changed all that much in my lifetime. It is tidier, many of the old close hedges and the hedgerow trees have gone, but the fretted field patterns still remain, albeit stretched, and the rivers wind through the crops, in the main unblemished by modern agriculture or development as far as their scenic qualities are concerned. Of course, there are exceptions. The country around Ashingdon, Rochford, Heybridge and Rayleigh has borne its inevitable increment of modern speculative development less well. Yet the distant views from the historic hill-top churches of Ashingdon and Canewdon, redolent of Saxon and Dane, across the river valley of the Crouch are delightful and restful. The corn, diluted by green pasture, presents a less compelling symmetry than that in the main granary lands.

To the south, in dramatic contrast, the urban sprawl has consumed almost all of the farmlands, marshlands and forested slopes and one must seek out those precious vestiges of the old rural and village scenes. Embedded in the vast suburban hinterland of the capital and the brooding dormitory growths towards the Thames estuary, the remaining symbols of the old Essex have struggled to survive. The 'village' at Walthamstow, the churchyard of St. Mary Magdalene in East Ham, the smock mill at Upminster, odd corners in Redbridge and the green at Havering are tenacious reminders of what was lost as the old manorial estates and village communities were fragmented. The notable exceptions still, in this generally lost campaign, are Epping and Hainault Forests. The sylvan beauty of Epping Forest that Essex shares with the capital, offers the most pleasing aspect of any of the main routes into London with which Essex has been entangled in this historic and decisive trend.

As topographers frequently remark, there are, in Essex, no large and burgeoning industrial cities like those that disfigure the Midlands and Merseyside. Apart from the Greater London conglomeration the urban foci of Essex are quite different in character. The county town, with its Georgian centre, has also some of the characteristics of the classic cities of the Victorian age that overtook the elegance of the eighteenth century. But, Chelmsford 'more prosperous than picturesque'[5] never attained the scale of those industrial giants of the English heartland. Colchester, a delight among the towns of eastern England and savouring an historic lineage that cities of more fashionable image might envy with reason, is the county's most prestigious and interesting town. Elsewhere, the spreading suburbs of Southend-on-Sea and its environs and the other riverside and sea-side towns that abut the North Sea have had to tolerate turgid burdens of residential, recreational and industrial development. At the sea-side resorts, especially Frinton, some dignity and style has survived. The depressing 'Arcadian'[6] legacy of the poignant aspirations of hopeful people escaping from the metropolitan squalor that has defined Jaywick, Canvey, Laindon and Hockley is being modified by time and public ambition. It has, nevertheless, left its incongrous blemish on the Essex scene. The new towns, Dagenham, Harlow and Basildon and the other residential growths such as those at Billericay and Wickford, have engulfed sizeable areas of the open countryside. They represent an historic social experiment and have earned their architectural accolades. In relieving the congestion in the London boroughs the new towns, self-sufficient and therefore, unlike the traditional relationship, largely independent of the surrounding countryside and villages, have created communities in which an introspective insularity could become a major social problem. Harlow was well sited for its purpose; Basildon suffers geographically because its location was largely dictated by the intention, laudable in itself, to clear away what had become a growing 'rural slum'.

The coastal towns like Clacton, Southend-on-Sea and Harwich, the latter now yielding its maritime role to Felixstowe, all enjoy the cultural flavour that they derive from their associations and contiguity with the sea. Shipping and the activities that are concomitant with the social and economic life of coastal communities determine that, whether the emphasis is on their commercial or recreational purposes. There is an atmosphere that is at once physical and metaphysical. It is quite impossible to see or feel a coastal town in the same mood as one experiences an inland city. Life, in all its aspects, is invariably more brisk, definable or elevating. The long and tortuously irregular coastline has clothed a large part of Essex life in this maritime mantle. The purposeful bustle of the sea-ports, the lugubrious or meretricious atmosphere of the resorts and the silent spaciousness of the islands, creeks and mud-flats together comprise an unique and major dimension of Essex topography and life.

A glance at the map of Essex will illustrate, more than words, the massive impact made by the historical development of manufacturing capacity and a world-wide seaborne trade on Thameside from Bow Creek through dockland, Beckton and across the Roding along to Dagenham, Purfleet, Grays, Tilbury and thence to Thameshaven, Canvey and the estuarine agglomerations. It became, in a comparatively brief episode of history, a land of serried roof-rows, chimneys, cranes, sheds, wharves, factories, pylons and containers. Bricks, concrete and metal were combined into harsh textures, where previously the riverside marshlands had exhibited a tranquil, apparently changeless scene and provided a life, hard and unhealthy, of its own. These ugly and depressing symbols of commercial enterprise despoiled the land. It must, however, be acknowledged that they were also the emblems of an amazing industrial initiative that improved the living standards and promoted the social well-being of the incoming communities that were attracted to the area in vast numbers. Local life was subsumed; but alongside the industrial squalor people were uplifted, better paid, better fed, better clothed and lived in greater dignity. In and around the factories the new housing estates spread northwards into the Essex countryside under the stimulus of public investment or private speculation to the general advantage. Planned locations of simple, often monotonous, but respectable housing absorbed the surplus population of London and assured the human resources needed for the new industries. More desirable owner-occupied housing estates in the newly developed areas enlarged the capital's dormitory and made irreversible demands on the Essex countryside. Today, it is not beautiful, but the low-lying river and creek-filled land and the still detectable nuclei of the old parishes and villages, give it a distinctive ambience the historic echoes of which murmur of Essex rather than Middlesex, Kent or Surrey, which counties also sacrificed territory to the pressure of the London overflow in the same historic process.

An evocative link between the contemporary scene and history is that provided by the names that locate discrete communities or features of the landscape. Indeed, one of the most important manifestations of an unique identity, whether one is concerned with people or places, is that of nomenclature. In Essex, place-names symbolise the continuity and charm of country life. The associations with personal names are of such importance that there are people whose names adorn every Essex history. Eorcenwald, Byrhtnoth, Fitzwalter, Elizabeth Tudor, Ray and Lister come readily to mind. They are relevant to Essex pride and its status as a definable unit of English life. In another sense so are the county's place-names. Those of Essex do not quite exude the glorious extravagance of those of Dorset; but they have an equally fine pedigree and a compelling resonance of their own. Who doubts that attractive names such as Saffron Walden, Earls Colne, Tolleshunt D'Arcy and Wendons Ambo enhance parochial pride and strengthen the fabric of local society by their connotations and comfortable familiarity? There are too, the splendied flourishes of other names, of French provenance, with their personal Norman affixes like Hatfield Peverel, Helions Bumpstead, Shellow Bowells, Norton Mandeville and Theydon Garnon. Moreover, who does not delight in idiosyncratic minor nomenclature such as Scrapfaggots Green (Great Waltham), Sparepenny Lane (Great Sampford), Tittymouse Wood (Hatfield Peverel), Porridge Pot Hall (Terling), Hopping Jack's Lane (Danbury) and Creep Mouse Alley (Saffron Walden)? These, as well as those of the nobler range should be enjoyed by those who love the secluded by-ways of Essex and the traditional flavour of its towns and villages. At the level of scholarship, place-names are for the philologists whose esoteric disciplines put their subject beyond the modest reach of lay enthusiasm. It is important that the technical analysis of place-names should be employed to illuminate and explain difficult or obscure historical problems. It is more important that whole communities should enjoy and cherish them as part of the Essex heritage. These are not mutually exclusive approaches to the art and science of place-names; each may be enriched by the other.

History is not, in essence, concerned with events or chronology. It is, or should be, devoted to the exploration and understanding of the condition and circumstances of people in relation to these phenomena. There were people living in what is now Essex long before recorded history. At the dawn of history Celtic peoples left their imprint on the land. We still cultivate their hard-won and irregularly-shaped fields as the deep reticulating lanes and the vestigial ragged hedgerows of the north Essex farmlands testify. Things do no always change beyond recognition, a consequence that validates John Betjeman's insight in referring to the sweet uneventful countryside of Essex. His reference to the uneventful nature of the Essex scene is, of course, to the reticent quality of the landscape; there has been no lack of drama in the pageant of Essex history.

On that note we may make brief reference to a few of the major strands that have determined the life of the county and the nature of its people. The earliest persistent strand has been the continuity of agriculture, the emphasis on corn in particular, as the basis of life in rural Essex. The symbolic ear of barley on Cunobelin's gold stater (A.D. 10–40) attests the importance of grain to the economy of the Trinovantian kingdom. It was overrun by the Catuvellauni who developed the great oppidum on the site of Camulodunum (Colchester) before the Romans and Saxons added their stature to what we now call Essex. The pre-eminence of corn has continued into the affluent era of the European Community even though there now seem to be market problems of serious proportions ahead. Ever was it so; under the pressure of trans-Atlantic competition corn became unprofitable in the late nineteenth century and many small Essex farms were bankrupted. Fields now laden with corn were then burdened with debt. Farmers and farm-workers suffered alike and the poor rates, at no more than subsistence levels, provided no substitute for a living wage. Essex agriculture has always had to adapt but, from the beginning, corn has always predominated. Nowadays, it is true, we speak more in terms of acreage and the rural scene than of people. In the early part of the nineteenth century more than half of the population of Essex was engaged in or supported by agriculture. Today it is a tiny percentage. In 1861, Coller could write 'It is chiefly upon its Agriculture that the importance and reputation of the county depend.'[7]

The coming of Christianity imparted another vital strand. After the false dawns of the Roman era and the abortive efforts of Mellitus, Bishop of London, who was inspired by Augustine from Canterbury in 604 A.D., the impetus came from the foundations laid by the Celtic church a half a century later. St. Cedd's endeavours were centred on the mission at Ithancester, on the site of the ruined Roman fort of Othona and another at Tilbury of which there is now no trace. The first great abbey at Barking, endowed by the East Saxon dynasty, was founded soon afterwards. Since then the life and history of every town and village in Essex has been replete with the presence and influence of the Christian churches.

In war, from the time of the Anglo-Saxon colonisation, Essex people have found their identity in common purposes and distinguished themselves in defence of their country. The inspiring example of the Saxons rallying round their leader at Maldon in 991 A.D., Elizabeth's stirring presence at Tilbury as the Armada was awaited in 1588, the battle honours borne upon the banners of the 'Pompadours', among them Waterloo, Inkerman, Sevastopol, Ypres, Loos and Gallipoli and the courageous bearing of the Essex Regiment and the people of Essex at home and in the armed forces during the darkest days of the last war, are focal points in an historic sequence that has bound the people of the county together in honour and pride. We may insist then, that in its historical stance, in its scenic aspects and in the mores of its people Essex can find those common threads that entitle it to claim the attributes of a commonalty that gives it an unique identity in British life. When Norden wrote the oft-quoted passage 'This shire is moste fatt, frutefull, and full of profitable thinges . . . . .'[8] he was alluding to economic, particularly agricultural prosperity. We may surely be allowed, in offering this tribute, to broaden that assertion so as to embrace the whole aspect of life in Essex.

References

1. John Norden, *Description of Essex* (1594)
2. Alison Cockburn, *Letters 1713–1794* (1900)
3. S. L. Bensusan, *Back of Beyond* (1945)
4. Michael Drayton, *Polyolbion* (1662)
5. John Hissey, *Tour in a Phaeton* (1889)
6. Denis Hardy and Colin Ward, *Arcadia for All* (1984)
7. D. W. Coller, *The People's History of Essex* (1861)
8. John Norden, *Description of Essex* (1594)

INDEX

Unless otherwise stated, places and subjects generally relate to Essex
Names *not* indexed: (1) East Saxon ealdormen and kings (pp. 57–95);
(2) taxpayers (pp. 143–145).

Abdy family: 246
Acts of Parliament: 18, 37, 39, 40–42, 143, 157, 160, 199, 200, 202
Adams, Robert, Theophilus: 153–61
Addison, Sir William: *The Making of the Essex Landscape*: 47–55
Admiralty court: 36
Ælfgar (and other ealdormen of Essex): 58–84
Æthelbert (and other kings of Mercia): 57–78
Ætheldred (and other kings of East Saxons): 60–95
Agas, Ralph: 247
agriculture: *see* farming
Aldham: 247
Alfred, King: 57, 63, 65
Allen, Henry: 250
Alresford: 70
America, North, Essex place-names:53; Harvard: 5
amusements *see* fairs
Anglo-Saxon Chronicle: 57, 60–77
Antiquaries, Society of: 2
Archaeological and Historical Societies, Essex Congress: vii, 2
archdeacon of Essex: 118, 174
archery societies: 229
Ardleigh: 195, 229
Archivists, Society of: 2, 4
Arkesden: 54
Army, British: 185–96
Arnold, Matthew: 55
assizes, early: 32
Augmentations, Court of: 85, 154
Aveley: 103–4, 247

Bacon family: 214
Baddow, Great: 238
Badlesmere, Bartholomew de: 34
Bardfield, Great: 31, 33, 256
Barking: 39, 42, 98–104; abbey: 85, 162; Saxon charter: 63, 72, 82; manor: 154, 60–65; fair: 232; Fulkes: 162; Westbury: 101–4
barns, brick: 53–4
Barnston: 122

Barrett-Lennard, Mr: 180–81
Bartlow Hills: 48
Bascombe, Dr K. N.: *Two Charters of King Suebred of Essex*: 85–96
Battle of Maldon: 72–78
Bedford: 1
Bedfordshire County Council and Record Office: 1–4, 15, 21, 22, 27
Bedfordshire Historical Record Society: 4, 22
Belchamp St. Paul: 233; fair: 238
Benfleet, North: 98–102, 105
Benfleet, South: 51, 98–9
Bensusan, S. L: 255
Beorhtwulf, ealdorman of Essex: 60, 65
Berden, early burgesses: 31, 33; fair: 234, 237–8
Berkshire: 57
Billericay: 50; fair: 234, 238
Bindoff, Prof. S. T.: 5
Birdbrook: Baythorne End, fair: 238
bishop's transcripts: 12
Black family: 116
Blackchapel (Great Waltham): 115–42
Black Death: 99, 172
Blackwater river: 47, 73
Blatch/Blecche family: 116
boards: ; burial: 41; guardians: 20, 41; health: 41; local: 41
Bocking: 103
borough records: 20, 27–45
boundaries: parish: 92–3; Saxon: 92–3
Boundary Commission: 201
Boxted: 229
Boycott, Thomas, William: 249
Boyes, John: *Essex and the 1871 Fairs Act*: 229–39
Bradwell on Sea; fair: 238
Braintree: 126
Bramston, Sir John: 180
Brentwood: 105; fair: 238
Brewer, Dr William: 200, 222
brick barns and churches: 53–4
brickmaking: 53
bridges: 246
British Academy: 19
British Museum: 19

British Record Society: 2, 23
British Records Association: 2, 8, 23
Bromley family: 214
Bulphan: 105
burgesses, early: 31–33
burhs: 28
Burial Boards: 41
Burley, R.: 248
Burstead, Great: 50
Bury St. Edmunds: 31
Byrd, William: 7
Byrhtnoth, ealdorman of Essex: 57, 66,
    70–76

cage, parish: 179–80
Cambridge: 29, 204, 217–8, 247
Cambridge University: 1, 156
canal companies: 37
Canewdon: 55, 98
Canfield, Great: 124–5; castle: 51
Canvey island: 51, 103; fair: 238
carpentry, medieval: 52
cartography in Kent and Essex: 241–52; in
    Bedfordshire: 3
castles: 31, 51, 55, 97, 250
Cecil, Robert: 154; Sir William: 5, 154–5
census records: 199, 200, 203, 210, 215, 218
Chadwell: 106
Chadwick, Sir Edwin: 40
chantries: 35, 154, 157
Chapel, Black: 115–42
chapels, nonconformist: 215
Chaplin, Philip: 231
Charity Commissioners: 116–28
charters: Saxon: 60–63, 85–96; borough:
    30–42; fairs: 229–31; forest: 110, 112
Cheeke, Thomas: 180
cheeses,: 100, 103
Chelmsford: 31, 32, 41, 48; fair: 235; map:
    249
Chelsea Royal Hospital: 193–96
Chesterford, Great: 47
Chesterford, Little: 52
Chigwell: 50, 54
Child, Jeffery: 120–21; Sir Josiah: 37
Chingford: 42
churches: 50, 51, 54
Civil War: 36, 250
Clacton, Little; fair: 234
cladding: 53
Clare, Gilbert de: 34
Clarke, William: 162–68
Clavering: 54, 232
clergy: 121–28, 173, 214–22, 229
clothmaking: 32, 37–39
coach, stage: 180
Coffyn, John: 243
Colchester: 28, 32, 65; burgesses: 28, 33,

110; borough charters: 33–35; borough
    records: 36–39; elections, parliamentary
    (Victorian): 199–227; garrison: 195, 203;
    histories: 38; maps: 248; market charter:
    30; parliamentary members: 40; Saxon:
    60, 71; school: 35; siege: 36–7;
    Kingswood Heath: 32, 110; Union: 40;
    see also Greenstead; Lexden; Mile End
Colnes: 51
Colne, Earls: school: 246; fair: 238
Commissioners, Boundary: 201
Commissioners for Charitable Uses: 116–18
Commissioners, Inclosure: 126
Commissioners of Sewers *see* Sewers
common fields: 32, 50, 242; Kent: 242
commons: 32, 110
concealed lands: 153–70
Congress of Archaeological Societies
    (national): 19
Congress of Archaeological & Historical
    Societies (Essex); vii, 2
Conservatives: 199–214
constable, high: 180
Copford: 55
Cornwall, Julian, *The Letter of the Law:
    Hatfield Peverel in the Lay Subsidy of
    1524–5*: 143–52
Corringham: 98–9, 104
Cosin, William: 248
county councils *see* individual counties
county record offices, origins: 11–25
Creighton, Bishop M.: 16, 17
Cressing fair: 238
cricket clubs: 229
Cromwell, T. History of Colchester: 39
Cunobelin: 48
custumal: 33
cutlery industry (Thaxted): 33–34

Dagenham: 42, 101–2, 105
dairy farms *see* wicks
Dale, Samuel: 38
Danbury: 28, 50; fair: 238
Danelaw: 61
Danes: 28, 50, 60–77
Darcy family: 245
David, Elizabeth: 5
Davids, Rev. Thomas: 215, 219–20
Dawes, Robert: 153, 159–63
Dedham: 53; school: 246
deer: 47, 53
defence: 194–5, 242
Defoe, Daniel: 97, 106
Dibben, Alan, *Blackchapel, Great Waltham*:
    115–42
Dickens, Prof. A. G.: Foreword: xiii
diocesan records: 12, 13, 17, 20
Doddinghurst: 105

Domesday Book: 29–31, 50–51, 71–72, 89, 97–108, 100, 103, 109, 179
Doncaster, Tony: 6
Donyland, East: 202
Dovercourt: 32, 36, 41, 70
drunkenness: 229–34
Dunmow, Great: charter: 35; medieval: 33; parliamentary borough: 40
Dyer, Sir Edward: 159–60

Ealdordom of Essex: 57–84
Easter, Good; fair: 231, 238
Easter, High: 121
East Saxons see Saxons, East
Eastwood: 101–2
Ecclesiastical Commissioners: 17
ecclesiastical records: 12, 20
Edward the Elder: 28–9, 60–65
elections, parliamentary (Colchester): 199–227
Elizabethan Life series: 5, 6
Eldred, William: 250
Elmdon: 54
Elwell, Rev. Henry: 235
Emmison, Dr F. G.: xiii–xv, 1–11, 21, 23, 27, 42, 78, 229, 251, 253; Mrs Margaret: 2, 3, 7, 8; Lesley, Martin: 2
enclosure see inclosure
ends (hamlets): 50, 51
entertainments see fairs
Epping Forest: 47–8, 51, 109
Errington, George: 209–10
Essex: appreciation: 253–60; boroughs: 27–45; county, original: 72; defence: 194–5; landscape: 47–55
Essex Archaeological Society: 2
Essex County Council see Essex Record Office
Essex Journal: 3
Essex Record Office: 2, 11, 27, 42, 50; Guides: 3, 42
Essex Wills: 6
Evans, Sir John: 15
Exchequer: 30, 110, 151, 154–63

Fairfax, Thomas: 36
Fairs Act: 229–30
fairs: medieval: 31, 36, 97, 104; Victorian: 211, 229–39
Family History, Society for Bedfordshire: 2; for Essex: 2
Fanshawe, Henry, Thomas, William: 163–65
farmhouses, Medieval: 51–53
farming: 32, 48–9, 53–4, 99, 150, 172–81, 222
Faulkbourne Hall: 53
Felgate, Robert: 247
Felsted: 52, 110, 116–26; Felsted School: 123–27

ferries, Tilbury: 104, 248
Fiddlers Hamlet, fair: 238
fields, common (open): 30, 50, 242; Kent: 242
Filmer family: 246
Finch, William: 165
Finchingfield: 256
fisheries: 39, 89, 99, 105
Fisher, W. R.: 109–14
Fitch, Dr Marc: 4
floods: 104
Fobbing: 99, 100, 104–6
forests: 32, 34, 47–8, 51, 90, 100, 109–13, 165
Foulness island: 98, 103, 255; fair: 238
Fowler, Dr G. H.: 1, 3, 21–24
Foyle, Miss Christina: 5
Francis family: 216
freemen (Colchester): 201–214
French Wars: 39
Friends of Historic Essex: 2, 6, 7

gaslighting: 40, 222
Geffe, Nicholas: 161–65
Genealogists, Society of: 2
geology of Essex: 47
Getty, Paul: 5
gilds: 30, 35, 145, 148
Gouge, James: 247
Gray, Victor: 3; The County Record Office: The Unfolding of an Idea: 11–25
Green family: 214
Green Belt: 55
Greenstead-juxta-Colchester: 210, 216–18
Greensted-juxta-Ongar: 50
Grieve, Hilda: 7
Grocers' Company: 155–57
Guardians, Boards of: 40, 41
Guides to Sussex Record Office
guildhalls: 38, 54
guilds see gilds

Hadleigh: 55, 104
Hainault Forest: 50
Hall, Joseph: 53
Halls family: 214
Hallingbury, Great: Woodside Green; fair: 239
Ham, East: 42, 98, 100, 105
Ham, West: 41, 98–100, 104–6; Plaistow: 41; Stratford: 41, 104–5
Hanningfield, West: 247
harbours: 37, 250
Hardy & Page: 15, 16
Hardy, W. le: 11, 23
Hardy, W. J.: 15
Harlow, early burgesses: 31; fair: 231, 238
Harridance, James: 185, 192, 196

Harrison, William: 52, 53
Hart, Dr Cyril: *The Ealdordom of Essex*: 57–84
Harvey, Sir Gawen: 160–61
Harwich, early burgesses: 31–2; charter: 36; parliamentary members: 32, 36, 40; guildhall: 38
Hatton, Sir Christopher: 156–58
Hatfield Broad Oak: 111
Hatfield Peverel: lay subsidy: 143–52
Havens, W. R.: 202, 205, 219
Havering: 28, 97; royal manor: 110–11, 171, 173
health, boards of: 41
heaths, 32, 47, 49
Hedingham, Castle: 51, 54; fair: 238; nunnery: 111
Hertfordshire: 60, 62
Hertfordshire County Council and Record Office: 11, 15, 18
Hervey *alias* Mildmay, Carew: 179
Hewes family: 214
Hickes, Sir Michael: 154
Historical Association: 2, 8
Historical Manuscripts Commission: 12, 13, 19, 22, 24
Historical Monuments Commission: 52, 53
Hockley: 99
Hogben, Henry: 247
Holland, Great: 190
Home Office: 230–39
Hornchurch: 97; manor of Suttons: 172; New College, Oxford, estate: 171–83; priory: 171
Horndon-on-the-Hill: 99–106; *burh*: 28; fair: 238
Horndon, West: 105
hospitals: 171, 193
Hospitallers: 105
houses, timber-framed: 52–3; rebuilding: 38
Hull, Felix: *Aspects of Local Cartography in Kent and Essex, 1585–1700*: 241–52
hundredal courts: 28, 40, 101

Ilford: 42; Hospital: 85; justices: 232–33
Improvement Act (1811): 39
Inclosure Commissioners: 126
Income Tax Commissioners: 20
industries *see* cloth; cutlery
inhabitants *see* population
Ingatestone: 54; inns: 235–6; map: 244, 249; Hall: 1, 4–7, 180
Institute of Heraldic and Genealogical Studies: 2
Institute of Historical Research: 23
islands *see* Canvey; Foulness; Mersea

Jeafferson, J. C.:14, 15

Jenkinson, Sir Hilary: 23
justices of the peace: 14, 34, 41, 120, 180, 230–37; Colchester: 40, 211

Karslake, E.: 200–222
Kelvedon fair: 238
Kent: 51, 60, 65, 104, 194; maps: 241–52; Archives Office: 241
kiddles: 105
kings, Mercian and Saxon: 57–84

Lambourne: Abridge fair: 238
Lancashire & Cheshire, Historic Society of: 18
Lancaster, Duchy of: 246
landscape (Essex): 47–55
Langley, Dr Baxter: 200, 219
Layer Marney: 53, 54, 146
lay subsidies: 143–52
Lea, river: 47, 60, 89
Learmouth, Col.: 200, 211, 222
Legatt, Thomas: 176
Leicester gild: 30
Leigh: 104
Leighs, Little: 115, 120
Lennard family: 247
Lenthall, John: 177
Lethieullier, Smart: 85
letters, 185–97
Lexden: 70, 199, 203, 210–11, 216–18; fair: 211
Leyton: 42
Liberals: 199–224
Liddell, William: *The Bounds of the Forest of Essex*: 109–13
Local Board: Chelmsford: 235
Local Government Act (1888): 41; (1894): 18
Lockwood, H. H.: *Those Greedy Hunters after Concealed Lands*: 153–70
London: 28, 37, 39, 60, 105, 172; bishops of: 16, 17, 60, 174; city companies: 156–8; Chelsea Hospital: 193–96; University: 2
Low Countries: 36
Luckyn, Sir Thomas: 120
Lucy, Richard de: 51
Lynn, King's: 31
Lyte, Sir H. Maxwell: 17

magistrates *see* justices of the peace
Maldon: admiralty court: 36; charter: 28, 30, 34; parliamentary members: 40; postal services: 185–98; *Battle of Maldon*: 69–73
Mandeville family: 51
Manningtree: 41, 236; early burgesses: 31
manors, early: 31–2, 51; maps of (Kent and Essex): 244

manor courts: 101, 116–7, 154, 216
mapmakers in Kent and Essex: 241–52; scales: 242–47
maps: 155; catalogues of Essex: 3, 155; of Kent: 241
markets, early Essex: 29–36, 97, 104–5; later: 39, 235; *see also* fairs
Marney, Lord: 146
Marsham, John: 247
marshes: 47, 50–1, 97–100, 103–6, 242, 244
Martin, Dr Geoffrey: *Essex Boroughs and their Records*: 27–45
Master of the Rolls: 21
McIntosh, Marjorie K.: *New College, Oxford, and its Hornchurch Estate, 1391–1675*: 171–84
McKay, George: 185–97
Melbourne, Lord: 186
members of parliament: 40; Colchester: 199–227
Mercia: 28, 51–65
Mersea: 71
Middlesex County Council and Record Office: 11–15
Mildmay, Humphrey: 160
Mile End, Colchester: 203, 210, 216, 218
military history: *see* Saxons, East; Army
Mill, John Stuart: 200
Miller, Taverner: 199–222
mills: medieval: 35, 53, 105; water: 53; wind: 53–4
mints, early Essex: 29
Mistley; fair: 236, 238
moats: 52
monasteries, dissolution of: 53
Moore, Sir John: 194
Morant, Philip: 38, 121, 153
Moy, Thomas: 217
Mucking: 98–9, 105
Municipal Corporations Act (1835): 40
musters: 146
music: 6–7, 22, 234

Napoleonic Wars: 39, 194–96
Navestock: 60, 89
Nazeing: 54, 86–89, 93
Navy, British: 38, 186
Neale, Sir John: 5
Neale, Kenneth: *Frederick G. Emmison: 1–10*; *Essex: An Appreciation*: 253–60
Newham: 28
Newport, early burgesses: 31; fair: 238
newspapers, Essex: 213, 220
Newton, Kenneth: 3
nonconformity: 36–7, 215–21
Norden, John: 97, 106
Norfolk: 31, 35, 247
Norman, Canon Charles: 236

Norman place-names: 50–1
Northamptonshire: 247
Northern & Eastern Railway: 41
Norwich: 31
Notley, Black: 116
Nutbrown, William: 161

Oakley, Great, fair: 238
occupations *see* trades
Ongar, Chipping: 231–2; castle: 51; fair: 238
open fields *see* fields, common
Orsett fair: 238
Osborne, Peter: 156–7
Oxford colleges: Magdalen: 246; New: 171–83; Trinity: 122
Oxford, Earls of *see* Vere, de
oysters: 39; from Scotland: 180

Paglesham: 103
Papillon, Philip O.: 199–222
pargetting: 52
parish boundaries: 49–50, 92–3
parish records: Bedfordshire: 3; Essex: 3
parish council records: 18
parish registers: 12
parks: 53, 101, 110, 174
parliamentary elections, Victorian (Colchester): 199–227
parliament, origin of: 31–2, 40; members of (Colchester): 199–227
Parliamentarian army: 36
Pattenden, John: 241, 249
Paving (etc.) Commissioners: 39
Peachye (or Petchye), Thomas: 247–8
Pease, Anne Robert: 161–62
Pebmarsh: 229
Peel, Robert: 186
Peirse, Mark, Samuel: 249
Petchey, Dr William: 7
Petre family: 180, 242–46; Sir William: 1, 4
Petty Sessions: 230
Phillips, Andrew: *Four Colchester Elections: Voting Behaviour in a Victorian Market Town*: 199–227
Pilgrim Fathers: 53
Pipe Rolls: 30, 110
place-names, origins of: 50; Norman: 51; North American: 53; Saxon: 90–93
plague *see* Black Death
Plaistow *see* Ham, West
Pleshey: early burgesses and market: 31, 33; castle: 31, 51
Plummer, Thomas: 244
Poker, Matthew: 250
police (Victorian): 41, 231
politics *see* parliamentary elections
pollbooks, election *see* parliamentary elections

Pollock, Sir F.: 19
poll tax returns: 99
population medieval: 97–100, 106; Hatfield Peverel: 146; *see also* censuses
poor relief, early: 35, 37; later: 4, 37, 39–40, 203
Poor, Guardians: 20; Unions: 37, 40
Poor Law Acts: 40
ports: 32
Portugal: 186
postal service: 185–97
preachers *see* clergy
Pridden, John: 122
priories: Hatfield Peverel: 145; Hornchurch: 171; Prittlewell: 98
Prittlewell: 104; Milton: 104; priory: 98
private records: 19
Prujean, Robert: 179
Public Health Act (1875): 41
Public Record Office: 12, 19, 20
puddingstones: 90–1
punishments: 179–80
Purfleet *see* Thurrock, West
Puritans: 36–7

Quarter Sessions: 229; rolls: 16
Queen Elizabeth the Queen Mother: 5

Radwinter: 52, 53, 256
railways: 41, 204, 219, 223
Rainham: 99, 104; fair: 238
Ramme, William: 179
Rayleigh: 97, 101, 104; fair: 238
Rebow, John Gurdon: 199–222
Record Commissioners: 12
record (offices): *see under* Essex; Middlesex; Worcestershire
records: borough: 27–45; county: 11–25; diocesan: 12, 13, 17, 20: ecclesiastical: 12, 20; parish: 3, 12, 18; private: 19; *see also* charters; maps; poll books; wills
record societies *see* individual counties
Redbridge: 28
Record Acts: 40, 199, 202, 212
registers, parish: 12
Regiment, 95th: 194
religion; *see* clergy; Puritans
Riche, Lord: 160, 245
riots *see* fairs
rivers *see* Lea; Roding; Stort; Stour; Thames
River Conservators: 20
roads: early: 48–50, 90; turnpike: 37
Robertson, Ian: *'Dear Betsy': Reflections on two letters from the First Carlist War*: 185–97
Rochford: 98, 100–1, 104–5
Roding river: 47, 89
Romans: roads: 48, 50, 90; settlement: 48–9

Romford: 39, 42, 97, 178, 247–8; chapel: 171–2; fair: 238
Roothings, The: 47, 50, 51; Abbess: 51; High: 124; Margaret: 127; White; fair: 239
Round, J. H.: 109–14
Rouse, Thomas: 221
Royal Historical Society: 2
Royalists: 36
Roydon: 93; fair: 238
Russell, George: 247–8, 250; Lord John: 11

saffron: 35
Saffron Walden *see* Walden, Saffron
Saint Osyth: 51, 235; fair: 239
Saint Paul's Dean and Chapel: 245
Salcott: 51
Salisbury, Earl of, *see* Cecil, Robert
Saltpans: 51
Sampfords: 256
Sandon, fair: 239
sanitary authorities: 41–42
Saxons: charters: 57–84
Saxons, East: 27–28, 49; ealdormen and kings: 57–84
Saxons, West: 28
Saxton, Christopher: 247, 250
schools, grammar: Colchester: 35; Earls Colne: 246, 248; Dedham: 246; Felsted: 123–27; Maidstone: 248; Rochester: 248
Scriveners' Company: 2
Seaman, Dr M.: 216
seal: 180
seaside resorts: 41
seawater bathing: 38
servants: hiring fairs: 229; *see also* trades and occupations
Sewers, Commissioners of: 241–2, 245, 248
Shakespeare, William: 51
sheep: 97, 100–1, 106; milch: 103
sheriff, origin of: 97
shire court: 32
Shopland: 104
Shrewsbury gild: 30
Shropshire Parish Register Society: 17
Sidney, Earls of Leicester: 245
Skill, Charles: 126
Sokens: 50
Southchurch: 99, 102, 105
Southend-on-Sea: 4; fair: 239
Southminster: fair: 239
Spain: 185–95
sports: 232
Springfield: 161
Sprye, R.: 11, 24
Stanford-le-Hope: 99, 105
Stane(s), William: 243
Stane Street: 48, 50, 110

Stanway: 70, 247
Stansted Mountfitchet: 110
Stebbing: 119; fair: 233, 239
Stisted: 118
stocks, parish: 179
Stock: 50
Storks, Sir Henry: 200–222
Stort, river: 47
Stour Valley: 54
Stratford: *see* Ham, West
Sturmer: 72
subsidies, lay: 143–52
Suebred, King of Essex: charters: 85–96
Suffolk: 35, 148, 194–5; Bury St Edmunds: 31
Surrey: 28, 57, 60, 65, 156, 247; Sutton Place: 5
surveyors, map: *see* map makers
Sussex: 18, 60, 65, 247
Sutton: 103–4
Symonson, Philip: 247–8, 250

Takeley: 124
Tanner, Thomas: 117
taxes *see* poll taxes; subsidies
Taylor, Silas: 38
Tendring Union: 40
Thames, river: 39, 41, 47, 65, 99, 104–6, 248, 250
Thaxted, 54; charter: 34; cutlery trade: 33–4; early burgesses: 31, 33; early records: 36; guildhall: 54; market and fair: 33; mayor: 34; windmill: 54
Theydon Garnon: 54
Thorpe-le-Soken: fair: 239
Threlfall, John B.: 6
Thundersley: 102
Thurland, Gervase: 157
Thurrock, Grays: 104–5
Thurrock, Little: 98–9, 106
Thurrock, West: 99, 104, 247, 249; Purfleet fair: 238
Tilbury: 41, 104
Tilbury, East: 105–6, 247
Tilbury, West: 99, 104
Tillingham: fair: 239
Tindal, Nicholas: 121
Tipper, William: 153, 156, 158–61
Tiptree Heath: 32
tithes: 31, 171–78
Tollesbury: fair: 239
Toppesfield, 53; fair: 239
Townsend, Sarah: 126
trade, medical: 29–34
trades and occupations: accountants: 222; agricultural labourers: 219, 221; architects: 222; auctioneers: 222 bailiffs: 222; bakers: 105, 225; baymakers: 38–9; beersellers: 201, 204; blacksmiths: 224; booksellers: 215; brewers: 224; bricklayers: 219; brickmakers: 224; builders: 224; butchers: 211, 219, 225; cabinet makers: 224; carpenters: 217, 219; carters: 223; chemists: 215, 225; clergy (see main index); clerks: 223; clothiers: 38, 224; coachmen: 223; coal merchant: 217, 224; coal porters: 217, 223; coopers: 224; corn merchant: 193, 224; costermongers: 219, 224; customs/ coast guard officers: 222; cutlers: 33, 34; dealers: 222, 225; dentists: 222; doctors: 222; drapers: 225; estate agents: 222; farmers: 222; farm servants: 223; farriers: 224; ferrymen: 223; fishermen: 105, 223; fishmonger: 211, 225; fullers: 104; gardeners: 203, 205, 219, 222; government officers: 222; greengrocers: 225; grocers: 225; hairdressers: 225; hawkers: 219, 224; innkeepers: 223; ironmongers: 225; labourers: 147–51, 193, 195, 203, 217–8, 221–3; leather workers: 224; livestock dealer: 222; lunatic asylum staff: 2; machine makers: 217; maltsters: 224; mapmakers: 242–5; mariners: 210–11, 219, 223; masons: 225; milkmen: 225; millers: 224; millwrights: 217, 224; musicians: 222; ostlers: 223; painters: 217, 224; photographers: 225; pipemakers: 211, 224; policemen: 223; porters: 223; printers: 217, 224; publicans: 201, 204, 211, 218–9, 221, 223; railway workers/ staff: 204, 219, 223; retailers: 221; rat catcher: 219; sawyers: 219, 224; schoolteachers: 222, 248; servants: 147–51, 223, 229; shipowners: 205, 224; shoemakers: 185, 215, 219, 224–5; shop assistants: 223; shopkeepers: 217, 219, 225; silk weavers: 224; soldier: 185–97, 223; solicitors: 126, 203, 210, 215, 222; surveyor: 210; sweeps: 224; tailors: 217, 225; tanner: 193; timber merchant: 224; town clerk: 211; upholsterers: 225; verderers: 110; veterinary (surgeon): 222; victuallers (licensed): 223; warehousemen: 223; watchmakers: 225; well sinker: 224; wheelwrights: 225; wine merchants: 225; miscellaneous: 226; unemployed: 225
tribal hidage: 72
Tudor England: 4
Tudor Secretary: 4
Tufton, Earls of Thanet: 245
turnpike trusts: 20, 37
Twisden family: 246
Tyack, Dr Sarah: 7
Tyrell family: 246

tyes: 50–51

Ugley: fair: 239
unions, trade: 217
universities *see* Cambridge; London; Oxford
urban sanitary authorities: 41

Vange: 28
Vaughan, J.:85
Velly, A. C.:126
Vere, de, family: 51, 111, 245
vestries: 39
Victorian elections: 199–227; fairs: 2
Vikings: 50, 72–3
vineyard: 97
visitations, episcopal: 126, 174
voting (electoral): 200–25

wages: 147, 151, 194–5
Wakering, Great: fair: 239
Waldegrave, Paul, William: 154, 163
Walden, Saffron: 30–39; charter: 34–5; gild: 30, 35
Walker, John, senior and junior, and Samuel, mapmakers: 3, 155, 243–51
Waltham Abbey (Holy Cross): 31, 33, 53, 95
Waltham, Great: 50; Blackchapel: 115–42
Waltham, Little: 120
Waltham Forest: 28, 109–15
Walthamstow: 42
Walton-on-Naze: 41, 50
Wanstead: 37, 42
Ward, George: 234; Dr Gladys: 3; Dr Jennifer: 37; *South Essex in the Middle Ages*: 171–84
Warley, Great: 195

warrens: 53, 111
watermills *see* mills
Watson, A. T.: 14
Watts, John: 249
Weald, South: 105
weather-boarding: 53
Wendens Ambo: 47, 54
Wentworth, Thomas Lord: 157–8
Wesleyans: 220
Wessex, kings of: 60–65
Wethersfield: 53
wicks: 51
Wigborough, Great: 247
wills, Elizabethan: 6
Winchester, bishop of: 172
windmills *see* mills
Wiseman, Anne: 126; John: 117; Thomas: 116
Witham: Newland: 29; *burh*: 28–9; Saxon: 62; fair: 239
Wivenhoe: 52, 199, 202, 205
Woodford: 42
Woodham Ferrers: fair: 239
Woodward, Michael, warden: 175–81
wool trade: 32, 35, 103, 105; *see also* cloth making
Wormingford: 217
Worcestershire County Council and Records: 16
Wrake, Thomas: 249
Writtle: 161, 180; early burgesses: 31–32; royal manor: 109, 111; fair: 239
Wykeham, William of: 172

Young, Arthur: 54